John Douglas's Guide to the
Police Officer Exams

ALSO AVAILABLE

John Douglas's Guide to Careers in the FBI

John Douglas's Guide to the
Police Officer Exams
Fourth Edition

KAPLAN

PUBLISHING

New York

© 2011 John Douglas

Published by Kaplan Publishing, a division of Kaplan, Inc.
395 Hudson Street
New York, NY 10014

Printed in the United States of America

10 9 8 7 6 5 4 3 2 1

ISBN-13: 978-1-60714-846-3

Kaplan Publishing books are available at special quantity discounts to use for sales promotions, employee premiums, or educational purposes. For more information or to purchase books, please call the Simon & Schuster special sales department at 866-506-1949.

Contents

How to Use This Book

Congratulations! By reading this book you are preparing yourself to start an exciting career in the police force. The detailed information, targeted review, and full-length practice tests in this book will help to make you an informed and desirable police officer candidate.

Chapter One, the first section in "Part One: Career Opportunities as a Police Officer," discusses the different types of jobs available in the police force. You will learn about entry-level officer positions, as well as the career path you might encounter during your years serving on the force. Information about the differences between rural and urban police forces is also provided.

Chapter Two explains the application process for becoming a police officer in detail. You will learn where to find job openings and recruitment postings, as well as exactly what is required of you before you are hired. This chapter also offers tips and tricks for acing the interview portion of the hiring process with grace and confidence.

Part Two of this book, "Preparing for the Police Officer Exam," offers targeted reviews for different sections of the Police Officer Exam you may encounter on test day. Use chapters three through six to study and review this material so you are comfortable with different question formats. These chapters also offer hints to ace grammar, math, spelling, and reading comprehension questions. The more comfortable you are with these basics, the more confident you will be on test day!

Finally, Part Three contains five practice tests based on general police officer situation questions from tests around the country. Each exam is followed by an answer key and detailed answer explanations for every question.

By using this manual, you are well on your way to obtaining the skills and scores you need to acquire a distinguished job as a police officer. Good luck!

PART ONE

Career Opportunities as a Police Officer

CHAPTER ONE

Careers in the Police Force

Congratulations! You have taken the first steps toward securing a career in law enforcement. By purchasing this book, you have demonstrated a commitment to stand alongside thousands of others who have entered this challenging and rewarding field.

Never in our nation's history has the security and law enforcement field been more important and challenging. The safety and security of all of our citizens, including your family and friends, are being threatened by the specter of terrorism. Since September 11, 2001, this new challenge has provided (and will continue to provide) opportunities for dedicated professionals who can remain alert under pressure and focused on the threats we face.

Even with these massive changes, there is also still the very important traditional side of police work. Police agencies are always looking for men and women who can effectively serve their fellow citizens. Service to one's community is an honorable calling—the term "public servant" is interchangeable with police officer. In the past, "customer service" was not always stressed as much as it is today. Now, agencies are increasingly looking for those who can communicate effectively and provide their clients with exceptional service. In fact, many of the psychological tests used in the recruiting process are designed to identify those who have a strong desire to serve others—to be effective public servants.

OPPORTUNITIES

The most demanding and probably the most rewarding job in a police agency is the police officer, also called the trooper or deputy sheriff position. This role is extremely important because it is a "front line" position. As a front line officer you are the most crucial in affecting people's lives and responding to their needs. The vast majority of the time, you will be a decision maker responsible for choices that influence the lives and welfare of the citizens you serve. These decisions may be life-changing for all involved, and you will be expected to make them without the benefit of counsel from others. Such a great amount of responsibility makes this career very demanding and rewarding. It is also why those who make law enforcement a career tend to stay for a long time and feel a great sense of accomplishment.

The career descriptions that follow are fairly general; the specific details for the department you are interested in will vary depending on your location.

GENERAL POLICE PATROL

Whether riding in a patrol car, riding on a bicycle, or walking a post (beat) in an urban setting, you are the first responder for those who need assistance. This is where you gain the most diverse experience in dealing with a wide variety of people in an endless array of circumstances and incidents. General patrol work can also include enforcing vehicle and traffic laws.

INVESTIGATORS, DETECTIVES, AND PLAIN CLOTHES OFFICERS

Police officers with these titles are considered the "next level" in a police department's organizational chain. In some departments, these positions are considered a promotion. In other departments, they are considered a reassignment or lateral transfer from the uniform function. In this second case, the assignment may only be temporary before you are returned to uniform patrol. This position sometimes involves the investigation of higher-grade crimes or the follow-up work needed to solve crimes or resolve incidents. Duties include conducting preliminary and follow-up investigations, preparing the required investigative reports, identifying and apprehending the suspect, and preparing a case for a successful prosecution. Depending on the agency, detectives may work on many different cases or they may specialize in certain areas, some of which are listed below.

SPECIALIZATION

Modern law enforcement demands provide a myriad of diverse and interesting specialty jobs. These positions offer police recruit candidates with the needed education and skill sets the opportunity to contribute to the agency. Areas such as forensic science (including DNA analysis), white collar computer crime, and criminal gang enterprises require people with science degrees, computer skills, and language skills. As previously mentioned, new terrorism threats have made people with these skills and abilities invaluable to the police profession and the security of our nation.

MANAGEMENT POSITIONS

Usually the first step into management is the first-line supervisor position, which may be a sergeant, a corporal, or a senior patrol officer. These are vital leaders who ensure that jobs are getting done. They also provide valuable training and guidance for patrol officers.

There may also be further advancement opportunities, depending on the size of the department. Middle management positions can include the ranks of lieutenant and captain. The scope widens at this level with more responsibilities that may include managing more personnel at the scene of more serious crimes and incidents as well as facility management and budgeting.

ON THE BEAT

"The patrolman should walk with purpose, energetically and on the alert, avoiding the appearance of one who has nothing to do but put in time. His movement should be unhurried, even while apprehending a criminal unless there is something definite to be gained by speed; a running policeman will attract a crowd quickly. The patrolman should ordinarily patrol to the left, that is, with his shield to the curb. This is done for the reason that superior officers patrol to the right and, therefore, can more readily find the patrolman. Patrolling should never under any circumstances be reduced to a habit so that the patrolman is ordinarily at a given spot at a given time; the patrol should be irregular. The competent beat patrolman stops occasionally and casually looks back to observe what is going on. He cuts through alleys, yards, and private passageways; he retraces his steps. At night he occasionally stands in dark spots in order to scrutinize closely all passersby. Patrolling after dark is ordinarily done along the property line in order to try more readily doors and windows. The patrolman keeps on the outside in patrolling a crowded thoroughfare so that he may be seen. That is the reason the patrolman wears a uniform; its presence distinctly acts as a deterrent to crime....

"Patrolling a beat properly is both a science and an art. Improper and incompetent patrolling is a nuisance to the public and a cause of unhappiness and dissatisfaction to the beat patrolman.

"The outstanding patrolman knows almost every person on his beat and has their unqualified confidence. They know him, they respect him, and they bring their troubles to him. Consequently, they admire him and look up to him; in a sense, his relationship with the people on his beat is like that of a father of a large family. No reward is as rich in the esteem of one's fellow men. The work of the beat patrolman can bring that and, therefore, be full of happiness. The beat patrolman has the opportunity to reap rewards far beyond his monetary salary."

—from *Basic Police Procedure*,
published by the Pennsylvania Chiefs of Police Association, 1940

Upper management positions can include deputy chief, deputy superintendent, or deputy commissioner. Responsibilities may include department-wide planning, hiring, and larger-scale operations. These upper management positions report directly to the head of the agency (chief, commissioner, superintendent, or sheriff). The agency head is the person who must answer to criticism when things go wrong (such as a controversial police shooting) and the person who can take credit for all the positive accomplishment (such as a reduction in the crime rate).

CHOOSING A LOCATION

For those of you who have decided to be a police officer but have not decided where or with what agency, consider the following:

The larger the agency, the greater the number of opportunities that are available. Agencies such as the Los Angeles Police Department, California Highway Patrol, New York City Police Department, and New York State Police serve large populations over vast amounts of geography. These large agencies have crime labs, SWAT teams, K-9, aviation, and marine units, and computer crime specialists. Their resources and missions are usually more diverse and greater than the small-town, ten-member police departments. However, all police agencies, regardless of size, provide a highly valued service to society and need to employ consummate, dedicated police professionals.

Just as a comparison, let's take a look at two police departments in two different jurisdictions in the same state: Saratoga Springs, NY and New York City.

Don't misunderstand me—I'm not making any sort of comparison between these two departments as far as the value of their work. The officers in Saratoga do important work and so do the folks in the NYPD. But if your fondest dream is to fly a police helicopter, Saratoga may not be the place for you.

Regardless of where you would like to work as a police officer, think about what your skills and goals are. Now do some research on the department, or departments, you are interested in. Is it a good match to your skills and your goals?

SARATOGA SPRINGS POLICE DEPARTMENT

The Saratoga Springs Police Department has 65 full-time officers who protect a population of more than 28,000 in a 28-square-mile area.

They handled approximately 29,789 service calls in 2009. The department has 1 captain and 4 lieutenants. There are 11 investigators who perform detective functions. To learn more about the Saratoga Springs Police Department, visit their website at *www.saratogapolice.org*.

NEW YORK CITY POLICE DEPARTMENT

The New York City Police Department employs 38,000 sworn members who protect a population of more than 8.2 million residents in a 322-square-mile area. The department has over 400 members of the elite Emergency Services Unit, which includes such specialties as SWAT and K-9. The Harbor Unit includes a Scuba Team of 30 divers and also deploys 27 marine vessels. There are approximately 750 captains and more than 1,500 lieutenants. To learn more about the NYPD, visit their website at *www.nyc.gov/html/nypd/home.html*.

PREPARE YOURSELF

Remember: The front line police officer is where everyone starts out. You gain experience, credibility, and a reputation for professionalism.

You have already taken a big step toward becoming a police officer: You've been proactive, seeking out this book to make yourself a better candidate. To learn more about how to find employment opportunities with police departments throughout the United States, as well as what the application process is like, turn to chapter two.

CHAPTER TWO

The Application Process

This chapter reviews in detail all the steps of the application process. It's important to know that the application process is not the same as being hired. You will usually have to pass each step before you can proceed and have the job you want. Remember, this is a general guide; you should always review the process specific to the police department to which you are applying. You may consider applying to numerous departments.

APPLICATION OVERVIEW

The application process varies somewhat from department to department. The following are different steps within the process, beginning with finding a job opening.

Find a Job Opening

↓

Review the Minimum Requirements

↓

Complete the Application

↓

Review All Materials Sent to You in Response to Your Application

↓

Take the Written Test

↓

Pass the Physical Test /Preliminary Medical Review

↓

Complete the Psychological Test

↓

Successfully Complete a Background Investigation

↓

Take the Polygraph Test

↓

Complete an Interview

FINDING JOB OPENINGS

Before you can apply for a job, you have to know that one is available. Fortunately, most police departments have websites. With access to the Internet, you also have access to all recruitment postings and job openings available within the department you are interested in. If you don't know the website address for the department you are interested in, use any search engine and type in "[city's name] police department." Once at the website, you should look for key words such as jobs, careers, employment, and recruitment.

If you do not have access to the Internet, you should call your local police department (you will find the number in the government pages of the phone book), go to your local library, or check your local newspaper or community bulletin board for job openings. In larger cities, such as New York, you may even see billboards and posters for upcoming recruitment drives. Today, many departments will also set up recruitment drives at shopping malls and on college campuses.

Many police agencies have walk-in examinations. The New York City Police Department (NYPD) offers a walk-in exam in some locations, such as on college campuses. It is usually limited to "first come, first served" candidates. The San Francisco Police Department gives an exam every month. All you need for these walk-ins is some form of valid identification and/or a driver's license. Check the announcements on the respective department websites for details.

MINIMUM REQUIREMENTS

Minimum requirements vary depending on the department in which you hope to work.

Some possible types of requirements are:

- **Citizenship.** Most departments require applicants to be citizens of the United States by the time of hiring.
- **Age.** Age requirements for prospective applicants can vary. The age requirement for taking the test can be lower than the age for hiring. The New York City Police applicants can file for the exam at 17.5 years old. Most agencies require applicants to be 21 years old at the time of actual hiring. The upper limit can also vary. The NYPD upper limit is 35 years old. There may be further allowance for military experience. Some police departments have abandoned this upper limit.
- **Education.** In most cases, a high school diploma or GED is required. Many agencies now require college credits (60 hours for the NYPD and the New York State Police (NYSP)). Some agencies will accept military experience in lieu of college credits.
- **Licensure.** A current, valid driver's license is usually required.
- **Convictions.** Applicants should NOT have any felony convictions or dishonorable discharges from the military.
- **Vision/Health.** Generally, applicants are required to have good or correctable vision, must have a reasonable height/weight ratio, and may not take illegal drugs.

FILLING OUT THE APPLICATION

Whether filling out an application online or submitting a written version, make sure it is *accurate, complete,* and *legible!* This application is actually the beginning of your background investigation. It is the first impression the agency will have of you!

Something you should always strive for regardless of the type of application you complete is *honesty. Don't try to hide anything on your application.* Tell the truth. If there is a gap in your work record because you took three months off to hike the Appalachian Trail, that's fine. Or, what if you dropped out of high school and drifted for a while before you got back on track and went back for your GED? Well, so what? Recruiters know they are dealing with human beings with different life situations.

Also, do not forget to proofread the whole application. Check your spelling and grammar. If you are not sure about something, look it up. Have someone else read what you have written to make sure it makes sense.

Once you have submitted your application, you just have to wait. Most departments will notify you when they receive your application. Even if they don't, have patience! Some agencies process thousands of applicants. The application itself should state what you will hear and when.

REVIEW ALL MATERIALS YOU RECEIVE

After you have received the good news that you are scheduled for the next round of testing, then what? The most important thing you can do is study the information you get from the agency to which you are applying. The application process can vary widely from one jurisdiction to another, so the information in this book may or may not apply to your application. But all law enforcement agencies want to make sure their applicants are well prepared. Most of the time, you will receive a packet of information about what you will be tested on, how well you need to do on those tests to move on, and everything else you might need to know. Even if there is no formal information booklet, the officer in charge of recruitment will be happy to answer your questions. If you are ever in doubt about what you are going to have to do, make a phone call. Some departments even offer applicants a test preparation course for the Police Officer Exam—take advantage of it!

MAKE A LIST OF QUESTIONS

If for whatever reason you still have questions about what is expected of you or what your next step in the application process will be, write them down. Leave your list of questions for a couple of hours or, better yet, a couple of days, then come back to it. Can you think of any other questions? Write them down. Once you have a good list of questions, call or email the recruiting office. You don't want to pester the recruiters with a bunch of phone calls or emails when you can probably get all of your questions answered at once.

THE POLICE OFFICER EXAM

You will definitely have to take a written test of some kind. And, unfortunately, that is about all I can tell you for sure. Some states have set up a statewide testing system. Applicants to all municipal police departments throughout the state take the same standardized test, often a civil service test. Each city will then set a cut-off point—or passing score. You can ask for your scores to be sent to as many different police forces as you like, but they will only go out to the departments you are eligible for. Even within this statewide system, some cities, especially the larger ones, may choose to administer their own tests. It just depends on the specific department.

Some cities have tests that are very specifically designed for that jurisdiction. For example, the department sends each of its applicants a booklet that covers local laws, including traffic laws. You are asked to memorize these laws and apply them to situations described in the test itself.

You can see why it is so important to pay attention to what you are told by the agency you are applying to. However the written test is designed, it almost always takes the form of a standardized, multiple-choice test, around 100 questions long.

Here are some of the topics that may be tested on different versions of the Police Officer Exam:

- **Basic grammar and spelling.** Nothing tricky—you just need to brush up on the basics, like subject/verb agreement.

- **Reading comprehension.** You will need to read a short passage (usually a description of a law-enforcement scenario) and answer questions about the most important aspects of the situation.

- **Mathematics.** Don't panic—there's no calculus or trigonometry, just standard addition, subtraction, and multiplication.

- **Police situations.** This covers the bulk of most written exams. For example, you may be given a description of a situation, a legal definition of a specific crime, or a police policy. Working from that information, you will be asked to make decisions that demonstrate your ability to make reasonable judgments and accurately interpret and apply written guidelines. The good news is, correct answers rely heavily on common sense.

You will understand more about the Police Officer Exam when you complete the review chapters and take the practice tests at the end of this book.

OTHER TOPICS

Memorization (sometimes called Observation): Before answering these questions you are required to observe and memorize either a picture or written text. Questions must be answered based only on memory.

Spatial Orientation (sometimes called Map Reading, Directional Orientation, or Visualization): These questions test your ability to understand the relationship between the location of two items or to visualize a route, location, or position based on a graph or text.

Written Expression (sometimes called Report Writing): You may have to write in correct English or recognize correct written English.

Information Ordering: These questions require you to place unordered text in a logical order.

Inductive Reasoning: These questions involve taking different observations, pieces of information, or specific answers to problems and forming a general conclusion or rule.

Deductive Reasoning: These questions involve using a general rule and applying it to different observations or problems, and then determining what is a reasonable, logical conclusion or answer.

Problem Sensitivity: These questions are most similar to Police Situation questions. Your task is to be able to identify causes and solutions to various problems.

Personality Profile or Attributes: Today many departments have added a line of questioning that is in the form of a statement about an attitude or a tendency that you may exhibit. You will be asked to respond as to how strongly you agree or disagree with the statement. Generally, these types of questions are used to see if a candidate's traits are a good "fit" for certain types of jobs.

THE PHYSICAL TEST/PRELIMINARY MEDICAL REVIEW

Many departments will conduct a preliminary medical review, which includes vision and hearing tests and height/weight ratios, when you show up for the physical agility testing segment of the application process. (If you successfully complete all the steps of the entire hiring process, you may undergo a more extensive medical examination prior to being offered a job.)

You need to be reasonably fit to do a good job as a police officer. If you don't already have some sort of physical fitness routine, start one immediately. Law enforcement agencies want people who have adopted a lifestyle of fitness; fit officers are more productive and have fewer injuries.

Your primary task is to pass a specific physical test. You should start immediately by researching what your test will entail and then train for those specific events. Agencies will require you to strictly adhere to the test protocols. If you are required to do 40 sit-ups in one minute, being able to do 100 crunches is meaningless unless you can do the 40 sit-ups.

The specific test you will have to pass will depend on the agency, but almost all of them include most or all of the following:

- **Distance run.** You will have to run a certain distance. Many agencies use the 40th or 50th percentile of the Cooper Institute for Aerobics Research Standards as the minimum standard to complete a 1.5 mile run. The requirements may be age and gender normed.

- **Obstacle course.** This involves a kind of rapid scramble over and through different kinds of barriers—fences, barrels, low monkey bars, whatever the department has set up.

- **Dummy drag.** You will have to drag a certain amount of dead weight, usually 150 pounds, for a specific distance. Even if you are strong and fit, this is harder than it sounds; it requires you to use muscles not often called upon. Definitely try to practice beforehand.

- **Weight lifting.** Usually, this involves basic bench press, squats, and curls. How much you have to lift and how many reps depends on your size and gender.

- **Sit-ups, push-ups, and pull-ups.** Find out the specific number of repetitions required; if it's more than you can comfortably do now, slowly work up to it.

Keep in mind, your performance on test day could suffer because of nervousness. Train to a level that will give you a cushion of 20 percent or more; however, don't over train just before the physical test. You might consider taking a day or two off before the event. If you haven't done your homework before this, cramming your workouts in at the last minute may only hurt you. It is always recommended that before starting any fitness plan, you consult with a physician first.

In general, being physically fit will help you handle stress (always a big part of any law enforcement job). Fitness increases your stamina and really does help you think more clearly.

Remember, always check with the department you are applying to. They will give you specifics about their standards. Some of the larger forces have scheduled training programs to help applicants get up to the required fitness level.

The Psychological Exam

In general, people tend to get nervous at the mention of "psychological" anything, but there's really no point in getting wound up about this portion of the application process. Actually, I think this is one of the easiest parts of the whole process—you can't study for this test and you can't outguess it, so there is really nothing to do to prepare. Here is some information about what the psychological test entails.

THE WRITTEN TEST

Almost all departments give applicants a standardized, multiple-choice test—either one they have designed themselves or one that is commonly used in psychological settings. The most common test is the Minnesota Multiphasic Psychological Inventory (MMPI). Updated versions of the test include the MMPI-2 and the MMPI-2RF. These tests are comprised of over 500 true-false statements, which you read and respond to. Just to give you some idea of what it's like, the statements range from things like, "I prefer romance novels to mysteries," to "My father is a good man," to "I am an important person." You mark your answers, depending on whether the statement never applies to you, sometimes applies to you, often applies to you, or always applies to you. And that's it. Another commonly used self-reporting instrument is the California Psychological Inventory. This instrument is comprised of over 400 similar questions.

Other tests may ask you to complete sentences or to react to specific phrases: "When I'm at home _____," or "My mother's favorite _____." Don't obsess over your answers. Answer honestly, but think about what you are writing. "My mother's favorite color is purple" will probably send a better message than "My mother's favorite was always my worthless brother." However, do not waste a lot of time trying to come up with the "right" or the "best" answers. You are better off just answering honestly. The MMPI and all psychological tests are specifically designed to pick up inconsistencies that indicate someone is manipulating the answers. You don't gain anything by being dishonest in your responses.

THE PSYCHOLOGICAL INTERVIEW

In some departments, you will have an interview with a psychologist, usually some time after you complete the written test. The psychologist will probably ask you some follow-up questions about the results of your written test, and he or she may also ask other questions to find out a little more about what kind of person you are.

Don't worry too much about this. Anything you say is private, and you are not going to leave the testing room in a straitjacket. You may be asked questions no one's ever asked you before—things like, "What's the worst thing you've ever done?" or "Do you have a happy marriage?" Don't say, "None of your business"—although that will probably be your first impulse. Just answer the questions as honestly as you can.

THE BACKGROUND INVESTIGATION

The background investigation can actually start with the scrutiny of the information you submit in your original application. The first major step is usually the verification of your eligibility to even pursue the application process. Part of the background may be a separate questionnaire regarding specific issues, such as how many traffic tickets you have been issued or traffic charges you have been convicted of or plead guilty to. Remember, this type of information can be verified, so honesty is best!

All other information that you have supplied is then followed up on. Usually, the majority of the background check is commenced once you have successfully completed the written exam, physical test, and psychological test.

Background investigators will look up your school transcripts, your credit report, and your medical, military, and employment history. They will also review any arrest records, vehicle and traffic violations, and motor vehicle accidents you may have had. Depending on the agency to which you are applying, that may be as far as the background check goes.

The background check will include interviewing the references and employers you have listed. They may interview former coworkers. The investigators ask the kinds of questions any employer would ask—how your work performance was, what kind of student you were, that sort of thing. You should tell your references that you are applying for a police job and that you have listed them as references so they may be contacted.

Of course, the investigators will gather other sources, too. There is no way you can alert every single person the investigators might speak to—which is really the point of a background check. But unless you had significant trouble with former neighbors or employers, you shouldn't have anything to worry about.

THE POLYGRAPH TEST

More and more police departments are requiring polygraphs. If you have never taken one before, the idea can be intimidating. You may be asking yourself the following: How does it work? What are they going to ask about? What if I'm nervous during the test? Can I beat the polygraph?

HOW DOES IT WORK?

The polygraph measures several involuntary physiological responses to stress—specifically, the stress involved in lying. When you are actually "hooked up," you will be seated in a chair near the polygraph. Three sensors will be attached:

1. Blood pressure cuff, to measure heart rate
2. Convoluted rubber tubes, attached around the abdomen and chest, to measure respiratory activity
3. Two small metal plates, attached to the fingers, to measure sweat gland activity

The questioning phase also has three parts:

Pretest: Before you are hooked up to the polygraph, the examiner asks you several questions. There are the baseline questions—"Is your name Jane Doe? Were you born in Peoria, Illinois?" Then there are the real questions—questions such as, "Have you ever manufactured, transported, or sold illegal drugs?" You are not going to lie about your name or where you were born; even if your heart is beating faster than it normally would because you are nervous, that elevated heart rate is going to register as the baseline for the test.

Chart Collection Phase: You are then hooked up to the polygraph, and the examiner goes through the questions again. Then, there is the follow-up—"Did you lie when you told me you haven't manufactured, transported, or sold illegal drugs?" This is the key to the use of the polygraph—the specific questioning and the immediate response.

Test Data Analysis Phase: The examiner reviews the charts and notes areas where deception is indicated. When appropriate, the examiner will ask the subject to explain or clarify any unusual physiological responses—something along the lines of, "You seemed to react strongly to the questions about theft. Is there a specific reason for that?"

WHAT ARE THEY GOING TO ASK ABOUT?

Law enforcement agencies maintain very high ethical standards among their employees. Even so, they are not looking for saints or robots. Drug use isn't defined as being in the same room as a marijuana cigarette; theft isn't defined as making a few personal phone calls on company time.

The questions on a polygraph are very carefully designed to be limited and specific, and thus useful. They won't ask you if you have stolen pens from work. They will ask questions like, "Have you ever significantly defrauded an employer?" or "Have you ever manufactured or sold illicit drugs?"

WHAT IF THE POLYGRAPH SHOWS I'M LYING WHEN I'M NOT?

During the pretest, the examiner will assess your emotional state and physical condition and allow for any effect these might have. The control questions help identify subjects who are extremely responsive or extremely nervous; there are specialized tests that are used in these circumstances. The examiners make every effort to get an accurate reading from the polygraph.

If you know a deceptive response on your polygraph is inaccurate, you can request a second polygraph with a second examiner, or you can ask to have the first polygraph reviewed by another examiner.

As far as trying to beat the polygraph—forget it. It is not the machine you are trying to fool, it's the examiner—and a skilled, experienced polygraph examiner is almost impossible to fool.

THE INTERVIEW

For most people, this is the most stressful part of the application process. Don't worry. Just prepare yourself ahead of time, and you will do fine.

BEFORE THE INTERVIEW

Do your homework. Find out about the interview process. If it's a small local department, they may want to ask you about your knowledge and interest in the community and the department. You may be directly interviewed by the chief. How many officers are on the force you are applying to? What is the major crime problem in the community? Have there been any big changes in policy or focus recently? Are there any cases or investigations that have been widely covered in the news? Who is the police chief? How long has he been there? Did he come in from outside or was he promoted from within? How does he get along with the mayor? You can get information like this from local newspapers or from the department itself; work it into your answers where appropriate, and you will impress your interviewers.

For example, if a question refers to gang graffiti, you can say something like, "Well, the gang problem is the main target of the new Street Shield unit, and they have been having some success—gang activity is down 12 percent since last year. In light of that, I would coordinate my efforts with the unit to build on their success."

Of course, you won't impress anyone if your information is wrong or doesn't really connect with what you are saying. Think about the information you are going to use; don't just blurt things out.

There are agencies in which the interviews are designed as a specific part of the background investigation. You will most likely be asked about your personal history in conjunction with certain results of the psychological exam and/or polygraph. Sometimes these types of questions are asked just for clarification purposes.

There are those departments that have a much more formal, structured interview process. These questions may be competency-based, can be more complex, and can revolve around a scenario you are given, with accompanying laws or regulations. You would then be given questions regarding what issues or problems you may see, and how you would respond. The questions are designed to elicit responses that indicate if the candidate has the abilities the department has determined are essential in good job performance. The line of questioning may also be more behavior-based. This means you may be asked about your past experiences and how you demonstrated competent behavior. An example might be how you exhibited good communication skills. Usually, such departments offer a more detailed preparatory guide for these interviews.

Anticipate the questions. I can't tell you exactly what the interviewers are going to ask you, but I can tell you what they are looking for. They want to know if you can deal with conflict, get along with other people, and learn from mistakes. To get at that information, they will ask you for details about your previous experience and education. To further probe for these qualities, they will sometimes give you a hypothetical situation and ask for your response. This also tests your ability to make good decisions and think on your feet.

Here are some general ways you can prepare yourself:

- Look at the interview process and your own application, and put yourself in the interviewers' shoes. They are going to push to find out if you have got what it takes to be a good, responsible police officer. Come up with your own questions and honest answers.

  Here is an example: "I see you left your job at Kasper Dry Cleaning after only three months. Why is that?" Do not say: "I had to quit because the manager was a pushy jerk, and he kept trying to make me do stuff that wasn't in my job description." That makes you sound like someone who is always looking for a scapegoat.

Instead, put it like this: "I had a personality conflict with the manager that we just weren't able to resolve. That was one of my first jobs out of school, and since then I've really worked on my people skills. In fact, at my current job, I was able to negotiate with the boss to get a better scheduling system set up for all the employees."

This shows that you are able to learn from your mistakes, and that you have developed the ability to work with others—both important aspects of being a good police officer.

This is an important step in your preparation, so take your time. Ask a friend to help you if you are having trouble coming up with difficult questions. You really can't overprepare; even if the interviewers don't ask exactly the same questions you come up with, they will probably be similar. It will also mean there is less chance you will be caught off guard.

- Imagine some difficult situations a police officer might face, and come up with your responses. You will need to have some practice at making good decisions quickly. These are the kinds of things you might be asked:

"You are on patrol and you see a car being driven erratically. You pull it over, and the driver is the police chief's 16-year-old daughter. There are empty beer bottles in the front seat and her eyes are red. She says they were left by her boyfriend, who she just dropped off, and her eyes are red because they had a fight and she was crying. What do you do?"

"You are working on a narcotics case, and you make a big bust. Another police officer, your partner's brother-in-law, pockets some of the cash before it's booked into evidence. You tell your partner, and he just shrugs and says that the guy's a bum but his sister loves him. What do you do?"

"The station gets an anonymous call about child abuse at a certain address. You are sent to check it out. When you get there, the man who answers the door says there is no problem. You hear a kid screaming in the background. When you ask to come in and take a look, the man tells you to come back with a warrant. What do you do?"

When you are in the interview, the officers will keep adding complications to the original situation. Don't rush into an answer, and don't change your answer once you have given it. Most of the time, there is no black-and-white answer they are looking for; they just want to see how you react to stress and whether you are able to make reasonable decisions under pressure. The only time you should take back your answer is if you realize that there really is a better solution than the one you first gave. Whatever you do, do not change any answer more than once.

Practice with a friend. Get someone you trust to do some role playing with you. Ideally, this will be a friend who is a police officer and who has been through the interview process. But whoever it is, make sure it is someone who can give you honest feedback.

Give that person the questions and situations you have come up with, along with your application. Ask him or her to write out some more questions and then put you through an interview. This might seem weird at first, and neither one of you may want to take it seriously, but keep at it. This is the best way to prepare yourself, so you can walk into that interview room feeling confident.

Take notes while you are practicing, and ask your friend to do the same. What do you need to work on? What are your strengths? Keep thinking about how to improve your performance, and incorporate those ideas into your notes.

Prepare a closer. At the end of the interview, you will almost always be asked, "Do you have any questions?" Have your answer prepared. If you have a couple of good questions, ask them. Don't ask about retirement benefits or how soon you can be promoted to detective. That really sends the wrong signal—that you are assuming you are going to be hired and that you are focused a bit too much on your own personal goals. If you can't think of any questions, just say something like, "I don't have any questions, but I would like to say that becoming a police officer has been a lifelong goal, and I believe my skills would make me an asset to this department."

Make sure you know how to get to the interview site. Do not assume it is at the police station. Check your notification form. Even if you have been to the station, or the courthouse, or wherever it is you are supposed to go, make another trip. If you can, go at the same time of day you will be heading in for your interview. Time the trip, then add a safety margin for traffic jams, subway delays, flat tires, or any other transportation disaster.

THE NIGHT BEFORE THE INTERVIEW

Check your transportation. If you are driving, do you have enough gas in the tank? Have you been having problems with your car? If so, arrange a backup—get a friend to stand by in case you need a ride, or make sure you have enough money for cab fare and the number of a good company. If you are using mass transit, make sure you have a ticket or money to pay for one.

Check your clothes. For some people, this is second nature, but others may need a little prompting here. Men should wear a suit or a sport coat and tie. Women should wear a dress or suit. Lay out every single thing you are going to wear to the interview, including your underwear. Make sure it is all clean, matching, with no buttons missing or seams ripped. If you haven't worn those clothes for a while, try them on now—while there is still time to find an alternative in case they don't fit. You want to minimize any nasty surprises in the morning.

Go over your notes. Read through your application so it is fresh in your mind. The interviewers will have read it and will probably have it in front of them, and you won't want to just repeat what you have already told them. Read the notes from your mock interview. Think about the positive aspects about yourself that you want to get across.

Get a good night's sleep. This is not the time to go out for a drink with your friends. Have a good dinner, and do something relaxing like watch TV or read a book.

THE DAY OF THE INTERVIEW

Make sure you get up early. You do not want to be rushed, so give yourself plenty of time to get ready. If you are a sound sleeper, set two alarms and have a friend call you.

Eat breakfast, but don't overdo the caffeine. You want to give yourself some fuel, but you don't want to be hyped up on caffeine. Have a sensible breakfast like cereal and fruit or eggs and toast.

Leave early. You want to be in the waiting room 15 minutes before your appointment—regardless of traffic or a slow bus. Believe me, people notice promptness, and it makes a good impression. Bring your notes, and you can use the waiting time for a little last-minute reviewing. If you are starting to get stressed out, take a few really deep breaths. Don't start worrying about all the things that could go wrong; instead, focus on doing well and making a good impression. That should be the image you carry into the room.

IN THE INTERVIEW

Acknowledge everyone. Someone will take the lead and introduce himself or herself and the other interviewers. This person may or may not be the chief decision maker in this situation, so you need to acknowledge and address all the interviewers—now and throughout the interview.

When you are introduced, smile, shake hands, and greet each of the interviewers. When you answer questions, make eye contact with everyone. I'm not saying you should sit there with your eyes darting from person to person, but you do need to acknowledge that you are addressing more than one interviewer.

Listen to the questions. One of the biggest mistakes people make is answering the question they think they have heard, instead of the question that has been asked. If you are in any doubt, ask for a clarification.

Don't blurt out your answer right away. You don't get extra points for speed. Give yourself a second or two to gather your thoughts and focus on the best answer to the question. You don't want to have to retract your answer later.

Identify the "bad cop." If one of the interviewers begins to play the heavy, the one who challenges your answers and tries to get you to back down, don't be aggressive with this person, but don't let him or her bully you either. Address this person directly; don't get thrown by the questions or by his or her tone. And don't take it personally. This person is not out to get you—the point is to see how you react to stress and confrontation.

Thank the interviewers. When you get up to leave, shake hands again with each of the interviewers and thank them for the opportunity to speak with them.

PART TWO

Preparing for the Police Officer Exam

CHAPTER THREE

Diagnostic Quiz

Before you begin reviewing grammar, reading, math, and the police situation concepts that you might face on the Police Officer Exam, it's a good idea to know the strength of your skills so you can spend more time on the subjects where you need more practice. The following diagnostic quiz offers a sampling of questions you might see tested on the exam. Answers and explanations are found at the end of the chapter. When you're done, turn to chapters four, five, six, seven, and eight for a review of material and for tips to help you face test day with confidence.

DIAGNOSTIC QUIZ

For the following questions, choose the right word from the italicized words in the sentence.

1. The courtroom had to be cleared of spectators before the trial could *precede/ proceed.*

2. Greed, along with gullibility, *cause/causes* many people to fall for Ponzi schemes and other financial scams.

3. Neither the attorneys nor the courthouse observers *expect/expects* the trial to last more than two weeks.

4. Some people believe it's difficult to *prosecute/persecute* Internet offenses because the statutes haven't been written to reflect the new technology.

5. Of the many recent advances in science, DNA analysis *has/have* the biggest impact on law enforcement.

Rewrite the following sentences to eliminate confusion or correct grammatical errors. Use the blank lines provided.

6. Officer Melton couldn't hardly see out the windshield because of the heavy rain.

    _____

    _____

    _____

    _____

7. Reflecting the glare of the cruiser's lights, the tall weeds in front of the factory almost hid the shards of broken glass.

    _____

    _____

    _____

    _____

8. Because Officer Wilson genuinely liked talking to people, he sometimes missing his days on the street.

    _____

    _____

    _____

    _____

9. Officer Kwame told Officer O'Neil herself to trade shifts over the weekend.

    _____

    _____

    _____

    _____

10. Street festivals being targets for pickpockets, because of the crowded conditions and many distractions.

    _____

    _____

    _____

    _____

Read the following short passage and answer the question that follows.

PASSAGE 1

The first detective stories were written by Edgar Allan Poe and Arthur Conan Doyle in the mid-1800s, a time of great public interest in science and scientific progress. Newspapers continually ran articles describing the latest scientific discoveries, and scientists were often treated like national heroes. Like the rest of the public, Poe and Conan Doyle were fascinated with the systematic, logical approach used by scientists in their experiments. Poe and Conan Doyle both endowed their detective heroes with outstanding powers of scientific reasoning.

The character of Sherlock Holmes illustrates Conan Doyle's admiration for the scientific mind. In every case that Holmes agrees to investigate, he is able to use the most unlikely pieces of evidence to track down and identify the criminal. Relying on his restless eye and phenomenal reasoning powers, Holmes pieces together the solution to the crime from details like the type of cigar ash left at a crime scene or the kind of ink used to write a letter. In fact, Holmes's careful attention to detail reminds the reader of Charles Darwin's scientific method in *The Origin of Species,* the revolutionary book on natural history published 20 years earlier.

11. Mark the following choices, indicating whether each is a main idea (MI), paragraph topic (PT), or detail (D).

    A. cigar ash _____

    B. Poe and Conan Doyle endowed their characters with great powers of scientific reasoning. _____

    C. Sherlock Holmes had an eye for detail. _____

    D. Sherlock Holmes had the mind of a scientist. _____

    E. Scientists use a methodical, step-by-step approach to thinking. _____

    F. Holmes can be compared to Charles Darwin. _____

    G. The detective story was created in the mid-1800s. _____

Each of the following statements ends with a keyword. Use the statement's main idea and the keyword in bold to figure out which of the four choices makes the most sense.

12. Some people seem to believe that stricter gun control would eliminate violent crime. **But**

    A. the causes of violent crime are too complicated for any one action, including gun control, to overcome by itself.

    B. gun control is favored by many law enforcement officers.

    C. these people really aren't part of the mainstream, since they tend to be vegetarians.

    D. many Americans feel that the Second Amendment guarantees an unrestricted right to gun ownership.

13. Many police officers find it difficult to maintain friendships and other relationships with people outside law enforcement, **because**
    A. other police officers compete with them for the most desirable assignments.
    B. people outside law enforcement always want to handle the officers' firearms.
    C. working in law enforcement makes it difficult to schedule get-togethers.
    D. only other police officers readily understand the stresses of the job.

For each of the following questions, fill in the blank with any word (or phrase) that makes sense.

14. When Yoshi moved from his parents' spacious house to his first apartment, a small studio, he had to be very _____ about the belongings he took with him.

15. The two horses crossed the finish line _____, so the race was declared a tie.

16. After I replaced the broken lamp, my bedroom was much _____.

For the following questions, choose the answer that is closest in meaning to the underlined word. Please note, underlined words are just made-up words so you cannot rely on anything but the context to choose the best answer.

17. Instead of actively job hunting, Sunil was <u>soddile</u>; he figured the right job would come to him.
    A. energetic
    B. enthusiastic
    C. charming
    D. passive

18. Because it features many <u>jictic</u> actors and actresses, the movie is expected to be a huge financial success.
    A. famous
    B. clumsy
    C. rich
    D. tall

19. At her Carnegie Hall debut, the young pianist easily played the most difficult music, impressing critics with her nasivity.

    A. spirit
    B. charm
    C. personality
    D. skill

Choose the answer that is closest in meaning to the underlined word or phrase.

20. Judge Connor was known for his placid temperament; his colleagues and even his subordinates felt comfortable speaking to him directly, even criticizing him when necessary.

    A. peaceful
    B. violent
    C. gloomy
    D. lucky

21. The light that came through the windows was fleeting. It faded before anyone could examine the scene carefully.

    A. moving
    B. blinding
    C. bright
    D. brief

22. She generally paints in an abstract style, using patterns and colors. The lifelike portrait of her cat was uncharacteristic for her work.

    A. drab
    B. fashionable
    C. unusual
    D. inspiring

Read the following short passage and answer the questions that follow.

PASSAGE 2

When selecting dogs for narcotic detection training, the behavior of an individual dog is more important than the dog's breed or background. Trainers have identified several different categories of behavior that all dogs display; from a forensic standpoint, investigative behavior is the most important of these categories. A high degree of investigative behavior indicates a very inquisitive nature and a desire to examine objects closely and thoroughly. Both of these qualities make the dog an excellent candidate for narcotic detection training. Several specific signs indicate investigative behavior in dogs. First, watch the dog in its kennel. Does it stop to look and listen when it hears an unusual sound? Then, introduce a new object. Does the dog investigate it thoroughly, sniffing and pawing it? When outside the kennel, other investigative behaviors include walking or running with nose to ground, sniffing; holding the head in air, sniffing; and holding the head raised, ears erect. Of course, all dogs display this behavior to some degree; the dog who's a good candidate for training will keep sniffing and investigating after other dogs have lost interest.

23. Summarize the passage in your own words.

   _____

   _____

   _____

   _____

   _____

   _____

24. The passage implies which of the following about dogs' behavior?
    A. A dog's breed has a major impact on its behavior.
    B. Some dogs display no investigative behavior.
    C. Any dog who shows investigative behavior would be a good candidate for narcotic detection training.
    D. Dogs who show strong investigative behavior tend to be very inquisitive and examine objects closely.

25. Calculate the perimeter of this room:

16 feet

12 feet

A. 384 feet^2

B. 192 feet^2

C. 96 feet

D. 56 feet

26. Simplify: $20 + 6^2 \div 4$

A. 14

B. 29

C. 169

D. 8

27. Simplify the following: $-10 + (-3) \times (-2) - 9$

A. -25

B. -13

C. 7

D. 17

28. $2.035 + 3.9 = $ _____?

A. 2.074

B. 5.935

C. .5395

D. 2,074

29. The ratio 3 to 5 can also be expressed as the ratio 15 to _____?

A. 9

B. 12

C. 25

D. 45

30. A police department decides to employ several multilingual officers. Which of the following would be the most logical explanation for this decision?

    A. This is in compliance with federal regulations.

    B. Officers that speak more than one language have the ability to communicate with citizens in the community whose primary language is not English.

    C. Multilingual officers are always smarter than those who speak only one language.

    D. If a case takes officers to another country, multilingual officers might know that country's language and be able to communicate with people there.

31. In which of the following situations would an officer be most likely to remove his weapon from its holster?

    A. An unarmed suspect tries to walk out of the police station to escape arrest.

    B. Two men are arguing in the parking lot of a bar.

    C. A woman who has shot several citizens turns and points her gun at the officer.

    D. A young man asks to see the officer's sidearm.

32. Officer Luttrell responds to a call from a woman who reports that she was bitten by a dog, and he gathers the following information:

Location:	#5 Terrence Place
Time:	4:40 P.M.
Complaint:	dog bite
Victim:	Sandy Flora-Lupino
Suspect:	black male chow
Injury:	gash in victim's right thigh
Action Taken:	a search for the dog was unsuccessful

    Officer Luttrell is writing his report. Which of the following expresses the information most clearly and accurately?

    A. At 4:40 P.M. a dog bit Sandy Flora-Lupino at #5 Terrence Place. The dog was described by the victim as a black male chow. The victim suffered a gash in her right thigh, and the dog got away.

    B. Sandy Flora-Lupino reported that at 4:40 P.M., she was bitten by a black male chow dog. She was at #5 Terrence Place when she was bitten, but the dog was not found.

    C. Sandy Flora-Lupino stated that at 4:40 P.M. at #5 Terrence Place, she was bitten by a black male chow dog and suffered a gash in her right thigh. A search for the dog was unsuccessful.

    D. At #5 Terrence Place at 4:40 P.M., Sandy Flora-Lupino reported that she was bitten on her right thigh by a black male chow, which was searched for and was not found.

33. Officer Leland is dispatched to a residence where a man reports that he found a small child wandering around his yard. Officer Leland gathers the following information:

Location:	350 Stone St.
Time:	6:00 P.M.
Police Contacted by:	Juan Phillips
Occurrence:	a small girl is found wandering in a stranger's yard
Description of Child:	about four years old with blonde hair and blue dress
Identification on Child:	"Mary Thomas" and phone number written in the tag of her dress
Action Taken:	parents contacted, child taken to the E.R.

Officer Leland has to write his report. Which of the following expresses the information most clearly and accurately?

A. Juan Phillips of 350 Stone St. found Mary Thomas, a small, blonde-haired girl of about three years of age, wandering in his yard and called the police. Mr. Phillips found the girl at about 6:00 P.M. Her name and phone number were found written on her dress's tag, and her parents were contacted. She was then taken to the emergency room for examination.

B. At 350 Stone St., a young girl who turned out to be four-year-old, blonde-haired Mary Thomas, was found in Juan Phillips's yard by Mr. Phillips at 6:00 P.M. The child's parents were contacted, and she was taken to the emergency room for examination.

C. Mary Thomas was found at the home of Juan Phillips of 350 Stone St. at 6:00 P.M. Mr. Phillips reported that the small, four-year-old, blonde child was wandering in his yard. The child's parents were contacted after her name and phone number were found in the child's dress tag. Mary Thomas was then taken to the emergency room for examination.

D. At 6:00 P.M., Juan Phillips reported finding a small, blonde-haired girl, about four years old, wandering in his yard at 350 Stone St. The child's name, Mary Thomas, and her telephone number were found in the tag of her blue dress. The child's parents were contacted, and she was taken to the emergency room for examination.

34. After work, Bill and Tony were walking to their cars, which were parked in a parking garage. As they approached their cars, a man jumped out from behind a kiosk, pointed a gun at them, stole their briefcases, and ran off. During his investigation of the incident, Officer Perez interviewed several witnesses, who gave him the following descriptions of the suspect. Which of these descriptions should Officer Perez consider most likely to be correct?

A. 5'10" male, about 200 pounds, wearing a black jumpsuit and black sandals

B. 6'10" male, about 200 pounds, wearing a black shirt, black pants, and black boots

C. 5'10" male, about 300 pounds, wearing a blue jumpsuit and black boots

D. 5'10" male, about 200 pounds, wearing a black jumpsuit and black boots

35. A produce salesman at a deli reported that a woman stole a bag of expensive cherries, two grapefruits, and a box of sugared pecans from the deli, then fled on foot. During her investigation, Officer Camden interviewed several witnesses. Of the following descriptions of the woman, given to Officer Camden by witnesses, which should she consider most likely to be correct?

   A. 5'2" and 150 pounds, wearing a yellow sundress and a brown straw hat
   B. 5'9" and 110 pounds, wearing a yellow sundress and a brown straw hat
   C. 5'2" and 150 pounds, wearing a green sundress and a brown straw hat
   D. 5'2" and 110 pounds, wearing a yellow sundress and a white straw hat

36. A person is guilty of **RECKLESS ENDANGERMENT OF PROPERTY** when he recklessly engages in conduct that creates a substantial risk of damage to the property of another person in an amount exceeding $250. Based solely upon this definition, which of the following is the best example of Reckless Endangerment of Property?

   A. At a party, Randolph drinks too much and carries his girlfriend's $200 stereo over his head as he wades through the shallow end of her swimming pool.
   B. At the mall, Inez grabs her friend's recently purchased vacuum cleaner, valued at $245, and stands on it in order to get a better look at a celebrity who is shopping there.
   C. Henry decides to chop down a sick, large tree that sits on the property line between his house and his neighbor's. The tree falls in the wrong direction and lands within inches of the neighbor's $7,500 car.
   D. Scott, an experienced sailor, takes his father's boat out onto a local lake without asking.

ANSWERS AND EXPLANATIONS

1. *The courtroom had to be cleared of spectators before the trial could* proceed.

2. *Greed, along with gullibility,* causes *many people to fall for Ponzi schemes and other financial scams.* Phrases containing *along with* do not contribute to a compound subject.

3. *Neither the attorneys nor the courthouse observers* expect *the trial to last more than two weeks.* Here you are dealing with a *neither/nor* linking two plural nouns, so the verb must agree with the closer subject. That means you will have a plural subject and a plural verb.

4. *Some people believe it's difficult to* prosecute *Internet offenses because the statutes haven't been written to reflect the new technology.*

5. *Of the many recent advances in science, DNA analysis* has *the biggest impact on law enforcement.* This is a singular subject, DNA analysis.

There are a few ways you could have fixed these sentences. Here are some sample rewrites:

6. Officer Melton could hardly see out the windshield because of the heavy rain. Or: Officer Melton couldn't see out the windshield because of the heavy rain.

7. The tall weeds in front of the factory almost hid the shards of broken glass, which reflected the glare of the cruiser's lights.

8. Because Officer Wilson genuinely liked talking to people, he sometimes missed his days on the street.

9. Officer Kwame asked Officer O'Neil if he would be willing to trade shifts with her over the weekend.

10. Street festivals are targets for pickpockets because of the crowded conditions and many distractions.

11. **A.** cigar ash
    Detail—Illustrates Holmes's outstanding reasoning powers.

    B. Poe and Conan Doyle endowed their characters with great powers of scientific reasoning.
    Main idea—The rest of the passage tries to show this is true, using Holmes as an example.

    C. Sherlock Holmes had an eye for detail.
    Detail—Illustrates Holmes's outstanding scientific reasoning powers.

    D. Sherlock Holmes had the mind of a scientist.
    Paragraph topic—All of paragraph two seeks to illustrate this.

    E. Scientists use a methodical, step-by-step approach to thinking.
    Detail—Introduces discussion of Poe and Conan Doyle.

    F. Holmes can be compared to Charles Darwin.
    Detail—Illustrates Holmes's reasoning skills.

    G. The detective story was created in the mid-1800s.
    Detail—Introduces discussion of Poe and Conan Doyle.

12. **A** is correct. *But* is a contrast keyword, so you are looking for an idea that would cast some doubt on the original statement. The only choice that does this is A. You might have picked D, a statement which is undoubtedly true and seems to oppose the original statement. But look again. The first sentence isn't just about favoring gun control; it links gun control with an automatic reduction in crime. The only answer that directly addresses that is A.

13. **D** is correct. *Because* is an evidence keyword. You are looking for evidence—an explanation for why police officers are most comfortable with other officers. Choice D is the only answer that makes sense.

14. *Selective* or *careful*. Because Yoshi can't take everything, he has to be careful how he chooses what he moves to the new apartment.

15. *Simultaneously* or *at the same time*. That's what a tie means.

16. *Brighter* or *lighter*. After you replace a broken lamp with one that works, you would expect the room to be brighter.

17. **D** is correct. Notice the contrast. If Sunil isn't actively looking for a job, he's doing the opposite—being passive.

18. **A** is correct. If a movie stars many famous actors, most people would expect it to make money.

19. **D** is correct. If the pianist easily played difficult music, she must have had a lot of skill.

20. **A** is correct. If people are comfortable criticizing the judge to his face, he must be a peaceful person.

21. **D** is correct. If the light faded before anyone could examine the scene carefully, that means the light didn't last long.

22. **C** is correct. If the artist generally paints in an abstract style, using patterns and colors, a lifelike painting would be unusual for her.

23. Sample summary: A dog who shows strong investigative behavior is the best candidate for training in narcotics detection.

24. **D** is correct. This sentence explains why dogs demonstrating high levels of investigative behavior tend to make good narcotics detection dogs.

25. **D** is correct. This question tests your ability to calculate the perimeter of a shape, which is the sum of all sides. Add 12 feet + 16 feet + 12 feet + 16 feet = 56 feet. Answer B, 192 feet^2, is the area of the room.

26. **B** is correct. Remember the order of operations and evaluate the exponent first: $6^2 = 36$. Next, evaluate division: $36 \div 4 = 9$. Finally, evaluate addition: $20 + 9 = 29$.

27. **B** is correct. This question tests the concept of using order of operations with integers. Using order of operations, multiply -3 and -2 first to get 6. The expression then becomes $-10 + 6 - 9$. Combine the values in order from left to right.

$$-10 + 6 = -4$$
$$-4 - 9 = -4 + -9$$
$$= -13$$

28. **B** is correct. This problem tests decimal addition. Remember, it is important to line up decimal points when adding and subtracting decimals. Tack two zeroes onto the end of 3.9 to get 3.900 and then add. 2.035 + 3.900 = 5.935.

29. **C** is correct. To compare the ratio 3 to 5 with another ratio, write the ratios in fraction form and set them equal to one another. Since 3/5 = 15/?, the values in the second ratio are 5 times larger than the first ratio. To find the solution, multiply 5 × 5 to get 25 in the denominator.

30. **B** is correct. Watch for the word "always," as in C. This is often an indication that a statement is exaggerated or incorrect.

31. **C** is correct, as it is the only instance in which there is a threat to public safety (not to mention the officer's safety).

32. **C** is stated most clearly and accurately.

33. **D** is the only statement that contains all the information.

34. **D** contains the most repeaters.

35. **A** is the best answer. Note that the descriptions of the woman's weight, "150 pounds" and "110 pounds," each appear twice, canceling each other out. Descriptions of the woman's height, dress, and hat should be used to eliminate possible answers.

36. **C** is the best answer, because it is the only situation in which the property in question is worth more than $250 and in which the individual "recklessly engages in conduct that creates a substantial risk of damage to the property."

CHAPTER FOUR

Grammar and Spelling

Depending on where you are applying, you may or may not run into specific questions on the Police Officer Exam testing grammar and spelling. If you need to brush up on these basics, here is the information most likely to show up on an exam. Remember, even if your department's test doesn't include specific grammar or spelling questions, both good grammar and accurate spelling are required for clear and effective writing—another skill that may also be tested. No matter what the actual exam covers, it won't be a waste of your time to review this chapter and to complete the practice questions that follow.

GRAMMAR

This is the structure of language—how words fit together to form meaningful sentences. Most of the grammatical mistakes people make fall into one of the following categories. Identify your weak spots and focus on those.

SENTENCE FRAGMENTS

Sentence fragments are usually pretty easy to spot. When you read one, your reaction is usually, "Huh?" There is something crucial missing. In more technical terms, a sentence fragment is a group of words that looks like a sentence, but it is either grammatically or logically incomplete. Here is the grammatical test: To be a sentence, the group of words has to contain both a subject and a verb related to one another.

Take a look at this example:

The man in the lineup wearing the plaid shirt.

Well, you have a subject—*the man*. And you seem to have a verb—*wearing*. But *wearing the plaid shirt* really just modifies the subject, giving us more details about the man. There is no verb. What *about* the man in the lineup? Did he do something? Or did someone do something to him? What was going on? Who knows?

You can complete the sentence by adding a verb:

The man in the lineup wearing the plaid shirt mumbled so much the witness couldn't understand him.

The man in the lineup wearing the plaid shirt was the witness's first choice.

But some sentence fragments do have a subject and verb; these are the sentences that are logically incomplete. Look at this:

When the sergeant has to fill out a lot of paperwork.

There is the subject, *the sergeant*. And there is a verb attached—*has to fill out a lot of paperwork*. But what about that *when*? That leads us to expect information that just isn't there. Here's how that fragment can be turned into a full sentence:

When the sergeant has to fill out a lot of paperwork, he gets very cranky.

The sentence may also be corrected by deleting *when*:

The sergeant has to fill out a lot of paperwork.

Subject/Verb Agreement

Okay, we have talked about what a sentence has to have—a subject and verb. But it can't be just any subject and verb; they have to match in person and number. So what does that mean?

Person indicates who the speaker or writer is talking about or talking to. *First person* means the speaker is referring to or describing himself or herself—*I am*. *Second person* means the sentence is addressed to or describing the audience—*you are*. *Third person*, or *he/she/it is*, describes or refers to someone or something that is neither the speaker nor the audience.

Then there is *number—singular* or *plural*. The previous examples are all singular in number. *We are, you are, they are*—that's first person plural, second person plural, and third person plural.

All the given examples match in person and number. You wouldn't say, *I are a good student*. That's a pretty easy mistake to spot, but it can get trickier. Here are some of the easy-to-miss situations.

Subject Separated from the Verb

Do not get distracted by phrases that come between the subject and verb. Take a look at this sentence and see if you can tell which verb is correct:

Officer Prince, who spends many days off jumping with an elite group of skydivers, remain/remains *calm under the most stressful circumstances.*

The right answer is the singular form, *remains*. Even though there is a plural noun right before the verb, the subject of the sentence is Officer Prince, a singular noun. Everything between the commas just gives you more information about the singular subject.

COMPOUND SUBJECTS

Another tricky situation occurs when you have a sentence in which the subject is a list of some kind:

> *The applicant told the interviewers that his drive, determination, and intelligence* makes/make *him an ideal recruit.*

The correct answer is *make*—that list of three singular nouns combined with the word *and* adds up to one compound subject, which requires a plural verb.

COMPOUND IMPOSTORS

As if compound subjects weren't difficult enough, there are some sentences that seem to have compound subjects when they really don't. Watch out for phrases containing or beginning with *neither/nor, either/or, along with, as well as,* or *in addition to.* These are the compound impostors.

> *Neither the rookie nor the old-timer* knows/know *how to handle the situation.*

Here, the right answer is the singular verb—*knows*—even though this looks like a list of two nouns. To make it clearer, rewrite the sentence as, *Neither* one *knows how to handle the situation.* That is the implied meaning of *either/or* and *neither/nor.*

However, what if you had *rookies* and *old-timers*? Then you are dealing with plural subjects in both situations.

> *Neither the rookie nor the old-timers* knows/know *how to handle the situation.*

Here the sentence takes a plural verb, *know.* That is because the verb is closer to the plural noun *old-timers.*

> *Officer Tremblay, along with half of the 9th Precinct,* was/were *a rabid softball player.*

The sentence takes a singular verb—*was.* Officer Tremblay is the real subject of the sentence. The phrase *along with half of the 9th Precinct* is just a kind of detour; grammatically, it doesn't become part of the subject.

AMBIGUOUS PRONOUN REFERENCE

Pronouns stand in for other nouns in a sentence. (Check out the following table listing the different kinds of pronouns.) They are used most often to eliminate repetitiveness. Here's an example:

> *The department offers a wide range of benefits for the department's employees.*

Using a pronoun, this sentence becomes:

> *The department offers a wide range of benefits for its employees.*

The original noun (department) is called the *antecedent*. You should always make sure that there is no confusion about which noun is the antecedent of a pronoun. This grammatical error is called ambiguous pronoun reference.

Here are a couple of examples:

> *I've always been interested in forensic psychology, so I've decided to be one.*

One what? No one can be a forensic psychology. Here is one way to make the sentence clearer:

> *I've always been interested in forensic psychology, so I've decided to make that my specialty.*

> *Officers Smith and Jones jumped into their cruiser and, hitting the siren, raced to the scene. It was brand new.*

What is new—*the scene, the siren,* or *the cruiser*? The way the sentence is written, it's impossible to tell. Here's a possible fix:

> *Officers Smith and Jones jumped into their brand-new cruiser and, hitting the siren, raced to the scene.*

PRONOUNS

Type of Pronoun	Purpose	Examples	Sample Sentence
personal pronouns	stand in for people or things	I, me, you, he, she, him, her, it, we, us, they, them, one	John and Latisha have been friends for years; they went to kindergarten together.
relative pronouns	used in clauses relating to someone or something	who, whom, which, that, where, whose	The suspect, who had been arrested many times before, seemed quite comfortable with the processing routine.
possessive pronouns	refer to things belonging to some individual or group	mine, yours, his, hers, theirs, ours, its	Enriqué did well on the screening test, but Sally did even better; in fact, hers was the highest score in the state.

MISPLACED MODIFIERS

Modifying phrases can help describe something more precisely, or explain something more fully. However, if they are not clearly linked to the noun they are modifying, these phrases can also make a sentence confusing. For example:

> *With its contents spilling onto the highway, Lieutenant Stanley ran toward the overturned tanker truck.*

The way this is written, it seems as though the contents of Lieutenant Stanley are spilling; it is actually the tanker truck's contents. To make this sentence clear and grammatically correct, it should be rewritten like this:

Lieutenant Stanley ran toward the overturned tanker truck, which was spilling its contents onto the highway.

DOUBLE NEGATIVES

In English, if a sentence contains two negatives—words such as *not* or *without*—the words cancel each other out. Sometimes people intentionally use double negatives, especially when they are trying to sound sophisticated. Saying that *the little bistro was not without charm* means it was a cute place. But it takes a second to figure that out. It is better to avoid double negatives altogether.

Watch out for the less obvious negatives—*hardly, barely, scarcely, cannot.* They do count as negatives.

Here are some examples of double negatives and ways to fix them:

The suspect said that he didn't commit no burglaries.

If you want to be clear and correct, you shouldn't write this way. *Didn't* is a contraction for *did not*—that is one negative. Combined with *no*, you have a double negative. Here are two ways to fix it:

The suspect said he didn't commit any burglaries.

The suspect said he committed no burglaries.

• • • • • • • • •

Recruit Smith hasn't hardly any worries about how he will do on the running portion of the test.

Hasn't is a contraction for *has not*, and *hardly* is one of those tricky negatives. You have one negative too many. Here are two ways to fix it:

Recruit Smith has hardly any worries about how he will do on the running portion of the test.

Recruit Smith hasn't any worries about how he will do on the running portion of the test.

• • • • • • • • •

With the new computerized databases, it doesn't take scarcely any time to run a license check.

Try these:

With the new computerized databases, it doesn't take any time to run a license check.

With the new computerized databases, it takes scarcely any time to run a license check.

SPELLING

In some languages, words are spelled pretty much the way they sound—not English. Take a look at *through* and *rough*. Or *through* and *threw*. Well, I'm afraid there aren't many shortcuts here. Other than the old standby—*I before E except after C, or when it sounds like A, as in neighbor and weigh*—I can't give you any helpful hints for remembering how to spell. You just have to memorize the words you have trouble with.

Here is a list of some of the most commonly misspelled words.

Incorrect	Correct
alot	a lot or allot
athelete	athlete
calender	calendar
definately	definitely
docter	doctor
eleminate	eliminate
excelerate	accelerate
oppertunity	opportunity
persued	pursued
seperate	separate

Do any of these words pose problems for you? Make a list of the words that you consistently have trouble spelling. Then write them on index cards and carry the cards around with you. Anytime you have a few minutes, take a look. Make yourself as familiar as possible with them, so you will be more likely to spot the correct spelling right away.

Then there are the cases when people confuse words that sound similar but mean totally different things. This confusion often arises when it comes to words with an apostrophe. So let's take a little punctuation detour, shall we?

THE APOSTROPHE

This bit of punctuation can indicate two totally separate ideas: possession or a contraction.

For instance, when you write, *That locker is Tammy's*, the apostrophe tells readers you are talking about a locker that belongs to Tammy, not a locker built out of several people named Tammy. And while we are on the topic of possessives—what if you are talking about something belonging to several people named Tammy? In other words, you want the plural possessive. In that case, you add the apostrophe after the *s* indicating the plural—*It turned out that all three of the Tammys' dates were named Todd.*

Then there is the other meaning of the apostrophe. If you write, *That locker can't be Tammy's*, the apostrophe in *can't* signals a contraction—a shortened combination of two words, with the apostrophe marking the place of the missing letter or letters.

SO WHY IS ENGLISH SPELLING SO CONFUSING?

For the answer to that, you have to know a little bit about *etymology*—the study of where words come from.

English contains a mishmash of words from all over the globe. There was the original Anglo-Saxon language, which had similarities to German. This language was adulterated by Latin brought over by Roman conquerors. Then Normans (from what's now France) took over, and a lot of their words became part of English. Because Romans and Normans made up the ruling class, their languages were considered more elegant and, therefore, more proper—a trend that continues today.

As English explorers traveled the globe, they picked up bits and pieces of other languages. Often, spelling was based either on the original language or was phonetically spelled out. And that's why English spelling can be so confusing!

Here are three English words we've borrowed from other languages:

- **assassin**—Off and on, during the 11th, 12th, and 13th centuries, Christian soldiers marched off to the Middle East on a mission to retake the Holy Land. These campaigns, known collectively as the Crusades, didn't accomplish much except to waste a lot of money and kill a lot of people. During the Crusades, the Christians encountered a Muslim sect that, like the Christians, took on murder as a religious duty. Unlike the Christians, this particular sect fueled themselves with hashish; their zeal apparently impressed the English Crusaders. The sect is commemorated in the English word *assassin*, which originated from the Arabic word *hashshashin*, meaning "eaters or smokers of hashish."

- **gorgeous**—Around the same time as the Crusades, in the late Middle Ages, the hot fashion for women was a *gorgias*, a cloth headdress wrapped over the hair and under the chin, so only the face showed. Fashion being what it is, anyone who had the resources decorated her gorgias with embroidery or jewels. Over time, the decorations became more and more elaborate and eye-catching. As an adjective, *gorgayse*, the word became a synonym for "beautiful" or "highly decorative."

- **cigar**—This word was lifted from the Spanish word *cigarro*, which means exactly the same thing. According to some sources, *cigarro* came from the Mayan verb sicar, "to smoke rolled tobacco leaves."

The real confusion arises when words sound identical but are spelled differently. Take a look and see if any of these present problems for you.

their/there/they're

- *Their* indicates possession by more than one person, not including the speaker—*That's* their *car*.
- *There* indicates distance from the speaker—*That's their car over* there.
- *They're* is a contraction for *they are*—*That's their car over there;* they're *sitting inside it*.

your/you're

- *Your* indicates possession by someone the speaker is talking to—Your *golf game has improved.*
- *You're* is another contraction, meaning *you are*—Your *golf game has improved a lot.* You're *just about to break par.* (Note that *a lot* is two words, not one.)

its/it's

- *Its* is the possessive form of *it*—The department has really raised its *standards.*
- *It's* is a contraction of *it is*—The department has really raised its standards, and it's *a great morale booster.*

SOUNDALIKE WORDS

Of course, the apostrophe isn't responsible for all sources of confusion. Certain words are close to others in sound and meaning, but different in spelling; it is important to know the difference so you can express yourself accurately.

lay/lie

- *Lay* is a transitive verb, one that indicates an action done to something or someone. Transitive verbs are incomplete without an object—*I'm going to* lay *tile in the new family room.*
- *Lie* is a regular verb, one that indicates an action done by something or someone— *I'm going to lay tile in the new family room, and then I'm going to* lie *down for a nap.*

raise/rise

This difference is similar to that between *lay* and *lie*.

- *Raise* is done to someone or something—The candidate is going to have to raise *a lot of money.*
- *Rise* is done by someone or something—The candidate is going to have to raise *a lot of money before he can rise in the political structure.*

accept/except

- *Accept* means taking possession or acknowledging ownership of something—The *professor said he wouldn't* accept *late papers.*
- *Except* indicates a special case—The professor said he wouldn't accept late papers, except *in situations involving medical or family emergencies.*

effect/affect

- *Effect* is a noun, a result of some action—The effect *of the earthquake is devastating.*
- *Affect* is a verb, resulting in an effect—The effect of the earthquake is devastating; *nothing this disastrous has ever* affected *the region before.*

site/sight

- *Site* indicates a location—*The* site *of the outdoor music festival was a pasture south of town.*

- *Sight* is related to vision, either the sense itself or something that is seen—*The site of the outdoor music festival was a pasture south of town. After three days of crowds and rain, the area was quite a* sight.

persecute/prosecute

- *Persecute* means inflicting some kind of torment on someone—*I don't know why he keeps* persecuting *his assistant with unkind comments.*

- *Prosecute* involves bringing legal action—*I don't know why he keeps persecuting his assistant with unkind comments. If he doesn't watch it, she might try to have him* prosecuted *for harassment.*

precede/proceed

- *Precede* means to come before—*A Secret Service team always* precedes *the president as he travels.*

- *Proceed* means to continue— *A Secret Service team always precedes the president as he travels. If the security team doesn't feel a site is secure, the event will not* proceed.

Now that you have reviewed these basic grammar and spelling rules, see if you can answer the following practice questions. These questions are an excellent way to find out your strengths and weaknesses in these subjects. Questions on the Police Officer Exam you take may be a little different than these.

GRAMMAR AND SPELLING PRACTICE

For the following questions, choose the right word from the italicized words in the sentence. Answers are found at the end of the chapter.

1. Pancakes, eggs, biscuits, and sausage *is/are* Officer Stone's favorite breakfast foods.

2. The one positive *affect/effect* of the accident was the subsequent installation of the stop sign at the dangerous intersection.

3. Both my mom and dad *supports/support* my decision to become a police officer.

4. Of all the injuries Officer Ruiz sustained in the fender bender, the bruising of her ribs *bothers/bother* her the most.

5. Officer Gill, along with the rest of the squad, *is/are* determined to apprehend the burglar before he strikes again.

6. Officer Washington tries to *rise/raise* early enough to run five miles every day.

7. Neither the approaching storm nor the warnings on all radio frequencies *persuades/persuade* Officer Norton to give up searching for survivors.

8. Polls show that the number of people who don't care about the latest government scandal *has/have* increased.

9. Many residents, especially those from the converted hotel, *were/was* extremely upset by the string of robberies.

10. The detective refused to *accept/except* the suspect's evasive answers and kept pressing him for the truth.

Rewrite the following sentences to eliminate confusion or correct grammatical errors. Write the revised sentences in the blank lines provided. Suggested answers are found at the end of the chapter.

11. Staggering and weaving, the officer approached the old man who had just left the bar.

    _____

    _____

    _____

12. Officer Ryan hadn't hardly been on duty but five minutes when the call came in about a burglary in progress.

_____

_____

_____

13. The desk sergeant, after weighing the pros and cons, deciding not to change the duty roster.

_____

_____

_____

14. Staring blankly, the computer screen flickered while Joanna sat at her desk.

_____

_____

_____

15. Upon discovering the theft in the office, the employees, suspecting one another.

_____

_____

_____

16. Officer Jasek drove the cruiser into the garage, running on only one cylinder.

_____

_____

_____

17. The actors on that TV cop show are great, but they're details of real-life police work aren't right.

_____

_____

_____

18. Officer Chang searched the available files to see what kind of rap sheets they had.

_____

_____

_____

19. The driver, traveling at a high rate of speed, losing control on the slick road.

_____

_____

_____

20. Don't believe everything you read in the papers because you don't know if they are telling the truth.

_____

_____

_____

ANSWERS AND EXPLANATIONS

1. *Pancakes, eggs, biscuits, and sausage* are *Officer Stone's favorite breakfast foods.* This is a compound subject because the items are combined with the word *and*; don't be thrown off by that singular word, *sausage*, just before the verb.

2. *The one positive* effect *of the accident was the subsequent installation of the stop sign at the dangerous intersection.* Remember, *effect* is the noun, *affect* is the verb.

3. *Both my mom and dad* support *my decision to become a police officer.* The two parents make up a compound, or plural, subject.

4. *Of all the injuries Officer Ruiz sustained in the fender bender, the bruising of her ribs* bothers *her the most.* The subject is *bruising*, which is singular. Again, don't be confused by the plural word just before the verb—*ribs* is not the subject.

5. *Officer Gill, along with the rest of the squad,* is *determined to apprehend the burglar before he strikes again.* Don't be fooled by the compound imposter *along with. Officer Gill* is the singular subject.

6. *Officer Washington tries to* rise *early enough to run five miles every day.* If the subject is doing the getting up himself, he's *rising. Raising* is something done to a person or thing—you raise money, or raise a flag.

7. *Neither the approaching storm nor the warnings on all radio frequencies* persuade *Officer Norton to give up searching for survivors.* Although *neither/nor* is a compound imposter, remember the verb agrees with the subject that is closest to the verb.

8. *Polls show that the number of people who don't care about the latest government scandal* has *increased.* The subject is not *people*, it's *number*, which is singular.

9. *Many residents, especially those from the converted hotel,* were *extremely upset by the string of robberies.* The subject is plural, *residents.* Again, don't be confused by the noun just before the verb; *hotel* isn't the subject of the sentence. *Residents* is the subject.

10. *The detective refused to* accept *the suspect's evasive answers and kept pressing him for the truth. Accept* is a verb. *Except* indicates a special circumstance.

There are a few ways you could have fixed these sentences. Here are some sample rewrites:

11. The officer approached the old man who, staggering and weaving, had just left the bar.

12. Officer Ryan hadn't been on duty five minutes when the call came in about a burglary in progress. Or, as an alternative: Officer Ryan had been on duty only five minutes when the call came in about a burglary in progress.

13. The desk sergeant, after weighing the pros and cons, decided not to change the duty roster.

14. The computer screen flickered while Joanna, staring blankly, sat at her desk.

15. Upon discovering the theft in the office, the employees began suspecting one another. Or, equally correct: Upon discovering the theft in the office, the employees suspected one another.

16. Officer Jasek drove the cruiser, which was running on only one cylinder, into the garage.

17. The actors on that TV cop show are great, but the show's details of real-life police work aren't right.

18. Officer Chang searched the available files to see what kind of rap sheets the suspects had. (*They* in the original sentence refers to a noun not included in the sentence.)

19. The driver, traveling at a high rate of speed, lost control on the slick road.

20. Don't believe everything you read in the papers because you don't know if the writers are telling the truth. (*They* in the original sentence refers to a noun not included in the sentence.)

CHAPTER FIVE

Reading Comprehension

As with grammar and spelling, you may or may not have a test section specifically covering reading comprehension. However, the entire Police Officer Exam will require you to read and apply skills encompassed in reading comprehension. This chapter includes strategies for effective comprehension and offers practice questions to help you hone your skills.

BASIC READING TECHNIQUES

Here are some basic tips for focusing on the important aspects of a written passage. As you prepare for your test, try applying these techniques to everything you read—from the morning paper, to your sports magazine, to the novel you are reading.

PREREADING

You can often get a pretty good idea of what a story or article is about by quickly glancing over it. Before you read the entire thing, put it through a quick prereading survey:

- Is there a title? If so, what does it tell you about the article?
- Are there pictures, charts, or illustrations? What information do they give you?
- What does the first sentence say?

Based on your prereading, you can often make an accurate prediction about the content of the text.

ACTIVE READING

It's probably been drilled into your head that you shouldn't write in books. Although this is the respectful choice if the book doesn't belong to you, you can mark up your own books, magazines, and newspapers. And you *should* mark them up. That's part of active reading, which will help you focus on the meaning of the text. Mark words that are repeated. Write down any questions you have as you read, or circle words you don't understand. Underline the sentence, or sentences, that introduce or sum up the author's main point.

This will help you spot the building blocks of any essay or article, which include:

THE PURPOSE

Why did the author write the material you are reading? To inform you? To persuade you? To motivate you? What particular issue does the text cover? In the margin, write down what you think the author's purpose is. It will be related to, but not exactly the same as, the main idea.

THE MAIN IDEA

The main idea is a specific idea that supports the author's broader purpose. Often, the first sentence clues you in to the main idea, or topic; sometimes, the first sentence is a straightforward statement of the topic. However, don't count on that. A writer may choose to leave the main idea unstated, expecting you to draw your own conclusions from the evidence and arguments assembled in the essay.

Think of the main idea as the spine of the essay; it is the long line that holds everything together.

Look for a statement of the main idea; underline it, if you find it. If there doesn't seem to be a sentence that sums up the topic, write your own statement of the main idea in the margin.

PARAGRAPH TOPICS

If the main idea is the spine of the essay, the paragraph topics are the bones; they provide the underlying structure. Each paragraph adds something slightly different to the author's argument; the supporting element contained in a paragraph is the paragraph topic. As with the main idea, paragraph topics may or may not be directly stated.

After you finish each paragraph, look for its topic sentence and underline it. If you can't find a topic sentence, write your own statement in the margin.

DETAILS

So far, we have the skeleton of an essay, with the basic substructure of main idea and paragraph topics in place. But it is still a bit flimsy. That's why the author adds details. The details are the muscle attached to that skeleton, making it stronger and more stable. These details can be examples or logical arguments, but they have to be directly connected to the paragraph topic they flesh out.

The details are always directly stated; otherwise, they wouldn't be very useful. Number the details the author gives to build up the paragraph topics. You will always have more details than anything else. After all, there can be only one main idea per passage, and one paragraph topic per paragraph. But within a single paragraph, the author may provide several supporting details.

KEYWORDS

Okay, now we have a fairly functional organism here: a stable structure made up of the main idea and the paragraph topics fleshed out with details. We can complete things with keywords, which will keep everything working together.

Keywords link the sentences within and between paragraphs; they also guide the reader through the author's argument. There are six types of keywords, each with a different function in the paragraph.

Type of Keyword	Purpose	Examples	Sample Sentence
continuation keywords	These tell you that you are getting more of the same kind of information. The new detail builds on the earlier one.	and, also, moreover, furthermore	The U.S. team won the gold medal in the 400-meter relay. Furthermore, it established a new world record.
illustration keywords	These let you know that the author is about to give you an example of an idea or concept.	for example, for instance	Psychology has many practical uses. For example, it is used regularly in advertising research.
contrast keywords	These tell you that the author is about to change direction in his or her argument or mention an opposing idea.	but, however, although, otherwise, nevertheless, by contrast	Yesterday was rainy and cold. However, today it's sunny and warm.
conclusion keywords	These let you know that the author is about to summarize or restate an important idea. Conclusion keywords often signal that the author is wrapping up the argument. Pay attention to conclusion keywords because they often relate directly to the main idea.	therefore, thus, in conclusion, consequently, hence	The score was tied after nine innings. Therefore, the game went to extended innings.
evidence keywords	These tell you that the author is going to offer a piece of evidence that supports an idea that was just stated. Often, the evidence has a cause-and-effect relationship with the idea it supports.	because, since	In today's job market, it is a good idea to know a second language because many employers demand bilingual skills.
importance keywords	These let you know that the author thinks a particular idea or fact is very important.	especially, above all, most of all, primarily, particularly	It is important to make eye contact during a job interview; most of all, you should always thank your interviewer.

AFTER READING

Before you move on, think about what you have just read and make sure you fully understand it:

- Identify the key points. What are the most important statements the author made? List them.

- Summarize. Try to shrink these statements down to one or two sentences.

- Any questions? If you wrote down questions that remain unanswered when you finish reading, take another look. Focus on the specific sentences or passages that prompted the questions.

USING CONTEXT INSTEAD OF A DICTIONARY

It's a good idea to read unfamiliar material with a dictionary close by. That way, you can easily look up any words you don't understand. But what if you aren't allowed to use a dictionary? In those situations, which include just about all standardized tests, you need to be able to make a good guess about the meaning of a word based on its context. Here is what I mean:

Even though they give her nightmares, Joyce likes gruesome movies.

Let's say you don't know exactly what *gruesome* means. But the sentence tells you that gruesome movies give Joyce nightmares, so it's a good bet that gruesome doesn't mean romantic or funny. What kind of movies would give someone nightmares? Just using context and your own common sense, you can figure out that gruesome means something close to scary or violent.

Once you are out of a testing situation, you can refine your definition by looking up those unfamiliar words in the dictionary. But your context definitions will keep you from getting stuck during a test.

SUMMARIZING

Being able to sum up the material you have read is an important aspect of reading comprehension. It demonstrates that you have understood the argument well enough to state the author's main idea in your own words. Here is an example of how to summarize material:

Hollywood movies and television series tend to show criminal profiling as a mysterious, supernatural talent, something like mind-reading or predicting the future. In fact, criminal profiling consists of close analysis of crime scene evidence, using a large body of information gathered from other offenders to make reasonable assumptions about the offender in a particular case. Like any other human activity, some people have more of a "knack" for profiling than others, but anyone can learn the basic principles and techniques of criminal profiling.

An accurate summary of the paragraph's topic would be something like this:

Criminal profiling is not a mysterious talent, but a set of principles and techniques that can be taught.

This sentence sums up the author's argument; everything else in the paragraph provides details. If you get stuck thinking of a summary, or have any other trouble with a passage, keep reading to learn ways to move past your problems.

WHEN YOU HIT A WALL

In a testing situation, it is natural to panic. Sometimes, you might go blank on a reading comprehension section. You might not be able to make any sense out of what you are supposed to be reading. Relax—here are some ways to break through that wall:

- **Reread.** Sometimes all it takes is another run through a sentence to make its meaning clear.

- **Stop and think.** Make notes to yourself. Look at sentences just above and just below the difficult passage.

- **Paraphrase.** If a sentence is especially baffling, try putting it into your own words.

The best way to avoid panic is to be prepared. Complete the following practice questions to test what you have learned in this chapter.

IDENTIFYING MAIN IDEAS, TOPICS, AND DETAILS PRACTICE

Read each passage and answer the questions that follow. Answers are found at the end of the exercise.

PASSAGE 1

Many people mistakenly believe that the average police officer often uses his or her firearm on duty. While all officers are trained in the use of firearms and are expected to be able to use a weapon when necessary, gunfire plays little role in the everyday duties of a law enforcement officer. It's not surprising that this misunderstanding exists; the media pays more attention to situations in which a suspect or bystander is shot by an officer than they do to any other police action. This widespread media coverage focused on relatively rare incidents has led to an exaggerated idea about officers' use of firearms. In fact, most officers rarely draw their weapons, and many officers retire after never having fired a shot for 20 years.

1. Select the paragraph's topic from the following choices:
    A. newspaper and television headlines
    B. people's beliefs about police officers' use of guns
    C. the increase in the use of weapons among police
    D. the reckless use of weapons

2. Which of the following best states the author's main idea?
   A. Newspapers shouldn't write about the police.
   B. News stories lead people to think police officers use their weapons more often than they actually do.
   C. Officers need to be better trained in the use of firearms.
   D. More stories are written about the use of firearms than any other police action.

PASSAGE 2

The early Dutch settlers on the island of Manhattan organized the formal security operations that eventually became the New York Police Department. In the early 1600s, New Amsterdam, as New York was then known, had only one formal peacekeeper, a "schout-fiscal," or "sheriff-attorney." As New Amsterdam grew, the colonists decided they needed better protection from wild animals, hostile tribes, and law-breakers. The settlers constructed a gated wall from river to river, across the northern end of the colony at the site of today's Wall Street. In 1658, the first "night watch" was formed as a group of volunteer colonists, who were soon replaced by a paid force of eight men. The night watch patrolled the settlement, carrying wooden noisemakers to awaken the colonists to fight fires, invasions, or other common threats. These clanking noisemakers led colonists to refer to the men as the "rattle watch." Each member of the rattle watch also carried a lantern with inserts of green glass. This distinctive lantern lit the watchman's way on the dark paths and streets, and also identified him to any passersby. Eventually, watch houses were built to shelter the watchmen on duty; a man returning from his rounds hung his lantern by the front door, showing he was in the watch house in case anyone needed his help. Even today, every NYPD precinct house has green lights at its doors, what the department calls a "symbol that the watch is present and vigilant."

3. What is the main idea of this passage?
   A. The first police officers in New York City were volunteers.
   B. Early colonists were most concerned about fire.
   C. New York City's law enforcement operations were first set up by Dutch colonists.
   D. Colonial cities needed only one peacekeeper.

4. List four supporting details mentioned by the author.

   _____

   _____

   _____

   _____

PASSAGE 3

Public safety professionals—a group that includes firefighters, paramedics, and law enforcement officers—deal with tremendous amounts of stress simply because of the nature of their work. However, police officers face added levels of stress because of the power of the badge and the dangers that go with it. A police officer is entrusted with powerful weapons such as firearms, batons, and Tasers. The officer can arrest citizens on his own authority; short of arrest, an officer can make traffic stops, write tickets, and in other ways police others. Officers must have this authority and autonomy in order to uphold their duty of protecting life and property; however, a good officer is always careful not to abuse his authority, and this can lead to second-guessing. The constant need for independent decision making in high-stakes situations creates further stress. Civilians may disagree with an officer's actions; they can become hostile and suspicious of the police, which causes problems for individual officers. Officers know that, at any time, they may be targeted by individuals seeking revenge, expressing hatred of authority, or acting from deranged motives. All these factors create stress unique to law enforcement.

5. State the author's main idea in your own words.

_____

_____

_____

_____

_____

6. List four supporting details mentioned by the author.

_____

_____

_____

_____

_____

ANSWERS AND EXPLANATIONS

1. **B** is correct. The first and last sentences of almost all paragraphs provide very important information. In this case, the first sentence of this paragraph tells you that the author will be discussing common beliefs about police officers' use of firearms.

2. **B** is correct. At the beginning of the paragraph, the author states that police use their weapons less often than people believe. Then, the author says that this is because incidents involving shootings by officers receive more media coverage out of proportion to their occurrence. Choice B is the best statement of this. Note that choice D is a supporting detail.

3. **C** is correct. The author begins by stating that the Dutch first set up the law enforcement system in what became New York City; the rest of the paragraph supplies supporting details. Choice C supplies the best summary of that idea.

4. Your answers may vary but here are some of the details you might have mentioned:

   - New Amsterdam's first law enforcement official was a "schout-fiscal" or "sheriff-attorney."
   - The settlers built a gated wall where Wall Street is today.
   - In 1658, a group of patrolmen was formed; the first volunteers were replaced by paid patrolmen.
   - The patrolmen guarded against common threats such as fires and attacks on the settlement.
   - These patrolmen carried green lanterns, which they hung outside their watch house when not on patrol; today, the green lights at NYPD precinct houses are a reminder of those early patrolmen.

5. Your wording may be different, but the author's main idea is this: While all public safety professionals face stress in their jobs, law enforcement officers face stresses that are unique to their job.

6. Here are some of the details you might have mentioned:

   - Police officers have authority that no one else is allowed.
   - This authority includes carrying weapons, the right to arrest anyone, and the right to police citizens.
   - A conscientious officer will always try to make sure he or she isn't abusing his or her authority.
   - Some citizens will always disagree with the way officers exercise their authority.
   - Officers are a target for people who have an argument against authority or police in general.

UNDERSTANDING KEYWORDS PRACTICE

Each of the following statements ends with a keyword. Use the statement's main idea and the keyword in bold to figure out which of the four choices makes the most sense.

1. Many scientific studies have shown that regular physical exercise helps people deal with psychological stress. **Therefore,**

    A. people who frequently experience stress should make physical exercise part of their regular routine.

    B. one study has found that people who never exercise tend to be older than people who exercise often.

    C. without more information, beginning an exercise program could prove dangerous.

    D. many people who experience stress aren't physically fit.

2. A crime scene should be kept off-limits to bystanders and most police officers until the forensics experts have completed their work; **otherwise,**

    A. old-fashioned magnifying glasses will have to be used.

    B. the forensics team will have nothing to do.

    C. important evidence may be damaged or lost completely.

    D the criminal may be among the bystanders.

3. The suspect benefited from the rookie officer's inexperience, **because**

    A. the officer had never handled a murder case before.

    B. the officer's flawed search warrant eventually led to the suspect's release.

    C. the suspect knew all the other officers at the precinct.

    D. the suspect had a lot of experience, judging from his criminal record.

4. It's very unlikely that two people will have the same genetic "fingerprint," **since**

    A. genetic research has made great advances in the last two decades.

    B. only identical twins, which are relatively rare, share the same DNA, or genetic material.

    C. practically all of the genetic research done has taken place in universities.

    D. human genetic codes are so similar to those of the chimpanzee.

5. The city jail was built to serve a much smaller population, and crime rates keep going up. **Consequently,**

    A. the jail is always filled with far more inmates than it was designed to hold.

    B. the mayor has blocked every attempt to improve the situation.

    C. the police officers have a hard time finding parking places.

    D. the population figures must be going up as well.

6. The purpose of the new task force is to reduce the rate of gang activity. **Therefore,**

    A. gangs are expected to accumulate more firearms.

    B. a large part of the department's budget is set aside for new equipment.

    C. more research into gang membership should be done.

    D. the task force's effectiveness will be judged on whether or not gang activity declines.

ANSWERS AND EXPLANATIONS

1. **A** is correct. *Therefore* is a conclusion keyword, so the answer must add a logical conclusion to the idea in the first sentence. Since exercise tends to help people handle stress, choice A makes sense. None of the other choices presents an idea that flows logically from the first sentence.

2. **C** is correct. *Otherwise* is a contrast keyword, one that signals a change in direction, or a kind of warning—"Get in out of the rain, otherwise you will get wet." The only logical connection is between protecting the crime scene and preserving evidence.

3. **B** is correct. *Because* is an evidence keyword, something that provides proof of an idea or statement—in this case, the statement that the suspect gained something from the officer's mistake. The only choice that does this is B.

4. **B** is correct. *Since* is another evidence keyword, something that gives support for the first statement. Go through the choices, and you'll see that B is the only one that would allow us to draw the conclusion that it's rare for two people to share identical genetic material.

5. **A** is correct. *Consequently* is a conclusion keyword, which signals a logical conclusion that can be drawn from the first statement. Only one of the choices follows logically from the original sentence. If the jail was built when the population was smaller, and a larger percentage of that larger population is being arrested, then the jail must be chronically overcrowded.

6. **D** is correct. *Therefore* is another conclusion keyword. You are looking for something that's logically connected to the original statement. If the whole point of creating a task force is to reduce gang activity, then its effectiveness will be measured by how much gang activity is reduced. Research, new equipment, or the gangs' weapons don't have the same direct connection with the task force's goals.

USING CONTEXT PRACTICE

EXERCISE 1

This first exercise will get you used to deducing meanings from context. For each of the following questions, fill in the blank with any word (or phrase) that makes sense. Answers are found at the end of Exercise 3.

1. Since I'm a loyal Yankees fan, I _____ whenever they play.

2. When I went shopping for earrings, I realized I couldn't afford a pair with _____ diamonds, so I bought earrings with imitation diamonds.

3. Unlike the more experienced members of the team, the _____ kept making obvious errors.

4. Joris had to stop practicing with the team after his injury; once the injury healed, he _____ practicing.

5. The movie was so _____ that everyone left the theater before the movie was even half over.

6. Stores are _____ from selling cigarettes to children; they may, however, sell cigarettes to adults.

7. When Joon had a part-time job, she was able to go to the gym regularly. But ever since her promotion, she's been extremely busy. She's only been able to get to the gym _____ .

8. Ronaldo had underestimated his favorite band's _____ . Even though he was in line at 6:00 A.M. on the first day concert tickets went on sale, the entire stadium was sold out by the time he got to the ticket window.

9. Buying the ticket with the winning numbers in the $10 million jackpot was lucky; losing the ticket was a _____ .

10. Veronica wanted to make sure the audience could understand her, so when she stepped up to the microphone, she spoke very _____ .

11. The student's excuse for not turning in his homework—his dog ate it— was especially _____ , considering he didn't even have a dog.

12. Strangely enough, Aarthi felt no _____ when she saw the deadly rattlesnake inches away from her.

EXERCISE 2

Here is another set of exercises for deducing meaning from context. This time, the questions are worded in a way that is closer to what you are likely to see on a standardized test.

For the following questions, choose the answer that is closest in meaning to the underlined word. Please note, underlined words are just made-up words so you cannot rely on anything but the context to choose the best answer. Answers are found at the end of Exercise 3.

1. To earn money, Rita goes from house to house <u>tumblying</u> newspapers.

   A. editing
   B. assembling
   C. selling
   D. writing

2. The instant replay was not <u>tortentous</u>; even after watching it repeatedly, the referees couldn't tell whether the receiver was out of bounds.

   A. available
   B. timely
   C. ambiguous
   D. conclusive

3. People who worked with him were <u>mickled</u> by Rashid's terrible job performance.

   A. disgusted
   B. delighted
   C. happy
   D. repudiated

4. After I showed my teacher he'd made an error while grading my paper, he <u>clecked</u> the grade in his grade book.

   A. noticed
   B. changed
   C. criticized
   D. ignored

5. Because she didn't want to be late to class, Evelyn gave us the <u>jutley</u> version of her vacation.

   A. brief
   B. fascinating
   C. painful
   D. detailed

6. She was such a <u>hirfle</u> collector of baseball cards that she had a complete set of all the cards that had been printed in the last three years.

    A. occasional
    B. devoted
    C. discerning
    D. interesting

7. The hyperactive twins <u>uppled</u> their babysitter so much that she took a nap as soon as she got home.

    A. bored
    B. surprised
    C. exhausted
    D. tripped

8. So many people want to go to the play-off game that the tickets are already <u>plonk</u>.

    A. hard to find
    B. easily available
    C. too variable
    D. very demanding

9. Taking the aspirin <u>binked</u> my headache.

    A. increased
    B. caused
    C. relieved
    D. continued

10. The mayor's series of illegal acts demonstrated that he was a <u>tewfey</u> man.

    A. depressed
    B. carefree
    C. respectable
    D. corrupt

11. Because the offices weren't being cleaned properly, the building manager <u>yopped</u> the contract with the cleaning company.

    A. extended
    B. renewed
    C. ended
    D. sold

12. Kevin's explanation for his behavior was <u>sleggish</u>; even after he told me, I still didn't know why he acted the way he did.

    A. long-winded

    B. hard to understand

    C. predictable

    D. tiresome

EXERCISE 3

Here is the last set of context exercises. These questions are closest to the ones you would encounter on a standardized test.

Choose the answer that is closest in meaning to the underlined word or phrase. Answers are found at the end of the exercise.

1. Strict vegetarians <u>eschew</u> not only meat, but also products that come from animals, such as eggs and cheese.

    A. sell

    B. like

    C. avoid

    D. grade

2. At his funeral, Malcolm X was <u>eulogized</u> by admirers such as Ossie Davis.

    A. praised

    B. rescued

    C. delighted

    D. forgotten

3. He didn't like his birthday present from his aunt, but <u>feigned</u> excitement to avoid hurting her feelings.

    A. hid

    B. suppressed

    C. pretended

    D. felt

4. The buzzing and biting of mosquitoes <u>vexed</u> the campers as they tried to sleep.

    A. soothed

    B. annoyed

    C. pleased

    D. lulled

5. Western accounts of Buddhism are often inaccurate. They tend to <u>distort</u> Buddhist thought by exaggerating some aspects of it and ignoring others.
   A. analyze
   B. explain
   C. praise
   D. misrepresent

6. Flooding is <u>anticipated</u> in the Brazos River valley, so sensible residents in the area are moving to higher ground.
   A. moderate
   B. expected
   C. rare
   D. beneficial

7. Because the explanation was so <u>verbose</u>, the lecture took much longer than necessary.
   A. serious
   B. intelligent
   C. wordy
   D. experienced

8. She was a <u>recluse</u>, living by herself and avoiding other people.
   A. loner
   B. adventurer
   C. fool
   D. homemaker

9. Members of the scouting patrol faced the greatest chance of being injured or killed; only the most <u>intrepid</u> soldiers volunteered for the assignment.
   A. careful
   B. clever
   C. polite
   D. brave

10. At home, the child was obedient and well behaved, but at school her teachers found her <u>intractable</u>.
    A. uncontrollable
    B. puny
    C. curious
    D. absentminded

11. The art collector has <u>eclectic</u> taste; she owns paintings and sculptures from all over the world, in many different styles.

   A. crude
   B. wide-ranging
   C. sturdy
   D. old-fashioned

12. The governor's opponents searched for evidence of wrongdoing in her background, but her record was <u>immaculate</u>.

   A. unbroken
   B. conclusive
   C. popular
   D. spotless

ANSWERS AND EXPLANATIONS

EXERCISE 1

1. *Watch.* A loyal Yankees fan would tend to watch every game.

2. *Real* or *genuine.* If you could only afford imitation diamonds, you wouldn't be able to buy real ones.

3. *Rookie* or *new player.* The missing word has to contrast with *more experienced members,* who don't make obvious mistakes.

4. *Resumed* or *went back to.* If he has stopped because of the injury, he can start again once it has healed.

5. *Bad* or *boring.* These are the most obvious reasons why an audience would walk out of a movie. Maybe you thought about using *long.* That's not as good an answer. If a movie is interesting enough, people will stay for the whole thing, no matter how long it is.

6. *Forbidden* or *banned. However* signals that there is a contrast between what stores can sell to adults and what they sell to children. If they can sell cigarettes to adults, then they must be forbidden from selling them to children.

7. *Occasionally* or *rarely.* Once Joon's schedule became *extremely busy,* she could no longer go to the gym regularly.

8. *Popularity.* If the tickets sell out so quickly, the band must be popular.

9. *Disaster, tragedy,* or *nightmare.* Think about how you would feel if that were your lottery ticket.

10. *Slowly, clearly,* or *loudly.* These words describe how you would speak if you wanted to make sure you would be heard.

11. *Unbelievable* or *far-fetched. His dog ate it* is already a doubtful excuse, but if the guy doesn't even have a dog, it's impossible.

12. *Fear* or *panic.* These are emotions you would expect someone to feel if she spotted a rattlesnake nearby.

Exercise 2

1. **C** is correct. If Rita is trying to earn money, the only way to do so by going house to house is by selling the papers.

2. **D** is correct. If the referees couldn't tell if the receiver was out of bounds, even after watching the instant replay, then the replay must not have been conclusive. Note that even if the replay were ambiguous, available, and timely, the sentence asks what the replay was *not*.

3. **A** is correct. People are not likely to be delighted or happy with a terrible job performance.

4. **B** is correct. If you showed a teacher an error in grading, you would expect him to change your grade.

5. **A** is correct. If you were concerned about being late, you would make your story brief. The story may or may not be fascinating, but the key information is that Evelyn was concerned about time.

6. **B** is correct. Someone who has a complete set of all the baseball cards printed recently must be a pretty devoted collector. She is probably not all that discerning; a discerning collector would try to judge which cards were most likely to increase in value, and keep only those.

7. **C** is correct. If the babysitter took a nap as soon as she got home, she must have been exhausted. People might nap when they are bored, but that is not likely to be the result of looking after active twins.

8. **A** is correct. If a lot of people want to go to the game, you would expect that the tickets would be scarce or hard to find.

9. **C** is correct. Aspirin usually relieves headaches; it generally does not cause them or make them worse.

10. **D** is correct. Someone who commits a series of crimes is corrupt, not respectable. He may be depressed or carefree, but we can't determine his mood from the sentence.

11. **C** is correct. Since the cleaning company wasn't doing a good job, you wouldn't expect the manager to extend or renew the contract; a contract generally isn't something you can sell.

12. **B** is correct. If Kevin explained his behavior and you were still puzzled by it, then his explanation must be hard to understand. It might also be long-winded and tiresome, but an answer can be long-winded, tiresome, and perfectly understandable.

EXERCISE 3

1. **C** is correct. Vegetarians probably don't like meat, and they may or may not sell or grade it, but they always avoid it.

2. **A** is correct. An admirer would probably praise someone at his funeral.

3. **C** is correct. If he didn't like the present, the best way to avoid hurting the giver's feelings is by pretending to like it.

4. **B** is correct. When's the last time you were pleased or lulled or soothed by mosquito bites? *Vexed* means annoyed.

5. **D** is correct. If the accounts of Buddhist thought are inaccurate, then they must misrepresent the religion.

6. **B** is correct. Moving to higher ground is sensible if flooding is expected. If the flooding is moderate, beneficial, or rare, leaving the area probably wouldn't be necessary or sensible.

7. **C** is correct. The word *verbose* means wordy.

8. **A** is correct. Someone living by herself and avoiding others is a loner.

9. **D** is correct. A soldier would have to be brave to volunteer for an especially risky task.

10. **A** is correct. The word *but* signals a contrast between the girl's behavior at home and her behavior at school. The word that contrasts with *obedient and well behaved* is *uncontrollable.*

11. **B** is correct. Collecting art from all over the world, in many different styles, indicates wide-ranging tastes.

12. **D** is correct. The word *but* lets you know the opponents didn't find what they were looking for. If they couldn't find wrongdoing, then the governor's record must be spotless. A record may be unbroken, popular, or conclusive and still contain incidents of wrongdoing.

SUMMARIZING PRACTICE

Read the following short passages and answer the questions about each one. Answers are found at the end of the practice.

PASSAGE 1

Though it's one of the most effective tools of forensic science, DNA testing can lead to delays in prosecuting—or clearing—suspects. While DNA testing is 99.99 percent accurate, it is also extremely time-consuming. A chemist in a crime lab can handle 75 to 100 drug tests a month; in that same period, an analyst can complete only one or two DNA tests. This lengthy processing time often causes a backlog in the lab. DNA testing also requires equipment and expertise that are too specialized and expensive for many smaller agencies; if the sample has to be sent out for analysis, the delays increase. For instance, it may take as long as a year to get DNA test results back from the FBI lab. While a DNA test can provide a highly accurate answer to the question of a suspect's guilt, everyone involved—the suspect, the victim, and the investigators—may have to wait a long time for that answer.

1. Write a one- or two-sentence summary of the passage's main idea.

   _____

   _____

   _____

   _____

   _____

   _____

   _____

2. DNA testing is very accurate, but:
   A. it's too expensive for many police departments to use.
   B. it can only be done at the FBI lab.
   C. it's also time-consuming.
   D. it takes too long to be widely useful.

PASSAGE 2

As disgusting as most people find them, maggots can help forensic entomologists solve murders. Forensic entomologists apply entomology, or the study of insects and other arthropods, to legal issues and investigations. In terms of this field, the most important aspect of arthropods is the fact that many varieties are carrion feeders; that is, they eat dead vertebrate bodies, including human corpses. A forensic entomologist classifies and analyzes the flies and larvae found on a body. Using his or her expertise in the life cycles of these creatures and the variables affecting the timing of each stage, the analyst can then estimate when the person died. By comparing the insects commonly found near the body with those on the body itself, a forensic entomologist can also help determine whether or not the corpse has been moved after death. In some instances, movement of suspects, goods, victims, or vehicles can be traced with the help of insects. Insect parts or whole insects can get caught in automobile headlights or radiators. By identifying these insects and plotting the distribution and biology of species, the forensic entomologist can create a map of where the suspect has been.

3. Summarize the passage in one or two sentences.

_____

_____

_____

_____

_____

_____

_____

4. The author would agree with all of the following statements about forensic entomology EXCEPT:

A. Forensic entomology applies the study of insects and arthropods to legal issues.

B. Forensic entomology can be used to estimate the time of death of a body.

C. Forensic entomology relies on the fact that many arthropods are carrion feeders.

D. Forensic entomology has no application in cases that lack a body.

PASSAGE 3

Private security firms are growing, despite a falling crime rate, as smaller law enforcement agencies privatize, and more affluent communities demand the round-the-clock presence no police force can offer. These private security officers must handle many of the same tasks as police, and many citizens mistake uniformed security officers for police. However, there is a big difference between private officers and the public force. While an applicant to a city or state police force must undergo a thorough background check, most private security firms lack the resources for the same kind of screening; this makes it easier for truly dangerous people to take on the authority of a gun and badge. In California, the serial killer known as the Hillside Strangler was able to become a security guard after he had been turned down by the Los Angeles Police Department and Sheriff's Department. In other states, private security officers have been accused of a variety of crimes, from theft to rape, while on duty. Furthermore, most private security officers don't receive the same thorough training as police. While police spend several months in training, and often are required to continue training throughout their careers, private security officers may have as little as 8 hours in training if they are unarmed, or 12 hours in training if they are armed.

5. Summarize the passage in your own words.

_____

_____

_____

_____

_____

_____

_____

6. More and more private security officers are being hired, even though:
   A. they are expected to assist the city police.
   B. they have to work around the clock.
   C. fewer applicants than ever pass the required background checks.
   D. the crime rates have been decreasing.

PASSAGE 4

The earliest European settlers in North America had no particular system of laws. The problems and disputes that arose between people were solved by using common sense. After England gained control over its colonies, however, the system based on common sense was gradually replaced by a formal system of laws, courts, and judges. Today, America's legal system still closely resembles that of England's.

7. Summarize the passage in your own words.

_____

_____

_____

_____

_____

_____

8. The author would agree that:

A. the American legal system is still based on common sense.

B. many legal systems around the world resemble the English legal system.

C. the American legal system has been strongly influenced by the English system.

D. there were relatively few disputes among the earliest American settlers.

ANSWERS AND EXPLANATIONS

1. Sample summary: Although DNA testing is accurate and important in investigating crimes, it can also create delays in those investigations.

2. **C** is correct. The fact that DNA testing takes a long time to complete is central to the passage's explanation of why such an accurate method can actually delay investigations. Notice that this does not mean the same thing as choice D. The author says that DNA testing is useful, even though it is time-consuming.

3. Sample summary: Forensic entomology allows investigators to use insects in investigating crimes, such as murder and smuggling.

4. **D** is correct. While much of the passage concerns the application of forensic entomology in murder cases, its application in cases of contraband, or smuggling, is also discussed.

5. Sample summary: While the number of private security officers is increasing, and their duties and appearance may be similar to those of police officers, their screening and training procedures are not as rigorous as are those for police officers.

6. **D** is correct. The author gives a couple of reasons for the growth of private security firms, but says specifically that the crime rate is decreasing.

7. Sample summary: While the earliest American colonists had no particular legal system, England eventually imposed its own system, which became the American legal system that we still know today.

8. **C** is correct. This choice is very close to the author's main idea, which is stated in the last sentence of the paragraph.

PUTTING IT ALL TOGETHER: LONG PASSAGE PRACTICE

In the pages that follow, you will read two long passages—twice. The first time you see each passage, it will be broken down into individual paragraphs with questions that follow each paragraph. This is to help you practice looking for and retaining details. The second time you read each passage, it will be presented in its entirety and followed by additional questions. Answers are found at the end of the practice.

PASSAGE 1

Taking accurate and useful fingerprints is one of the most cost-effective investigative techniques a police officer can use. Three simple tools—fingerprint powder, a brush, and some tape—will allow an officer to handle about 70 percent of normal crime scene fingerprinting. A few simple techniques will help you lift clear, useful fingerprints every time.

1. What's the author's primary topic?

   _____

   _____

   _____

2. Does the author believe that fingerprinting is a worthwhile investigative technique?

   _____

   _____

   _____

One thing inexperienced investigators often forget to keep in mind is the color of the print card. That's more important than the color of the surface you are printing. If you use a light powder, then lift the print and place it on a white or clear card, you will make the print almost invisible, and therefore useless. Black powder is a better choice and can be used even on black or dark surfaces. If you have trouble seeing the powdered print on the dark surface, use a high-powered flashlight and slant the beam at an angle until you can see the print clearly enough to lift it.

3. The author uses this paragraph primarily to:
   A. discuss an important aspect of fingerprinting that is often mishandled.
   B. explain what light and dark fingerprint powders are made of.
   C. make an argument against using white or clear print cards.
   D. remind officers to put batteries in their flashlights.

Now read the two paragraphs together.

Taking accurate and useful fingerprints is one of the most cost-effective investigative techniques a police officer can use. Three simple tools—fingerprint powder, a brush and some tape—will allow an officer to handle about 70 percent of normal crime scene fingerprinting. A few simple techniques will help you lift clear, useful fingerprints every time.

One thing inexperienced investigators often forget to keep in mind is the color of the print card. That's more important than the color of the surface you are printing. If you use a light powder, then lift the print and place it on a white or clear card, you will make the print almost invisible, and therefore useless. Black powder is a better choice and can be used even on black or dark surfaces. If you have trouble seeing the powdered print on the dark surface, use a high-powered flashlight and slant the beam at an angle until you can see the print clearly enough to lift it.

4. The most important function of the techniques discussed in the second paragraph is to:
   A. shorten the time needed to take fingerprints.
   B. discuss the different colors of powder available and what they are made of.
   C. make sure that the fingerprints are readable and useful once they are lifted.
   D. create a step-by-step procedure for fingerprinting.

5. The author describes fingerprinting as:
   A. tricky and complicated.
   B. simple and cost-effective.
   C. troubling and useless.
   D. difficult but worthwhile.

6. Based on the passage, the author would be most likely to support which of the following statements about fingerprinting?
   A. It's an old-fashioned and outdated investigative technique.
   B. It's expensive, but well worth the cost.
   C. It can't be used at 70 percent of crime scenes.
   D. It can be extremely useful if it's done properly.

PASSAGE 2

A few years ago, the U.S. Department of Justice released a report entitled "Convicted by Juries, Exonerated by Science." The report contains case studies of 28 individuals convicted of sexual assaults and murders. These individuals were released when postconviction DNA testing proved they could not have committed the crimes. In 24 of the 28 cases, eyewitness identification was a significant factor in convicting these individuals. But in all 24 cases the eyewitnesses were wrong. This isn't uncommon; studies have shown that eyewitness identification is wrong almost 50 percent of the time. This doesn't mean witnesses are lying or deliberately concealing the truth; most often, they are trying to help solve a crime and make an honest mistake in their identification. Why do so many eyewitnesses make mistakes? To understand this, we need to know something about how memory works, and how it can change over time.

7. State the topic in your own words.

    _____

    _____

There's a common belief that the brain stores memories like a videotape stores images; the brain records events and, once recorded, the recollection of those events doesn't change. However, years of research have shown that memory is fluid, not static. First, no one remembers everything about an event. Instead, fragments are noticed and registered. Once stored, these fragments can be changed by information taken in later, as the person recalls the incident. All of this takes place on an unconscious level; the person believes that what he remembers seeing is what actually happened.

Psychological experts divide the process of memory into three stages. The first is the acquisition stage, which is the individual's immediate perception of the event and the entry of the information into the memory system. This is followed by the retention phase, which covers the time elapsed before the witness tries to recall the event. The final stage is the retrieval stage, which occurs when the witness actually tries to retrieve the stored information. The memory can change at any point in this process.

8. The author uses the second paragraph primarily to:
    A. describe the ways in which the brain is like a videotape.
    B. describe the fluidity of memory.
    C. argue that faulty eyewitnesses are consciously lying.
    D. convince the reader of the accuracy of memory.

9. In the third paragraph, the author:
    A. describes the biological structure of the human brain.
    B. describes three ways in which memory is erased.
    C. lists three stages of memory.
    D. gives three reasons to suspect the accuracy of memory.

The acquisition stage is influenced by both *event factors* and by *witness factors*. Event factors are related to the incident itself: how well-lit the environment was, how long the event lasted, how far away the witness was, and how much violence occurred. Witness factors include personal qualities that can affect a witness's memory. These are internal factors such as fear, any previous experience with similar situations, or expectations the witness has of his or her own behavior or the behavior of those he or she is witnessing. These factors, and many others, influence what bits of information the witness first notices and remembers.

10. Based on this paragraph, the author probably would agree with which of the following statements?

   A. The acquisition stage is most strongly affected by the qualities of the event itself.

   B. Both event factors and witness factors have little effect on a witness's expectations.

   C. Dim lighting often frightens witnesses, especially witnesses who often work in badly lighted rooms.

   D. As memories are formed, they can be affected by factors that are both internal and external to the witness.

The retention or storage phase also is influenced by two sets of factors. The first is *retention interval*, or the length of time between when the memory is acquired and when it is retrieved. Research indicates that as the retention interval increases, the accuracy and details of the memory decrease. The second factor at this stage is *post-event information*, or information learned after an event takes place, which is then integrated into the memory of the event. Once witnesses have blended post-event information into memory, it's nearly impossible to separate what information came from the event itself and what was learned later. Because the witness doesn't consciously add post-event information, there is no way for him or her to distinguish between original memory and later revision. Witnesses can gather post-event information from sources such as leading questions, talking with other witnesses about the event or hearing other witnesses' conversations, or reading or watching stories about the event in the media.

11. The retention interval is:

   A. relatively unimportant in the process of memory.

   B. always more than 30 days.

   C. the period before the event takes place.

   D. the period between acquiring and retrieving a memory.

External factors can have a tremendous influence on memory during the third stage, the retrieval of information. Sociologists and psychologists describe the Experimenter Expectancy Effect: The interviewer unintentionally and unconsciously signals the subject, encouraging the desired response. The subject, also unintentionally and unconsciously, tailors his or her responses to fit the interviewer's expectations. The only way to prevent the interviewer from affecting the outcome of the interview is to create a "double-blind" situation, in which the interviewer is not aware of the desired outcome. The Experimenter Expectancy Effect is so strong that scientific experiments generally must be double-blind for their results to be accepted by the scientific community.

The responses a witness receives after recalling a memory can also affect the memory itself. The witness can become more confident in the accuracy of a memory—and less likely to recall conflicting information—if he or she receives positive feedback. On the other hand, people become less sure if given negative feedback or no feedback at all. This feedback can come from repeated questioning, or even casual conversation with others. A witness who is strongly confident seems more credible than a witness who is more tentative; however, studies demonstrate that confidence is a poor indicator of accuracy.

None of this suggests that eyewitness testimony has no value, or shouldn't be used. It does suggest that investigators should be aware of its potential weaknesses and seek as much supporting evidence as possible.

12. Based on the preceding paragraphs, which of these statements would the author DISAGREE with?

   A. Once memory is recalled, it remains fixed.

   B. An interviewer's expectations can affect the responses of the interviewee.

   C. Scientists feel that double-blind experiments provide more accurate results than those in which the experimenter is aware of the desired outcome.

   D. A confident witness may be no more accurate than a witness with less confidence.

Now read the entire passage again.

A few years ago, the U.S. Department of Justice released a report entitled "Convicted by Juries, Exonerated by Science." The report contains case studies of 28 individuals convicted of sexual assaults and murders. These individuals were released when postconviction DNA testing proved they could not have committed the crimes. In 24 of the 28 cases, eyewitness identification was a significant factor in convicting these individuals. But in all 24 cases the eyewitnesses were wrong. This isn't uncommon; studies have shown that eyewitness identification is wrong almost 50 percent of the time. This doesn't mean witnesses are lying or deliberately concealing the truth; most often, they are trying to help solve a crime and make an honest mistake in their identification. Why do so many eyewitnesses make mistakes? To understand this, we need to know something about how memory works, and how it can change over time.

There's a common belief that the brain stores memories like a videotape stores images; the brain records events and, once recorded, the recollection of those events doesn't change. However, years of research have shown that memory is fluid, not static. First, no one remembers everything about an event. Instead, fragments are noticed and registered. Once stored, these fragments can be changed by information taken in later, as the person recalls the incident. All of this takes place on an unconscious level; the person believes that what he remembers seeing is what actually happened.

Psychological experts divide the process of memory into three stages. The first is the acquisition stage, which is the individual's immediate perception of the event and the entry of the information into the memory system. This is followed by the retention phase, which covers the time elapsed before the witness tries to recall the event. The final stage is the retrieval stage, which occurs when the witness actually tries to retrieve the stored information. The memory can change at any point in this process.

The acquisition stage is influenced by both *event factors* and by *witness factors*. Event factors are related to the incident itself: how well-lit the environment was, how long the event lasted, how far away the witness was, and how much violence occurred. Witness factors include personal qualities that can affect a witness's memory. These are internal factors such as fear, any previous experience with similar situations, or expectations the witness has of his or her own behavior or the behavior of those he or she is witnessing. These factors, and many others, influence what bits of information the witness first notices and remembers.

The retention or storage phase also is influenced by two sets of factors. The first is *retention interval*, or the length of time between when the memory is acquired and when it is retrieved. Research indicates that as the retention interval increases, the accuracy and details of the memory decrease. The second factor at this stage is *post-event information*, or information learned after an event takes place, which is then integrated into the memory of the event. Once witnesses have blended post-event information into memory, it's nearly impossible to separate what information came from the event itself and what was learned later. Because the witness doesn't consciously add post-event information, there is no way for him or her to distinguish between original memory and later revision.

Witnesses can gather post-event information from sources such as leading questions, talking with other witnesses about the event or hearing other witnesses' conversations, or reading or watching stories about the event in the media.

External factors can have a tremendous influence on memory during the third stage, the retrieval of information. Sociologists and psychologists describe the Experimenter Expectancy Effect: The interviewer unintentionally and unconsciously signals the subject, encouraging the desired response. The subject, also unintentionally and unconsciously, tailors his or her responses to fit the interviewer's expectations. The only way to prevent the interviewer from affecting the outcome of the interview is to create a "double-blind" situation, in which the interviewer is not aware of the desired outcome. The Experimenter Expectancy Effect is so strong that scientific experiments generally must be double-blind for their results to be accepted by the scientific community.

The responses a witness receives after recalling a memory can also affect the memory itself. The witness can become more confident in the accuracy of a memory—and less likely to recall conflicting information—if he or she receives positive feedback. On the other hand, people become less sure if given negative feedback or no feedback at all. This feedback can come from repeated questioning, or even casual conversation with others. A witness who is strongly confident seems more credible than a witness who is more tentative; however, studies demonstrate that confidence is a poor indicator of accuracy.

None of this suggests that eyewitness testimony has no value, or shouldn't be used. It does suggest that investigators should be aware of its potential weaknesses and seek as much supporting evidence as possible.

13. The word *tentative* in the next-to-last paragraph means:
    A. severe.
    B. eager.
    C. careful.
    D. uncertain.

14. The author suggests that:
    A. witnesses must be interrogated repeatedly and severely in order to weed out liars.
    B. witnesses should be protected as much as possible from exposure to outside influences that, consciously or not, could taint their memories.
    C. witnesses consciously try to give investigators the answers they want because they crave the investigators' approval.
    D. witnesses who block out portions of their memory could retrieve these portions under hypnosis.

15. Based on this passage, which of these statements would the author be likely to AGREE with?

    A. Eyewitness testimony can be very persuasive to a jury and is estimated to be accurate in over 80 percent of the cases in which it is used.

    B. Police officers and other investigators often make deliberate efforts to manipulate witnesses' recollections of an event.

    C. While juries consider eyewitness testimony extremely strong evidence, a witness's memory of an event can be flawed, even if the witness honestly believes the memory is accurate.

    D. The common image of memory as a faithful recording of an event, like a videotape, is a good representation of the way memory works; flaws in memory can be compared to tracking problems when playing a videotape.

ANSWERS AND EXPLANATIONS

1. The primary topic is fingerprinting.

2. Yes. The author calls it *cost-effective*.

3. **A** is correct. The second paragraph spells out one way to keep from lifting unreadable prints.

4. **C.** is correct The second paragraph describes one common mistake and how to avoid it.

5. **B** is correct. Although the second paragraph describes a common problem, the author never describes fingerprinting as difficult or complicated.

6. **D** is correct. According to the passage, fingerprinting is useful when done correctly.

7. Sample topic: The general topic is eyewitness testimony. More specifically, the author is arguing that eyewitness testimony is less reliable than most people believe.

8. **B** is correct. In the second paragraph, the author argues that the image most of us have of memory as a kind of recording is not accurate, and that memory is subject to change.

9. **C** is correct. The author divides the process of memory into three steps or stages.

10. **D** is correct. *Event factors* and *witness factors* are external and internal to the witness and affect the witness's initial memory of an event.

11. **D** is correct. According to the passage, the retention interval is the time between when a memory is acquired and when it is retrieved.

12. **A** is correct. These paragraphs are intended to show that memory can be affected even as it is recalled, and afterwards. In other words, it is not fixed.

13. **D** is correct. The author is comparing a confident witness with a tentative one; *uncertain* is the only word that contrasts with *confident*.

14. **B** is correct. The author never actually recommends this, but protecting witnesses from outside influences is a logical extension of his or her arguments.

15. **C** is correct. This is a good summary of the author's argument.

CHAPTER SIX

Mathematics

Some police officer exams may test basic mathematics to ensure you are comfortable working with numbers. This chapter reviews some of the building blocks of math. If you are comfortable with the concepts presented in this chapter, facing everyday problems that require a basic knowledge of addition, subtraction, multiplication, and division will be a smooth process.

Most of you have encountered these rules and practices in school, though it may have been a while since you've reviewed the exact terms and concepts. For some of you, this chapter will just be a basic brush-up of skills you are comfortable with. Others may have to study this chapter carefully to relearn the basics. Like grammar and spelling, no matter what your actual exam tests, reviewing this chapter and completing the practice questions can only enhance your confidence going into test day.

ORDER OF OPERATIONS

No matter what line of work you are in, you will always encounter formulas in everyday life. When traveling abroad, you may need to convert a temperature from degrees Celsius to degrees Fahrenheit to better understand it. You may need to calculate the perimeter or area of a room in order to accurately describe it. Formulas exist for all kinds of situations.

When simplifying a mathematical expression after you have plugged values into your formula, you do not simply work from left to right, as you do when you read a book. Just as there are rules for driving an automobile, there are rules for order when performing arithmetic operations. There is a predetermined order of operations used to evaluate expressions. Perhaps you remember the mnemonic for remembering the order of operations: PEMDAS. Some of you may have the used memory tool "Please Excuse My Dear Aunt Sally" to recall the correct order.

The order of operations is:

P	Parentheses (grouping symbols)
E	Exponents
MD	Multiply and divide from left to right
AS	Add and subtract from left to right

The *P* in PEMDAS stands for parentheses, or grouping symbols. Grouping symbols include parentheses, brackets, the absolute value symbol, and a fraction bar. So to simplify $\frac{18 + 10^2 - 4 \times 2}{20 - 27 \div 3}$, treat the fraction bar as a grouping symbol and first evaluate the top (the numerator) then the bottom (the denominator). Then you will divide for the final step.

To simplify the numerator, first simplify your exponent: $10^2 = 100$. Second, multiply 4 times 2 to get 8. The top is now $18 + 100 - 8$. Evaluate from left to right: $118 - 8 = 110$. To simplify the denominator, first divide 27 by 3 to get 9. Then subtract: $20 - 9 = 11$. Finally, divide 110 by 11 to get 10.

When plugging numbers into formulas, a working knowledge of the order of operations is essential. For example, to convert a temperature from degrees Fahrenheit to degrees Celsius, you use the formula $C = \frac{5}{9}(F - 32)$, where *F* is the degrees in Fahrenheit and *C* is the degrees in Celsius. If you have a temperature of 77 degrees Fahrenheit, and you want to know the equivalent degrees in Celsius, substitute in 77 for *F* in the formula: $C = \frac{5}{9}(77 - 32)$. First, subtract 32 from 77, because parentheses are evaluated first: $C = \frac{5}{9}(45)$. Now, multiply $\frac{5}{9}$ by 45 (or $5 \times 45 \div 9$) to get 25 degrees Celsius.

NUMBER PROPERTIES

There are common properties of numbers that are frequently used to make adding and multiplying easier. You most likely use these properties without even realizing it when you do mental arithmetic or when you add a column of numbers. These properties give you the license to change the order of operations in certain situations. In addition to making addition and multiplication of number terms easier to calculate, these three properties are frequently used in solving algebraic equations.

THE COMMUTATIVE PROPERTY OF ADDITION

The commutative property of addition states that changing the order of the addends in a sum does not change the sum:

$a + b = b + a$, where *a* and *b* are any real numbers.

For example:

$12.3 + 6.9 + 7.7 = 12.3 + 7.7 + 6.9$

The order of operations would dictate that 12.3 would first be added to 6.9. But the addition is easier if you first add 12.3 to 7.7 because the sum will equal a whole number. The commutative property gives you this freedom.

THE COMMUTATIVE PROPERTY OF MULTIPLICATION

Similar to the commutative property of addition, the commutative property of multiplication states that changing the order of the factors in a product does not change the product: $a \times b = b \times a$, where *a* and *b* are any real numbers.

For example:

$2 \times 8 \times 5 \times 7 = 2 \times 5 \times 8 \times 7$

If you scan a group of factors to find subproducts to equal 10, 100, or 1,000, It Is easiest to multiply these factors first. The commutative property allows you to make these changes to the order of operations.

THE ASSOCIATIVE PROPERTY

The associative property also pertains to either the addends in a sum or the factors in a product.

The associative property of addition or multiplication states that changing the grouping (parentheses or brackets) of addends in a sum or the grouping of factors in a product does not change the resulting sum or product:

$a + (b + c) = (a + b) + c$, where a, b, and c are any real numbers.

$a \times (b \times c) = (a \times b) \times c$, where a, b, and c are any real numbers.

For example, to add $9.8 + (10.2 + 6.1) + 4.9$, the order of operations would call for you to evaluate inside the parentheses first and then to add from left to right. But the sum of 9.8 and 10.2 is 20, and the sum of 6.1 and 4.9 is 11. The associative property allows you to change the grouping by adding: $(9.8 + 10.2) + (6.1 + 4.9)$, to get $20 + 11 = 31$. Notice in the example that the order of the addends did not change, just the grouping.

To multiply, consider the expression $7 \times 20 \times 5 \times 8$. Notice that $20 \times 5 = 100$, so change the grouping to make the multiplication easier: $7 \times (20 \times 5) \times 8$. Now, evaluate from left to right: $7 \times 100 = 700$. Finally, $700 \times 8 = 5,600$.

You can also use a combination of the properties. For example, to simplify the expression $2.1 + 8.07 + 7.9 + 24.93$, scan the addends and recognize that $(2.1 + 7.9)$ and $(8.07 + 24.93)$ will produce whole numbers. Use the commutative property to get $2.1 + 7.9 + 8.07 + 24.93$. Then use the associative property to get $(2.1 + 7.9) + (8.07 + 24.93)$. Now the addition is easy to finish: $10 + 33 = 43$.

THE DISTRIBUTIVE PROPERTY

The distributive property involves two operations: addition and multiplication or subtraction and multiplication.

The distributive property of multiplication over addition or subtraction states that multiplication distributes over addition and subtraction:

$a \times (b + c) = (a \times b) + (a \times c)$, where a, b, and c are real numbers.

$a \times (b - c) = (a \times b) - (a \times c)$, where a, b, and c are real numbers.

For example, if you want to multiply 16 by 8, you may not know the multiples of 16. However, you do know the multiples of 10 and 6. The distributive property allows you to rewrite 8 × 16 as 8 × (10 + 6), or simply 8(10 + 6). Because multiplication distributes over addition, this problem becomes (8 × 10) + (8 × 6), which can be evaluated as 80 + 48 = 128. Likewise, 8 × 16 could be written as 8 × (20 − 4) or (8 × 20) − (8 × 4) = 160 − 32 = 128.

You can also use the distributive property in reverse. For example, if you were instructed to simplify (12 × 6.4) + (12 × 3.6), order of operations would have you evaluate parentheses first, which involves decimal multiplication. If you notice that both terms are multiplied by 12, use the distributive property to factor out the 12: (12 × 6.4) + (12 × 3.6) = 12 × (6.4 + 3.6) = 12 × 10 = 120.

INTEGERS

This section focuses on learning about the set of numbers known as integers. You encounter integers in many different places each day. They are used to express temperatures above and below 0, a loss or gain of yards when playing certain sports, and the highs and lows of the stock market, to name a few. Integers provide a foundation for the real number system.

Integers are the set of whole numbers and their opposites. As a set, the integers are written as {…, −3, −2, −1, 0, 1, 2, 3, …}. It is important to remember that the number 0 is neither positive nor negative.

ORDERING INTEGERS

The value of an integer is determined by its location on the real number line, where negative numbers appear to the *left* of 0, and positive numbers are located to the *right* of 0. When comparing integers, first determine their locations on the number line. A number farther to the right will be larger in value than a number farther to the left. For example, when comparing −8 and −9, −9 is farther to the left on a number line—therefore, −9 is less than −8. This concept can also be written using the symbol for less than, and would appear as −9 < −8.

For practice with ordering, try the following exercise:

Place the following integers in order from smallest to largest (ascending order): 1, −10, −1, −100.

Start with the value that is the *farthest* to the left on a number line, which would be −100. This is the smallest value in the list. The next smallest is −10 and then −1. The only positive number in the list, 1, is the largest number. The integers listed in ascending order would be −100 < −10 < −1 < 1. If working with negative numbers is confusing to you, here's a tip: Think of positive and negative numbers in terms of money in your pocket. −100 versus +1. Which is a greater amount? If you have −$100, you actually owe someone $100. Whereas if you have $1, it may be only $1 but at least it's a positive amount!

ADDING INTEGERS

When adding integers, the sign of the numbers involved is very important. In order to help you visualize adding integers, think of any positive integer as a group of that many positives and any negative integer as a group of that many negatives.

Now, keep in mind that any time one positive and one negative of the same value are grouped together, they cancel each other out, making a neutral. You can consider this as $+1 + -1 = 0$.

When adding integers that have the same sign, just add the absolute values of the numbers and keep the sign. For example, $+6 + +7 = +13$ and $-4 + -8 = -12$.

A general rule for adding integers with different signs is to subtract their absolute values and keep the sign of the number with the larger absolute value as your answer. In the example $18 + -25$, subtract the absolute values to get $25 - 18 = 7$. Since -25 has a larger absolute value, take the negative sign for your answer. The final answer is -7.

SUBTRACTING INTEGERS

The subtraction of any two integers can also be expressed as adding the opposite of the number being subtracted. This way, the concept can be simplified into an addition problem, and you only have two rules to commit to memory.

Here are a few examples to demonstrate how this works:

Find the value of $19 - (-2)$.

Since this is a problem subtracting integers, change the problem so that it is adding the opposite of the number subtracted. So the subtraction sign changes to an addition sign and the -2 changes to a $+2$. The problem now becomes $19 + (+2)$. Follow the rules for addition. Since the signs are both positive, add 19 and 2 to get 21 and keep the solution positive. $19 - (-2) = 21$.

Find the value of $-45 - 9$.

As in the previous example, change the subtraction sign to an addition sign and change the $+9$ to a -9. The problem now becomes $-45 + (-9)$. Since the signs are both negative, add the absolute values to get $45 + 9 = 54$ and keep the solution negative. $-45 - 9 = -54$.

The temperature on a certain day dropped from $-4°$ F to $-17°$ F. What is the difference in temperature for that day?

This example illustrates how negative integers can be used to show temperature. Since you are looking for the difference between the two temperatures, subtract the two values. $-4 - (-17)$ then becomes $-4 + 17$ after the subtraction sign is changed to addition and the sign of -17 is changed to a positive. Since the signs are now different, subtract the absolute values and take the sign of the larger absolute value. $17 - 4 = 13$. The difference in temperature is 13 degrees.

MULTIPLYING AND DIVIDING INTEGERS

Multiplication and division of integers is a bit more straightforward than adding and subtracting. Regardless of the numbers' signs, you multiply or divide the absolute values of the numbers just as you would when you first learned how to multiply and divide. The only question is whether the solution is positive or negative.

Whether you're multiplying or dividing, here's a quick way of determining positive and negative values:

positive × *positive* = *positive*
positive ÷ *positive* = *positive*

negative × *negative* = *positive*
negative ÷ *negative* = *positive*
  (An even number of negatives cancel each other out.)

positive × *negative* = *negative*
positive ÷ *negative* = *negative*
  (An odd number of negatives results in a negative product or quotient.)

For the problem (–5) × (–3), the two negatives cancel each other out. This would have a result of 15.

Since division follows the same principle, a problem such as –12 ÷ 4 would result in an answer of –3. There is only one negative in the problem, so the answer will also be negative.

In the example –4 × –9 × –2, the result will be the opposite of the product of 4, 9, and 2, which is –72. The solution here is negative because there are three negatives.

AREA AND PERIMETER

When writing a report, investigating a crime scene, or just making observations, it will be important for you to be able to calculate (even if you're just estimating) areas and perimeters of rooms, open areas such as parks, and other types of spaces. Here's a quick review of how to calculate the area and perimeter of spaces.

AREA

Mathematically speaking, the area of a space is the two-dimensional surface occupied by that space. You will likely encounter areas when reporting square footages of a room or building. Area is a fairly easy formula to remember, particularly since most rooms, buildings, parking lots, etc., are approximate squares or rectangles. Triangles and circles get a bit trickier. But how often do you encounter a triangular room or a circular parking lot? For these reasons, I am going to focus solely on squares and rectangles.

In the example below, the room's dimensions are 15 feet by 22 feet. Assuming that the parallel walls are the same size, the area of this room is calculated by multiplying the length (l) times the width (w) or 15 feet $\times$ 22 feet = 330 feet^2.

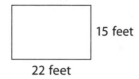

15 feet

22 feet

Calculating the area of a square space is even simpler. Since a square has four equal sides, you simply *square* the length of one side, often written as s^2. So for the square playground below, the calculation for its area would be (40 feet)^2 = 1,600 feet^2.

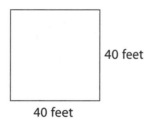

40 feet

40 feet

PERIMETER

Perimeter is a term you've likely heard on TV cop shows. *"Secure the perimeter of the park with 20 officers."* You know what a perimeter is—the outer edge of a space—but do you remember how to calculate it? Let's use the room and the playground examples from above.

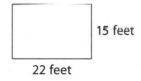

15 feet

22 feet

A perimeter of a shape is the sum of all its sides. So, in this case, the perimeter of this room = 22 feet + 15 feet + 22 feet + 15 feet, simplified as 2 $\times$ (22 feet + 15 feet) = 74 feet.

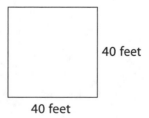

40 feet

40 feet

Likewise, the perimeter of the playground above is 40 feet + 40 feet + 40 feet + 40 feet, simplified as 4 $\times$ 40 feet = 160 feet.

ORDER OF OPERATIONS PRACTICE

1. Simplify: 56 − 24 + 12
   A. 68
   B. 20
   C. 44
   D. 92
   E. 42

2. Simplify: 36 + 8 ÷ 2
   A. 40
   B. 22
   C. 52
   D. 25
   E. 88

3. Simplify: $32 - 4^2 \times 2$
   A. 32
   B. 0
   C. 48
   D. 16
   E. 80

4. Simplify (40 + 20) ÷ 10
   A. 3
   B. 42
   C. 5
   D. 1
   E. 6

5. Simplify: 48 ÷ 2 + 4 × 4 − 2
   A. 110
   B. 3
   C. 38
   D. 30
   E. 56

6. Simplify: $(15 - 12)^3 \div 9 \times 3$

    A. 9

    B. 3

    C. $\frac{1}{3}$

    D. 1

    E. 27

7. Simplify: $10^2 \div (80 \div 4 \times 2)$

    A. $\frac{2}{3}$

    B. 10

    C. $\frac{5}{2}$

    D. $\frac{1}{2}$

    E. 25

8. Simplify: $(126 - 56) + (3 + 2)^3 \div 3$

    A. 77

    B. 39

    C. 225

    D. 17

    E. 95

ANSWERS AND EXPLANATIONS

1. **C** is correct. First subtract 24 from 56; 56 − 24 = 32. Now add this result to 12: 32 + 12 = 44.

2. **A** is correct. Evaluate division first: 8 ÷ 2 = 4. Then add: 36 + 4 = 40.

3. **B** is correct. The order of operations is exponents, then multiplication, and finally subtraction. 4^2 = 16, then 16 × 2 = 32. Finally, 32 − 32 = 0.

4. **E** is correct. Evaluate parentheses first: 40 + 20 = 60. Then divide: 60 ÷ 10 = 6.

5. **C** is correct. Work from left to right, evaluating all division and multiplication first. Thus, 48 ÷ 2 = 24. Next, 4 × 4 = 16. Then, 24 + 16 = 40. Finally, 40 − 2 = 38.

6. **A** is correct. Evaluate parentheses first: 15 − 12 = 3. Next, evaluate the exponent: 3^3 = 3 × 3 × 3 = 27. Next, divide: 27 ÷ 9 = 3. Finally, multiply: 3 × 3 = 9.

7. **C** is correct. First, simplify within the parentheses. Division is located to the left of multiplication, so divide first: 80 ÷ 4 = 20. Now, multiply: 20 × 2 = 40. The expression within parentheses is simplified, so evaluate the exponent next. 10^2 = 100. The final step is to divide: 100 ÷ 40.

   Thus: $\frac{100}{40} = \frac{50}{20} = \frac{5}{2}$

8. **E** is correct. Address the parentheses first (126 − 56) = 70 and $(3 + 2)^3 = 5^3$. Next, complete the exponent, so 5^3 = 125. Now the equation becomes 70 + 125 ÷ 5. By the order of operations, division comes next, so 70 + 125 ÷ 5 = 70 + 25 = 95.

INTEGERS PRACTICE

1. Which of the following answer choices are NOT in ascending order?

   A. 0, 2, 4

   B. −5, −7, −8

   C. −21, −20, −19

   D. −90, −80, −70

   E. none of these

2. Evaluate: −13 + −6

   A. −19

   B. −7

   C. 7

   D. 18

   E. 19

3. Evaluate: 20 + (−5)

   A. −25

   B. −15

   C. −4

   D. 15

   E. 25

4. Evaluate: −19 + 4 + (−2)

   A. −25

   B. −21

   C. −17

   D. −13

   E. 13

5. Evaluate: −4 × −1 × −9

   A. −14

   B. 14

   C. −36

   D. 36

   E. −32

6. Evaluate: $-6 + (14 - (-2)) - 3^2$

   A. 1
   B. 4
   C. 13
   D. -3
   E. 0

7. Marty checks her bank account and finds that she has a balance of $231.28. She then writes checks in the amounts of $64.75, $122.20, and $49.08 to pay some of her bills. What is the balance in her account after paying the bills?

   A. -$236.03
   B. -$4.75
   C. $4.75
   D. $236.03
   E. $467.31

8. Starting from the second floor, a person takes an elevator down 1 floor, up 14 floors, down 6 floors, and then down another 2 floors. On what floor does this person end up?

   A. 2nd
   B. 5th
   C. 7th
   D. 21st
   E. 23rd

ANSWERS AND EXPLANATIONS

1. **B** is correct. Each of the answer choices is listed in order from smallest to largest except for the numbers in choice (B). Since –5 is greater than –7, and –7 is greater than –8, these numbers are listed in descending, or decreasing, order.

2. **A** is correct. Since you are adding and the signs of the numbers are the same, add the absolute values and keep the sign. –13 + –6 = –19.

3. **D** is correct. Since you are adding and the signs are different, subtract the absolute values of the numbers and keep the sign of the larger absolute value for your answer. 20 – 5 = 15; the sign of the larger is positive so the final answer is +15.

4. **C** is correct. Since you are adding and the signs of the first two numbers are different, subtract the absolute values and keep the sign of the number with the larger absolute value. –19 + 4 = –15. Now add –15 + –2 by adding the absolute values and keeping the negative sign. –15 + –2 = –17.

5. **C** is correct. Multiply 4 × 1 × 9 to get 36. Since there is an odd number of negatives in the problem, the final answer is –36.

6. **A** is correct. Evaluate this expression by using the order of operations. The first step is to evaluate within the parentheses. In the expression 14 – (–2), change the subtraction sign to addition and the sign on –2 to +2. It then becomes 14 + 2 = 16. Then, evaluate the exponent of 2 on the base of 3. $3^2 = 9$. The entire expression is now –6 + 16 – 9. Combine –6 and 16 to get 10 by subtracting the absolute values and making the result positive. To complete the problem subtract 10 – 9 to get a final answer of 1.

7. **B** is correct. Since Marty has a starting balance of $231.28, take that amount and subtract the amount of each check. 231.28 – (64.75 + 122.20 + 49.08) = 231.28 – 236.03 = 231.28 + –236.03 = –4.75. Marty has a negative balance of $4.75.

8. **C** is correct. Write an expression for the elevator trip that starts at the second floor: 2 – 1 + 14 – 6 – 2. Changing each subtraction sign to addition, the expression becomes 2 + –1 + 14 + –6 + –2. Use the commutative property from chapter one to change the order of the expression to 2 + 14 + –1 + –6 + –2. Combining the negative values and the positive values yields 16 + –9 = 7. The person ended up on the seventh floor.

AREA AND PERIMETER PRACTICE

1. The area of a triangle is given by the formula $A = (b \times h) \div 2$, where b is the length of the base and h is the height of the triangle. What is the area of a triangle with base of 5 cm and height of 8 cm?

   A. 40 cm^2

   B. 20 cm^2

   C. 160 cm^2

   D. 10 cm^2

   E. 200 cm^2

2. Your team has been asked to secure the perimeter of the outside of a building. The base of the building is 100 feet by 78 feet. What is the total perimeter of the building?

   A. 7,800 feet^2

   B. 178 feet

   C. 356 feet

   D. 3,900 feet^2

   E. 712 feet

3. A suspect has escaped a crime scene, and your superior officer asked your team to search an area covering 15 city blocks by 20 city blocks. What is the total area of the space you are searching?

   A. 300 square blocks

   B. 35 blocks

   C. 70 blocks

   D. 140 square blocks

   E. 150 square blocks

4. Calculate the total perimeter of the house and its detached garage. The length of the house is 85 feet; the width of the house is 40 feet; and the detached garage is a square, where one side is 40 feet.

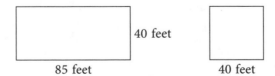

85 feet   40 feet   40 feet

   A. 165 feet

   B. 410 feet

   C. 316 feet

   D. 338 feet

   E. 3400 feet^2

ANSWERS AND EXPLANATIONS

1. **B** is correct. Multiply base times height and then divide by 2: $5 \times 8 = 40$; $40 \div 2 = 20$ cm^2.

2. **C** is correct. The perimeter of the building is the sum of all its sides, so 100 feet + 100 feet + 78 feet + 78 feet = 356 feet.

3. **A** is correct. The total area of the space you're searching is 300 square blocks: 15 blocks $\times$ 20 blocks.

4. **B** is correct. The perimeter of the house is 85 feet + 40 feet + 85 feet + 40 feet = 250 feet; the perimeter of the garage is 4×40 feet = 160 feet. So, the total perimeter of the house plus the detached garage is 250 feet + 160 feet = 410 feet.

CHAPTER SEVEN

Police Situations

Questions pertaining to situations you might face as a police officer will make up a significant portion of your exam. There are several reasons for this. First, they are closely related to actual police work and decisions you will face on the job. This is where you are tested on the basic tasks of police work, and these types of questions give the agency an indication as to whether or not you use good common sense and judgment in making decisions. These questions also show how well you understand, interpret, and apply legal statutes or rules and procedures. They provide an opportunity to show how well you sift through conflicting and overlapping information and understand the English language.

Previous knowledge about police work is not necessary to do well on these questions, but of course it's helpful. Visit your local library and check out a few books on criminal justice and law enforcement. Look up specialized magazines for police. Look online; there are thousands of websites that can illuminate the life of a police officer. Several are provided in the box on page 105. The best preparation? Read your test packet carefully. That's where you will get the most accurate and useful information about the test itself. Beyond that, always keep in mind the following general guidelines that define the police officer's hierarchy of duties.

HIERARCHY OF DUTIES

As a police officer, you have to assume a lot of different roles every single day. In the course of one shift, the work of a police officer can resemble that of a social worker, a career advisor, and a soldier. But there is a definite hierarchy that governs a police officer's various functions.

First: Help anyone in danger. You need to protect innocent victims and bystanders and assist anyone who's wounded or otherwise injured. You also need to protect yourself and fellow officers.

Second: Secure public order. If a riot threatens, you need to do everything you can to defuse the situation. Any acts of aggression or destruction must be stopped, without inciting further action.

Third: Uphold the law. Assess the situation, determining what laws may apply. Arrest those who are, in your judgment, violating those laws. Protect crime scenes to preserve any evidence that may assist in investigation and prosecution.

Fourth: Customer service—help those needing assistance. This can cover anything from helping the victim of a purse-snatching write up a report, to giving directions to tourists. You will also be required to respond appropriately to people who can't adequately care for themselves and require your help. These can include the elderly, children, the mentally or physically handicapped, the homeless, and others in similar situations.

Fifth: Tend to your beat or patrol area. As any police officer will tell you, the job isn't as well plotted as a TV series. In real life, you don't get a weekly jolt of heart-stopping drama. Most of your job consists of keeping an eye on your little piece of the world. This is especially true now, as community policing becomes more and more widespread. So you've got to know what "normal" looks like, and spot anything that's out of place. Is there anyone around who looks like he doesn't belong? A light on in a store at a time when the owner's never been there before? If you want to know about what's going on in the neighborhood, who do you go to?

Then there are the ethical issues. Your day to day interactions with peoples of all races, nationalities, or diverse beliefs reflect not only on you, but your agency and all other police officers as well. Ethical issues aren't easy to prioritize, but keep some of the basics in mind as you make decisions.

Remember your oath to serve. You have made a commitment to perform certain duties; you are expected to respond, as a cop, in any situation that requires law enforcement assistance.

Avoid even the appearance of corruption. This is one of the hot-button areas of law enforcement. Police corruption, or the suspicion of it, has set off more investigations and ruined more careers than any other single issue. Don't put yourself in the neighborhood of this accusation.

Don't play favorites. As you work a beat, you will inevitably develop opinions and attitudes about the people you see regularly. It's just human nature. You are going to like some of these folks, and others are going to drive you up a wall. You can't help that, but you can't let your personal feelings influence your responses. All people are entitled to equal treatment under the law—even really irritating people.

Police Department Websites for the 20 Largest Cities in the United States in descending order of population	
New York	www.nyc.gov/html/nypd/html/home/home.shtml
Los Angeles	www.lapdonline.org/
Chicago	www.cityofchicago.org/city/en/depts/cpd.html
Houston	www.hpdcareer.com/
Phoenix	www.phoenix.gov/joinphxpd/
Philadelphia	www.phillypolice.com/
San Antonio	www.sanantonio.gov/sapd/
San Diego	www.sandiego.gov/police/
Dallas	www.dallaspolice.net
San Jose	www.sjpd.org/
Detroit	www.detroitmi.gov/Departments/PoliceDepartment/tabid/141/default.aspx
San Francisco	http://sf-police.org/
Jacksonville	www.coj.net/Departments/Sheriffs+Office/Default.htm
Indianapolis	www.indy.gov/eGov/City/DPS/IMPD/Pages/home.aspx
Austin	www.ci.austin.tx.us/police/
Columbus	www.columbuspolice.org/
Fort Worth	www.fortworthpd.com/
Charlotte	charmeck.org/city/charlotte/CMPD/Pages/default.aspx
Memphis	www.memphispolice.org/
Boston	www.cityofboston.gov/POLICE/

POLICE SITUATION QUESTION TYPES

Police entrance exams can contain several types of questions. The examples described below are most likely the types of questions you will encounter on the test.

OFFICER RESPONSE

These are the "What should you do?" questions. You are presented with a situation typical of what an officer might face, along with any relevant definitions or circumstances. You have to select the best answer of the four provided. Some of these questions apply specifically to law enforcement situations; others simply test your common sense or reasoning.

You know yourself better than anyone else—are you levelheaded and logical? Can you make decisions under pressure? These are important qualities in a police officer—qualities that can be demonstrated in your responses to these question types.

COMMON ELEMENTS OR REPETITIOUS FACTS (REPEATERS)

When you are answering questions about witness reports, look for overlaps in the information and information that is repeated by other sources. Eyewitness reports come from several sources and will vary, and the first thing to do is to assess where those reports coincide. These are the areas most likely to be accurate, and therefore useful. Look for and focus on the elements that are repeated in eyewitness descriptions.

When you are answering these questions, circle the repetitive information. The choice with the most circled items should be the correct answer.

RELEVANT FACTS

Whenever you are investigating *any* incident, even a kid's cat stranded up in a tree, you will get about five times more information than you can possibly use. You have to sift through all the facts and factoids, determine what's relevant, and then set the rest aside. Then you have to sort through the relevant information and figure out what is essential in dealing with the case.

One kind of sift-and-sort question tests your ability to write a useful report. A report has to contain all the relevant information that would allow any other officer to handle the situation, just from reading the report. These questions often contain the words "clearly and accurately," so watch out for those. You will get a short list of facts about a police situation, and you will be asked to choose the best answer from among four short narratives built up from this information.

There are two principles to keep in mind here:

1. *Is everything there that ought to be?* Make sure the answer you choose includes all relevant information: names, addresses, results.

2. *Is there anything there that shouldn't be?* A report is not a place for an officer to express his opinions or show off her wit. Remember the old *Dragnet* slogan: "Just the facts, ma'am."

Another kind of sift-and-sort is much closer to a standard reading comprehension question. You will read a description of a police situation, like the situations in the "clearly and accurately" questions, and answer several questions about the situation. But these descriptions contain more than just relevant facts; to answer the questions, you will have to pay attention to the details and focus on what's important. As you are reading, remember to notice and underline the relevant bits of information. Who's the victim? Who's the suspect? Are there any times or dates given? Are there witnesses? What do they say? You will have to sift through a lot of details that really aren't relevant from a police officer's point of view; that's exactly what you will have to do on the job, every single day.

APPLICATION OF THE LAW
(INCLUDING DEPARTMENTAL RULES OR POLICY)

As a police officer, you are the front line of the country's legal system. You have to know the statutes of your particular jurisdiction and apply them responsibly and accurately. And you have to be able to do this on the spot, under pressure, without ducking out for a quick trip to the library. You will also have to know and follow departmental rules, regulations, and policy.

As far as the test goes, pay careful attention to the test booklet you get from your agency. They may give you specific legal information you are expected to memorize before the test. This is not something you want to discover as you are reading the test itself. When reading the questions, pay attention to the details: What are the elements of the law? What conduct do you have to engage in?

Remember: As with any exam, these rules apply:

- *Read each question carefully.* Use the active reading strategies; underline or in some way mark the relevant information.

- *Watch out for absolutes.* Words like *always, never, first,* and *last* are often placed in a question to see how focused the reader is. They can radically change a situation.

- *Don't overanalyze.* Don't read into the question or add to the question. Just take it as it's written.

So here we go with some sample questions in each area.

OFFICER RESPONSE EXERCISE

1. In the city, there is a marked increase in the number of bank robberies near the 1st and 15th of every month. Given this information, which of the following is the most logical explanation?

   A. The banks have fewer security guards on duty near the 1st and 15th of the month.

   B. Many bank robbers have jobs that prevent them from robbing banks at other times of the month.

   C. Banks see increased activity near the 1st and 15th of the month due to payroll traffic.

   D. The phases of the moon affect the behavior of bank robbers in the city.

2. Officer Davis reports to the scene of a robbery where the suspect has been apprehended by a security guard. The suspect tells Officer Davis that the security guard has been beating him ever since he apprehended him, even though the suspect is unarmed and insists that he has not tried to escape. Officer Davis should:

   A. ignore the suspect's complaints.

   B. arrest both the suspect and the security guard.

   C. detain the security guard for questioning about the suspect's accusations after the suspect has been processed.

   D. say nothing, but report the security guard's actions to his supervisor and insist that he be fired.

3. If Officer Rivera is pursuing a man who is suspected of stealing five dollars from a gas station attendant and who has sped away from the station onto a busy thoroughfare, Officer Rivera should:

   A. open fire on the suspect, attempting to shoot out one of his rear tires.

   B. pursue the suspect without endangering any civilian lives.

   C. set up a roadblock a few miles ahead of the suspect.

   D. call for helicopter backup to pursue the suspect.

4. An industrial section of Officer Griffin's patrol area has been hit by a recent rash of burglaries of large equipment. About which of the following scenarios should Officer Griffin be most concerned while patrolling this industrial section?

   A. two men walking a dog and carrying toolboxes

   B. a man dressed in black who is parking a windowless van

   C. a pair of teenagers sharing a cigarette

   D. a woman carrying a pair of jumper cables

5. Under which of the following circumstances would a police officer be most likely to wear a bullet-resistant soft body armor?

   A. when visiting an elementary school to explain what a police officer does

   B. when patrolling in heavy traffic

   C. when confronting a suspect who is known to be armed

   D. whenever departmental policy advises to wear it

6. While on patrol in a quiet residential area, Officer Riley sees a young woman who is crying and who has a large bruise on her face. She tells Officer Riley that she was struck several times by her boyfriend, who is in the backyard of the house across the street. Officer Riley should:

   A. arrest the woman on suspicion of prostitution.

   B. administer a lie detector test to the woman.

   C. take a statement from the man.

   D. take the woman's statement, arrest the boyfriend, and detain him for questioning.

7. The police department selects a particular sidearm as its departmentally issued weapon. Which of the following is the most logical reason for this?

   A. The manufacturer pays for the privilege of making the selected weapon.

   B. The department selects the most efficient and accurate weapon available.

   C. The department does not want to waste time training officers on more than one weapon.

   D. The department selects the least expensive weapon available and orders it in bulk.

8. Officer Pettiford is told to focus his attention on drug dealing in his patrol area. Of the following, about which location should the officer be least concerned?

   A. a 24-hour community center staffed by social workers

   B. an underpass where juveniles sometimes congregate

   C. an abandoned building where several drug arrests have been made in the past year

   D. a vacant lot where prostitutes sometimes gather

ANSWERS AND EXPLANATIONS

1. **C** is the best answer. Since many companies and government agencies do issue paychecks on the 1st and 15th of the month, this statement is the most logical of the four.

2. **C** is correct. Officer Davis should not ignore the complaints (A), but there is no reason to take any action beyond questioning the security guard at this point.

3. **B** is the best answer. Such a minor crime does not warrant any of the other three actions, especially A, which could endanger the lives of other motorists on the "busy thoroughfare."

4. **B** is correct. While the other scenarios might be somewhat suspicious, Officer Griffin should be most concerned about B.

5. **D** is the best answer. Departmental policy should be followed.

6. **D** is the best answer. Probable cause has been established by the woman's statement, and the man should be arrested. There certainly is no reason for Officer Riley to presume that the woman is a prostitute (A), nor for him to administer a lie detector test (B).

7. **B** is the most logical statement. A is illogical; police departments do not use weapons as a means of endorsing them, and manufacturers do not pay for the privilege. C and D imply that saving money is the top priority in this situation, which is untrue.

8. **A** is correct. A "community center staffed by social workers" is the least likely location for a drug deal to take place.

RELEVANT FACTS EXERCISE

1. Officer Church records the following information at a residence at which a woman reports a robbery:

Location:	4949 Cherry Hill Lane
Time:	8:15 A.M.
Victim:	Mrs. Alice Berry
Crime:	robbery
Suspect:	male, approx. 6', covered in black clothing, except his hands, which are white
Weapon:	a switchblade knife
Status of Suspect:	fled on foot
Items Missing:	a watch, a ring, and six pairs of earrings

Officer Church calls in an alert for the suspect. Which of the following expresses the information most clearly and accurately?

A. A robbery suspect, male, approximately six feet tall, covered in black with white hands exposed, is armed with a switchblade knife and was last seen fleeing on foot from 4949 Cherry Hill Lane in an unknown direction shortly after 8:15 A.M. The suspect allegedly stole a watch, a ring, and six pairs of earrings from Mrs. Alice Berry at said location.

B. A watch, ring, and six pairs of earrings were stolen from Mrs. Alice Berry who warns that the armed and dangerous suspect, who is carrying a switchblade knife, fled on foot from her house at 4949 Cherry Hill Lane shortly after he robbed her, which happened at 8:15 A.M. Suspect is described as six feet tall, male, and covered in black clothing.

C. Shortly after 8:15 a.m., a six-foot-tall man robbed Mrs. Alice Berry at 4949 Cherry Hill Lane with a switchblade knife. He allegedly stole a watch and six pairs of earrings. The suspect fled on foot. He is described as wearing black all over his body except for his hands, which are exposed and white.

D. A robbery suspect, approximately six feet tall and covered in black clothing with his white hands exposed, is fleeing on foot from 4949 Cherry Hill Lane, where Mrs. Alice Berry describes him as male and armed with a switchblade knife. The incident occurred at 8:15 A.M., and the suspect fled shortly thereafter.

2. Officer Smith responds to a report of a larceny and gathers the following information:

Location:	980 First Street
Time:	11:45 P.M.
Victim:	Mr. Clay Vale
Crime:	larceny
Suspect:	black male, approx. 5'5", wearing overalls
Location of Suspect:	unknown
Item Stolen:	red 1965 Ford Mustang

Officer Smith is writing his report. Which of the following expresses the information most clearly and accurately?

A. Mr. Clay Vale's prized vintage 1965 Ford Mustang, which is red, was stolen at 11:45 P.M. from his house at 980 First Street by a black male who Mr. Vale, the victim, describes as about 5'5" tall. The suspect is wearing overalls.

B. Mr. Clay Vale, of 980 First Street, reported that his red 1965 Ford Mustang was stolen at 11:45 P.M. by a suspect he describes as a black male, approximately 5'5", wearing overalls. The suspect's location is unknown.

C. A black man, approx. 5'5" tall, wearing overalls, is suspected of stealing a red Ford Mustang at 11:45 P.M. from 980 First Street. The whereabouts of the suspect and the vehicle are unknown. The vehicle is owned by Mr. Clay Vale of the aforementioned address, and is a red 1965 Ford Mustang.

D. At 11:45 P.M., a red Ford Mustang was stolen from Mr. Clay Vale at 980 First Street. The car was manufactured in 1965. The suspect's location is unknown, as is the vehicle's. The suspect is described as a black male, 5'5" tall.

3. Responding to the report of an assault at a local elementary school, Officer Shawn gathers the following information:

Location:	Eubanks Elementary School
Time:	4:45 P.M.
Crime:	assault
Victim:	Mrs. Lebotnik, a teacher
Suspect:	Evan Meredith, a fourth-grade student
Injury:	Mrs. Lebotnik is unconscious and has a concussion
Weapon:	a soccer trophy
Action Taken:	Mrs. Lebotnik was taken to the hospital by an ambulance
Status of Suspect:	Evan Meredith confessed and was taken to the precinct, where he is awaiting a visit from a juvenile court service worker

Officer Shawn is filling out his report on the incident. Which of the following expresses the information most clearly and accurately?

A. Mrs. Lebotnik, a teacher at Eubanks Elementary School, stated that she was assaulted by Evan Meredith, a student at the school, at 4:45 P.M. at Eubanks Elementary School and suffered a concussion. Evan Meredith confessed and is waiting for a court service worker from juvenile court to talk to him at the precinct, where he is.

B. Evan Meredith, a student at Eubanks Elementary School, assaulted Mrs. Lebotnik, a teacher, at Eubanks Elementary School with a soccer trophy. She has a concussion and is unconscious and at the hospital. He is at the precinct awaiting a visit from juvenile court. Evan Meredith confessed to assaulting Mrs. Lebotnik at 4:45 P.M., at which time the assault took place on school grounds.

C. Mrs. Lebotnik, a teacher at Eubanks Elementary School, reported that at 4:45 P.M. at the school, a fourth-grade student named Evan Meredith assaulted her with a soccer trophy. Mrs. Lebotnik suffered a concussion and remains unconscious at the hospital, where she was taken by ambulance. Evan Meredith confessed to the assault and is at the precinct, where he awaits a visit from a juvenile court service worker.

D. Mrs. Lebotnik was assaulted with a soccer trophy by a student, Evan Meredith, who assaulted Mrs. Lebotnik at the school where he went and she worked, Eubanks Elementary School. Evan Meredith confessed to the assault, and Mrs. Lebotnik was taken by ambulance to the hospital, where she is unconscious and has a concussion. Evan Meredith is at the precinct.

4. Officer Escalante follows up on a report of a fire. He gathers the following information:

Location: 850 Hiram Boulevard
Time: 9:15 P.M.
Crime: arson
Victim: Jamal Ferrell
Suspect: Kennedy Cochran
Damage: carport destroyed by fire
Action Taken: suspect arrested and taken into custody

Officer Escalante is writing his report. Which of the following expresses the information most clearly and accurately?

A. Jamal Ferrell reported that at 9:15 P.M. at his home at 850 Hiram Boulevard, Kennedy Cochran started a fire that destroyed Ferrell's carport. Kennedy Cochran was arrested and was taken into custody.

B. At 9:15 P.M., a fire lit by someone at 850 Hiram Boulevard destroyed a carport. The owner of the carport was Jamal Ferrell. The arsonist was Kennedy Cochran. Kennedy Cochran was taken into custody after having been arrested for arson.

C. A carport at 850 Hiram Boulevard was destroyed by a fire lit by alleged arsonist Kennedy Cochran, who did not own the property. The owner is Jamal Ferrell, whose carport was destroyed at 9:15 P.M. Kennedy Cochran was arrested and taken into custody.

D. Jamal Ferrell's carport was destroyed by arson at 850 Hiram Boulevard by a man he says is Kennedy Cochran, who was arrested and taken into custody. The fire destroyed the carport at 9:15 P.M., which was before Kennedy Cochran was arrested.

5. At the scene of an accident, Officer Broadbent gathers the following information:

Location:	intersection of Elderberry and Vincent Streets
Time:	7:30 P.M.
Occurrence:	automobile collision
Driver Struck:	Helen Sinclair
Driver at Fault:	Wade Wairubi
Damage:	both cars were badly damaged and had to be towed away
Action Taken:	Wade Wairubi was given a traffic ticket for failing to yield the right-of-way

   Back at the precinct, Officer Broadbent is attempting to write his report. Which of the following expresses the information most clearly and accurately?

   A. Wade Wairubi should have yielded the right-of-way to Helen Sinclair. Since he did not, his automobile hit hers at the intersection of Elderberry and Vincent Streets, and he was given a traffic ticket. The collision occurred at 7:30 P.M.

   B. At 7:30 A.M. at the intersection of Elderberry and Vincent Streets, Wade Wairubi's vehicle struck Helen Sinclair's after Mr. Wairubi failed to yield the right-of-way. Both cars were badly damaged. Mr. Wairubi was given a traffic ticket. The cars were towed away.

   C. At the intersection of Elderberry and Vincent Streets, Wade Wairubi's and Helen Sinclair's vehicles were badly damaged and had to be towed away after Mr. Wairubi hit Ms. Sinclair after he failed to yield the right-of-way at 7:30, for which he was given a traffic ticket.

   D. At 7:30 P.M., a vehicle driven by Wade Wairubi struck a vehicle driven by Helen Sinclair at the intersection of Elderberry and Vincent Streets. Both vehicles were badly damaged and had to be towed away. It was determined that Mr. Wairubi was at fault, and he was given a traffic ticket for failing to yield the right-of-way.

6. Officer Lyman responds to a report of a robbery and gathers the following information:

Location:	First Light Studios
Time:	12:30 P.M.
Crime:	robbery
Victim:	Aaron Roos, employee
Suspect:	white male, 6'4", wearing only blue shorts, unarmed
Injury:	Mr. Roos was struck by the suspect and has a broken nose
Items Stolen:	four EZ-meraldi microphones
Status of Suspect:	last seen boarding an uptown bus at Hem Road and Fire Street

Officer Lyman calls in an alert for the suspect. Which of the following expresses the information most clearly and accurately?

A. Four EZ-meraldi microphones were stolen from Aaron Roos, an employee at First Light Studios at 12:30 P.M. by a suspect who then jumped on an uptown bus at Hem Rd. and Fire St. The suspect is a white male and was wearing only blue shorts and is unarmed. Aaron Roos was struck by the suspect during the robbery and has a broken nose.

B. A suspect described as a white male, 6'4", wearing only blue shorts, boarded an uptown bus at Hem Rd. shortly after 12:30 P.M. The suspect is unarmed but possibly, as he reportedly struck Aaron Roos, an employee at First Light Studios, from whom the suspect stole four EZ-meraldi microphones. Aaron Roos has a broken nose.

C. A robbery suspect, described as a white male, 6'4", wearing only blue shorts and unarmed, boarded an uptown bus at Hem Rd. and Fires St. shortly after 12:30 P.M., at which time he forcibly stole four EZ-meraldi microphones from First Light Studios, striking employee Aaron Roos and breaking Mr. Roos's nose.

D. Aaron Roos reports that his nose was broken at 12:30 P.M. by a suspect described as a white male, 6'4", wearing blue shorts and nothing else. The suspect was unarmed. The suspect stole four EZ-meraldi microphones from First Light Studios then boarded an uptown bus at Hem Rd. and Fire St.

7. Officer Drake responded to a call from a restaurant manager who reported that he had seen an employee vandalizing his parking lot. Officer Drake gathered the following information:

Location: La Conda Diner
Time: 4:30 A.M.
Crime: vandalism
Victim: Mr. Biscardi, the owner
Suspect: Elsa Manuela, an employee
Damage: the lines in the parking lot were painted black
Action Taken: suspect arrested

Officer Drake is filling out a report on the incident. Which of the following expresses the information most clearly and accurately?

A. La Conda Diner owner Mr. Biscardi reported that employee Elsa Manuela vandalized his property by painting the lines in the parking lot black at 4:30 A.M. She was arrested.

B. At 4:30 A.M., Elsa Manuela painted the lines in the La Conda Diner parking lot black. The restaurant's owner, Mr. Biscardi, reported the incident, and Ms. Manuela was arrested.

C. Elsa Manuela took black paint to the lines in the parking lot where she worked at La Conda Diner. The diner's owner, Mr. Biscardi, called the police and she was arrested.

D. At La Conda Diner, the parking lot lines were painted black by employee Elsa Manuela at 4:30 P.M. and were reported painted black by owner Mr. Biscardi. Elsa Manuela was arrested.

8. Officer Guarna responds to a call from a skating rink, where the manager says a fight broke out in the parking lot between two men who were arguing over a parking space. Officer Guarna gathers the following information:

Location: Rockin' Rink, 1414 Belmont
Time: 9:00 P.M.
Crime: assault
Victim: Jerry Arundel
Suspect: Indio West
Injury: fractured skull
Weapon: tire iron
Action Taken: suspect confessed and was arrested, victim hospitalized
Witness: Rod Shilling, rink manager

Officer Guarna has to write his preliminary report back at the precinct. Which of the following expresses the information most clearly and accurately?

A. Rod Shilling, the manager of Rockin' Rink at 1414 Belmont, reported that at 9:00 P.M. he saw Indio West hit Jerry Arundel on the head with a tire iron in the parking lot of Rockin' Rink. The victim is in the hospital with a fractured skull. The suspect confessed and was arrested.

B. At 1414 Belmont at Rockin' Rink at 9:00 P.M., an assault occurred. Jerry Arundel was struck on the head by a tire iron by Indio West, who was arrested. Jerry Arundel has a fractured skull and is in the hospital and manager Rod Shilling saw the whole thing.

C. At 9:00 P.M., an assault occurred at Rockin' Rink, located at 1414 Belmont. Indio West struck Jerry Arundel with a tire iron, fracturing Arundel's skull. West was arrested.

D. At Rockin' Rink, at 1414 Belmont, a fight ensued over a parking space that became an assault. Indio West confessed to striking Jerry Arundel on the head with a tire iron and was arrested. Arundel was hospitalized with a fractured skull. Rod Shilling saw this at 9:00 P.M.

To answer Questions 9, 10, 11, and 12, use the information in the following passage.

Shortly after 2 A.M. on March 3, the burglar alarm at Fulton Ford, an automobile dealership, was triggered, and Officers Klebold and Jones were dispatched to investigate. When they arrived at the dealership, they heard the alarm still going off. They saw that a new Ford Explorer had been driven halfway through a plate glass window at the front, or north side, of the showroom. The Explorer was still running; when the officers approached, they saw that keys were in the ignition. Apparently, the Explorer had become stuck on a pillar and was abandoned. The officers disabled the alarm, called in for forensic specialists, and began to investigate the showroom; Toby Fulton, owner of the dealership, arrived and helped them determine what had been disturbed or was missing.

A key cabinet in the manager's office had been pried open and several sets of master keys were missing. Mr. Fulton said that the cabinet was always kept locked, and only he and the manager, Jennifer Watts, had the keys. He and Ms. Watts also were the only two people who knew the alarm codes. Mr. Fulton identified one automobile missing from the showroom: a new, red Ford Tempo. Another large window on the eastern side of the showroom had been shattered; the officers noticed residue of red paint on the post at the right-hand side of the window. They also found a nearly empty bottle of Chives Regal Scotch just outside the shattered window. The officers called in the information on the missing automobile.

Sergeant Cutter, a qualified fingerprint expert, arrived and was able to lift latent prints from the key cabinet, the manager's office door jamb, the Scotch bottle, and the door, dashboard, and steering wheel of the Explorer. Sergeant Cutter also took samples of the red paint.

Officers Klebold and Jones took a statement from Mr. Fulton. He said he had come to the dealership because the alarm system was set up to go off at his home as well as at the police station. The system had been installed over four years ago, and this was the third time it had gone off. The first alert, six months after the system was installed, had apparently been a false alarm, or a burglar had been scared away; no one was found on the premises. After the second alert, about a year later, two teenagers had been arrested trying to climb the high fence at the edge of the used-car lot. Mr. Fulton reported no conflicts or disagreements with his employees; he said his service manager had been with the dealership for over 20 years, and the sales manager had started working at the dealership as a secretary and worked her way up to her current position. He said he'd had to fire two people in the past year: one, an assistant in the service area, had been caught driving customer's cars without authorization; another, a salesman, had what Mr. Fulton described as a "drinking problem" that caused problems at work. Mr. Fulton remembered the service assistant's last name, which was Algernon; the salesman's name was Nelson Fontaine. The service assistant had been angry at his firing and threatened to "get back at" Mr. Fulton; the salesman had left without protesting. Mr. Fulton estimated that another 10 employees had quit in the past year. He agreed to consult his files to get the names and any other relevant information about these 12 former employees.

As the officers questioned Mr. Fulton, they received a call that a red Ford Tempo had been stopped after driving erratically on Main Street. The Tempo had no plates, and the driver could not produce registration, insurance, or a driver's license. He refused to give his name and carried no wallet or identification. He smelled strongly of alcohol and had failed a field sobriety test; he refused to take a Breathalyzer test. Officers on the scene had arrested him and were on their way to the station. Mr. Fulton agreed to view the car and the suspect.

9. Why did Officers Klebold and Jones go to Fulton Ford?

    A. They received an anonymous call that the dealership was being burglarized.

    B. They were passing the dealership while on regular patrol.

    C. They were dispatched to investigate because the dealership's alarm had gone off.

    D. Officer Klebold was considering purchasing a vehicle and wanted to look at the cars.

10. How long had the dealership's alarm system been in service, and how many times had it gone off before this particular night?

    A. four years; twice

    B. four years; three times

    C. two years; once

    D. one year; four times

11. Which two pieces of evidence were recovered at the scene?

    A. blood and hair samples

    B. fingerprints and paint samples

    C. fingerprints and blood samples

    D. footprints and fingerprints

12. Based on the information above, who is the most likely suspect and why?

    A. The sales manager; she has a very close relationship with the owner of the dealership and may even be his mistress.

    B. The fired salesman; he would know where the key cabinet was, and his reported drinking problem fits with evidence at the scene.

    C. The fired service assistant; he made threats against the owner and may have had difficulty obtaining a new job without a good recommendation.

    D. There's not enough information to make any conclusion about a possible suspect.

ANSWERS AND EXPLANATIONS

1. **A** is the only statement that contains all the information.

2. **B** is the only statement that accurately conveys the information without repetition.

3. **C** is stated most clearly. Note that in B, the statement "He is…awaiting a visit from juvenile court" is oversimplified; Evan Meredith is awaiting a visit from a juvenile court service worker.

4. Only **A** is stated clearly and in a logical order.

5. **D** expresses the information most clearly and accurately. Note that in statement C, the time of the accident is incomplete. A and B are poorly worded and inaccurate.

6. **D** is stated in the clearest order and is the most accurate.

7. There is information missing from three of the four statements and D has the wrong time; only **A** is clear and complete.

8. Answers B and D are awkwardly worded and unclear, and C is incomplete, so **A** is correct.

9. **C** is correct.

10. **A** is correct.

11. **B** is correct.

12. **D** is correct. There is no evidence at this point in the investigation to render a possible suspect. One would have to find out if the car that was stopped was the stolen car, and if it was, positively identify the driver in order to call him a suspect.

REPEATERS EXERCISE

In the following questions, examine the details provided in the witness responses and determine which set of details seems most likely based on how many times each detail is repeated.

1. After a hit-and-run accident, eyewitnesses told Officer Samuelson that they saw a man fleeing the scene of the accident in a white truck. Of the following license plate numbers given to Officer Samuelson by the eyewitnesses, which should he consider most likely to be correct?

   A. JPH 217
   B. JPK 217
   C. JRH 277
   D. JPH 216

2. On a Saturday evening, three shots were fired from a vehicle traveling south on Main Street. No one was hurt, and several witnesses said they got a good look at the vehicle, which they described to Officer Tomkins. Of the following descriptions of the vehicle given to Officer Tomkins by the witnesses, which should she consider most likely to be correct?

   A. black two-door, with a dented right-rear fender and black-tinted windows
   B. navy blue sedan, with a dented left-rear fender and blue-tinted windows
   C. black sedan, with a dented right-rear fender and black-tinted windows
   D. black sedan, with no dents and black-tinted windows

3. While walking to the corner deli, Marge was shoved down by a man who attempted to steal her purse, but only managed to tear the strap. The man ran off and into a subway station. Officer Mendez interviewed Marge, who did not get a good look at the man, as well as several witnesses who said that they did. Of the following descriptions given to Officer Mendez by the witnesses, which of the following should he consider most likely to be correct?

   A. white male, 35 years old, wearing a red cap with a blue feather
   B. black male, 25–30 years old, wearing a red cap with a blue feather
   C. white male, 35 years old, wearing an orange cap with a blue feather
   D. white male, 25–30 years old, wearing a red cap with a gray feather

4. Four bank tellers were present when a suspect entered the bank and snatched a customer's purse. The tellers each described the man to Officer Whale, who arrived on the scene after the suspect had fled on foot. Of the following descriptions given to Officer Whale by the witnesses, which should he consider most likely to be correct?

   A. male with a deep voice and a stutter, wearing a ski mask and black gloves

   B. male with a high-pitched voice and a stutter, wearing a ski mask and black gloves

   C. male with a deep voice and no stutter, wearing a ski mask and black gloves

   D. male with a deep voice and a stutter, wearing a ski mask and brown gloves

5. Around Christmas, the owner of a Christmas tree lot reported that a man stole one of his prize firs and drove away before he could be apprehended. Officer Jackson reported to the scene, where witnesses described the vehicle driven by the suspect. Of the following four descriptions given to Officer Jackson by the witnesses, which should she consider most likely to be correct?

   A. blue Toyota truck, with a camper top, missing right brake light, and cracked windshield

   B. blue Chevy van, with a missing right brake light and cracked windshield

   C. gray Chevy van, with a missing left brake light and cracked windshield

   D. blue Chevy van, with a missing right brake light and no apparent dents or cracks

6. On the Fourth of July, several people reported that two people were setting off fireworks in a nearby park. Officer Jimenez investigated the reports and interviewed witnesses. Of the following descriptions given to Officer Jimenez by the witnesses, which should he consider most likely to be correct?

   A. two teenage boys, both wearing yellow tank tops

   B. one teenage boy and a young girl, both wearing yellow T-shirts

   C. two teenage boys, both wearing yellow T-shirts

   D. two teenage boys, both wearing pink T-shirts

7. At the corner of First Street and Myrtle Avenue, someone struck a parked car and sped off. Officer Peters reported to the scene to investigate and interviewed witnesses. Of the following license plate numbers given to Officer Peters by witnesses, which should she consider most likely to be correct?

   A. XP 8501

   B. XR 8801

   C. ZP 8500

   D. XP 7591

8. A street vendor reported that someone stole a six-pack of cold drinks from his stand on Front Street on a busy Sunday afternoon. Officer Blakely interviewed witnesses at the scene. Of the following descriptions given to Officer Blakely by the witnesses, which should he consider most likely to be correct?

A. black male, wearing green pants, a blue stocking cap, with his left arm in a sling

B. black male, wearing green pants, a black hooded sweatshirt, with his left arm in a sling

C. black male, wearing blue pants, a black hooded sweatshirt, with only one arm

D. white male, wearing green pants, a black hooded sweatshirt, with his left arm in a sling

ANSWERS AND EXPLANATIONS

1. **A** contains the most repeaters.

2. **C** is the best answer. Note that, while it only appears twice, "dented right-rear fender" (A and C) is a repeater.

3. **A** is the answer. Note that each description of the man's age is given twice; "35 years old" in A and C and "25–30 years old" in B and D. These descriptions cancel each other out, so the other three types of descriptions should be used to eliminate possibilities.

4. **A** contains the most repeaters. Note that, since the descriptions "male" and "wearing a ski mask" are included in all four answers, they cannot be used to eliminate any possibilities.

5. **B** contains the most repeaters.

6. **C** contains the most repeaters. Note that, while the difference between tank tops and T-shirts is somewhat minor, it is important in this case to differentiate between the two in order to eliminate possible answers.

7. **A** contains the most repeaters.

8. **D** contains the most repeaters. Note that there is more than one way to eliminate the incorrect answers.

APPLICATION OF THE LAW EXERCISE

1. A person is guilty of **BURGLARY IN THE THIRD DEGREE** when he knowingly enters or remains unlawfully in a building with intent to commit a crime therein. Based solely upon this definition, which of the following is the best example of Burglary in the Third Degree?

    A. Julie, an employee at Snack World, hides in the back room in order to slip out of the restaurant's rear exit so she can avoid seeing her boss, who wants her to work an extra shift.

    B. Frank climbs the exterior stairs of a university building so he can watch the sunset.

    C. Dimitri, a clerk at Big Foods, climbs through an open window after operating hours to retrieve his wallet, which he left after his shift.

    D. Harris enters the public library through a door that does not lock securely in order to steal several valuable rare books.

2. A person is guilty of **CUSTODIAL INTERFERENCE IN THE SECOND DEGREE** when, being a relative of a child less than 16 years old, he takes the child from his lawful custodian, with intent to hold the child permanently or for a long period, knowing he has no legal right to do so. Based solely upon this definition, which of the following is the best example of Custodial Interference in the Second Degree?

    A. Minnie picks up her nephew from day care every Wednesday to help her sister, who has class on Wednesdays.

    B. Jack picks up his five-year-old daughter from school and leaves the country with her while his ex-wife, who has legal custody of the child, is at work.

    C. While babysitting her neighbors' son, Tonya takes the child to the movies, but does not let the child's parents know that she is taking him out of the house.

    D. On a break from college, Sam picks up his 17-year-old brother, Mitch, from high school and takes him to Canada, where the two brothers plan to start a new life without telling their parents.

3. A person is guilty of **PERJURY IN THE THIRD DEGREE** when he swears falsely; this occurs when a person intentionally makes a false statement that he does not believe to be true either while giving testimony or while under oath in a written instrument. Based solely on this definition, which of the following is the best example of Perjury in the Third Degree?

    A. Jan testifies under oath that a toaster she bought from the defendant was not stolen, when, in fact, she knew that it was stolen.

    B. Ida signs a sworn statement attesting to the fact that she owns a piece of lakefront property that she is selling to someone else, when, in fact, her husband sold the property years ago without telling her.

    C. Fred testifies accurately in court as to his whereabouts on the evening that a crime was committed.

    D. Wendy confuses the dates in a sequence of events about which she is being questioned under oath in court, but corrects herself when she realizes her mistake.

4. A person is guilty of **SPORTS BRIBING** when he confers, or offers or agrees to confer, any benefit upon a sports participant with intent to influence him not to give his best efforts in a sports contest. Based solely upon this definition, which of the following is the best example of Sports Bribing?

    A. Stanley tells his wife that he'd give two weeks' pay to see a certain power hitter stop hitting home runs during a series against his favorite team.

    B. Steven's mother asks him if he would perform better in his next swim meet if she bought him the swim cap he's been admiring at a local sports store.

    C. Victor tells his son that he'll buy him his own large pizza if he strikes out three batters during a little league game.

    D. Matthew offers a high school's star quarterback $50 to purposely allow the opposing team to score by intentionally fumbling the football during a big game against Matthew's younger brother's team.

5. A person is guilty of **FALSE IMPERSONATION** or **FALSE PERSONATION** when, after being informed of the consequences of such an act, he knowingly misrepresents his actual name, date of birth, or address to a police officer or peace officer with intent to prevent the officer from ascertaining such information. Based solely upon this definition, which of the following is the best example of False Impersonation?

   A. A man is so drunk that his name cannot be clearly understood by the police officer who is questioning him. When the officer informs the man that he needs to know his correct name, the man passes out.

   B. Caught with a stolen bicycle, Ryan Jones tells Officer Wright that his name is Eric Jones. When Officer Wright warns him of the consequences of misinforming a police officer about his identity, he repeats that his name is Eric Jones.

   C. Officer Black's good friend, Robert, who is a lawyer and who knows the consequences of misinforming a police officer about his identity, calls Officer Black and pretends to be Officer Black's wife, of whom he does an amazing impression.

   D. Three-year-old Sally Jackson is found wandering around a local mall, and will not tell Officer Sampson her name or address, even after he asks her repeatedly for the correct information so that he can help her find her parents.

6. A person is guilty of **EAVESDROPPING** when he unlawfully engages in wiretapping, mechanical overhearing of a conversation, or intercepting or accessing of an electronic communication. Based solely upon this definition, which of the following is the best example of Eavesdropping?

   A. Greg comes home early from work and listens to a message for his wife about a party to which he has not been invited.

   B. Due to a headquarters-based computer error, Pedro begins receiving emails that are meant for a coworker and reads one of the messages before he realizes it is not meant for him.

   C. While recording street sounds for a movie, Chris overhears an argument between two cast members through his audio equipment.

   D. A landlord places tiny microphones in his tenants' apartments and listens to their activities and conversations on a headset in his apartment.

7. A person is guilty of **PETIT LARCENY** when he steals property. A person is guilty of **ROBBERY IN THE THIRD DEGREE** when he forcibly steals property.

    Kyle steals his neighbor's bicycle. Later that week, when the neighbor accuses him of stealing the bicycle, he beats the neighbor unconscious. Based solely upon the above definitions, which of the following is true?

    A. Kyle should be charged with Petit Larceny.

    B. Kyle should be charged with Robbery in the Third Degree.

    C. Kyle should be charged with both Petit Larceny and Robbery in the Third Degree.

    D. Kyle should not be charged with either crime.

8. A person is guilty of **INCITING TO RIOT** when he urges ten or more persons to engage in tumultuous and violent conduct of a kind likely to create public alarm. Based solely upon this definition, which of the following is the best example of Inciting to Riot?

    A. José encourages his 15 friends, who have gathered to cook steaks and watch the World Series, to loudly cheer for their favorite team.

    B. At a high school assembly, Colin removes his shirt and announces that he would like for the 800 other students there to do likewise.

    C. After a massive series of layoffs at the factory, which resulted in Andrew and 175 other people losing their jobs, Andrew gathers all the former employees and encourages them to storm the plant and set it on fire.

    D. Megan and her seven-member antidrinking sorority gather in Megan's backyard and throw bottles of liquor that they have been given by the most recent inductee into a bonfire to celebrate their collective sobriety.

ANSWERS AND EXPLANATIONS

1. **D** is the best answer, as it is the only instance in which the person intended to commit a crime.

2. **B** is correct. The only other answer in which the adult has "intent to hold the child permanently or for a long period" is D, but since Mitch is 17 years old, his brother is not breaking this law by taking him to Canada.

3. **A** is the best answer. B is not correct because, while Ida is signing a statement that is not true, she does believe it to be true, so she is not committing this crime. C and D are both honest actions.

4. **D** is correct. Choice A is simply an example of innocent wishful thinking. And while B and C are both examples of people offering a benefit to a sports participant, neither person is attempting to "influence him not to give his best efforts."

5. **B** is the best answer. None of the other three answers are examples of someone committing this crime, since none of the people in these three scenarios has "intent to prevent the officer from ascertaining such information."

6. **D** is the best answer, as it is obviously an instance in which someone "unlawfully engages in…mechanical overhearing of a conversation" or conversations.

7. **A** is correct. While Kyle may be committing another crime when he "beats the neighbor unconscious," he is not committing Robbery in the Third Degree because he is not forcibly stealing property. If he had beaten the neighbor in the process of stealing the bicycle, then he would have been forcibly stealing property; in this case, he would have been committing Robbery in the Third Degree.

8. **C** is the best answer. Choice A is obviously incorrect. While the activity that is being encouraged in B could cause a stir, it is not "tumultuous and violent conduct of a kind likely to create public alarm." The liquor bonfire in D could "create public alarm," but since the group is made up of only seven people, Megan is not committing this crime.

CHAPTER EIGHT

Additional Skills

WRITING

At some point in the application and/or the exam process, you are going to have to write *something*. You may not see an essay portion on the test you take, but you will have to give extended answers to some questions in the application itself. Some exams also have you write sample reports.

No one is expecting Pulitzer Prize material here. You just need to get your point across clearly and honestly—using correct grammar also helps.

Here are some suggestions for writing effective responses:

WRITE AN OUTLINE

Whether you're writing a sample report or a response to a question, developing a strong structure before you begin writing will save you time in the long run. It doesn't really matter what style you use to write your outline. You are the only one who is going to see it. But you should always start with an outline to keep your thoughts focused and organized.

First, write down the most important thing you want to say. Don't worry about how you write it now; it doesn't even have to be a complete sentence at this point. Just summarize your main point. Think of it as the direct answer to the question.

Now you have to come up with some support for your main point. If your main point is the direct answer to the question, the supporting examples are the answers to the follow-up questions. The support material can be examples from your own experience or reasoning that you've worked out; the examples can be more or less separate, or one can build on top of another.

Finally, you need to wrap it up with a conclusion. You don't need to get fancy; you can just restate your original main point.

Be Clear

Once you've got your outline finished, you are more than halfway there. All you have to do is flesh out the sentences or sentence fragments, and you are done.

The big mistake people make here is they get a little too fancy. Remember, you are writing to express, not impress. No one reading a police report cares about the writer's literary craft. So skip the ten-dollar words and the mile-long sentences. Just say what you want to say and stop.

Be Active

Verbs can be categorized as active or passive. Some people think that the passive voice is more formal; it's really just blander and more boring. You will automatically sound like a better candidate if you just eliminate any passive verbs in favor of active verbs.

Here are some examples:

Passive

I was introduced to the importance of hard work by my grandfather.

Active

I learned the importance of hard work from my grandfather.

Passive

While a senior in high school, I was named to the All-Region football team as an offensive lineman.

Active

During my senior year in high school, I played offensive line for the All-Region football team.

Passive

My most difficult situation occurred shortly after my older brother was diagnosed with leukemia.

Active

I faced the most difficult period of my life after my older brother was diagnosed with leukemia.

Give It a Rest and a Reread

Once you have written your first draft, let it sit for a day or two and then come back to it. You will be able to see mistakes or awkward sentences that you didn't notice when you wrote them down.

Obviously, on a timed test you won't *have* a couple of days to mull over what you've written. But you should *always* reread your written material before turning in the test. Look for misspellings and grammatical errors, along with holes in your logic and other structural mistakes.

MEMORY AND OBSERVATION

You know that one of the requirements for being a police officer is vision correctable to 20/20. Well, that perfect vision won't do you any good if you can't use it intelligently. And that's where memory and observation come in.

As a police officer, you need to be able to observe a scene and sort through all the thousands of details to come up with the relevant information. And you've got to do it quickly—almost unconsciously. Of course, you will develop this skill with experience, but the force you are applying to wants to know whether you've got the basics in place already. A good tip to remember is to try to memorize information in some sort of order— top to bottom or left to right. You will probably see some questions about memory and observation on your application test.

THE "INSPECTOR CLOUSEAU" QUESTIONS

One category might test your ability to detect disguises. I call it the "Inspector Clouseau" category, because the questions usually involve looking at a set of goofy drawings showing even goofier disguises. One drawing shows the subject, and four or five other drawings represent possible disguises adopted by the subject. You are asked to determine which of the possibilities is most likely to be the actual subject. These tests are slowly being phased out, so they're not as common as they once were. But if you do come across this category, here's how you handle it:

- Focus on facial characteristics that can't easily be changed: nose breadth and length, the shape of the chin, the size of the eyes, the way the ears are set on the head.
- Don't be distracted by differences (or similarities) in qualities that are easier to manipulate: hair length, color, and texture; facial hair; size and shape of eyebrows; general shape of the face, which can be affected by weight gain or loss. These days, even eye color can be disguised with contacts.

Don't rush your decision; take your time and evaluate all your choices. Stick to the underlying facial structure, and the right choice will become obvious.

THE STREET SCENE

Another slightly more sophisticated test of your memory and observation skills involves an illustration or photo of a busy urban street scene. You will be given a certain length of time to look at the scene, then be asked to answer several questions about the action and details shown.

If you are lucky, you already have a good memory. But you can always sharpen it. And even if your memory isn't so great, you can learn better memory skills.

Think of the drawing you are given as a movie scene, and focus on the three basics you would find in any movie:

CHARACTERS

- How many people are there?
- Ages? Gender?
- Use two words to describe the physical appearance of each person. For instance, "tall, hairy man" or "plump, elderly woman."
- If one of the characters has an especially distinctive physical characteristic, note it: "tall, hairy man with eye patch."
- What about their facial expressions?
- What, if anything, is each character carrying?

ACTION

- What is each person doing?
- Group them, using your two-word descriptions: "Tall, hairy man escorting plump, elderly woman across the intersection."
- What can you infer about the relationships among the members of the group? Are they boss/coworkers, friends, spouses, strangers?
- Are any of the groups interacting? For instance, "Tall, hairy man escorting plump, elderly woman across intersection. Young, slender man with blond ponytail is running behind them, reaching toward her shopping bag."

SETTING

- Take note of any numbers, such as street addresses and license plate numbers.
- Look for other useful identifiers—business signs, names on buildings, statues, or other landmarks.
- Does the area seem prosperous or struggling? Crowded or deserted? Can you tell whether it's a weekday or weekend, daytime or evening or night?

The best way to prepare for this kind of test is to practice noticing. For the next few days, make a point of going through this exercise with as many things as you can—news photographs, advertisements, even the crowd in a movie theater or sports arena. Do this often enough, and it will become second nature.

PART THREE

Practice Police Exams

The following five tests are loosely based on the screening tests given by police departments around the country. The test administered by the department you are applying to might or might not resemble these tests. Regardless of the actual form of the test you will take, you will only help your chances by developing your skills at standardized test taking.

Give yourself a total of two hours for each of the following tests. Take the first test, then check your answers against the answer key directly following the questions. Then look at the questions you have the most trouble answering correctly. Go back and review that section before you take the next test. You should show improvement right away.

Practice Test 1

ANSWER SHEET FOR PRACTICE TEST 1

For each question, select the best answer choice. Use the answer sheet to mark your choices. Answers and explanations follow the test.

1. Ⓐ Ⓑ Ⓒ Ⓓ	26. Ⓐ Ⓑ Ⓒ Ⓓ	51. Ⓐ Ⓑ Ⓒ Ⓓ	76. Ⓐ Ⓑ Ⓒ Ⓓ
2. Ⓐ Ⓑ Ⓒ Ⓓ	27. Ⓐ Ⓑ Ⓒ Ⓓ	52. Ⓐ Ⓑ Ⓒ Ⓓ	77. Ⓐ Ⓑ Ⓒ Ⓓ
3. Ⓐ Ⓑ Ⓒ Ⓓ	28. Ⓐ Ⓑ Ⓒ Ⓓ	53. Ⓐ Ⓑ Ⓒ Ⓓ	78. Ⓐ Ⓑ Ⓒ Ⓓ
4. Ⓐ Ⓑ Ⓒ Ⓓ	29. Ⓐ Ⓑ Ⓒ Ⓓ	54. Ⓐ Ⓑ Ⓒ Ⓓ	79. Ⓐ Ⓑ Ⓒ Ⓓ
5. Ⓐ Ⓑ Ⓒ Ⓓ	30. Ⓐ Ⓑ Ⓒ Ⓓ	55. Ⓐ Ⓑ Ⓒ Ⓓ	80. Ⓐ Ⓑ Ⓒ Ⓓ
6. Ⓐ Ⓑ Ⓒ Ⓓ	31. Ⓐ Ⓑ Ⓒ Ⓓ	56. Ⓐ Ⓑ Ⓒ Ⓓ	81. Ⓐ Ⓑ Ⓒ Ⓓ
7. Ⓐ Ⓑ Ⓒ Ⓓ	32. Ⓐ Ⓑ Ⓒ Ⓓ	57. Ⓐ Ⓑ Ⓒ Ⓓ	82. Ⓐ Ⓑ Ⓒ Ⓓ
8. Ⓐ Ⓑ Ⓒ Ⓓ	33. Ⓐ Ⓑ Ⓒ Ⓓ	58. Ⓐ Ⓑ Ⓒ Ⓓ	83. Ⓐ Ⓑ Ⓒ Ⓓ
9. Ⓐ Ⓑ Ⓒ Ⓓ	34. Ⓐ Ⓑ Ⓒ Ⓓ	59. Ⓐ Ⓑ Ⓒ Ⓓ	84. Ⓐ Ⓑ Ⓒ Ⓓ
10. Ⓐ Ⓑ Ⓒ Ⓓ	35. Ⓐ Ⓑ Ⓒ Ⓓ	60. Ⓐ Ⓑ Ⓒ Ⓓ	85. Ⓐ Ⓑ Ⓒ Ⓓ
11. Ⓐ Ⓑ Ⓒ Ⓓ	36. Ⓐ Ⓑ Ⓒ Ⓓ	61. Ⓐ Ⓑ Ⓒ Ⓓ	86. Ⓐ Ⓑ Ⓒ Ⓓ
12. Ⓐ Ⓑ Ⓒ Ⓓ	37. Ⓐ Ⓑ Ⓒ Ⓓ	62. Ⓐ Ⓑ Ⓒ Ⓓ	87. Ⓐ Ⓑ Ⓒ Ⓓ
13. Ⓐ Ⓑ Ⓒ Ⓓ	38. Ⓐ Ⓑ Ⓒ Ⓓ	63. Ⓐ Ⓑ Ⓒ Ⓓ	88. Ⓐ Ⓑ Ⓒ Ⓓ
14. Ⓐ Ⓑ Ⓒ Ⓓ	39. Ⓐ Ⓑ Ⓒ Ⓓ	64. Ⓐ Ⓑ Ⓒ Ⓓ	89. Ⓐ Ⓑ Ⓒ Ⓓ
15. Ⓐ Ⓑ Ⓒ Ⓓ	40. Ⓐ Ⓑ Ⓒ Ⓓ	65. Ⓐ Ⓑ Ⓒ Ⓓ	90. Ⓐ Ⓑ Ⓒ Ⓓ
16. Ⓐ Ⓑ Ⓒ Ⓓ	41. Ⓐ Ⓑ Ⓒ Ⓓ	66. Ⓐ Ⓑ Ⓒ Ⓓ	
17. Ⓐ Ⓑ Ⓒ Ⓓ	42. Ⓐ Ⓑ Ⓒ Ⓓ	67. Ⓐ Ⓑ Ⓒ Ⓓ	
18. Ⓐ Ⓑ Ⓒ Ⓓ	43. Ⓐ Ⓑ Ⓒ Ⓓ	68. Ⓐ Ⓑ Ⓒ Ⓓ	
19. Ⓐ Ⓑ Ⓒ Ⓓ	44. Ⓐ Ⓑ Ⓒ Ⓓ	69. Ⓐ Ⓑ Ⓒ Ⓓ	
20. Ⓐ Ⓑ Ⓒ Ⓓ	45. Ⓐ Ⓑ Ⓒ Ⓓ	70. Ⓐ Ⓑ Ⓒ Ⓓ	
21. Ⓐ Ⓑ Ⓒ Ⓓ	46. Ⓐ Ⓑ Ⓒ Ⓓ	71. Ⓐ Ⓑ Ⓒ Ⓓ	
22. Ⓐ Ⓑ Ⓒ Ⓓ	47. Ⓐ Ⓑ Ⓒ Ⓓ	72. Ⓐ Ⓑ Ⓒ Ⓓ	
23. Ⓐ Ⓑ Ⓒ Ⓓ	48. Ⓐ Ⓑ Ⓒ Ⓓ	73. Ⓐ Ⓑ Ⓒ Ⓓ	
24. Ⓐ Ⓑ Ⓒ Ⓓ	49. Ⓐ Ⓑ Ⓒ Ⓓ	74. Ⓐ Ⓑ Ⓒ Ⓓ	
25. Ⓐ Ⓑ Ⓒ Ⓓ	50. Ⓐ Ⓑ Ⓒ Ⓓ	75. Ⓐ Ⓑ Ⓒ Ⓓ	

1. Officer Jones is dispatched to an apartment building where a section of the parking deck has collapsed, and she gathers the following information:

Location: Waterfront Apartments
Time: 5:15 A.M.
Problem: section of parking deck collapsed
Damage: 10 cars destroyed
Injuries: none

Officer Jones must write her report. Which of the following expresses the information most clearly and accurately?

A. At 5:15 10 cars were destroyed by a collapsing section of the parking deck at Waterfront Apartments.

B. At 5:15 A.M., a section of the parking deck at Waterfront Apartments collapsed, destroying 10 cars. No one was injured.

C. At 5:15, 10 cars were destroyed but no one was injured when a section of the parking deck collapsed. The cars were parked in the parking deck at Waterfront Apartments.

D. At 5:15 A.M., Waterfront Apartments' parking deck collapsed in one section but did not cause anyone to be injured except for the cars.

2. Officer Greene is dispatched to a residence at which a "peeping Tom" has been reported. There, Officer Greene gathers the following information:

Location: 14 Liberty Avenue
Time: 8:15 P.M.
Incident: a man was seen peering in the bathroom window
Victim: Rachel Winters, resident
Suspect: short, heavyset male, wearing a stocking cap
Location of Suspect: fled on foot in unknown direction

Officer Greene must prepare a report on the incident. Which of the following expresses the information most clearly and accurately?

A. A short, heavyset man in a stocking cap was reported by Rachel Winters to have been peering into her bathroom window at 14 Liberty Avenue at 8:15 P.M. The man fled on foot in an unknown direction.

B. A short, heavyset man in a stocking cap peered in the window of Rachel Winter's bathroom at 14 Liberty Avenue. The man fled on foot shortly after 8:15 P.M.

C. At 8:15 P.M., Rachel Winters reported that in her bathroom window at 14 Liberty Avenue a man was peering in. He was heavyset, Ms. Winters said, and short. He also wore a stocking cap. He fled on foot in an unknown direction.

D. Rachel Winters reported that at 8:15 P.M., she saw a short, heavyset man, who was wearing a stocking cap, peering in her bathroom window at 14 Liberty Avenue. The suspect fled in an unknown direction.

3. In State X, a person is guilty of the **UNLAWFUL USE OF CREDIT CARD** when, in the course of obtaining property or a service, he uses or displays a credit card which he knows to be revoked or canceled.

   Carla Jones attempts to pay for her purchases at a local pharmacy by presenting her MasterCard, not realizing that her husband recently canceled the MasterCard account. Given only the above definition, is Mrs. Jones guilty of the Unlawful Use of Credit Card?

   A. No, because she did not know the credit card was canceled.

   B. Yes, because it is her responsibility to keep up with her credit card accounts.

   C. No, but only because the card was rejected.

   D. It is impossible to determine whether or not she is guilty without knowing whether she paid for her purchases by some other means.

4. Officer Starks sees a young man shoot a young woman at point blank range at an automatic teller machine. Officer Starks approaches the young man from behind, identifies himself, and tells the young man to drop the weapon and turn around. The young man spins on his heels, points his gun at Officer Starks, and shoots. Officer Starks shoots back. The young man's shot misses, but Officer Starks's shot does not. He approaches the young woman and determines that she is dead. He then approaches the young man, who lies unconscious and is bleeding heavily from his abdomen. He calls for an ambulance and is told that the ambulance will arrive in about 10 minutes. Which of the following would be the least logical action for Officer Starks to take while waiting for the ambulance?

   A. attempt to stop the young man's bleeding by applying direct pressure

   B. read the young man his rights

   C. try to ascertain the young man's identity by looking for a wallet

   D. scan the area for witnesses to question about what led to the shooting

5. Officer McDonald reports to an intersection where a traffic light is malfunctioning. He gathers the following information:

Location: corner of Long Street and First Avenue
Time: 8:30 A.M.
Problem: malfunctioning traffic light
Action Taken: Officers Hay and Ramirez on the scene, directing traffic; repair workers on the way

Officer McDonald is writing a report on the incident. Which of the following expresses the information most clearly and accurately?

A. At 8:30 P.M., Officers Hay and Ramirez were directing traffic at the intersection of Long Street and First Avenue. A traffic light was malfunctioning, and repair workers were on the way.

B. Officers Hay and Ramirez had the situation under control with a malfunctioning traffic light and were directing traffic at Long Street and First Avenue, with repair workers on the way at 8:30 A.M.

C. At 8:30 A.M., a traffic light at the corner of Long Street and First Avenue was malfunctioning. Officers Hay and Ramirez were directing traffic, and repair workers were on their way.

D. Officers Hay and Ramirez would be directing traffic and awaiting repair workers at the corner of Long Street and First Avenue, where malfunctioning traffic light at 8:30 A.M. meant they had to direct traffic.

6. Officer Flanagan responds to a call from a worker at a fast-food restaurant who explains that an elderly man has collapsed at his table. Officer Flanagan gathers the following information:

Location: Burger Binge
Time: 1:00 P.M.
Victim: Timothy Sanderson, age 81
Suffering From: heart attack, according to paramedics
Action Taken: Mr. Sanderson taken by ambulance to the hospital

Officer Flanagan is writing his report. Which of the following expresses the information most clearly and accurately?

A. At 1:00 P.M., a man eating at Burger Binge had a heart attack and collapsed on his table. The man, 81-year-old Timothy Sanderson, was taken to the hospital by an ambulance, whose paramedics were the ones that determined that it was a heart attack.

B. Timothy Sanderson, 81, had a heart attack at Burger Binge at 1:00 P.M. He was taken to the hospital.

C. At 1:00 P.M. at Burger Binge, Timothy Sanderson, age 81, collapsed from what paramedics later determined was a heart attack. Mr. Sanderson was taken by ambulance to the hospital.

D. At Burger Binge, 81-year-old Timothy Sanderson was taken by ambulance to the hospital after paramedics determined that what caused his collapse was a heart attack that occurred when he collapsed on his table.

7. A suitcase, whose presence no one could explain, exploded at Castlewood Elementary School's annual Field Day activities. Several witnesses described the suitcase's appearance before it exploded to Officer Jenwalter. Of the following descriptions given by the witnesses, which should Officer Jenwalter consider most likely to be accurate?

A. brown leather, with two red stripes in the center and two silver buckles

B. black leather, with one red stripe in the center and one silver buckle

C. brown leather, with two orange stripes in the center and two silver buckles

D. black leather, with two red stripes in the center and two gold buckles

8. Officer Chow is dispatched to the scene of a robbery, where she gathers the following information:

Location:	The Kitchen Sink
Time:	8:00 P.M.
Crime:	robbery
Victim:	Ann Kitchen
Injury:	badly bruised back
Items Missing:	$400 in cash
Suspect:	Buster Reed
Weapon:	a large vase
Witness:	Joy Kitchen
Status of Suspect:	arrested and in custody

Officer Chow must write a report on the incident. Which of the following expresses the information most clearly and accurately?

A. At 8:00 P.M. at The Kitchen Sink, Joy Kitchen saw Buster Reed hit Ann Kitchen and steal $400 in cash. Reed was arrested and is in custody. Ann Kitchen has a badly bruised back.

B. At The Kitchen Sink, Buster Reed reportedly stole $400 after hitting Ann Kitchen with a large vase, badly bruising her back. Reed was arrested and is in custody.

C. Buster Reed hit Ann Kitchen at The Kitchen Sink with a large vase, badly bruising her back, then stole $400 in cash, all of which Joy Kitchen saw. Reed was arrested and is in custody.

D. Joy Kitchen reported that at 8:00 P.M. at The Kitchen Sink, she saw Buster Reed hit Ann Kitchen using a large vase, badly bruising Ann's back. Joy Kitchen reported that she then saw Reed steal $400 in cash. Reed was arrested and is in custody.

9. In State X, a person is guilty of **COMPUTER TAMPERING IN THE FOURTH DEGREE** when he uses a computer and, having no right to do so, intentionally alters or destroys another person's computer data. Given this definition alone, which of the following is the best example of Computer Tampering in the Fourth Degree?

   A. After Ralph makes up an exam that he had previously failed, Mr. Petrovich, Ralph's teacher, changes Ralph's grade in the school's grading and scoring database.

   B. Jacob Johns, a brilliant designer for a private Internet company, gains access to his bank's computer system and adds $100 to his checking account.

   C. Dr. Aaron, a veterinarian in private practice, logs onto his billing system and deletes the charges billed to a poor man for an operation Dr. Aaron performed on the man's dog.

   D. Louise George, a restaurant supervisor, uses her computer password to enter the payroll system and manually correct the number of hours entered for an employee with a malfunctioning time card.

10. A man held a gun to the head of Jim Wise, a street vendor, then loudly demanded Mr. Wise's money, took it from him, and ran. Investigating the robbery, Officer Blanco interviewed several witnesses, who each gave a description of the suspect. Of the following descriptions, which should Officer Blanco consider most likely to be accurate?

    A. 6' tall, with a dark mustache and a deep voice

    B. 5' tall, with a dark mustache, a deep voice, and a stutter

    C. 5' tall, with no facial hair, a deep voice, and a stutter

    D. 5' tall, with a dark mustache, a high-pitched voice, and a stutter

11. Officer Bates is dispatched to a record store, where an alleged shoplifter has been detained by store security. At the store, Officer Bates gathers the following information:

Location:	Big Records
Time:	4:00 P.M.
Witness:	Pam Adams, employee
Item Taken:	one CD player
Suspect:	Ralph Clark
Status of Suspect:	detained by store security after he walked out of the store with the CD player without paying; suspect arrested

Officer Bates must write her report on the incident. Which of the following expresses the information most clearly and accurately?

A. At 4:00 P.M., Ralph Clark was detained by store security at Big Records after employee Pam Adams saw him walk out of the store with a CD player without paying for it. Ralph Clark was arrested.

B. Walking out of Big Records with an unpaid-for CD player at 4:00 P.M., Ralph Clark was seen by an employee and was detained by Big Records security. He was arrested.

C. A CD player belonging to Big Records was attempted stolen at 4:00 P.M. by Ralph Clark, who walked out of the store with the player without paying for it. Pam Adams, an employee, saw it. Ralph Clark was arrested.

D. After being seen by Pam Adams, an employee of Big Records, walking out of the store with a CD player that he had not paid for, Ralph Clark was detained by store security and arrested.

12. Rose Franklin was pushed in front of a bus by someone who then ran away. Although Ms. Franklin was unconscious and on her way to the hospital when Officer Perez arrived at the scene of the crime, several witnesses approached Officer Perez to offer the following descriptions of the suspect. Which of the descriptions should Officer Perez consider most likely to be accurate?

A. white male, 5'2" tall, wearing a black robe over red pajamas

B. black male, 5'9" tall, wearing a black blazer over red pajamas

C. white male, 5'10" tall, wearing a blue robe over red pajamas

D. black male, 5'10" tall, wearing a blue robe over orange pajamas

13. Officer Bradley is dispatched to a residence where a larceny has been reported. He gathers the following information:

Location: 750 River Road
Time: 5:30 P.M.
Crime: larceny
Victim: Mr. Stone
Item Missing: gas grill
Suspect: Michael Smith (victim reports seeing him take the grill)
Location of Suspect: unknown

Officer Bradley is writing his report. Which of the following expresses the information most clearly and accurately?

A. Michael Smith stole a gas grill from Mr. Stone at 5:30 P.M. Michael Smith's location since stealing the grill from 750 River Road is unknown.

B. From 750 River Road, the home of Mr. Stone, a gas grill was stolen at 5:30 P.M. The location of the suspect, whom Mr. Stone saw stealing the grill, is unknown.

C. At 5:30 P.M., a gas grill was stolen from Mr. Stone, who reported seeing Michael Smith, whose location is unknown, stealing the grill.

D. Mr. Stone reported that at 5:30 P.M., he saw Michael Smith steal a gas grill from his residence at 750 River Road. Michael Smith's location is unknown.

14. A truck carrying bags of garbage sped into a residential neighborhood toward a cul-de-sac. Then, a few minutes later, it sped out of the neighborhood without the garbage bags. Mr. Zartanian, who lives in the cul-de-sac, called the police to report that someone dumped 15 bags of putrid garbage on his front lawn. When Officer Crain arrived at Mr. Zartanian's house, neighbors who had witnessed the truck's entry and exit described the vehicle to Officer Crain. Of the following descriptions given by the witnesses, which should Officer Crain consider most likely to be correct?

A. a light green Ford, with a broken right brake light

B. a cream-colored Dodge, with a broken left brake light

C. a cream-colored Ford, with a broken left brake light

D. a white Ford, with a broken left brake light

15. Officer Spears follows up on a call from a restaurant where two people have left without paying their bill. At the restaurant, Officer Spears gathers the following information:

Location: Spaghetti Sam's
Time: 7:30 P.M.
Crime: two women ate and left without paying
Person Reporting Crime: Cindy Altman, waitress
Value of Meals: $77
Suspects: twin sisters, 5'10", black hair
Location of Suspects: drove off on a motorcycle

Officer Spears is writing a report on the incident. Which of the following expresses the information most clearly and accurately?

A. At 7:30 P.M., waitress Cindy Altman was stiffed for a $77 bill by two twin sisters, 5'10" with black hair, who fled on a motorcycle from Spaghetti Sam's, where they ate but did not pay for their meals.

B. Cindy Altman, a waitress at Spaghetti Sam's, reported that at 7:30 P.M. a pair of twin sisters, whom she describes as 5'10" with black hair, ate $77 worth of food and then left the restaurant without paying. Altman reported that the sisters drove off on a motorcycle.

C. At Spaghetti Sam's, $77 worth of food was eaten but not paid for by twin sisters described by the waitress, Cindy Altman, as 5'10" with black hair. This happened at 7:30 P.M.

D. Twin sisters, described as 5'10" with black hair, drove away from Spaghetti Sam's on a motorcycle after having eaten $77 worth of food and not paying for it, waitress Cindy Altman reported the incident as having occurred at 7:30 P.M.

16. In State X, a person is guilty of **HAZING IN THE FIRST DEGREE** when, in the course of another person's initiation or affiliation with any organization, he intentionally or recklessly engages in conduct that creates a substantial risk of physical injury to such other person. Given this definition alone, which of the following is the best example of Hazing in the First Degree?

A. The president of a fraternity, Sam Sloan, invites the fraternity's new pledges to go on a guided white-water rafting excursion to celebrate their brotherhood.

B. Mary Gruber, a church youth minister, organizes a Saturday afternoon trip to the beach for the newest members of the youth group.

C. Freshman girls hoping to join a sorority are told by Nell Davis, the sorority's president, that they must participate in a rum-guzzling contest in order to become sisters.

D. Marcus Roberts, the head of the Caribou Lodge men's club, adds a cigar-smoking room onto their clubhouse for the voluntary use of Lodge members.

17. Officer Levine responds to a call from a businessman whose storefront has been vandalized. At the scene, Officer Levine gathers the following information:

Location:	Approximate Investments
Time:	10:30 A.M.
Incident:	a rock was thrown through the front window
Business Owner:	Marcus Torres
Suspect:	tall, black male
Location of Suspect:	fled on foot toward the train station

Officer Levine must write a report on the incident. Which of the following expresses the information most clearly and accurately?

A. At 10:30 A.M., Marcus Torres's business called Approximate Investments had a rock thrown through its window by someone described by Mr. Torres as a tall, black male. The suspect fled on foot toward the train station.

B. Marcus Torres reported that at 10:30 A.M., a tall, black male threw a rock through the front window of his business, Approximate Investments. The suspect fled on foot toward the train station.

C. A rock was thrown through the front window of Approximate Investments, the business of Marcus Torres, who says the suspect, who is a tall, black male, threw the rock at 10:30 A.M. and then fled on foot toward the train station.

D. The owner of Approximate Investments reported that at 10:30 A.M., a man threw a rock through the front window of the business. The suspect, described as a tall, black male, fled on foot toward the train station.

18. While trying on shoes at an expensive designer shoe store, a well-dressed woman asked to try out a pair on the sidewalk. The sales clerk, Agnes Miller, agreed. The lady took a few cautious steps out onto the sidewalk, glanced back into the store, and then ran off. Ms. Miller called the police. When Officer Wehru arrived at the store, several witnesses offered descriptions of the lady who had run off with the shoes. Of the following descriptions given by the witnesses, which should Officer Wehru consider most likely to be accurate?

A. 5'1" tall, wearing a pink silk dress with a wide white belt

B. 5'2" tall, wearing a white silk pantsuit with a wide white belt

C. 5'3" tall, wearing a white silk dress with a wide pink belt

D. 5'11" tall, wearing a white silk pantsuit with a wide white belt

19. Officer Terry reports to the scene of a robbery and gathers the following information:

Location:	40 Brown Street
Time:	3:00 A.M.
Victim:	Tom Carpenter
Injury:	none
Suspect:	Jeff Ford
Weapon:	handgun (shown to victim but not fired)
Items Missing:	wallet containing $50 and credit cards
Status of Suspect:	found with gun and wallet, arrested

Officer Terry must write a report on the incident. Which of the following expresses the information most clearly and accurately?

A. At 3:00 A.M., Tom Carpenter's wallet, containing $50 and credit cards, was stolen from him by a man with a handgun, who showed Mr. Carpenter a handgun but did not fire it. Mr. Carpenter reported that the man was Jeff Ford, who was found with a gun and the wallet and was arrested.

B. Tom Carpenter reported that at 3:00 A.M. at 40 Brown Street, Jeff Ford showed him a handgun and stole his wallet, which contained $50 and credit cards. Jeff Ford was found with a gun and the wallet and was arrested.

C. After being found with the handgun and Tom Carpenter's wallet, Jeff Ford was arrested for robbery. The handgun was not fired but was shown to Tom Carpenter at 3:00 A.M. at 40 Brown Street, when Mr. Ford stole the wallet.

D. At 3:00 A.M., Jeff Ford reportedly showed a handgun to Tom Carpenter and stole Mr. Carpenter's wallet, with which, along with the gun, he was later found, and which contained $50 and credit cards. Jeff Ford was arrested.

20. In State X, a person is guilty of **PROMOTING A SUICIDE ATTEMPT** when he intentionally causes or aids another person to attempt suicide. Given this definition alone, which of the following is not an example of Promoting a Suicide Attempt?

A. Billy helps Allison, who has told him that she wants to die, determine the number of prescription pills necessary to stop her heart. She swallows the pills, but is resuscitated at the hospital.

B. Mr. Esteban jumps from a 10th-floor ledge after being helped onto the ledge by his son, who knew that his father was going to jump.

C. Sue Ann lends a gun to her father so he can shoot nuisance pigeons; he shoots himself instead.

D. Roger dies of carbon monoxide poisoning after being shown how to kill himself in this manner by his friend Ed, who knew Roger was suicidal.

21. Officer Reese responds to a report that an elderly man has been seen wandering in the street. Officer Reese gathers the following information:

Location:	Beach Highway near Chambers Street
Man's Name:	Arnold Harris
Age:	73
Address:	200 Oak Street
Situation:	Mr. Harris was wandering in the street
Medical Information:	suffers from occasional loss of memory
Status:	unharmed, returned to his home

Officer Reese is writing a report on the incident. Which of the following expresses the information most clearly and accurately?

A. A 73-year-old man named Arnold Harris who lives at 200 Oak Street was returned to his home unharmed. He was wandering in the street at Beach Highway near Chambers Street.

B. After being found wandering Beach Highway near Chambers Street, 73-year-old Arnold Harris was returned to his house unharmed. Mr. Harris suffers occasional loss of memory.

C. At Beach Highway near Chambers Street, Arnold Harris, 73, of 200 Oak Street, was found wandering in the street. Mr. Harris, who suffers from occasional loss of memory, was unharmed and was returned to his home.

D. Arnold Harris is 73 years old and was wandering in the street at Beach Highway and Chambers Street. He lives at 200 Oak Street and suffers from occasional loss of memory. He was unharmed.

22. Just before dusk in a busy downtown business and entertainment district, Officer Floyd is patrolling Main Street on horseback. As he turns a corner, he sees a young man prying at the trunk of a car with a metal rod. What should Officer Floyd do first?

A. approach the young man and read him his rights

B. approach the young man slowly, while calling for backup from a nonmounted officer

C. approach and arrest the young man

D. radio the dispatch, approach, and question the young man about his activities

23. When the young man sees Officer Floyd, he immediately hurls the metal rod at the officer and flees. Which of the following is the most logical assumption?

A. The young man was trying to break into the trunk of someone else's car.

B. The young man is afraid of horses.

C. In this community, police have a frightening reputation for mistreating suspects.

D. The young man does not work in the area.

24. In State X, a person is guilty of **APPEARANCE IN PUBLIC UNDER THE INFLUENCE OF NARCOTICS OR A DRUG OTHER THAN ALCOHOL** when he appears in a public place under the influence of narcotics or a drug other than alcohol to the degree that he may endanger himself or other persons or property, or annoy persons in his vicinity. Which of the following is the best example of Appearance in Public Under the Influence of Narcotics or a Drug Other Than Alcohol?

    A. Having taken a hallucinogenic drug, Roderick panics in a public park and screams incessantly.

    B. Jim drinks 20 cans of beer and drunkenly stumbles into many people on the street.

    C. After taking several narcotic capsules, P.J. lies on a lawn chair on his patio.

    D. Letitia has several cocktails at an outdoor wedding reception and punches a groomsman.

25. If Officer Sarah Smith intends to enforce an 11:00 P.M. curfew for everyone under the age of 18, she should focus her attention most closely on which of the following sections of her beat?

    A. a quiet all-night coffee shop frequented by college students

    B. a neighborhood bar with a strict policy of allowing only adults over the age of 21 to enter

    C. a movie theater running midnight shows

    D. a bank with an external 24 hour teller machine

26. Officer Simmons answers a call from a woman who reports that her car has been stolen. He gathers the following information:

Location:	75 Astor Avenue
Time:	between 9:00 P.M. and 10:00 P.M.
Crime:	larceny
Item Missing:	white 1998 Volvo
Owner:	Mrs. Reynolds
Suspect:	unknown, no witnesses

    Officer Simmons is writing his report. Which of the following expresses the information most clearly and accurately?

    A. Between 9:00 P.M. and 10:00 P.M., a white 1998 Volvo was stolen, but there were no witnesses. The owner is Mrs. Reynolds of 75 Astor Place and the suspect, who probably stole the car, is unknown.

    B. A white 1998 Volvo was reported missing from her home at 75 Astor Avenue by Mrs. Reynolds. The car became missing between 9:00 P.M. and 10:00 P.M. There were no witnesses.

    C. Mrs. Reynolds reported that sometime between 9:00 P.M. and 10:00 P.M., her white 1998 Volvo was stolen from 75 Astor Avenue. The suspect is unknown, and there were no witnesses.

    D. There were no witnesses to describe the suspect in a reported car theft from 75 Astor Avenue. The car, a white 1998 Volvo, was stolen from Mrs. Reynolds between 9:00 P.M. and 10:00 P.M.

27. Mrs. Hancock, who lives at 3075 Teak Street, returns home from taking her kids to school and finds her expensive brick mailbox broken and laying on her front lawn. She calls the police. When Officer Lee arrives, Mrs. Hancock shows him the damage and says she is certain that her neighbor's 20-year-old son, Ronnie Fielding, is guilty because he speeds around the neighborhood recklessly and has never held down a job.

    Mrs. Hancock gives Officer Lee a description of Ronnie and tells him that Ronnie and his parents live around the corner, at 2828 Oak Drive, and that Ronnie drives a red Jeep with an obscene cartoon sticker on his windshield. Officer Lee writes down the information and calls in an alert for Ronnie Fielding and his vehicle. He then returns to the station house.

    Did Officer Lee choose the best plan of action?

    A. No, because Officer Lee should have stayed around and asked Mrs. Hancock to list other neighbors with bad reputations.

    B. Yes, because Mrs. Hancock's instincts were probably correct, since she knows her neighborhood, and Ronnie Fielding could cause more damage to personal property if a concentrated effort to apprehend him is not made.

    C. No, because Officer Lee should have visited the Fielding residence in an attempt to question Ronnie as to whether or not he might have been involved.

    D. Yes, because even if Ronnie Fielding is not guilty, Mrs. Hancock's suspicion is the only lead Officer Lee has, and he needs to get back to the precinct right away to type up his report.

28. In State X, a person is guilty of **LOITERING IN THE FIRST DEGREE** when he loiters or remains in any place with one or more persons for the purpose of unlawfully using or possessing a controlled substance.

    Armand stands on a corner for an extended amount of time, hoping for a quiet moment to use a drug that is defined by State X as a controlled substance. Officer Smith arrests Armand, and Armand is subsequently charged with Loitering in the First Degree. Given only the definition above, is Armand guilty as charged?

    A. Yes, because he remained in one place.

    B. No, because he was alone.

    C. Yes, because he intended to use a controlled substance.

    D. Armand is guilty only if he actually possessed a controlled substance at the time of his arrest.

29. Officer Melendez reports to the southwest corner of Wythe and Crystal Avenues, where a fire hydrant is reportedly gushing water into the street. Officer Melendez gathers the following information:

Location: southwest corner of Wythe and Crystal Avenues
Time: 4:00 P.M.
Incident: fire hydrant opened; water is pouring into the street
Action Taken: fire department called
Witnesses: no one saw the hydrant being tampered with

Officer Melendez must write a report on the incident. Which of the following expresses the information most clearly and accurately?

A. At 4:00 P.M. at the southwest corner of Wythe and Crystal Avenues, a fire hydrant had apparently been opened and was pouring water into the street. The fire department was called. No one in the area witnessed anyone tampering with the fire hydrant.

B. At the southwest corner of Wythe and Crystal Avenues, an open fire hydrant that no one saw anyone tamper with was pouring water into the street. The fire department was called.

C. The fire department was called after a fire hydrant at the southwest corner of Wythe and Crystal Avenues was reported to be open and pouring water into the street at 4:00 P.M.

D. A fire hydrant at the corner of Wythe and Crystal Avenues was reported to be pen and pouring water into the street at 4:00 P.M. after no one saw anyone else tampering with the hydrant. The fire department was called.

30. Walter Washington, an off-duty police officer who lives in a densely populated residential neighborhood, is trimming his hedges on a Saturday afternoon. While taking a break from his yard work, Officer Washington takes a few sips of beer. He then hears what he is certain are two gunshots coming from the eastern end of his block. What should Officer Washington do first?

A call in and report the shots

B. call in and request to be put on duty so he can investigate

C. nothing, as he is off duty and has been drinking

D. get his gun and run in the direction of the shots

31. Angela Branch was about to make a cash deposit into her checking account at an automatic teller machine when someone grabbed her deposit envelope and shoved her, face first, onto the ground. The suspect ran away. During his investigation, Officer Wayne interviewed witnesses who described the suspect. Of the following descriptions given by witnesses, which should Officer Wayne consider most likely to be correct?

    A. tall, light-skinned male with long, blonde, braided hair
    B. short, dark-skinned male with long, black, braided hair
    C. tall, light-skinned male with long, black, braided hair
    D. tall, dark-skinned male with long, black, straight hair

32. Officer White responds to a report of an assault at a convenience store. At the store, Officer White gathers the following information:

Location:	ABC Convenience
Time:	8:45 P.M.
Crime:	assault
Victim:	Jay Alberts
Injury:	broken wrist
Suspect:	white teenage boy, about 5'7"
Weapon:	large rock
Location of Suspect:	fled on a green bicycle

    Officer White is writing a report on the incident. Which of the following expresses the information most clearly and accurately?

    A. Jay Alberts reported that at 8:45 P.M. at ABC Convenience, a white teenage boy, about 5'7", struck him with a large rock then fled on a green bicycle. Mr. Alberts suffered a broken wrist.

    B. At 8:45 P.M., Jay Alberts reported that a white teenage boy hit him with a large rock, breaking his wrist. The assault occurred at ABC Convenience, and the boy fled on a green bicycle. Mr. Alberts's wrist was broken.

    C. At ABC Convenience there was an assault involving Jay Alberts, who was hit with a large rock, breaking his wrist, and a white teenage boy, about 5'7", who fled on a green bicycle. The incident occurred at 8:45 P.M.

    D. A white teenage boy, about 5'7", allegedly struck Jay Alberts, breaking his wrist, with a large rock at 8:45 P.M. The boy fled ABC Convenience on a green bicycle.

33. John Ruiz, a traffic officer, pulls a motorist over for driving 10 miles per hour over the speed limit. Officer Ruiz discovers that the driver is his close friend's mother, Mrs. Sandemeier, who has never been issued any sort of citation. Officer Ruiz should:

    A. apologize and let her go because he knows her, and police officers have a certain amount of flexibility in protecting those close to them from fines and prosecution.

    B. give her a warning and advise her to drive carefully. A good driver will almost always be more careful after being issued a warning, and police officers are allowed to use their own discretion in deciding when a ticket or a warning would be best.

    C. write her a ticket, because she has probably gotten away with driving too fast many times.

    D. write her a ticket, because all drivers breaking the law should always be issued tickets.

34. Later that same afternoon, Officer Ruiz pulls over another driver for exceeding the speed limit by 15 miles per hour, driving through a red light, changing lanes without signaling, and making a U-turn in an area in which it is unlawful to do so. Officer Ruiz recognizes the driver as Mrs. Sandemeier's husband, Dr. Sandemeier. He asks Dr. Sandemeier if he is answering an emergency call. Dr. Sandemeier apologizes for his driving and says that he is only trying to get home quickly after a bad day. Dr. Sandemeier has been given three speeding tickets in the previous year. Officer Ruiz should:

    A. give Dr. Sandemeier a warning, because he apologized for his bad driving.

    B. give Dr. Sandemeier a warning, since Officer Ruiz does not want to give Dr. Sandemeier the impression that he likes Mrs. Sandemeier better.

    C. write Dr. Sandemeier a ticket, because he broke several laws and endangered the lives of others.

    D. apologize to Dr. Sandemeier and let him go.

35. In State X, a person is guilty of **SPORTS BRIBE RECEIVING** when, being a sports participant, he solicits, accepts, or agrees to accept any benefit from another person upon an agreement that he will be influenced not to give his best efforts in a sports contest, or, being a sports official, he solicits, accepts, or agrees to accept any benefit from another person upon an agreement that he will perform his duties improperly. Given this definition alone, which of the following is the best example of Sports Bribe Receiving?

   A. Johnny, a soccer referee, is offered $100 to overlook fouls committed by the Stanford Stingers' star forward, but he refuses.

   B. Sven accepts $50 from a parent to umpire a baseball game in a new kids' league.

   C. Joey, a guard for State College's basketball team, accepts a new car from a gambler in return for intentionally getting himself thrown out of a game by committing too many fouls.

   D. During a softball game, the ball hits Sylvia in the eye. Following doctor's orders, Sylvia sits out the next game, and her parents console her with a new glove.

36. Officer Wells is dispatched to the scene of an automobile accident, where she gathers the following information:

Location:	corner of Main Street and Ohio Avenue
Time:	11:15 A.M.
Incident:	two cars collided after one of the drivers ran a stop sign
Driver at Fault:	Mr. Clark
Victim:	Ms. Eastman
Action Taken:	Mr. Clark received a traffic ticket

   Officer Wells must write her report on the incident. Which of the following expresses the information most clearly and accurately?

   A. At 11:15 A.M., two cars collided at the corner of Main Street and Ohio Avenue after the car driven by Mr. Clark ran a stop sign. The other car was driven by Ms. Eastman. Mr. Clark received a traffic ticket, as he was at fault for running the stop sign.

   B. At 11:15 A.M. at the corner of Main Street and Ohio Avenue, Mr. Clark ran a stop sign, causing a collision between his car and the car driven by Ms. Eastman. Ms. Eastman was not at fault, so she did not receive a traffic ticket, as Mr. Clark did.

   C. At the corner of Main Street and Ohio Avenue at 11:15 A.M., Mr. Clark ran a stop sign, causing a collision between his car and the car driven by Ms. Eastman. Mr. Clark received a traffic ticket.

   D. Ms. Eastman's car was hit by Mr. Clark's at the corner of Main Street and Ohio Avenue after Mr. Clark's car ran a stop sign. Mr. Clark was at fault.

37. Jim Davis was out walking his dog when a car sped around a corner and knocked them both onto the curb. The car did not stop. Officer Walker answered the call to investigate this hit-and-run. Which of the following descriptions of the vehicle, given by witnesses, should Officer Walker consider most likely to be correct?

    A. brown Mazda, tag JND 149
    B. yellow Toyota, tag JND 149
    C. brown Toyota, tag JBD 149
    D. yellow Toyota, tag JNO 149

38. On each of the past eight Saturday nights, between 8:00 P.M. and 1:00 A.M., an apartment near the local university has been broken into, and stereo equipment has been stolen. About which of the following scenarios should officers patrolling the area on a Saturday be most concerned?

    A. a man carrying a boxed stereo component system into an apartment at 1:00 P.M.
    B. a van circling the neighborhood at 9:00 P.M.
    C. a pair of men, dressed in black, shining flashlights onto the fire escape of one of the apartment buildings at 12:30 A.M.
    D. three teenagers driving through the neighborhood in a compact car at 1:30 A.M.

39. Officer Barron is dispatched to a club, where the owner reports that a minor attempted to enter with a fake I.D. At the club, Officer Barron gathers the following information:

Location:	Jack's Club
Time:	12:30 A.M.
Incident:	a minor attempted to enter with a fake I.D.
Minor:	Joel Haynes
Club Owner:	Jack Redmond
Action Taken:	fake I.D. confiscated, Joel Haynes arrested and taken into custody

    Officer Barron must write a report on the incident. Which of the following expresses the information most clearly and accurately?

    A. At 12:30 A.M., Jack's Club owner Jack Redmond refused entry, wisely, to a minor trying to get in with a fake I.D. Joel Haynes, the minor, was arrested after his I.D. was confiscated.
    B. At Jack's Club, Joel Haynes, who is a minor, attempted to enter by giving a fake I.D. to owner Jack Redmond. The minor's I.D. was confiscated and he was arrested.
    C. At Jack's Club, owner Jack Redmond was presented with a fake I.D. by minor Joel Haynes who wanted to enter his club but was not old enough. The minor's fake I.D. was confiscated and he was arrested after attempting this at 12:30 A.M.
    D. At 12:30 A.M., Joel Haynes, a minor, attempted to enter Jack's Club by presenting a fake I.D. to owner Jack Redmond. The I.D. was confiscated and the minor was arrested.

40. While patrolling an industrial section of town on a Saturday afternoon, Officers Sloan and Dividny observe five teenagers skateboarding in an empty concrete reservoir. The area is marked "PRIVATE PROPERTY: NO TRESPASSING" by a sign that hangs on only one side of the adjacent building, which might not be visible to those approaching from the other sides.

    Officers Sloan and Dividny escort the teenagers home and explain to their parents that the teens were breaking the law, although they may not have realized it, and endangering their lives. The officers then call the owners of the property and advise them to construct a fence and post more signage around the reservoir to prevent this from happening again. Further, the officers resolve to keep a watch out for other teenagers who try to skateboard there in the future.

    The officers' actions were:

    A. good, as they removed the teenagers from a potentially dangerous situation and advised the property owners on how to make the area safer.

    B. bad, as they have no jurisdiction over what happens on private property.

    C. bad, as they should have arrested the parents for neglecting to closely supervise their children.

    D. It is impossible to tell whether they acted correctly until the property owner either does or does not erect a fence.

41. A homeowner reports the following items stolen from his residence:

Large-screen television	$1,500
Home-cinema sound system	$3,000
DVD player	$ 445
14k gold necklace	$ 330
Diamond ring	$1,500
Emerald bracelet	$ 750
Cash	$3,271

    Later, the homeowner reports that the diamond ring was found under the sofa. What is the total value of the items stolen?

    A. $13,796

    B. $17,396

    C. $ 9,296

    D. $10,796

42. Officer Rainier responds to a report of a missing child and gathers the following information:

Location:	414 Rodeo Boulevard
Child Reported Missing by:	his mother, Stephanie Johnson
Name of Missing Child:	C.J. Johnson, age 6
Status of Child:	came home unharmed shortly after Mrs. Johnson called the police

Officer Rainier is filling out his report. Which of the following expresses the information most clearly and accurately?

A. A six-year-old boy was reported missing shortly before he came home by his mother, Stephanie Johnson, at 414 Rodeo Boulevard. The child, C.J. Johnson, was unharmed.

B. C.J. Johnson, age 6, of 414 Rodeo Boulevard, was reported missing by his mother, Stephanie Johnson. Shortly after she reported him missing, C.J. came home unharmed.

C. C.J. Johnson returned home shortly after he was reported missing. His mother, Stephanie Johnson, reported that the child, age 6, was missing, shortly before C.J. came home, unharmed, to 414 Rodeo Boulevard.

D. After calling the police to report that her son, age 6, was missing, Stephanie Johnson's son came home to 414 Rodeo Boulevard unharmed.

43. In State X, a person is guilty of **AGGRAVATED DISORDERLY CONDUCT** when he makes unreasonable noise while at a lawfully assembled religious service or within 100 feet thereof, with intent to cause annoyance. Based solely upon this definition, which of the following is the best example of Aggravated Disorderly Conduct?

A. In the midst of a heated sermon, Reverend Hightower yells at his congregation.

B. During his ex-girlfriend's wedding, Greg drives in circles around the parking lot of the church with his stereo blaring and his windows down.

C. A.J., an 18-month-old baby, begins to cry loudly during Mass.

D. Emotionally driven to commit her life to the church, Ada runs screaming down the aisle during a service and throws herself on the altar.

44. A speeding motorist, driving down a busy road in a shopping district, refuses to pull over, even after Officer Sandoval indicates by flashing lights and several amplified verbal announcements that the motorist should do so. Officer Sandoval leans out of his window and fires a shot at the motorist's right rear tire. Officer Sandoval's action was:

    A. good, because the motorist might be dangerous and should be stopped immediately.

    B. bad, because his actions might have endangered the lives of innocent people on this busy stretch of road.

    C. good, because this will deter others from attempting to evade a pursuing officer in the future.

    D. bad, because Officer Sandoval clearly had a better shot at the left rear tire.

45. Mrs. Ethel Jackson called the police to report that at some point during the previous night, the screen on her bathroom window had been slashed, and her window had been forced open. While Mrs. Jackson could not determine whether or not anything was missing from her house, she did see strange footprints in a few rooms, along with signs of someone having disturbed her belongings. Officer Murphy spoke with Mrs. Jackson at her house and then interviewed several people who saw someone near Mrs. Jackson's bathroom window the night before. Of the following descriptions of the suspect given by those witnesses, which should Officer Murphy consider most likely to be accurate?

    A. tall, thin male, dressed in tight black clothing and brown boots

    B. tall, heavyset male, dressed in tight black clothing and black sneakers

    C. short, thin male, dressed in tight black clothing and black boots

    D. short, heavyset male, dressed in tight blue clothing and black boots

46. After receiving a report of a minor in possession of alcohol, Officer Nesbitt reports to the scene and gathers the following information:

Location: Deep Center Batting Cages
Time: 9:30 P.M.
Crime: possession of alcohol by a minor
Minor: Gary Russell
Action Taken: beverage in question nonalcoholic; no action taken

Officer Nesbitt must write a report. Which of the following expresses the information most clearly and accurately?

A. At 9:30 P.M., a report of a minor named Gary Russell was received saying the minor possessed alcohol and was at Deep Center Batting Cages. The drink was nonalcoholic, and no action was taken.

B. At 9:30 P.M., minor Gary Russell was reported to be in possession of alcohol at Deep Center Batting Cages. The beverage in question was determined to be nonalcoholic, so no action was taken.

C. At Deep Center Batting Cages, a minor named Gary Russell was supposedly in possession of alcohol. Investigators found that his drink was nonalcoholic, though, so no action was taken.

D. At Deep Center Batting Cages, a minor was reported to be in possession of alcohol. The minor's drink was determined to be nonalcoholic, so no action was taken.

47. Officer Mitchell, who works for her local municipal police department, is driving south in one of the two southbound lanes of a state highway on her way home from her shift. Suddenly, an 18-wheeler headed north flies past her in the other southbound lane. A concrete median divides the two sides of the highway. What should Officer Mitchell do first?

A. call in to report the situation

B. turn her car around and pursue the 18-wheeler

C. nothing, because she is a municipal officer and the incident occurred on a state highway

D. cross the median and pursue the 18-wheeler from the other side so that she is traveling in the proper direction

48. In State X, a person is guilty of **ESCAPE IN THE THIRD DEGREE** when he escapes from custody. **CUSTODY** is defined as restraint by a public servant pursuant to an authorized arrest or an order of a court. Based solely on these definitions, which of the following is the best example of Escape in the Third Degree?

    A. While his supervisor is not looking, Jason Cunningham, a janitor at the sheriff's office, leaves work 30 minutes before the end of his shift.

    B. Joanie, who has been arrested by a police officer after he saw her steal a skirt from a department store, runs away from the officer.

    C. After answering several questions at the police precinct about an ongoing investigation, Jesus is thanked for his time and told he is free to go. Being late for a softball game, he runs out of the precinct.

    D. Harrison becomes physically ill during a scheduled visit to his parole officer and asks to be excused before the visit is over.

49. Smoke is billowing from a window many floors above the street in a high-rise apartment building. Officer Chin sees the smoke from his patrol car and immediately calls the fire department. His decision was:

    A. correct, as the fire department needs to be alerted as soon as possible so that they can contain what is probably a fire.

    B. incorrect, as he should have gotten a closer look at the type of smoke before calling the fire department.

    C. incorrect, as he should have called his own precinct first for instructions from a supervisor.

    D. It is impossible to tell without knowing whether or not there actually is a fire.

50. Officer Major responds to a report of the smell of natural gas at an apartment building, where he gathers the following information:

Location:	Bear Village Apartments
Time:	8:00 P.M.
Caller:	Paula Oak
Problem:	the smell of natural gas was permeating her apartment
Action Taken:	the gas company was contacted; an emergency repair person arrived in minutes and fixed the leak

    Officer Major is writing his report. Which of the following expresses the information most clearly and accurately?

    A. At 8:00 P.M., Paula Oak reported that the smell of natural gas was permeating her apartment. The gas company was contacted, and an emergency repair person arrived in minutes and fixed the leak.

    B. At 8:00 P.M., Paula Oak reported that the smell of natural gas was permeating her apartment at Bear Village Apartments. The gas company was contacted.

    C. At 8:00 P.M., Paula Oak reported smelling natural gas. The gas company was contacted and an emergency repair person arrived in minutes to fix the leak, which was causing the smell at Bear Village Apartments.

    D. At 8:00 P.M., Paula Oak reported that the smell of natural gas was permeating her apartment at Bear Village Apartments. The gas company was contacted, and an emergency repair person arrived in minutes and fixed the leak.

51. An officer on traffic patrol should be most concerned about which of the following drivers?

    A. Lee Severinstone, who does not immediately dim her lights when the officer's patrol car approaches in an oncoming lane of traffic

    B. Mr. Johnston, who has a sneezing fit while driving and swerves a few inches into the next lane

    C. Ann Ramirez, who fails to turn on her windshield wipers as soon as raindrops begin to fall

    D. Josie Farmer, who changes lanes on a busy street several times without signaling

52. Michelle Lucas was eating lunch at a sidewalk cafe when someone ran up and stole a bottle of wine from her table. Those sitting near Ms. Lucas offered the following descriptions of the suspect to Officer Cole. Which of the descriptions should Officer Cole consider most likely to be accurate?

    A. white male, wearing a sleeveless white shirt, with several tattoos of black bars on his left arm

    B. black male, wearing a sleeveless pink shirt, with several tattoos of black bars on his right arm

    C. white male, wearing a short-sleeved blue shirt with black stripes, with several tattoos of black bars on his right arm

    D. white male, wearing a sleeveless pink shirt, with several tattoos of black bars on his right arm

53. Officer Kaurismaki is sent to the local elementary school following a call from the school principal, who reported seeing several teenagers spray-paint an obscene image and phrase on the slide in the school's playground. Officer Kaurismaki asks the principal a few questions. Which of the following is least likely to be among Officer Kaurismaki's questions?

    A. "What did the suspects look like?"

    B. "What time did the vandalism occur?"

    C. "Did anyone else see the vandalism occur?"

    D. "How long have you been the principal at this school?"

54. In State X, a person is guilty of **PROMOTING PRISON CONTRABAND IN THE FIRST DEGREE** when he knowingly and unlawfully introduces any dangerous contraband into a detention facility, or, being a person in a detention facility, he knowingly and unlawfully obtains or possesses any dangerous contraband. **DANGEROUS CONTRABAND** is defined as material that is capable of such use that may endanger the safety or security of a detention facility or any person therein.

    Based solely upon these definitions, which of the following is true if Samantha brings her incarcerated husband, Dick, his collection of miniature knives, which he takes back to his cell?

    A. Neither Samantha nor Dick should be charged with any crime, as the knives are not dangerous contraband.

    B. Samantha and Dick should be charged with Promoting Prison Contraband in the First Degree.

    C. Only Dick should be charged with Promoting Prison Contraband in the First Degree.

    D. Only Samantha should be charged with Promoting Prison Contraband in the First Degree.

55. Officer Robinson responds to a call from a man who reports that a woman tried to sell drugs to him. Officer Robinson gathers the following information:

Location:	Silver Screen Multiplex
Time:	midnight
Person Reporting Incident:	Danny Singh
Crime:	attempting to sell drugs
Suspect:	40-year-old woman
Location of Suspect:	left the theater lot in a white Lincoln

Officer Robinson must write a report on the incident. Which of the following expresses the information most clearly and accurately?

A. At midnight, at Silver Screen Multiplex, a woman of about 40 years old tried to sell drugs to Danny Singh. The woman left the theater lot in a white Lincoln, according to Danny Singh, to whom the woman tried to sell the drugs.

B. Danny Singh reported that at midnight, a 40-year-old woman tried to sell him drugs. The woman then left the theater lot in a white Lincoln, after which time Mr. Singh called the police to report the attempted sale.

C. At the Silver Screen Multiplex at midnight, a 40-year-old woman attempted to sell Danny Singh some drugs. The woman was described as 40 years old, and left the theater in a white car.

D. Danny Singh reported that at midnight at the Silver Screen Multiplex, a woman who appeared to be around 40 years of age attempted to sell him drugs, then left the theater lot in a white Lincoln.

56. If Officer Banks, who is assigned to direct traffic in a busy intersection with malfunctioning traffic signals, sees a collision occur at an intersection two blocks away, what should she do first?

A. call the incident in to her precinct

B. ask a responsible citizen to take over directing traffic while she investigates the accident

C. assume that someone near the accident has a cellular phone and will report the accident, as traffic is much too heavy for her to be distracted

D. fire a shot from her gun over her head to alert all nearby motorists to the situation

57. Driving through the parking lot of a public pool during a routine patrol, Officers Quinton and LeFarge overhear three boys discussing a plan to attack one of the girls at the pool and pull her swimsuit top off while forcing her to stand on the diving board so everyone can see. Which of the following should Officers Quinton and LeFarge do first?

    A. draw their guns and approach the boys, who are obviously demented and possibly dangerous

    B. call for backup from an officer from juvenile court

    C. determine which girl the boys are targeting, call her parents, and get her out of the pool

    D. approach the boys and discuss with them the crime they have already committed by conspiring to attack the girl and what would happen to them if they carried out their plan

58. In State X, a person is guilty of **RESISTING ARREST** when he intentionally prevents or attempts to prevent a police officer or peace officer from effecting an authorized arrest of himself or another person. Based solely on this definition, which of the following is the best example of Resisting Arrest?

    A. Wally yells at and grabs at a police officer who is attempting to arrest his friend, Sam.

    B. In order to alert the officer to an assault occurring across the street, Sinead jumps in between a police officer and the man the officer is attempting to arrest.

    C. After being chased from court by his screaming ex-wife, Theodore refuses to accompany the bailiff back into the courtroom to proceed with a custody hearing.

    D. Colin, in shock after being attacked on a train, runs from the police, who want to get him to a hospital.

59. Officer Reynolds is patrolling on foot and watching for a suspect described as just over six feet tall, weighing about 150 pounds, with brown hair and a gold wristwatch. A man fitting that description passes by, pushing an elderly woman in a wheelchair while having a friendly conversation with her. Which would be the most logical action for Officer Reynolds to take?

    A. follow the man to his destination and observe his behavior before approaching him

    B. arrest the man immediately and call for a helpful civilian to escort the elderly woman to her destination

    C. call for backup after pulling his gun

    D. call for another officer to replace him at his current location, then wait until that officer arrives, even if it means losing the man who fits the suspect's description

60. Officer Petty responds to the scene of a reported domestic dispute, where she gathers the following information:

Location:	88 DeVaro
Time:	3:30 P.M.
Incident:	loud fighting and crashing sounds coming from the house
Person Reporting Incident:	Chung Lee, a neighbor
Residents at 88 DeVaro:	Jay and Ida Lindsay
Action Taken:	the couple explained that they were practicing Judo together; no action taken

Officer Petty has to write her report. Which of the following expresses the information most clearly and accurately?

A. At 88 DeVaro, a Judo practice session between Jay and Ida Lindsay, the residents, alarmed their neighbor, Chung Lee, who called the police. No action was taken.

B. Chung Lee reported that his neighbors at 88 DeVaro were fighting and that crashing sounds were loudly coming from their house at 3:30 P.M. Jay and Ida Lindsay said they were just practicing Judo.

C. At 3:30 P.M., Chung Lee reported that loud fighting and crashing sounds were coming from his neighbors' house at 88 DeVaro. The residents, Jay and Ida Lindsay, explained that they were practicing Judo together, so no action was taken.

D. Jay and Ida Lindsay were practicing Judo in their home at 88 DeVaro, causing loud fighting and crashing sounds to be heard by their neighbor, Chung Lee, who became concerned and called the police. No action was taken.

61. Eight-year-old Leslie Smalls was reported missing by her parents. Officers Pearl and August, in the course of investigating Leslie's disappearance, interviewed several people who saw Leslie get into a vehicle just a few hours before she was reported missing. Of the following descriptions of the vehicle given by the witnesses, which should Officers Pearl and August consider most likely to be accurate?

A. black truck, tag number JG 1501

B. charcoal grey truck, tag number JC 1509

C. black truck, tag number JC 1501

D. black truck, tag number JC 1587

62. Officer Patrizio is certified in the lifesaving techniques of First Aid and CPR. He comes upon a man who has collapsed on the sidewalk and is flailing and clutching his chest. Officer Patrizio calls for an ambulance as the man becomes unconscious and stops moving. When Officer Patrizio checks the man's pulse, he finds that the man's heart has stopped beating. What should Officer Patrizio do first?

    A. attempt to revive the man using CPR

    B. give the ambulance a reasonable amount of time to arrive before attempting to use CPR to revive the man on his own

    C. scour the surrounding area for a doctor or a nurse

    D. place the man in his squad car immediately and take him to a hospital

63. As a result of a recent series of thefts of lawn furniture and yard sculptures, Captain Dryden warns officers on patrol to watch for large vehicles whose contents are not visible from the outside. Which of the following should officers who heed Captain Dryden's warning be most concerned about?

    A. a florist's van with no side or rear windows

    B. a 40-foot motor home with large windows

    C. a pickup truck with completely opaque tinted windows

    D. an unmarked van with no side or rear windows

64. Officer London is stopped by a girl who asks that Officer London take her friend, who has been stung multiple times by hornets, to the hospital. At the hospital, Officer London gathers the following information:

Victim:	Reggie Planks, age 8
Condition:	stable after a severe allergic reaction to hornet stings
Friend:	Hanna Reynolds, age 7
Action Taken:	Hanna Reynolds provided Reggie Planks's phone number, and his parents were contacted

    Officer London must fill out her report. Which of the following expresses the information most clearly and accurately?

    A. Reggie Planks, age 8, was stung multiple times by hornets and suffered a severe allergic reaction. Reggie was taken to the hospital, where he is in stable condition. His friend, Hanna Reynolds, provided Reggie's phone number, and his parents were contacted.

    B. After suffering a severe allergic reaction to multiple hornet stings, Reggie Planks, age 8, is in stable condition. His parents were contacted.

    C. Hanna Reynolds, age 8 and a friend of hornet sting victim Reggie Planks, age 7, provided Reggie's phone number so that his parents could be contacted after Reggie suffered a severe allergic reaction. Reggie is now in stable condition.

    D. In stable condition after suffering a severe allergic reaction to multiple hornet stings, the parents of Reggie Planks, age 8, have been contacted, thanks to his friend Hanna Reynolds, age 7, who provided their phone number.

65. Officer Kittridge, who is on a plainclothes patrol, sees a gun-shaped bulge in the ankle of a pair of pants worn by a man standing in line at a convenience store. The man is wearing sunglasses, does not have any items with him to purchase, and glances nervously around the store. Officer Kittridge waits until the man reaches toward his ankle then grabs both of the man's arms and pins him to the floor. Upon searching the man, Officer Kittridge finds that the bulge in his ankle is a wallet. Officer Kittridge apologizes, asks the man if he is okay, and helps him up.

Officer Kittridge's actions were:

A. good, because he had to let the man get as close as possible to committing the crime before attempting to apprehend him or he would have had a weak case.

B. bad, because to prevent any possible harm from coming to the clerk or others in the store, Officer Kittridge should have asked the man to show him what was in the ankle of his pants before allowing the man to reach for what might have been a weapon.

C. good, because the man will now have a healthy fear of police officers and will not be as inclined as he might have been to commit a crime.

D. bad, because he did not owe the man an apology as he had every reason to suspect the man was about to rob the clerk.

66. In State X, a person is guilty of **CRIMINALLY POSSESSING A HYPODERMIC INSTRUMENT** when he knowingly and unlawfully possesses or sells a hypodermic syringe or needle. Based solely upon this definition, which of the following is the best example of Criminally Possessing a Hypodermic Instrument?

A. Benny uses hypodermic syringes to inject himself with prescribed allergy medication.

B. After finding a baby deer alone in the woods, veterinary student Keisha uses a hypodermic syringe from her school's veterinary clinic to inject vitamins into the deer.

C. Elaine obtains hypodermic syringes from the hospital where she works then sells the syringes to intravenous drug addicts.

D. K.C. finds hypodermic needles on the corner outside his apartment. He gathers them in a plastic bag with the intention of taking them to the police to demonstrate that drug users have been gathering on the corner.

67. Officer Westover arrives at a residence that has been spray-painted with obscenities. At the residence, Officer Westover gathers the following information:

Location: #15 Tanner Circle
Crime: vandalism; house was spray-painted with obscenities
Victim: Mrs. Hersch
Suspect: Grant Patrick
Witness: Geri Budd, a neighbor
Status of Suspect: arrested

Officer Westover must write her report. Which of the following expresses the information most clearly and accurately?

A. Mrs. Hersch's home at #15 Tanner Circle was reportedly vandalized by Grant Patrick, who spray-painted obscenities on the house while a neighbor was watching. Mr. Patrick was arrested.

B. Geri Budd, who lives near Hersch's home at #15 Tanner Circle, witnessed Grant Patrick spray-painting the Hirsch residence with obscenities. Mr. Patrick was arrested.

C. At #15 Tanner Circle, Mrs. Hersch reported that her neighbor, Geri Budd, had seen Grant Patrick spray-paint her house with obscenities. Mr. Patrick was arrested.

D. Grant Patrick was arrested after a witness, Mrs. Hersch's neighbor Geri Budd, saw him spray-paint obscenities onto the house at #15 Tanner Circle, where Mrs. Hersch lives.

68. An elderly man suffering from occasional blackouts and memory loss is reported missing by his daughter. Officer Ortega answers the call and interviews the man's family. Which of the following facts would be least important to Officer Ortega's attempt to find the missing man?

A. The man is 73 years old and has short, white hair.

B. He was wearing tan slacks, a peach-colored shirt, and blue sneakers when he disappeared.

C. He loves the water and often wanders off to a nearby lake or to one of the rivers that feeds it.

D. He had spaghetti with meatballs for lunch just before he disappeared.

69. Officer Latke has noticed that some types of crimes occur more frequently in certain areas and at certain times of day than others. He has noticed that most of the robberies take place on Henderson between 8th Street and 10th Street, most of the rapes occur on Front Street between Miller Avenue and Robidaux Place, and most of the larcenies happen on the block around Pushkin Park. Most of the robberies take place between 6:00 P.M. and 1:00 A.M., the rapes between 8:00 P.M. and 4:00 A.M., and the larcenies between 10:00 A.M. and 4:00 P.M. Most of the robberies take place on Fridays. Most of the rapes occur on Tuesdays and Saturdays, and most of the larcenies happen on Sundays.

    Given this information, which of the following patrol schedules would enable Officer Latke to most effectively reduce the number of larcenies?

    A. Pushkin Park area, Saturdays and Sundays, 9:30 A.M. to 6:00 P.M.

    B. Front Street between Miller Avenue and Robidaux Place, Sundays, 9:00 A.M. to 5:00 P.M.

    C. Pushkin Park area, Sundays and Mondays, 8:00 P.M. to 4:00 A.M.

    D. Front Street between Miller Avenue and Robidaux Place, Sundays, 9:00 P.M. to 5:00 A.M.

70. Based on the information in Question 69, which of the following patrol schedules would be most effective in reducing the number of rapes?

    A. Front Street between Miller Avenue and Robidaux Place, weekdays, 8:00 P.M. to 4:00 A.M.

    B. Henderson between 8th Street and 10th Street, Saturdays, 6:00 P.M. to 6:00 A.M.

    C. Front Street between Miller Avenue and Robidaux Place, Tuesdays and Saturdays, 7:00 P.M. to 7:00 A.M.

    D. Henderson between 8th Street and 10th Street, 7:00 A.M. to 5:00 P.M.

71. Officer Mandrake arrives at a residence where a burglary has been reported and gathers the following information:

Location: 600 Springdale Court
Time: between 6:00 P.M. and midnight, while victim was out
Crime: break-in, burglary
Victim: Frances Blackmore
Items Missing: TV and microwave oven
Suspect: unknown

Officer Mandrake is writing a report on the incident. Which of the following expresses the information most clearly and accurately?

A. At 600 Springdale Court a burglary reportedly occurred between 6:00 P.M. and midnight. The resident at that address is Frances Blackmore, who was out at the time. Reported missing are a TV and microwave oven. The suspect is unknown.

B. Frances Blackmore, of 600 Springdale Court, reported that between 6:00 P.M. and midnight, while she was out, an unknown suspect broke into her house and stole a TV.

C. Frances Blackmore reported that between 6:00 P.M. and midnight, while she was out, an unknown suspect broke into her home at 600 Springdale Court and stole a TV and a microwave oven.

D. An unknown suspect broke into the home of Frances Blackmore at 6:00 P.M. at the earliest and midnight at the latest, during which time Ms. Blackmore was out. A TV and a microwave oven were taken.

72. Officer Clemente reports to a public park where visitors have complained that a man exposed himself to their children. Officer Clemente gathers the following information:

Location:	Diamondback Park
Time:	11:00 A.M.
Crime:	indecent exposure
Victims:	several children whose parents witnessed the incident from a nearby picnic table
Suspect:	red-haired man wearing only a black raincoat
Location of Suspect:	drove out of the park in a yellow Camaro

Officer Clemente must prepare a preliminary report on the incident. Which of the following expresses the information most clearly and accurately?

A. At 11:00 A.M., a redhead exposed himself to several children whose parents witnessed the incident from a nearby picnic table. The man drove away in a yellow Camaro, wearing only a black raincoat.

B. At Diamondback Park at 11:00 A.M., a man reportedly exposed himself to several children whose parents witnessed the incident from a nearby picnic table. The suspect, who has red hair and is wearing only a black raincoat, drove out of the park in a yellow Camaro.

C. At Diamondback Park, several children were exposed to the nude body of a red-haired man in a black raincoat who fled in a yellow Camaro after exposing himself to them at 11:00 A.M. Several parents witnessed the incident from a nearby picnic table.

D. At Diamondback Park at 11:00 A.M., a man described as having red hair and wearing only a black raincoat exposed himself to several children whose parents witnessed the incident from a nearby picnic table.

73. Officer Sanjay is told to scour a section of crowded beach for an armed and dangerous male suspect. Unfortunately, no description of the suspect is available. Given the situation, Officer Sanjay should be least concerned about:

A. a man in a bikini swimsuit and sunglasses running along the beach.

B. a man laying on the sand in his underwear with a pile of clothes under his head.

C. a man dressed in jeans and a long-sleeved shirt walking in the surf.

D. a man in a suit climbing the stairs to a lifeguard tower.

74. In State X, a person is guilty of **HARASSMENT IN THE FIRST DEGREE** when he intentionally and repeatedly harasses another person by following such person or by engaging in a course of conduct or by repeatedly committing acts that place such person in reasonable fear of physical injury. Given this definition alone, which of the following is the best example of Harassment in the First Degree?

    A. Josh accompanies his girlfriend to school after a series of early morning rapes are reported along her route.

    B. Moira follows her ex-boyfriend to his chess club meetings several nights in a row then waits outside during his meetings, swinging a crowbar and yelling about his lack of loyalty.

    C. Trevor surprises his mother by picking her up from school five days in a row.

    D. One evening, Dale follows his father, whom he suspects is having an affair, to determine where he is going.

75. Officer Vasquez is dispatched to the scene of a collision between two taxis. He gathers the following information:

    Location: the intersection of Russet Lane and King Drive
    Time: 7:10 A.M.
    Incident: two taxis collided
    Drivers: Jackson Freeman and Peter Josephs
    Action Taken: both drivers were issued traffic tickets

    Officer Vasquez is writing his report on the incident. Which of the following expresses the information most clearly and accurately?

    A. At 7:10 A.M. at the intersection of Russet Lane and King Drive, two taxis collided. Both drivers, Jackson Freeman and Peter Josephs, were issued traffic tickets.

    B. Jackson Freeman and Peter Josephs were both issued traffic tickets shortly after their two taxis collided. The accident occurred at the intersection of Russet Lane and King Drive.

    C. At the intersection of Russet Lane and King Drive, a collision occurred. The two cars were both taxis, and the drivers, Jackson Freeman and Peter Josephs, were issued traffic tickets.

    D. Two taxis collided, driven by Jackson Freeman and Peter Josephs, at the intersection of Russet Lane and King Drive at 7:10 A.M. Both drivers, Mr. Freeman and Mr. Josephs, were given traffic tickets.

76. Officer Conroy is dispatched to a senior citizens' home where a man was found dead in his room. Officer Conroy gathers the following information:

Location:	Shady Acres
Time:	4:00 P.M.
Victim:	Anderson Savage
Status of Victim:	deceased for several hours, found in his room
Action Taken:	an ambulance took Mr. Savage's body to the hospital

Officer Conroy is writing his report. Which of the following expresses the information most clearly and accurately?

A. At 4:00 P.M. at Shady Acres, Anderson Savage died in his room several hours ago and was found. An ambulance took his body to the hospital.

B. At 4:00 P.M., Anderson Savage's body was found dead in his room at Shady Acres. He had been dead for several hours, and his body was taken to the hospital in an ambulance.

C. At 4:00 P.M. at Shady Acres, a body was found in Anderson Savage's room that had been dead for several hours. The body was identified as Anderson Savage and was taken by ambulance to the hospital.

D. At 4:00 P.M. at Shady Acres, Anderson Savage's body was found in his room. Mr. Savage had been dead for several hours. His body was taken by ambulance to the hospital.

To answer Questions 77, 78, and 79, use the information in the following passage.

At 11:30 P.M., while parked in front of 945 Garfield Avenue, Police Officers Nelson and Frame received a radio call of a family dispute at 779 Blossom Street, Apartment 428. The radio dispatcher informed the officers that the call came from Mrs. Debra Lacoste, who lives in Apartment 430. The officers arrived at the location; when they reached the fourth floor, they heard yelling and screaming. When the officers knocked on the door, a woman answered. She was wearing a blue skirt and a white blouse and was crying hysterically. The officers could hear kitchen cabinets being slammed and a man muttering.

The woman, Gloria Ross, informed the officers that her husband, Sam Ross, was in her apartment. They were in the process of getting divorced, and she had moved to her present apartment six months earlier. She said her husband had arrived at her door at about 10:30 P.M., drunk and demanding to see his children. She'd tried to get him to go home, but when he began yelling at her, she let him in, fearing her neighbors would be disturbed. Once inside, he'd again demanded to see the children. When she told him they were staying with her sister, he accused her of lying and threatened to hurt her if she did not let him see them. The argument had continued until the police arrived.

Mrs. Ross said she had an order of protection issued by Family Court, which stated that Mr. Ross was not to be seen anywhere near his wife, including her residence and place of employment. Mrs. Ross told the officer that she wanted her husband arrested for violating the order of protection. Officer Frame asked to see the order. While Mrs. Ross was retrieving it, Mr. Ross emerged from the kitchen. He was walking unsteadily and smelled of alcohol. He was wearing blue jeans and a polo shirt; there was a large stain on the shirt. He said his wife had invited him in, and he had a right to be there and a right to see his children. When Mrs. Ross returned, Officer Frame quickly read the order of protection and informed Officer Nelson that the order was valid. Officer Nelson ordered Sam Ross to turn around with his hands behind his back. Officer Nelson handcuffed him and placed him under arrest.

77. Which of the following persons first made the authorities aware of the domestic dispute?

    A. a neighbor
    B. the wife
    C. a child
    D. the dispatcher

78. Where did the police officers respond to a disturbance?

    A. 779 Blossom Street, Apt. 430
    B. 945 Garfield Avenue
    C. 779 Blossom Street, Apt. 428
    D. 430 Garfield Avenue

79. Why was Mr. Ross arrested?

    A. He was drunk, which indicated he was likely to do something foolish.
    B. He wasn't properly dressed, which showed he was losing control.
    C. He was disturbing the neighbors, which threatens the peace.
    D. He was at his wife's apartment, which violated a valid court order.

80. After stopping a suspect who fits the description of a man seen peering in windows at a college dormitory, Officer Hines should first:

    A. call campus security to let them know the man has been caught, so the students can relax.
    B. handcuff the man and take him to the precinct.
    C. escort the man to the dormitory to see if any witnesses can positively identify him.
    D. detain the man for questioning.

81. Observing a street fight that involves more than a dozen men brandishing broken bottles, Officer McCormick, who is armed but off duty, should first:

    A. identify herself and demand to speak with the two men who started the fight.
    B. call in, report the fight, and request backup.
    C. do nothing, as she is off duty.
    D. fire a warning shot from her pistol into the air to get the attention of the fighting men.

82. Officer Arias is dispatched to a department store where a fight between two customers has been reported. Officer Arias gathered the following information at the department store:

Location:	Herald's Department Store
Time:	4:30 P.M.
Incident:	fight between two customers
Customers Involved:	Harriet Snow and Lucinda Blake
Action Taken:	women were removed from the store

Officer Arias is writing a report on the incident. Which of the following expresses the information most clearly and accurately?

A. At 4:30 P.M. at Herald's Department Store, two customers were fighting. They were removed from the store. The customers were Harriet Snow and Lucinda Blake.

B. Two women customers, Harriet Snow and Lucinda Blake, were fighting at Herald's Department Store. They were removed from the store shortly after 4:30 P.M., when their fighting occurred.

C. At 4:30 P.M., a fight occurred between two Herald's Department Store customers, Harriet Snow and Lucinda Blake. The women were removed from the store.

D. Harriet Snow and Lucinda Blake were shopping at Herald's Department Store when they were removed from the store shortly after 4:30 P.M., which was when they were fighting.

83. In State X, a person is guilty of **ASSAULT IN THE THIRD DEGREE** when, with criminal negligence, he causes physical injury to another person by means of a deadly weapon or a dangerous instrument. **CRIMINAL NEGLIGENCE** is defined as the failure to perceive a substantial risk of such nature that failure to perceive it is a gross deviation from the care that a reasonable person would observe. Based solely upon these definitions, which of the following is not an example of Assault in the Third Degree?

A. Happy to have driven in the last of the stakes needed for his garden, Kenny throws his sledge hammer over his head into his neighbor's yard. The sledge hammer strikes his neighbor in the head and cracks the neighbor's skull.

B. Mrs. Isher fires pellets at birds nesting in the eaves of her house. A dead bird falls from the eaves onto the shoulder of a pedestrian, whose jacket is ruined by the bird's blood.

C. During recess at an elementary school near his house, Hank practices throwing his javelin. He misjudges the distance on one of his throws and impales a child with the javelin, severely injuring the child.

D. Attempting to catch an elusive fish in a rocky, shallow stream crowded by fishermen, Dack pulls his pistol from its holster and begins shooting at the fish. A bullet ricochets off a rock and pierces the thigh of one of the other fishermen.

84. Officer Lon answers a call to a school where a teacher reports that a new student is causing a disturbance by intermittently screaming, kicking, and yelling obscenities. Officer Lon ascertains from a bracelet on the student's arm that she has a medical condition that may be causing the outbursts. Officer Lon handcuffs the student to keep her still, speaks to her in soothing tones, and escorts her to the hospital.

    Officer Lon's actions were:

    A. bad, as the handcuffs were unwarranted and could have caused the student to injure herself.

    B. good, as the student needed medical attention as soon as possible.

    C. bad, as it is never an officer's responsibility to take sick people to the hospital.

    D. good, as the student was probably very upset until Officer Lon began to try to calm her down.

85. Darnell Ross, a student at Fillmore School for Boys, decides to organize a protest against the school's uniform policy. He holds a meeting in the school's library, which is open to the public. During the meeting, he and nine other students become louder than what is normally tolerated by the librarian. When the librarian asks the students to be quiet, Darnell calls for the students to throw books at her, which they do.

    If State X defines **INCITING TO RIOT** as the urging of ten or more persons to engage in tumultuous and violent conduct of a kind likely to create public alarm, which of the following is true?

    A. Because he was only urging nine people, Darnell should not be charged with Inciting to Riot.

    B. Because the library is open to the public, Darnell should be charged with Inciting to Riot.

    C. Because, including Darnell, there were ten people involved in violent conduct, Darnell should be charged with Inciting to Riot.

    D. Only the students who threw books at the librarian should be charged with Inciting to Riot.

86. Officer Drew answered a call to a high-rise apartment building where Harry Polk, a resident, was attacked in the building's elevator by someone who ran through the lobby and out onto the street when the elevator reached the ground floor. Officer Drew proceeded to interview witnesses in the lobby and on the street outside the apartment building. Of the following descriptions of the suspect given by the witnesses, which should Officer Drew consider most likely to be accurate?

    A. female, just over five feet tall, wearing coveralls and a ski mask

    B. female, about six feet tall, wearing coveralls and a ski mask

    C. male, about six feet tall, wearing coveralls and nylons over his face

    D. male, about six feet tall, wearing jeans, a shirt, and a ski mask

87. Officer Brown responds to a call from a man who is stuck on his roof. He gathers the following information:

Location: 17 Smith Lane
Resident: Mr. Waters
Situation: Mr. Waters, home alone, was stuck on his roof after his ladder fell
Caller: Mr. Waters used his cellular phone
Action Taken: ladder was replaced, Mr. Waters safely climbed down

Officer Brown is writing his report. Which of the following expresses the information most clearly and accurately?

A. At 17 Smith Lane, Mr. Waters used his cellular phone to call the police after his ladder fell, leaving him stuck on his roof. He was home alone. The ladder was replaced, and then Mr. Waters, who was no longer stuck, safely climbed down.

B. Mr. Waters, who lives at 17 Smith Lane, was stuck on his roof when his ladder fell. He was home alone and safely climbed down when his ladder was replaced after he used his cellular phone to call the police.

C. Mr. Waters was stuck on his roof at 17 Smith Lane after his ladder fell. He was home alone, so he used his cellular phone to contact the police. His ladder was replaced, and he safely climbed down.

D. Mr. Waters was helped safely down his ladder after it was replaced at his home at 17 Smith Lane. Mr. Waters was on his roof when his ladder fell, and was home alone, but used his cellular phone to call the police.

88. Officer Sherri Handley is asked to remove any dangerous jewelry or other accessories from a female witness who is experiencing major drug withdrawal and who may present a danger to herself. Of the following accessories, which should Officer Handley be least concerned about?

A. a pair of shoes with six-inch spike heels
B. a plastic watch
C. a butterfly lapel pin
D. a rope belt

89. A large number of robberies have occurred in recent weeks near an amusement park. All the robberies have been committed by women. Officer Weiss has been instructed to watch for suspicious behavior as he patrols the area around the amusement park. Which of the following people should Officer Weiss watch most closely?

A. a woman sneaking into a pay-toilet by sliding under the door
B. a teenage boy asking strangers for change
C. a man sleeping in the back of a truck in the amusement park's parking lot
D. a woman crouching between cars in the amusement park's parking lot

90. Officer Dillon responds to an anonymous report of an unattended dog at a school playground. He gathers the following information:

Location: Peabody School playground
Time: 3:00 P.M.
Caller: anonymous
Complaint: unattended dog
Action Taken: a dog was unattended and wandering around the playground; Animal Control notified

Officer Dillon must write his report. Which of the following expresses the information most clearly and accurately?

A. At the Peabody School playground at 3:00 P.M., there was an anonymous person who reported an unattended dog. The dog was unattended.

B. A 3:00 P.M. anonymous report of an unattended dog at the Peabody School playground turned out to be correct, and Animal Control was notified after the dog's presence on the playground was verified.

C. At 3:00 P.M., an unattended dog at the Peabody School playground was reported by an anonymous caller. The dog was found wandering in the school playground, and Animal Control was notified.

D. Animal Control was notified after an anonymous report of an unattended dog at the Peabody School playground was verified.

PRACTICE TEST 1 ANSWER KEY

1. B	26. C	51. D	76. D
2. A	27. C	52. D	77. A
3. A	28. B	53. D	78. C
4. B	29. A	54. B	79. D
5. C	30. A	55. D	80. D
6. C	31. C	56. A	81. B
7. A	32. A	57. D	82. C
8. D	33. B	58. A	83. B
9. B	34. C	59. A	84. A
10. B	35. C	60. C	85. A
11. A	36. C	61. C	86. B
12. C	37. B	62. A	87. C
13. D	38. C	63. D	88. B
14. C	39. D	64. A	89. D
15. B	40. A	65. B	90. C
16. C	41. C	66. C	
17. B	42. B	67. C	
18. B	43. B	68. D	
19. B	44. B	69. A	
20. C	45. C	70. C	
21. C	46. B	71. C	
22. D	47. A	72. B	
23. A	48. B	73. A	
24. A	49. A	74. B	
25. C	50. D	75. A	

PRACTICE TEST 1 ANSWERS AND EXPLANATIONS

1. There is information missing from every statement except **B**, which is correct.

2. **A** is correct, as it is most clearly stated. Note that the phrase "on foot" is missing from D.

3. **A** is the best answer, because Carla Jones has not used a credit card that she "knows to be revoked or canceled."

4. **B** is correct. Because the young man is unconscious, the least logical action for Officer Starks to take next is to read him his rights.

5. **C** is the clearest and most accurate statement

6. **C** is correct. There is information missing from B and D, and A is poorly written.

7. **A** contains the most repeaters. Note that the phrases "brown leather" and "black leather" each appear twice, canceling each other out, so neither can be used to eliminate any descriptions. The number and color of the suitcase's stripes and buckles are the keys to eliminating descriptions here.

8. There is information missing from A, B, and C, so **D** is correct.

9. **B** is correct. In every other instance, the person has the right to alter the computer data in question. Only Jacob Johns, who "gains access to his bank's computer system and adds $100 to his checking account," has acted without the right to do so.

10. **B** contains the most repeaters.

11. **A** is the clearest statement. The order of the wording in the other statements is confusing, and information is missing from B and D.

12. **C** contains the most repeaters. Note that the phrases "white male" and "black male" each appear twice, canceling each other out, so neither can be used to eliminate any descriptions. This is also the case for the descriptions of the color of the suspect's outer layer of clothing. The phrases to watch are those describing the suspect's height, type of outer layer ("robe" or "blazer"), and the color of his pajamas.

13. **D** is the clearest and most accurate statement. Note that the name of the suspect is missing from choice B.

14. **C** contains the most repeaters. Note that the phrase "cream-colored" is a repeater, appearing in two of the descriptions of the truck's color, while "light green" (A) and "white" (D) each appear only once. This means that, after B has been eliminated because of its inclusion of "Dodge" (the repeater "Ford" appears in the other three descriptions), A and D can be eliminated.

15. **B** is the clearest and most accurate statement. A and D are awkwardly worded, and there is information missing from C (the fact that the twins drove off on a motorcycle).

16. **C** is the best answer, as it is the only situation in which a person "intentionally or recklessly engages in conduct that creates a substantial risk of physical injury" to another person. Note that, while the "guided white-water rafting excursion" (A) could be dangerous, it is not as dangerous as a "rum-guzzling contest" (C). The same holds true for the "trip to the beach" (B) and the "cigar-smoking room" (D).

17. **B** is the clearest and most accurate statement.

18. **B** contains the most repeaters. Note that there is no true repeater among the phrases describing the suspect's height, but the height (5'11") in D is very different from those in A (5'1"), B (5'2"), and C (5'3"), so D can be immediately eliminated.

19. **B** is the clearest and most accurate statement. Note, in D, the awkwardness of the phrase "with which, along with the gun, he was later found, and which contained $50 and credit cards."

20. The only situation in which someone does not intentionally cause or aid "another person to attempt suicide" is **C**. Sue Ann could not have known that her father would use the gun to shoot himself, rather than to "shoot nuisance pigeons." In each of the other three situations, the individual has reason to believe that the person he or she is helping or instructing will commit suicide.

21. A and D are unclear, and there is information missing from A and B (Mr. Harris's address), so **C** is correct.

22. **D** is the best answer. The young man could be trying to get into the trunk of his own car. It is inadvisable for Officer Floyd to take any action other than approaching and questioning the young man about his activities without first getting more information.

23. **A** is the most logical assumption, given the young man's behavior. There is no information to suggest that any of the other three assumptions might be valid.

24. **A** is the only example of a person appearing "in a public place under the influence of narcotics or a drug other than alcohol" who endangers or annoys anyone. Jim (B) and Letitia (D) have been drinking, so their activities in public do not constitute a violation of the defined law. P.J. (C) is at home, so his activities are not a violation of the defined law either.

25. **C** is most logical answer. Teenagers attempting to stay out later than allowed under the curfew would be most likely to go to the movie theater, where they might not be questioned about their age and where large numbers of them could get together.

26. **C** is the clearest and most accurate statement.

27. **C** is the best answer. Note that the statement in B ("Ronnie Fielding could cause more damage to personal property if a concentrated effort to apprehend him is not made") is based on the presumption that Ronnie Fielding is guilty; all suspects are presumed innocent until proven guilty in our criminal justice system.

28. **B** is correct. Armand is not guilty as charged because he was alone, and the definition indicates that a person must loiter or remain in any place "with one or more persons" for the purpose of using drugs in order for that person to be guilty.

29. **A** is correct. Note that there is information missing from B, C, and D.

30. The first thing an officer should do in such a situation is call in, so **A** is correct. An officer should call in rather than take action on his or her own without alerting the department to a potentially dangerous situation. Instructions as to how to proceed will come from a supervisor.

31. **C** contains the most repeaters. Note that in this question, both of the phrases that are used to describe the suspect's skin tone, "light-skinned" (A and C) and "dark-skinned" (B and D), appear twice. Thus, they effectively cancel each other out, so no eliminations can be made based on the repetition of those phrases.

32. **A** is the clearest and most accurate statement.

33. **B** is the best answer. While it is true that officers have a degree of discretion when it comes to issuing traffic tickets, they do not have "a certain amount of flexibility in protecting those close to them from fines and prosecution," as is inaccurately stated in A. Also, note the words "all" and "always" in D. These should serve as warning signals that the statement in which they are included might be either exaggerated or incorrect.

34. **C** is the only logical answer. B is particularly absurd and irrelevant, as an officer should not let his or her personal feelings affect his or her judgment.

35. The only example of Sports Bribe Receiving is given in **C**. Since Johnny (A) refuses the offer, he has not committed a crime. And it is obvious that neither Sven (B) nor Sylvia (D) has committed a crime.

36. A and B are unclear, and there is information missing from D, so **C** is correct.

37. **B** contains the most repeaters.

38. **C** is the best answer. Note that, while the "van circling the neighborhood" (B) is suspicious, officers should be most concerned about "a pair of men…shining flashlights onto the fire escape" (C).

39. A and C are unclear, and there is information missing from B (the time), so **D** is correct.

40. **A** makes the most sense of the four answers. Police officers definitely have jurisdiction over what happens on private property, so B includes an incorrect statement. The other answers are illogical.

41. **C** is correct. Although the diamond ring was originally included on the list of stolen items, it was later found, so its value is not included in the total.

42. A and C are unclear, and there is information missing from D, so **B** is correct.

43. **B** is the best answer. Since he "drives in circles around the parking lot of the church with his stereo blaring and his windows down," Greg's behavior is the best example of Aggravated Disorderly Conduct. The other individuals are displaying appropriate and perfectly legal emotion.

44. Without a doubt, Officer Sandoval's actions are "bad, because his actions might have endangered the lives of innocent people," so the answer is **B**. While D is partially correct, as Officer Sandoval's actions are definitely bad, the reason is not that he "clearly had a better shot at the left rear tire."

45. **C** contains the most repeaters. Note that in this case, the words "thin" and "heavyset" as well as the words "tall" and "short" each appear twice, so they cancel each other out even though they are repeaters. The only phrases that allow for elimination are those describing the suspect's clothing and shoes.

46. A is unclear, and there is information missing from C and D (the time), so **B** is correct.

47. Officer Mitchell should "call in to report the situation," so the correct answer is **A**. An officer should call in rather than take action on his or her own without alerting the department to a potentially dangerous situation. Instructions as to how to proceed will come from a supervisor.

48. **B** is the best answer. Joanie runs from the officer after she has been arrested. According to the definition given, none of the individuals in the other situations are in custody, so none of them could attempt to escape from custody.

49. **A** is the best answer. Since fires spread quickly, the fire department always needs as much time as possible to fight them.

50. There is information missing from every statement except **D**, which is correct.

51. **D** is correct. Josie Farmer is the only one of the four drivers whose actions present an immediate danger to others.

52. **D** contains the most repeaters. Note that the phrase "with black stripes" in C is unimportant to the process of elimination; the phrase "short-sleeved" allows C to be eliminated, since the shirt is described as "sleeveless" in A, B, and D.

53. **D** is correct. The other three questions are much more pertinent to the crime that has been committed. While Officer Kaurismaki could conceivably ask the principal a question about his career and experience, he would be much more likely to ask questions like A, B, and C.

54. **B** is correct. Miniature knives could be used to "endanger the safety" of someone in the facility, so the collection should be considered dangerous contraband. Since Samantha "introduces" the contraband and Dick "obtains" and "possesses" the contraband, both Samantha and Dick should be charged.

55. **D** is the clearest and most accurate statement.

56. **A** is the only logical answer. Note that the key word in this question is "first"; calling in to the precinct is the best first step for an officer to take. Also note that the other three answers do not present logical steps for the officer to take at all, in any order.

57. **D** is the best answer. The officers should not "draw their guns" (A), because the boys do not present an immediate danger. They should not call for backup "from juvenile court" (B) because a court does not provide backup, a police department does. And C, while presenting a good way for the officers to remove that particular girl from danger, does not offer them the opportunity to prevent the boys from harming anyone else.

58. **A** is the best answer, as it includes the only situation in which someone attempts to prevent an officer from "effecting an authorized arrest."

59. **A** is correct, as observing the man would be the most logical action for Officer Reynolds to take. There is not enough evidence to arrest the man (B). Note that "pulling his gun" (C) would be unnecessary and illogical in this situation, as there is no immediate danger.

60. There is information missing from every statement except **C**, which is correct.

61. **C** contains the most repeaters. Note that the number "1501" is a repeater, appearing in two of the descriptions of the tag number, while "1587" and "1509" each appear only once. This means that each of the four digits in "1501" is more likely to be correct than any differing digit in "1587" or "1509."

62. The officer should do everything he can to save the man's life, so **A** is correct. Any delay could cost the man his life.

63. The most suspicious vehicle is the "unmarked van with no side or rear windows," so the correct answer is **D**. Note that, while the "florist's van with no side or rear windows" (A) is suspicious, it is less suspicious than the unmarked van, particularly with regard to the type of crime to which Captain Dryden's warning pertains.

64. **A** is correct. There is information missing from B and C, and D is unclear; note that in C, in addition to the unclear wording, the children's ages have been reversed.

65. **B** is the best answer. An officer should always be more concerned about preventing crime and protecting citizens than he or she is about having "a weak case" (A). C and D imply that an officer's ego should be a factor in his or her decisions, which is untrue.

66. **C** is correct. None of the other individuals "unlawfully possesses or sells" a hypodermic instrument.

67. There is information missing from A and B, and D is unclear, so **C** is correct.

68. The most important information would pertain to the missing man's appearance and location, so **D** is the correct answer. Knowing what the man had for lunch would not be of immediate use to Officer Ortega.

69. **A** is correct. Most larcenies occur on the block around Pushkin Park on Sundays between 10:00 A.M. and 4:00 P.M., and the patrol schedule given in A is the only one of the four that provides coverage of that area on that day of the week at those times. Note that the patrol schedule given in C would work if the hours were 8:00 A.M. to 4:00 P.M. It is important to pay attention to whether a given time is A.M. or P.M.

70. **C** is correct. Most rapes occur on Front Street between Miller Avenue and Robidaux Place on Tuesdays and Saturdays between 8:00 P.M. and 4:00 A.M., and the patrol schedule given in C is the only one of the four that provides coverage of that area on those days of the week at those times. Note that A is incorrect because the patrol schedule does not include Saturdays.

71. A is unclear, and there is information missing from B and D, so **C** is correct.

72. There is information missing from A and D, and C is unclear, so **B** is correct.

73. The "man in a bikini swimsuit and sunglasses running along the beach" is the only one of the four possible suspects who could not possibly be armed and dangerous, so the answer is **A**.

74. **B** is the best answer, because Moira, in addition to following him, repeatedly commits acts that place her ex-boyfriend "in reasonable fear of physical injury." Note that in D, Dale only follows his father once and does not threaten him physically, so D is incorrect.

75. There is information missing from B and C, and D is unclear, so **A** is correct.

76. **D** is the clearest and most accurate statement.

77. **A** is correct. Note that although the dispatcher notified the officers, the dispatcher is a member of "the authorities."

78. **C** is correct. Apartment 430 is the neighbor's.

79. **D** is correct. Mr. Ross is indeed drunk and badly dressed, but these are not crimes. While disturbing the neighbors could be an offense, violating a court order is the more serious charge and should be addressed first.

80. Officer Hines should "detain the man for questioning," so the answer is **D**. Alerting "campus security to let them know the man has been caught" (A) would be grossly premature and unwise, as it presumes that the man is definitely the suspect, which is uncertain at this point. By the same token, there is not enough evidence for Officer Hines to "handcuff the man and take him to the precinct," so B is incorrect. C is entirely illogical. Witnesses are asked to identify suspects in lineups, where there are certain controls in place to decrease the chances that witnesses will be influenced into identifying the wrong person.

81. **B** is correct. An officer should call in rather than take action on his or her own without alerting the department to a potentially dangerous situation. Instructions as to how to proceed will come from a supervisor. Note that firing a "warning shot… to get the attention of the fighting men" (D) is unwarranted and could be dangerous.

82. **C** is the clearest and most accurate statement.

83. **B** is correct because, while the pedestrian's jacket may be ruined, the pedestrian did not suffer "physical injury."

84. **A** is correct. If the girl's behavior had necessitated some sort of restraints, handcuffs should not have been used; rather, an ambulance should have been called to take her to the hospital. The other three possible answers include incorrect statements, such as "it is never an officer's responsibility to take sick people to the hospital" (C). Often, police officers are required to do just that, if an ambulance is not readily available and the person requiring treatment needs that treatment immediately. Note the word "never" in that statement; this type of word should serve as a warning signal that the statement in which it is included might be either exaggerated or incorrect.

85. **A** is correct. The definition stipulates that someone must urge "ten or more persons" to engage in the type of activities prohibited by the defined law, and Darnell only urges nine. Location is not taken into consideration in the law so B is incorrect. Darnell would not be counted as one of the persons urged, so C is incorrect. And D is entirely illogical.

86. **B** contains the most repeaters. Note that the words "female" and "male" each appear twice, canceling each other out, so neither can be used to eliminate any descriptions.

87. **C** is the clearest and most accurate statement.

88. **B**, the "plastic watch," is correct. All the other items listed could be used to cause injury.

89. The "woman crouching between cars in the amusement park's parking lot" is the only one of the four people who fits the profile of the robber or robbers, so **D** is the best answer. Note that, while the "woman sneaking into a pay-toilet by sliding under the door" (A) is committing a crime, her activities should be of much less significance to Officer Weiss, whose attentions are focused on watching for at least one potentially dangerous felon.

90. There is information missing from A and D, and B is unclear, so **C** is correct.

Practice Test 2

ANSWER SHEET FOR PRACTICE TEST 2

For each question, select the best answer choice. Use the answer sheet to mark your choices. Answers and explanations follow the test.

1. Ⓐ Ⓑ Ⓒ Ⓓ   26. Ⓐ Ⓑ Ⓒ Ⓓ   51. Ⓐ Ⓑ Ⓒ Ⓓ   76. Ⓐ Ⓑ Ⓒ Ⓓ

2. Ⓐ Ⓑ Ⓒ Ⓓ   27. Ⓐ Ⓑ Ⓒ Ⓓ   52. Ⓐ Ⓑ Ⓒ Ⓓ   77. Ⓐ Ⓑ Ⓒ Ⓓ

3. Ⓐ Ⓑ Ⓒ Ⓓ   28. Ⓐ Ⓑ Ⓒ Ⓓ   53. Ⓐ Ⓑ Ⓒ Ⓓ   78. Ⓐ Ⓑ Ⓒ Ⓓ

4. Ⓐ Ⓑ Ⓒ Ⓓ   29. Ⓐ Ⓑ Ⓒ Ⓓ   54. Ⓐ Ⓑ Ⓒ Ⓓ   79. Ⓐ Ⓑ Ⓒ Ⓓ

5. Ⓐ Ⓑ Ⓒ Ⓓ   30. Ⓐ Ⓑ Ⓒ Ⓓ   55. Ⓐ Ⓑ Ⓒ Ⓓ   80. Ⓐ Ⓑ Ⓒ Ⓓ

6. Ⓐ Ⓑ Ⓒ Ⓓ   31. Ⓐ Ⓑ Ⓒ Ⓓ   56. Ⓐ Ⓑ Ⓒ Ⓓ   81. Ⓐ Ⓑ Ⓒ Ⓓ

7. Ⓐ Ⓑ Ⓒ Ⓓ   32. Ⓐ Ⓑ Ⓒ Ⓓ   57. Ⓐ Ⓑ Ⓒ Ⓓ   82. Ⓐ Ⓑ Ⓒ Ⓓ

8. Ⓐ Ⓑ Ⓒ Ⓓ   33. Ⓐ Ⓑ Ⓒ Ⓓ   58. Ⓐ Ⓑ Ⓒ Ⓓ   83. Ⓐ Ⓑ Ⓒ Ⓓ

9. Ⓐ Ⓑ Ⓒ Ⓓ   34. Ⓐ Ⓑ Ⓒ Ⓓ   59. Ⓐ Ⓑ Ⓒ Ⓓ   84. Ⓐ Ⓑ Ⓒ Ⓓ

10. Ⓐ Ⓑ Ⓒ Ⓓ   35. Ⓐ Ⓑ Ⓒ Ⓓ   60. Ⓐ Ⓑ Ⓒ Ⓓ   85. Ⓐ Ⓑ Ⓒ Ⓓ

11. Ⓐ Ⓑ Ⓒ Ⓓ   36. Ⓐ Ⓑ Ⓒ Ⓓ   61. Ⓐ Ⓑ Ⓒ Ⓓ   86. Ⓐ Ⓑ Ⓒ Ⓓ

12. Ⓐ Ⓑ Ⓒ Ⓓ   37. Ⓐ Ⓑ Ⓒ Ⓓ   62. Ⓐ Ⓑ Ⓒ Ⓓ   87. Ⓐ Ⓑ Ⓒ Ⓓ

13. Ⓐ Ⓑ Ⓒ Ⓓ   38. Ⓐ Ⓑ Ⓒ Ⓓ   63. Ⓐ Ⓑ Ⓒ Ⓓ   88. Ⓐ Ⓑ Ⓒ Ⓓ

14. Ⓐ Ⓑ Ⓒ Ⓓ   39. Ⓐ Ⓑ Ⓒ Ⓓ   64. Ⓐ Ⓑ Ⓒ Ⓓ   89. Ⓐ Ⓑ Ⓒ Ⓓ

15. Ⓐ Ⓑ Ⓒ Ⓓ   40. Ⓐ Ⓑ Ⓒ Ⓓ   65. Ⓐ Ⓑ Ⓒ Ⓓ   90. Ⓐ Ⓑ Ⓒ Ⓓ

16. Ⓐ Ⓑ Ⓒ Ⓓ   41. Ⓐ Ⓑ Ⓒ Ⓓ   66. Ⓐ Ⓑ Ⓒ Ⓓ

17. Ⓐ Ⓑ Ⓒ Ⓓ   42. Ⓐ Ⓑ Ⓒ Ⓓ   67. Ⓐ Ⓑ Ⓒ Ⓓ

18. Ⓐ Ⓑ Ⓒ Ⓓ   43. Ⓐ Ⓑ Ⓒ Ⓓ   68. Ⓐ Ⓑ Ⓒ Ⓓ

19. Ⓐ Ⓑ Ⓒ Ⓓ   44. Ⓐ Ⓑ Ⓒ Ⓓ   69. Ⓐ Ⓑ Ⓒ Ⓓ

20. Ⓐ Ⓑ Ⓒ Ⓓ   45. Ⓐ Ⓑ Ⓒ Ⓓ   70. Ⓐ Ⓑ Ⓒ Ⓓ

21. Ⓐ Ⓑ Ⓒ Ⓓ   46. Ⓐ Ⓑ Ⓒ Ⓓ   71. Ⓐ Ⓑ Ⓒ Ⓓ

22. Ⓐ Ⓑ Ⓒ Ⓓ   47. Ⓐ Ⓑ Ⓒ Ⓓ   72. Ⓐ Ⓑ Ⓒ Ⓓ

23. Ⓐ Ⓑ Ⓒ Ⓓ   48. Ⓐ Ⓑ Ⓒ Ⓓ   73. Ⓐ Ⓑ Ⓒ Ⓓ

24. Ⓐ Ⓑ Ⓒ Ⓓ   49. Ⓐ Ⓑ Ⓒ Ⓓ   74. Ⓐ Ⓑ Ⓒ Ⓓ

25. Ⓐ Ⓑ Ⓒ Ⓓ   50. Ⓐ Ⓑ Ⓒ Ⓓ   75. Ⓐ Ⓑ Ⓒ Ⓓ

1. Officer Yang is dispatched to a battery plant where a man has reportedly been beaten. Officer Yang gathers the following information:

Location:	Acid Batteries, 1010 Fletcher Street
Time:	10:00 A.M.
Crime:	assault
Victim:	Mike Ziegler, employee
Suspect:	Dave Finley, supervisor
Status of Suspect:	confessed, was arrested, and is in custody

   Officer Yang must prepare an initial report on the incident. Which of the following expresses the information most clearly and accurately?

   A. Mike Ziegler reported that at 10:00 A.M. at Acid Batteries, which is located at 1010 Fletcher Street and at which Mr. Ziegler is an employee, he was beaten by Dave Finley, his supervisor. Mr. Finley confessed, was arrested, and is in custody.

   B. At 10:00 A.M., at the location of Acid Batteries, which is at 1010 Fletcher Street, a supervisor, Dave Finley, beat up an employee, Mike Ziegler. Mr. Finley is in custody.

   C. Mike Ziegler, an employee of Acid Batteries, was beaten at 10:00 A.M. at the location of Acid Batteries at 1010 Fletcher Street by his supervisor. The supervisor confessed and was arrested.

   D. Dave Finley, a supervisor at Acid Batteries at 1010 Fletcher Street, beat an employee at Acid Batteries at 10:00 A.M. Mr. Finley confessed. Mr. Finley was arrested and is in custody.

2. In Normaltown, noise pollution and excessive noise, especially between midnight and 6:00 A.M., are strictly regulated by city ordinances. Normaltown Officer Jimmy Juarez answers a call to a row house where Harry Robb, a resident, complains that his next-door neighbor, Benny Gold, is loudly playing an electric guitar at 1:00 A.M. Officer Juarez instructs Mr. Gold to put the guitar away until morning, and Mr. Gold apologizes and agrees to follow Officer Juarez's instructions. Officer Juarez circles the block then parks on the street next to the row house. He hears guitar-playing coming from Mr. Gold's apartment windows. What should Officer Juarez do?

   A. visit Mr. Gold again and ask him to close his windows

   B. determine that it is Mr. Gold's guitar that he hears and then arrest Mr. Gold

   C. call Mr. Robb and ask him if the guitar-playing is bothering him, since it may seem louder from the street

   D. issue a second warning to Mr. Gold and indicate that if a third visit is warranted he will be arrested

3. Officer Evans responds to a call from a woman who complains about the noise her neighbor is making. He gathers the following information:

Location:	775 Bucket Street
Time:	2:30 A.M.
Complaint:	late-night lawn-mowing is creating too much noise
Person Making Complaint:	Ruby Fields
Person Mowing Lawn:	Hiram Stanley, Mrs. Fields's neighbor
Action Taken:	Mr. Stanley was asked to mow his lawn during daylight hours; he complied

Officer Evans must write a report on the incident. Which of the following expresses the information most clearly and accurately?

A. At 2:30 A.M., Mrs. Ruby Fields of 775 Bucket Street reported that her neighbor, Mr. Hiram Stanley, was mowing his lawn, which created too much noise. Mr. Stanley was asked to mow his lawn during daylight hours, and he complied.

B. Mr. Hiram Stanley decided to mow his lawn at 2:30 A.M., disturbing his neighbor, Mrs. Ruby Fields, who called the police to complain about the noise coming from the mower. Mr. Stanley will now mow his lawn during daylight hours, as he was instructed by police.

C. At 775 Bucket Street, Mrs. Ruby Fields was kept awake by too much noise from Mr. Hiram Stanley's lawn mower, which he was using at 2:30 A.M. He was instructed to mow during daylight hours.

D. Mrs. Ruby Fields stated that her neighbor, Mr. Hiram Stanley, was mowing his lawn at 2:30 A.M. and was making too much noise. Mr. Stanley was asked to mow during daylight hours, and complied.

4. In State X, a person is guilty of **PETIT LARCENY** when he steals property. Given this definition alone, which of the following is the best example of Petit Larceny?

A. Jason borrows his father's lawn mower and forgets to return it.

B. Leaving a meeting, Alejandro mistakes another man's briefcase for his own and takes it.

C. At a coworker's party, Fred slips a crystal ashtray into his pocket and takes it home.

D. Merle uses the last of the lipstick in a sample tube at her local drugstore.

5. During the summer, three robberies have occurred near a local mall. The suspect for the first robbery is described as male, black, 5'2" and 200 pounds, with a graying beard and mustache and a parrot tattoo on his left forearm. The suspect for the second robbery is described as male, black, 5'1" and 180 pounds, with a graying mustache and only four fingers on his left hand. The suspect for the third robbery is described as male, black, 5'10" and 185 pounds, with a graying beard and mustache and no visible tattoos or markings.

Over Labor Day weekend, Officer Verrick arrests a man after witnessing the man commit a robbery. The man is black, 5'11" and 190 pounds, with a graying mustache and no visible tattoos or markings. In addition to the crime for which he was arrested, for which of the following should Officer Verrick and other investigating officers consider the man a suspect?

A. the first robbery only

B. the first, second, and third robberies

C. the second and third robberies only

D. the third robbery only

6. Four-year-old Jeffrey Langhorne was reported missing by his parents. Officers Kerchner and Semel, in the course of investigating Jeffrey's disappearance, interviewed several people who saw him get into a vehicle just a few hours before he was reported missing. Of the following descriptions of the vehicle given by the witnesses, which should Officers Kerchner and Semel consider most likely to be accurate?

A. red truck, tag number JG 1702

B. navy blue truck, tag number JC 1703

C. red truck, tag number JC 1702

D. red truck, tag number JD 1751

7. Officer Marino responds to a call from a stranded motorist and gathers the following information:

Location:	intersection of Juno and Hidalgo Streets
Time:	7:15 A.M.
Incident:	stranded motorist
Problem:	car stalled and would not restart
Motorist:	Greta Bailey
Action Taken:	drove Ms. Bailey to her husband's office

    Officer Marino must write a report on the incident. Which of the following expresses the information most clearly and accurately?

    A. At 7:15 A.M., a woman became stranded in her car when it would not start after stalling. Her name is Greta Bailey, and she was driven to her husband's office.

    B. At the intersection of Juno and Hidalgo Streets, Greta Bailey's car stalled and would not restart. She was driven to her husband's office shortly after her car problems began at 7:15 A.M.

    C. At 7:15 A.M., Greta Bailey was stranded at the intersection of Juno and Hidalgo Streets when her car stalled and would not restart. She was driven to her husband's office by Officer Marino.

    D. The best idea was to drive Greta Bailey to her husband's office after her car stalled and would not restart at 7:15 A.M. at the intersection of Juno and Hidalgo Streets, so that was the plan Officer Marino executed.

8. The stop sign on the corner of Front Street and Third Avenue was broken off by a driver who sped off after hitting the sign. Witnesses gave the following descriptions of the vehicle to Officer Plummens. Which of the descriptions should Officer Plummens consider most likely to be correct?

    A. white Chevy Blazer, with gold rims and purple fog lights

    B. white Ford Explorer, with silver rims and blue fog lights

    C. light blue Chevy Blazer, with silver rims and purple fog lights

    D. white Ford Explorer, with silver rims and purple fog lights

9. Officer Pierre arrives at the scene of a collision between two bicycles and gathers the following information:

Location: intersection of Second Street and University Drive
Time: 2:15 P.M.
Incident: bicycle collision
Riders: Sam Collins and Steve Black
Action Taken: both riders were taken by ambulance to the hospital

Officer Pierre is writing his report. Which of the following expresses the information most clearly and accurately?

A. Sam Collins and Steve Black were both taken by ambulance to the hospital after colliding with each other on bicycles at the intersection of Second Street and University Drive.

B. At the intersection of Second Street and University Drive, two bikers, riding bicycles, Sam Collins and Steve Black, collided and were taken to the hospital in ambulances shortly after the collision occurred at 2:15 P.M.

C. At 2:15 P.M. at the intersection of Second Street and University Drive, two bicycles collided. The riders, Sam Collins and Steve Black, were both taken by ambulance to the hospital.

D. Ambulances took both riders, Sam Collins and Steve Black, to the hospital after they collided on their bikes at 2:15 P.M.

10. Over three weeks, three rapes have occurred in Fairfield. The suspect in the first rape is described as male, black, 5'9" and 180 pounds, with a receding hairline and pockmarks on his throat. The suspect in the second rape is described as male, black, 5'3" and 185 pounds, with excessive chest hair and long fingernails. The suspect in the third rape is described as male, black, 5'10" and 190 pounds, with a receding hairline and a full beard.

A fourth rape occurs, and a suspect is arrested. He is male, black, 5'10" and 185 pounds, with a receding hairline, a hairy chest, and pock marks on his throat. In addition to the rape for which he was arrested, for which of the following should the investigating officers consider the man in custody a suspect?

A. the first rape only
B. the first and third rapes only
C. the second and third rapes only
D. the third rape only

11. Officer Terry responds to a call from a woman who reports that she heard gunshots near her house. Officer Terry gathers the following information:

Location: 809 Heard Street
Time: 8:15 P.M.
Occurrence: gunshots heard
Reported by: Mrs. Sandra Stephens
Action Taken: several patrols of the area turned up nothing

Officer Terry is writing her report about the incident. Which of the following expresses the information most clearly and accurately?

A. At 8:15 P.M., Mrs. Sandra Stephens heard gunshots near her home at 809 Heard Street. Several patrols of the area turned up nothing. The patrols took place after police arrived at her home.

B. Mrs. Sandra Stephens, of 809 Heard Street, stated that there were gunshots near her home at 8:15 P.M. Nothing turned up.

C. Mrs. Sandra Stephens reported that at 8:15 P.M., she heard gunshots near her home at 809 Heard Street. Several patrols of the area turned up nothing.

D. At 809 Heard Street at 8:15 P.M., there were gunshots that were reported by the resident, Mrs. Sandra Stephens. Several patrols were done in the neighborhood, turning up nothing.

12. A man whom Officer Hidalgo is arresting for driving under the influence of alcohol claims to be the mayor's nephew. What should Officer Hidalgo do?

A. escort the man home safely, since his uncle is the mayor

B. call the precinct to make sure the man is actually the mayor's nephew, and escort him home only after this has been verified

C. arrest the man and take him to the precinct, as he should not be given preferential treatment

D. agree to let the man go but only on the condition that he get counseling for his drinking

13. In State X, a person is guilty of **CRIMINAL SOLICITATION IN THE FIFTH DEGREE** when, with intent that another person engage in conduct constituting a misdemeanor, he requests or otherwise attempts to cause such other person to engage in such conduct. A person is guilty of **CRIMINAL SOLICITATION IN THE FOURTH DEGREE** when, with intent that another person engage in conduct constituting a felony, he solicits or otherwise attempts to cause such other person to engage in such conduct.

    Wayne Stubbs attempts to talk his younger brother, Chris, into helping him rob a convenience store clerk at gunpoint, which would be a felony. Chris turns Wayne down, insisting that they should play it safe and cash a bad check at the convenience store, which would be a misdemeanor.

    Based solely upon the two definitions above:

    A. Wayne and Chris should both each be charged with Criminal Solicitation in the Fifth Degree.
    B. Wayne should be charged with Criminal Solicitation in the Fifth Degree, but Chris should not be charged with any crime.
    C. Chris should be charged with Criminal Solicitation in the Fourth Degree, and Wayne should be charged with Criminal Solicitation in the Fifth Degree.
    D. Chris should be charged with Criminal Solicitation in the Fifth Degree, and Wayne should be charged with Criminal Solicitation in the Fourth Degree.

14. Under which of the following circumstances would an officer be most likely to call for assistance from a supervisor, rather than relying strictly on his or her own experience and instincts?

    A. A water main breaks, spilling water into the street.
    B. A busload of tourists is hijacked by a terrorist.
    C. There is an accident on a busy downtown street, and traffic has to be rerouted.
    D. A terrible storm causes a tree to fall into a hospital parking lot, blocking the emergency room entrance and exit.

15. Officer Kent confronts a teenage boy whom he has observed attempting to break into an apartment window. The boy insists that the apartment belongs to his aunt and that she has asked him to house-sit for her while she is on vacation. He explains that he cannot find the key his aunt gave him, but that he needs to get in to take care of her cat. Which of the following should Officer Kent do first?

    A. ask the boy for identification
    B. find a neighbor who might be able to authenticate the boy's story
    C. take the boy to the precinct and call his parents
    D. help the boy get inside to find out if there really is a cat who may need food and water

16. Officer Blum is dispatched to a home where a larceny has been reported. There, Officer Blum gathers the following information:

Location: 80 Cane Street
Time: around 11:00 P.M.
Crime: larceny
Victim: Hobart Austin
Item Missing: table saw
Suspect: no description; no witnesses

Officer Blum is writing a report on the incident. Which of the following expresses the information most clearly and accurately?

A. At around 11:00 P.M. at 80 Cane Street an unknown suspect allegedly stole a table saw. The owner of the saw, who called the police, was Hobart Austin.

B. At around 11:00 P.M., a table saw belonging to Hobart Austin was stolen. There is no description of the suspect because there were no witnesses.

C. Hobart Austin reported that at around 11:00 P.M., his table saw was stolen from 80 Cane Street. There were no witnesses, so no description of the suspect is available.

D. At 80 Cane Street, a man or woman stole a table saw belonging to Hobart Austin at 11:00 P.M. There were no witnesses, so no description is available of the suspect.

17. Officer Curry observes that a great number of larcenies have been occurring in different sections of the area he patrols. He has determined that bicycles are stolen from the high school quad, newspapers are stolen from the business district, and hats are stolen from the shopping district. Bicycles are stolen between 1:00 P.M. and 3:30 P.M., newspapers are stolen between 6:00 A.M. and 10:30 A.M., and hats are stolen between 10:00 A.M. and 4:00 P.M. Bicycles are stolen on Wednesdays and Fridays, newspapers on Mondays, Tuesdays, and Thursdays, and hats on Thursdays.

Given this information, which of the following patrol schedules would enable Officer Curry to most effectively reduce the number of hats stolen?

A. the shopping district, Wednesdays and Fridays, 9:00 A.M. to 5:00 P.M.

B. the business district, Thursdays, 10:00 P.M. to 4:00 A.M.

C. the business district, weekdays, 10:00 A.M. to 4:00 P.M.

D. the shopping district, Thursdays, 9:30 A.M. to 5:15 P.M.

18. Based on the information in Question 17, which of the following patrol schedules would be least effective in reducing the number of bicycles stolen?

    A. the high school quad, weekdays, 10:00 A.M. to 4:00 P.M.

    B. the high school quad, Wednesdays and Fridays, noon to 4:00 P.M.

    C. the high school quad, weekdays, 10:00 A.M. to noon

    D. the high school quad, Wednesdays and Fridays, 9:00 A.M. to 3:30 P.M.

19. In State X, a person is guilty of **CRIMINAL SIMULATION** when, with intent to defraud, he makes or alters any object in such a manner that it appears to have an antiquity, rarity, source, or authorship that it does not in fact possess. Given this definition alone, which of the following is the best example of Criminal Simulation?

    A. Art, the owner of Art's Antiques, buys a truckload of brand-new statuettes, paints them so that they appear to be very old, and advertises them for sale as 19th-century antiques.

    B. Stephen, a tile maker, paints scenes from antiquity on tiles, which he sells.

    C. Regan, the owner of a rare book store, offers for sale a set of Hemingway's books with forged signatures, stipulating to his customers that the signatures are fake.

    D. Sahara airbrushes copies of paintings by famous artists like Monet onto T-shirts, which she sells at the beach.

20. Officer Patrick responds to a report of an assault and gathers the following information:

Location: Ben's Lounge
Time: 10:15 P.M.
Victim: Ben Howard, the owner
Weapon: box cutter
Injury: cut arm required 40 stitches
Suspect: Jane Howard, Mr. Howard's ex-wife
Action Taken: Ms. Howard was arrested

Officer Patrick is writing his report. Which of the following expresses the information most clearly and accurately?

A. Ben Howard reported that at 10:15 P.M. at Ben's Lounge, which he owns, his ex-wife, Jane Howard, assaulted him with a box cutter. The resulting cut on his arm required 40 stitches. Ms. Howard was arrested.

B. Jane Howard assaulted her ex-husband, Ben Howard, at the place he owns, Ben's Lounge, at 10:15 P.M. with a box cutter, and he required 40 stitches to his cut arm. She was arrested.

C. At 10:15, Jane Howard assaulted her ex-husband at Ben's Lounge, which he, Ben Howard, owns. She cut his arm with a box cutter, and he needed 40 stitches. She was arrested.

D. After reportedly assaulting her ex-husband at 10:15 P.M., Jane Howard was arrested. Ben Howard, the victim, needed 40 stitches for his arm, which she cut with a box cutter.

21. In State X, a person is guilty of **CRIMINAL IMPERSONATION IN THE SECOND DEGREE** when he impersonates another and does an act in such assumed character with intent to obtain a benefit or to defraud another. Based solely upon this definition, which of the following is the best example of Criminal Impersonation in the Second Degree?

A. June pretends to be a coworker in order to receive her coworker's Christmas bonus, which is paid in cash, and keep it for herself.

B. A famous comedian, Steven Sanborn, imitates the president on a nationally televised program and is paid millions of dollars for it.

C. Loretta dresses up like her mother as a gag for her mother's 50th birthday party.

D. At the video store, Phil is mistaken for his twin brother.

22. Officer Grand responds to a call from a man who reports that he has found a wallet. Officer Grand gathers the following information:

    Location: the curb in front of Slippery Water Park
    Time: 1:00 P.M.
    Person Finding the Wallet: Ronnie Sawyer
    Wallet Description: black leather wallet with $400 in cash inside
    Action Taken: wallet matched the description of one that had been reported missing; wallet returned to owner

    Officer Grand is writing a report. Which of the following expresses the information most clearly and accurately?

    A. At 1:00 P.M., a black leather wallet was found to contain $400 by Ronnie Sawyer, who called the police, who were able to match the wallet to one that had been reported missing and return the wallet to its owner.

    B. At 1:00 P.M., Ronnie Sawyer found a black leather wallet containing $400 in cash on the curb in front of Slippery Water Park. Mr. Sawyer notified the police. The wallet matched the description of a wallet that had been reported missing and was returned to its owner.

    C. An owner got their wallet containing $400 in cash back after Ronnie Sawyer found it at 1:00 P.M. on the curb in front of Slippery Water Park and called the police. The wallet had been reported missing.

    D. Ronnie Sawyer reported that he found a wallet containing $400 in cash on the curb in front of Slippery Water Park at 1:00 P.M., and the wallet matched the description of one that had been reported missing. It was returned to the owner.

23. Officer Seely receives a call from the precinct advising her to watch for a stolen vehicle, which is described as a vintage white Cadillac convertible, with blue polka dots. Fifteen minutes later, a vehicle that fits the description passes Officer Seely at a high rate of speed on a busy street. What should Officer Seely do first?

    A. follow the vehicle from a distance, carefully avoiding being seen by the driver

    B. call in to report that she has spotted the vehicle

    C. turn on her lights and sirens and follow the car, as it is too unique to be mistaken for another

    D. contact the car's owners to let them know that the car has been found

24. In State X, a person is guilty of **ROBBERY IN THE THIRD DEGREE** when he forcibly steals property. Given this definition alone, which of the following is least likely to be an example of Robbery in the Third Degree?

    A. Chris twists his roommate's arm, shoves him against a wall, and steals his wallet.

    B. Johanna pushes a child off of his bicycle and then takes the bike.

    C. Carl takes the mail out of his neighbor's mailbox and keeps it.

    D. Gerard pins a woman against the hood of her car and takes her purse.

25. On a routine foot patrol of a crowded section of town in which many bars and clubs operate late into the night, Officer Prejean sees a man pinning a woman against the wall of an alley, holding a knife to her throat. Officer Prejean approaches, pulls his gun, identifies himself as a police officer, and demands that the man drop the knife and let the woman go. The man calmly follows instructions and tells the officer that he and the woman are simply acting out a scene from an independent film he is making. The officer asks the woman, who is shaking and crying, if this is true. The woman responds to the officer in a language the officer does not recognize. He asks her if she speaks English, and the woman shakes her head *no*. As his next step, Officer Prejean should:

    A. call the precinct and request assistance from a language expert.

    B. ask the man to show him the script to prove that he is telling the truth.

    C. arrest the man and take the man and the woman to the precinct, where someone can be found to interview the woman in her language.

    D. consult with witnesses as to whether the man's story might be true.

26. Officer Wang has observed that a chain of restaurants called Sugar's, with several locations in Officer Wang's patrol area, has become a gathering place for certain types of criminals. At Sugar's East, violent gang members gather. At Sugar's West, robbers gather. And at Sugar's Underground, prostitutes gather. Officer Wang has observed that the gang members tend to get together from 10:00 P.M. to 1:00 A.M., robbers from 5:30 P.M. to 11:00 P.M., and prostitutes from 11:00 A.M. to 5:30 P.M. The get-togethers at Sugar's East tend to occur on Fridays. Those at Sugar's West take place on Mondays, Tuesdays, and Thursdays, and those at Sugar's Underground tend to happen on Saturdays and Sundays.

    Given this information, which of the following patrol schedules would enable Officer Wang to most effectively observe the prostitutes?

    A. the area near Sugar's Underground, weekdays, 11:00 A.M. to 6:00 P.M.

    B. the area near Sugar's West, Saturdays and Sundays, noon to 7:00 P.M.

    C. the area near Sugar's Underground, weekends, 9:00 A.M. to 6:00 P.M.

    D. the area near Sugar's West, weekdays, 11:00 P.M. to 7:00 A.M.

27. Given the information in Question 26, which of the following patrol schedules would be least likely to allow Officer Wang to observe the violent gang members?

    A. the area near Sugar's East, weekdays, 9:00 A.M. to 2:00 P.M.

    B. the area near Sugar's East, weekdays, 9:00 P.M. to 2:00 A.M.

    C. the area near Sugar's East, Fridays, 10:00 P.M. to 3:00 A.M.

    D. the area near Sugar's East, Fridays, 6:00 P.M. to 6:00 A.M.

28. In State X, a person is guilty of **CRIMINAL POSSESSION OF A DANGEROUS WEAPON IN THE FIRST DEGREE** when he possesses any explosive substance with intent to use the same unlawfully against the person or property of another. Given this definition alone, which of the following is the best example of Criminal Possession of a Dangerous Weapon in the First Degree?

   A. Luke, a demolition foreman, possesses a case of explosive material for use in legally demolishing a building.

   B. Jimmy has a knife under the seat of his car, with which he plans to slash his mother's face.

   C. Violet buys a case of dynamite, with which she plans to blow up her sister's car.

   D. Franco has five bundles of fireworks, which he plans to set off in his yard on July 4.

29. Officer Holmes reports to the scene of a fire. He gathers the following information:

Location:	1515 Armory Boulevard
Time:	11:00 P.M.
Incident:	fire destroyed one floor of an office building
Injuries:	none, building was empty
Cause of Fire:	under investigation; faulty wiring is suspected

   Officer Holmes is writing a report on the incident. Which of the following expresses the information most clearly and accurately?

   A. At 11:00 P.M., a fire caused by faulty wiring destroyed one floor of an office building at 1515 Armory Boulevard. The building was empty, so no one was injured.

   B. Faulty wiring is suspected in a fire that destroyed one floor of an office building at 1515 Armory Boulevard. The cause of the fire, that injured no one, is under investigation.

   C. At 11:00 P.M. at 1515 Armory Boulevard, one floor of an office building was destroyed by a fire whose cause, which is under investigation, is suspected to have been faulty wiring. The building was empty, and no one was injured.

   D. Faulty wiring may have caused the fire at 11:00 P.M. at 1515 Armory Boulevard that injured no one because the office building was empty. Officially, the cause is under investigation.

30. In State X, a person is guilty of **PROSTITUTION** when such person engages or offers to engage in sexual conduct with another person in return for a fee. Based solely upon this definition, which of the following is the best example of Prostitution?

    A. Heather tells her deadbeat boyfriend, Jay, that he will have to sleep on the couch until he pays his half of the rent.

    B. Dressed in a tight skirt and halter top, Sara approaches an unmarked police car on a dark street corner to ask the driver for directions.

    C. June tells a strange man that she can guarantee him "an hour's worth of good time" in her hotel room for fifty dollars.

    D. After a long walk back to her apartment from the movie theater, Ina invites her date to come inside.

31. As he crossed the street to buy a newspaper, Mr. Harris was struck by a cyclist who jumped back on his bicycle and sped off. Officer Harold was sent to investigate. Of the following descriptions of the suspect given by witnesses, which should Officer Harold consider most likely to be correct?

    A. tall, thin white man, about 30 years old, wearing yellow sunglasses and blue unitard

    B. tall, thin black man, about 35 years old, wearing yellow sunglasses and a black unitard

    C. tall, thin white man, about 20 years old, wearing red sunglasses and a black unitard

    D. tall, thin white man, about 30 years old, wearing yellow sunglasses and a black unitard

32. Officer Anthony responds to a call from a man who was blocked into a parking space by another vehicle and gathers the following information:

Location:	Merry Hill Courthouse
Time:	3:00 P.M.
Incident:	man blocked into parking space by illegally parked car
Victim:	Joe Bond
Illegally Parked Car:	black Monte Carlo, tag JWQ 577
Action Taken:	in accordance with posted courthouse policy, the illegally parked car was impounded

    Officer Anthony has to write her report on the events. Which of the following expresses the information most clearly and accurately?

    A. At 3:00 P.M., Joe Bond reported that his car was blocked into a space at the Merry Hill Courthouse by an illegally parked black Monte Carlo, tag number JWQ 577. In accordance with posted courthouse policy, the Monte Carlo was impounded.

    B. Joe Bond parked at the Merry Hill Courthouse and then emerged at 3:00 P.M. to find that his car was blocked into a space by an illegally parked car. The car that blocked him in was a black Monte Carlo, tag number JWQ 577.

    C. At the Merry Hill Courthouse at 3:00 P.M., Joe Bond's car was blocked into a space by an illegally parked black Monte Carlo. The Monte Carlo, tag number JWQ 577, was impounded. This impounding was done in accordance with posted courthouse policy.

    D. After being illegally parked at the Merry Hill Courthouse in a manner that blocked in the car of Joe Bond at 3:00 P.M., a black Monte Carlo, tag number JWQ 577, was impounded, in accordance with posted courthouse policy.

33. Officer Albright overhears a conversation between two detectives about a rash of robberies in an area of town in which Officer Albright's father runs a shoe store. The detectives are discussing an undercover operation to bust what they believe is a robbery ring, and they emphasize that the success of their operation depends upon the operation remaining undercover. Officer Albright wants to warn her father about the robberies so that he can come up with better security for his store, but she does not want to compromise the detectives' plan. What should Officer Albright do?

    A. tell her father about the robberies, but not about the undercover operation

    B. say nothing to her father and trust that the detectives' operation will end the robbers' spree before her father's store is a target

    C. tell the detectives about her father's store and insist that they keep a close watch on it for her, in return for her promise not to divulge their plans

    D. say nothing to her father, but spend a lot more time at his store during her patrols of the area

34. Under which of the following circumstances would it be least appropriate for an officer to remove his weapon from its holster?

    A. A driver is speeding down a busy road, firing shots from his pistol in a random fashion.

    B. Three women fight over a lunch bill. One of the women pulls a knife from her purse, holds the arm of one of the other women against the table top, and threatens to slice her wrist open.

    C. A college professor is demonstrating the evolution of the firearm when a student pulls his gun from his pants to show it to the class.

    D. A bank robber appears to have a gun in his pocket, which he points at the teller as he demands money.

To answer Questions 35, 36, 37, and 38, use the information in the following passage.

Police Officers Jennings and Lincoln were working a 4:00 P.M. to midnight tour of duty on Friday, December 5, when they were assigned to investigate a burglary. At 7:00 P.M., they were told to respond to 35-45 Grand Street, Apartment 1402, and to speak to the complainant, Ms. Phoebe Frost. Upon arrival, Officer Jennings interviewed Ms. Frost, who stated that when she returned home from work at approximately 6:10 P.M., she was unable to unlock her door because the keyhole had been stuffed with toothpicks. The building superintendent wasn't home, so she had a cup of coffee at the diner on the corner. When she returned to the building, the superintendent had arrived home and was able to open the door for her. Once she entered her apartment, she saw that her TV and DVD player were gone, and her jewelry box had been emptied and was lying on the floor. She immediately left the apartment and called the police from the super's apartment.

Officer Lincoln, who is qualified in fingerprint recovery, dusted the jewelry box and the front door in an attempt to recover any fingerprints that the burglar may have left. The officers also interviewed several other residents of the floor: Mrs. Lenore Caputo, who lives in Apartment 1404 next door to Ms. Frost; Ms. Frida Kalish, who lives in Apartment 1400 on the other side of Ms. Frost; and Mr. William Babbit, who lives in Apartment 1407 across the hall. None of the individuals had been at home during the day, and none had seen or heard anything unusual. Mrs. Caputo had come home earliest, at about 4:30 P.M. Ms. Kalish had returned at 5:45, and Mr. Babbit between 5:45 and 6:00.

At 4:30 in the afternoon on Saturday, December 6, Officers Jennings and Lincoln responded to Apartment 1514 in the same building on a call of burglary. The complainant, Ms. Lee Chung, stated that she left her apartment at about 2:00 to go shopping and run errands. When she returned home, she discovered that the lock on her apartment door had been stuffed with chewing gum. She found the super, who let her in. She discovered that her apartment had been burglarized. Her TV and DVD player were missing, along with her laptop computer, her answering machine, and her microwave oven. Officer Lincoln dusted for prints, focusing on the front door and a dresser, which had been left with its drawers ajar. The officers interviewed several neighbors: Mr. Stuart Lyon, in Apartment 1512 next door; Mrs. Eunice Colón, in Apartment 1516, and Ms. Petra Gruber, in Apartment 1520 across the hall. Ms. Gruber had been home studying all afternoon, but had heard nothing; Mr. Lyon had just returned from a trip to Washington, D.C., and hadn't been home; Mrs. Colón had heard "suspicious footsteps" at approximately 3:00 P.M., but hadn't seen anyone when she looked through the apartment door's peephole.

At the precinct, Detective Melendez was assigned to investigate the burglaries. Three days after the second burglary, Mr. Allen Hunt of the fingerprint identification unit informed Detective Melendez that the prints matched those of Peter Reilly, whose last known address was 355 Gavel Street, Apartment 1705. Later that evening, after obtaining an arrest warrant, Detective Melendez arrested Peter Reilly for the burglaries.

35. Who lived on the same floor as Ms. Frost?

    A. Mrs. Eunice Colón
    B. Mr. Allen Hunt
    C. Mr. Stuart Lyon
    D. Mr. William Babbit

36. When was the suspect arrested?

    A. December 9
    B. December 5
    C. December 6
    D. December 12

37. Why was Ms. Chung unable to unlock her door?

    A. A pickpocket had stolen her key.
    B. The lock was stuffed with chewing gum.
    C. The lock had been loosened so it no longer worked.
    D. The lock was stuffed with toothpicks.

38. Did the officers gain any important information from interviewing the neighbors?

    A. Yes, because the neighbors are very attentive.
    B. No, because the nearby apartments are vacant.
    C. No, because only one neighbor heard or saw anything, and her report was vague.
    D. No, because all of the neighbors were away from home when the burglaries occurred.

39. State X defines **MANSLAUGHTER IN THE SECOND DEGREE** as recklessly causing the death of another person. Given this definition alone, which of the following is the best example of Manslaughter in the Second Degree?

    A. Ivan stalks his ex-girlfriend, memorizes her schedule, and, after weeks of planning, kills her in her apartment.

    B. Don serves a pasta dinner to his extended family, and his aunt chokes to death on a long noodle.

    C. Driving too fast on a curvy, one-lane road, Fiona crashes her car into a tree and dies.

    D. Larry has too much to drink during a pool party and pushes a friend off of the second-story balcony toward the pool; the friend lands on the concrete and dies.

40. During recent months, three buildings have been burned down by arsonists. The suspect in the first fire is described as female, white, 5'4", with short black hair. The suspect in the second fire is described as female, black, 5'6", with short dark hair. The suspect in the third fire is described as female, white, 5'5", with short black hair.

    Officer Ling arrests a woman suspected of burning down a fourth building. She is white, 5'5", and has short, dyed-blonde hair with black roots. In addition to the arson for which she has been arrested, for which of the following should Officer Ling and other investigating officers consider the woman in custody a suspect?

    A. the first fire only

    B. the first and second fires only

    C. the first and third fires only

    D. the third fire only

41. On a routine patrol of a busy avenue, Officers Jenkins and Lowery observe a vehicle several car lengths in front of them that is weaving from lane to lane, endangering the lives of other drivers on the avenue. At this point, which of the following is the most logical assumption for the officers to make?

    A. The driver of the vehicle is intoxicated.

    B. The driver of the vehicle has been physically incapacitated, perhaps by a heart attack.

    C. The vehicle's steering has malfunctioned and is suddenly difficult to control.

    D. There is not enough evidence at this point to make any sort of assumption.

42. Officer Daniels answers a call to a campground where a girl has been reported missing and gathers the following information:

Location: High Pines Campground
Child Reported Missing by: her mother, Angela Bass
Name of Missing Child: Penny Bass
Description of Missing Child: 10 years old, short brown hair, red shorts
                                   and red shirt
Child Last Seen: near nightfall yesterday, walking toward river

Officer Daniels has to radio in an alert for the missing girl. Which of the following expresses the information most clearly and accurately?

A. Alert: A girl's mother, Angela Bass, reports that her daughter, Penny, who is 10 and has short brown hair and is wearing red shorts and a red shirt has been missing since nightfall yesterday, when she was last seen walking toward the river at the High Pines Campground.

B. Be on alert for a missing girl named Penny Bass, who is 10 years old, has short brown hair, and is wearing red shorts and a red shirt. The girl was last seen near nightfall yesterday, walking toward the river at High Pines Campground. Her mother, Angela Bass, is still at the campground.

C. Please watch for little Penny Bass. She is 10 years old and her mother, Angela Bass, reports that she was wearing red shorts and a red shirt when she disappeared last night after walking toward the river at High Pines Campground.

D. Keep an eye out for Angela Bass's daughter, 10-year-old Penny Bass, who was last seen last night on her way to the river at High Pines Campground. Penny has short brown hair and is wearing red shorts and a red shirt.

43. In State X, a person is guilty of **CRIMINAL MISCHIEF IN THE FIRST DEGREE** when, with intent to damage property of another person and having no right to do so, he damages property of another person by means of an explosive. Based solely upon this definition, which of the following is not an example of Criminal Mischief in the First Degree?

A. Fred frequently buys plants from a nursery that, he believes, could use a man-made pond. While the nursery is closed so that the owners can take their annual vacation, he uses dynamite to blow a hole in the ground and fills the hole with water.

B. Cass's sister asks him to build an underground playroom for her children. He uses explosives to excavate part of a hill on his sister's property and begins construction.

C. Sarah Ann buries dynamite in five places on school grounds and sets the explosives off with a remote detonator.

D. Billy uses dynamite to blow up the decorative gargoyles that line the walkway to a wealthy family's mansion because he believes the gargoyles are offensive pagan symbols.

44. While Officer Meyer is on foot patrol, a man approaches him, carrying a zippered bag. The man introduces himself as Jeffrey Holcombe. Mr. Holcombe says he is a jeweler, and he found the bag on the sidewalk in front of his shop when he arrived this morning. Mr. Holcombe has prepared a list of the contents of the bag and their estimated value and shows it to Officer Meyer:

One stainless steel man's watch $3,000
Two ladies' dress watches $1,800 (each watch)
One heavy gold chain $ 900
One cultured pearl bracelet $ 450
Three rings (semiprecious stones) $2,700 (total)
One diamond solitaire $4,500

What is the total value of the jewelry in the bag?

   A. $13,350
   B. $15,150
   C. $18,750
   D. $20,550

45. Given the situation described in Question 44, what should Officer Meyer do?

   A. Tell Mr. Holcombe to keep the jewelry, since it's probably stolen goods, and no one is likely to claim it.
   B. Take possession of the bag, carry it to the precinct house, have it filed in the evidence room, and issue Mr. Holcombe a receipt.
   C. Tell Mr. Holcombe to take the bag to the precinct house and file a report there.
   D. Arrest Mr. Holcombe, since he's almost certainly running some sort of scam.

46. Officer Little responds to a report of a robbery and gathers the following information:

Location:	9292 Sixth Street
Time:	8:20 P.M.
Victim:	Mrs. Hendricks
Weapon:	knife
Injury:	none (victim was threatened with the knife, but not hurt)
Item Missing:	jewelry box
Suspect:	Joe Hicks
Status of Suspect:	arrested

Officer Little is writing a report on the incident. Which of the following expresses the information most clearly and accurately?

A. Mrs. Hendricks reported that at 8:20 P.M. at 9292 Sixth Street, Joe Hicks threatened her with a knife and stole her jewelry box. Joe Hicks was arrested. Mrs. Hendricks was uninjured.

B. Joe Hicks was arrested after threatening and stealing with a knife the jewelry box belonging to Mrs. Hendricks from 9292 Sixth Street at 8:20 P.M. She was not hurt.

C. Mrs. Hendricks was uninjured after being threatened with a knife by Joe Hicks who stole her jewelry box at 9292 Sixth Street. After that, which happened at 8:20 P.M., Joe Hicks was arrested.

D. Joe Hicks did not hurt Mrs. Hendricks when he threatened her with a knife and stole her jewelry box, but was arrested after the robbery at 8:20 P.M. at 9292 Sixth Street.

47. In State X, a person is guilty of **ASSAULT IN THE FIRST DEGREE** when, with intent to cause serious physical injury to another person, he causes such injury to such person or to a third person by means of a deadly weapon. Based solely upon this definition, which of the following is not an example of Assault in the First Degree?

A. Joseph Sullivan runs down the hallway of his apartment building, carrying a knife. He trips and falls toward Miss Holker, a resident, severely cutting her with the knife.

B. Helen Moon plans to severely beat Andrea, a competitive coworker, with a pair of brass knuckles. Helen mistakenly attacks a stranger who resembles Andrea with the weapon, breaking four bones in the stranger's face.

C. Armed with a heavy chain, Scott Chu waits for his brother-in-law, Alex, in a dark alley. When Alex enters the alley, Scott whips him with the chain, breaking several bones and causing substantial internal bleeding.

D. Kim brings a baseball bat to school and waits for Ms. Tinker, a teacher whom Kim despises, to take her daily walk around the school grounds. When Ms. Tinker leaves for her walk, Kim attacks her with the bat and leaves her unconscious and bleeding heavily.

48. Since March 13, three larcenies have occurred near an outdoor green market. The first suspect is described as male, white, 6'7", with red hair, long fingernails, and a bright red birthmark on his right wrist. The second suspect is described as male, white, 5'7", with red hair and a red tattoo on his right shoulder. The third suspect is described as male, white, 5'6", with red hair and a tattoo on his right shoulder.

    On April 28, Officer Lensky arrests a man for a fourth larceny in the area. The man is white, 5'7", with red hair, long fingernails, and a red tattoo on his right shoulder and no other visible tattoos or markings. In addition to the crime for which the man has been arrested, for which of the following should Officer Lensky and other investigating officers consider the man a suspect?

    A. the first larceny only
    B. the first and second larcenies only
    C. the second and third larcenies only
    D. the third larceny only

49. After a team wins a big victory in a home game, Officers Connor and Novochek are assigned to crowd control duties near the stadium, where fans stream out into the street, celebrating. About which of the following should Officers Connor and Novochek be most concerned?

    A. A woman riding on a man's shoulders pulls her shirt off, baring her breasts.
    B. A dozen teenage boys begin setting off fireworks in the middle of the crowd.
    C. A man begins chanting the team's fight slogan, and soon hundreds of people chant with him.
    D. A man runs with a souvenir bat, telling everyone that he stole it from the stadium gift shop.

50. Officer De Nova, who has been assigned to patrol a busy area of town, is asked by a prominent businessman to accompany him as he makes a large cash deposit into his bank account. Officer De Nova politely declines, advises the man to take an employee or a security guard with him to the bank, and continues his patrol.

    Officer De Nova's actions were:

    A. good, because he should not do special favors instead of his assigned duties.
    B. bad, because if the man were robbed it would be Officer De Nova's fault.
    C. good, because rich people tend to look down on police officers and do not deserve their help.
    D. bad, because it is an officer's job to prevent crime at all times, even if it means defying a direct order from a supervisor.

51. In State X, a person is guilty of **UNLAWFUL POSSESSION OF A WEAPON UPON SCHOOL GROUNDS** when he knowingly possesses a weapon in or upon a building or grounds of any school without the written authorization of such institution. Given this definition alone, which of the following is true if Jerry, after obtaining verbal permission from a professor, brings his father's rifle to class as a visual aid?

    A. Jerry should not be charged with any crime because he obtained permission to bring the weapon to class.

    B. Jerry and his professor should both be charged with Unlawful Possession of a Weapon upon School Grounds, as they conspired to have the weapon brought to class.

    C. Jerry should be charged with Unlawful Possession of a Weapon upon School Grounds because he did not obtain written permission to bring the weapon to class.

    D. Jerry should be charged with a lesser crime than Unlawful Possession of a Weapon upon School Grounds, as he obtained permission to bring the weapon to class but did not get that permission in writing.

52. Officer Harbin is dispatched to a concession stand at the beach, where a robbery has been reported. There, Officer Harbin gathers the following information:

Location:	Cool It Snacks
Time:	12:30 P.M.
Crime:	robbery
Victim:	Ron Terry, employee
Injury:	broken jaw
Item Taken:	one case of lemonade
Weapon:	brass knuckles
Suspect:	Jeb Edge
Action Taken:	suspect was apprehended by a customer and held until police arrived; suspect arrested and now in custody

    Officer Harbin is writing his report on the incident. Which of the following expresses the information most clearly and accurately?

    A. At 12:30 P.M., a customer apprehended Jeb Edge who had just stolen one case of lemonade after striking Ron Terry, an employee of Cool It Snacks, with brass knuckles. Edge was arrested and is in custody.

    B. At 12:30 P.M. at Cool It Snacks, employee Ron Terry was struck by Jeb Edge, who used brass knuckles, and his jaw was broken. Edge stole a case of lemonade but was luckily apprehended by a customer. He was arrested and is in custody.

    C. At 12:30 P.M., Jeb Edge stole a case of lemonade from Cool It Snacks after striking employee Ron Terry with brass knuckles, breaking Terry's jaw. A customer apprehended Edge, who was arrested and is in custody.

    D. At 12:30 P.M., Ron Terry's jaw was broken by brass knuckles held by Jeb Edge, who struck Terry in an effort to successfully steal a case of lemonade. Edge was apprehended by a customer, was arrested, and is now in custody.

53. There have been several wallet-snatchings reported near a police precinct in recent weeks. After the fourth reported wallet-snatching, a man brings a wallet, which he says he found near a trash can, to the precinct. The man refuses to identify himself, turns in the wallet, and runs out of the precinct. When police match the wallet with the report filed by its owner, they find that the cash that was in the wallet is missing, but the credit cards and identification are there.

What is the most logical assumption?

A. The man stole the wallet and is trying to cover his tracks.

B. The man does not want the police department to know who he is, for any number of reasons.

C. The wallet was stolen by someone else, but the man who turned it in took the money.

D. The man stole the wallet and then felt guilty about taking it, so he turned it in.

54. Officer Vandy has been instructed to watch for a teenage runaway who left home seven days ago and was last seen near the area Officer Vandy is patrolling. The runaway is described as a black female, 5'2" and 110 pounds, with short, curly hair and four earrings in her left ear. On which of the following people should Officer Vandy focus most of her attention?

A. a 5'2" and 110 pound black woman, who is carrying a baby on her hip

B. a 5'3" and 105 pound black teenager with no earrings and a shaved head, who is begging for change

C. a 5'2" and 115 pound black woman, who is carrying a briefcase and talking on a cellular phone

D. a 5'3" and 140 pound black teenager with four earrings in her left ear, who is carrying schoolbooks and getting on a city bus

55. In State X, a person is guilty of **LARCENY** when, with intent to deprive another of property, he wrongfully takes or withholds such property from an owner thereof. Based solely upon this definition, which of the following is the best example of Larceny?

A. Lance claims as his own an idea for saving his company, when the idea is really a coworker's.

B. While Lee is at lunch, Joe takes an important disk from Lee's computer and hides it in his desk.

C. Olga borrows her neighbor's edger and neglects to return it.

D. Henry tells the cashier that the ginger ale he is purchasing is on sale, when he knows it is not.

56. Officer Long responds to a call from a man who reports that a burglary is in progress. Officer Long gathers the following information:

Location: 500 Last Lane
Time: 8:45 P.M.
Person Reporting Incident: Hal Simpson, of 490 Last Lane
Incident: man seen breaking into the house
Suspect: Greg Lewis
Status of Suspect: caught breaking into the house, was arrested

Officer Long is writing a report. Which of the following expresses the information most clearly and accurately?

A. At 8:45 P.M., Hal Simpson, who lives next to 500 Last Lane at 490 Last Lane, reported seeing a man breaking into that house. Greg Lewis was caught breaking into the house and was arrested.

B. Hal Simpson of 490 Last Lane reported at 8:45 P.M. that he saw a man breaking into his neighbor's house at 500 Last Lane. The man was caught breaking in and was arrested.

C. At 500 Last Lane, a man was caught breaking into the house and was arrested. Greg Lewis, the man who was arrested, was seen by neighbor Hal Simpson, of 490 Last Lane.

D. At 8:45 P.M., Hal Simpson, who lives at 490 Last Lane, reported seeing a man breaking into the house at 500 Last Lane. The man, Greg Lewis, was caught breaking into the house and was arrested.

57. Freshest Supermarket is one of many businesses that hires parolees as part of a coordinated effort between the courts, the prison system, and the private sector to reintroduce parolees into society. Freshest's manager, Oscar Grand, calls the police to report that $200 is missing from the previous day's receipts, and he believes it was stolen from a cash register by a parolee named Patricia Story, who works in the store's meat department. Officer Punch arrives at the store to investigate. He interviews the accused parolee, Patricia Story, who insists that she is innocent and that she does not have access to the cash registers. Which of the following should Officer Punch do next?

A. interview all the employees who were working the day before
B. arrest Patricia Story
C. encourage Mr. Grand to dismiss Patricia Story
D. get a warrant to search Patricia Story's belongings, car, and home

58. Officer Greer is dispatched to a high-rise building, where a man has been reported to be on the ledge of one of the highest floors. Officer Greer gathers the following information:

Location: Tall Towers
Time: 3:00 P.M.
Incident: man spotted on 20th-floor ledge
Name of Man: Jay Klein
Action Taken: negotiators talked Mr. Klein inside, and he was taken in for psychiatric evaluation

Officer Greer must fill out a report on the incident. Which of the following expresses the information most clearly and accurately?

A. At 3:00 P.M., Jay Klein was spotted on the 20th floor ledge at Tall Towers. Negotiators talked Mr. Klein into coming back inside, and Mr. Klein was then taken in for psychiatric evaluation.

B. Jay Klein was taken in for psychiatric evaluation after being talked into coming back inside after he was spotted on the 20th floor ledge. This happened at and after 3:00 P.M.

C. At Tall Towers, Jay Klein was spotted at 3:00 P.M. on the 20th floor ledge, from which he was talked back inside.

D. After being spotted on the 20th floor ledge of Tall Towers, Joe Klein was talked back inside and taken in for psychiatric evaluation.

59. In State X, a person is guilty of **AUTO STRIPPING IN THE SECOND DEGREE,** a misdemeanor, when he intentionally destroys or defaces any part of a vehicle without the permission of the owner. A person is guilty of **AUTO STRIPPING IN THE FIRST DEGREE**, a felony, when he commits the offense of Auto Stripping in the Second Degree after he has been previously convicted within the last five years of Auto Stripping in the Second Degree.

Oscar, who is angry with his mother's boyfriend, Eric, smashes the headlights and windshield of Eric's car but is not caught. Four years later, again angry with Eric, who is now his stepfather, Oscar smashes Eric's headlights and windows again. This time, the police catch him in the act and he is arrested. Based solely upon the above definitions, what should Oscar be charged with?

A. Auto Stripping in the Second Degree

B. Auto Stripping in the First Degree

C. both Auto Stripping in the Second Degree and the First Degree

D. nothing, because the car he was caught defacing belongs to a family member

60. An anonymous citizen calls the police department and reports that a man is mistreating his child at a public park. The caller declines to describe the man or the child further and hangs up the phone. Officer Reingold is dispatched to the park to follow up on the call. Of the following parents and children, about which should Officer Reingold be most concerned?

    A. a father who spanks his small son after the son jumps into the lake
    B. a mother who leaves her toddler unattended in a sandbox and drives away
    C. a father who shows his small son how to feed bread crumbs to the ducks, who are taller than the boy
    D. a mother who yanks her small son off the monkey bars

61. Officer Cannon is dispatched to the scene of a domestic dispute. He gathers the following information:

Location:	150 Willow Lane
Time:	10:00 P.M.
Person Reporting Incident:	anonymous caller
Incident:	screaming and gunshots coming from inside the house
People Involved:	Mary and Todd Hanson
Action Taken:	both were found holding handguns; there were bullet holes in several walls of the house; both arrested

    Officer Cannon is writing a report on the incident. Which of the following expresses the information most clearly and accurately?

    A. At 10:00 P.M., an anonymous caller reported that there were bullet holes in several walls of the house at 150 Willow Lane, along with screaming coming from the house. Mary and Todd Hanson were arrested after both were found holding handguns.
    B. At 150 Willow Lane, a domestic dispute involving screaming and gunshots was found to involve Mary and Todd Hanson, who were found with handguns. There were several bullet holes in the walls of the house. Both Mary and Todd Hanson were arrested shortly after 10:00 P.M.
    C. At 10:00 P.M., an anonymous caller reported that screaming and gunshots were coming from the house at 150 Willow Lane. Mary and Todd Hanson were found in the house, each holding a handgun. There were several bullet holes in the walls of the house. Both Mary and Todd Hanson were arrested.
    D. At 150 Willow Lane an anonymous caller reported screaming and gunshots from Mary and Todd Hanson at 10:00 P.M. Found with handguns, both were arrested.

62. During the past several months, Officer Kim has observed that certain types of assaults tend to occur in different sections of the area he patrols at different times. Assaults with broken bottles occur on Sixth Street between Whistler and Boone, assaults with chains occur near the Greyfield Memorial, and assaults with baseball bats happen on Finley Avenue between Trinidad and Hope. Assaults with broken bottles happen most commonly on Wednesdays, assaults with chains on Thursdays, Fridays, Saturdays, and Sundays, and assaults with baseball bats on weekdays. Assaults with broken bottles generally occur between midnight and 4:00 A.M., assaults with chains between 1:00 P.M. and 10:00 P.M., and assaults with baseball bats between 5:00 P.M. and 2:30 A.M.

    Given this information, which of the following patrol schedules would enable Officer Kim to most effectively reduce the number of assaults with broken bottles?

    A. Greyfield Memorial, Wednesdays, midnight to 6:00 A.M.
    B. Sixth Street between Whistler and Boone, weekdays, 10:00 P.M. to 6:00 A.M.
    C. Greyfield Memorial, weekdays, 10:00 A.M. to 6:00 P.M.
    D. Sixth Street between Whistler and Boone, Wednesdays, midnight to 2:00 A.M.

63. Given the information in Question 62, which of the following would be the best day and time for someone who wishes to avoid being assaulted with a chain to visit the Greyfield Memorial?

    A. Thursday from 10:00 A.M. to noon
    B. Friday from 9:00 P.M. to 10:30 P.M.
    C. Saturday from 11:30 A.M. to 2:00 P.M.
    D. Sunday from 5:00 P.M. to 6:30 P.M.

64. In State X, a person is guilty of **THEFT OF SERVICES** when he obtains or attempts to obtain a service by the use of a credit card or debit card that he knows to be stolen. Given this definition alone, which of the following is the best example of Theft of Services?

    A. Ramona reaches for her credit card to pay for her groceries and realizes that her purse, in which she keeps her credit cards, has been stolen.
    B. Geoff presents his mother's credit card, which she gave him with the stipulation that he use it only for school expenses, to pay for gas and motor oil for his car.
    C. Lysette attempts to buy a case of beer with her roommate's credit card, which she stole from him while he slept.
    D. Oscar accidentally takes his brother's debit card to the store with him instead of his own. Since he knows his brother's debit card code, he decides to use the card and repay his brother later.

65. Officer Santos is dispatched to the scene of a reported larceny, where she gathers the following information:

Location: 80 Avenue K
Time: between 9:00 P.M. and 1:00 A.M.
Victim: Nick Flowers
Item Missing: black skateboard, which was on the front stoop
Suspect: unknown
Witnesses: none

Officer Santos is writing a report. Which of the following expresses the information most clearly and accurately?

A. Between 9:00 P.M. and 1:00 A.M., a black skateboard was stolen from the front stoop at 80 Avenue K from Nick Flowers. There were no witnesses.

B. A black skateboard that was on the front stoop of 80 Avenue K was stolen between 9:00 P.M. and 1:00 A.M. The owner of the skateboard is Nick Flowers, and the suspect is unknown.

C. Nick Flowers reported that between 9:00 P.M. and 1:00 A.M., his black skateboard was stolen from the front stoop at 80 Avenue K. There were no witnesses, and the suspect is unknown.

D. The suspect is unknown who stole Nick Flowers's black skateboard from the front stoop at 80 Avenue K between 9:00 P.M. and 1:00 A.M. There were no witnesses.

66. Four men fitting the description of a robbery suspect pass in front of Officer Fugard, who has been told to watch for the armed and dangerous suspect. Which of the four men should Officer Fugard consider most likely to be the suspect?

A. the first man, who is walking a dog and thumbing through a train schedule

B. the second man, who is walking briskly and has a visible bulge in his pocket

C. the third man, who begins to run when he sees Officer Fugard

D. the fourth man, who is dressed too warmly for the weather and appears nervous

67. Officer Henry is dispatched to the scene of a robbery, where he gathers the following information:

Location: 50 Fifth Street
Time: 3:00 A.M.
Victim: Sheila Carter
Injury: broken cheekbone (suspect struck her)
Items Missing: engagement ring and watch
Suspect: tall, white male, dressed in navy blue from head to toe
Status of Suspect: fled on foot in an unknown direction

Officer Henry must write a report on the incident. Which of the following expresses the information most clearly and accurately?

A. At 3:00 A.M., a tall, white male, dressed in navy blue from head to toe, stole an engagement ring and a watch after striking the cheekbone and breaking it of Sheila Carter at 50 Fifth Street, from which the suspect fled on foot.

B. Sheila Carter's cheekbone was broken where a suspect described as a tall, white male, dressed in navy blue from head to toe, struck her and then stole her engagement ring and watch. The suspect fled on foot in an unknown direction from 50 Fifth Street after this occurred at 3:00 A.M.

C. At 50 Fifth Street at 3:00 A.M., Sheila Carter's cheekbone was broken where she was struck by a tall, white male who stole her engagement ring and watch and who fled on foot in an unknown direction.

D. Sheila Carter reported that at 3:00 A.M. at 50 Fifth Street, a tall, white male, dressed in navy blue from head to toe, struck her and stole her engagement ring and watch. The suspect fled on foot in an unknown direction. Ms. Carter suffered a broken cheekbone.

68. In State X, a person is guilty of **MANUFACTURE OF UNAUTHORIZED RECORDINGS** when he knowingly, and without the owner's consent, transfers any sound recording with the intent to sell such article to which the recording was transferred. Based solely upon this definition, which of the following is the best example of the Manufacture of Unauthorized Recordings?

A. Gisela records the Top Forty countdown off of the radio and listens to it later.

B. In preparation for a class project, Nina makes 15 CD copies of a famous speech by Winston Churchill to give to her classmates.

C. After attending a rock concert, Ricardo gives his girlfriend a videofile copy of the concert, which he recorded with a pocket video recorder concealed in his vest.

D. Sela makes several copies of a new CD then sells the copies to her friends.

69. Officer Waite has observed that most of the robberies in the area he patrols occur on Saturday and Sunday nights between 4:00 A.M. and 6:30 A.M. He also observes that most of the assaults occur on Friday and Sunday nights between midnight and 3:00 A.M. Which of the following patrol schedules would most effectively enable Officer Waite to reduce the number of robberies and assaults?

    A. weekdays, midnight to 7:00 A.M.

    B. Fridays, Saturdays, and Sundays, 6:30 A.M. to 4:00 P.M.

    C. Fridays, Saturdays, and Sundays, midnight to 8:00 A.M.

    D. Fridays and Sundays, midnight to 6:30 A.M.

70. Given the information in Question 69, which of the following is the most logical statement?

    A. On Mondays, Tuesdays, Wednesdays, and Thursdays, fewer crimes occur in the area Officer Waite patrols.

    B. On some Sundays, it is possible that one or more robberies and one or more assaults may occur in the area Officer Waite patrols.

    C. There are no assaults on Saturdays in Officer Waite's patrol area.

    D. There are more robberies than assaults in Officer Waite's patrol area.

71. In State X, a person is guilty of **CRIMINAL NUISANCE IN THE SECOND DEGREE** when he knowingly owns or maintains any place where persons gather for purposes of engaging in unlawful conduct. Based solely upon this definition, which of the following is the best example of Criminal Nuisance in the Second Degree?

    A. The owner of the Shoebox, a live-music club, is unaware of the fact that a group of kids regularly gathers in his courtyard to use drugs.

    B. Deciding that it is good for business, the owner of The Big Bar overlooks the group of prostitutes that enters his bar every evening to invite men to have sexual relations with them for money.

    C. A campus outreach representative arranges to have on-campus meetings for men and women recently paroled from prison who are interested in furthering their education.

    D. A wealthy philanthropist opens his home on Sunday evenings to panhandlers, drug dealers, homeless people, and others in need, offering them a hot meal and some encouragement.

72. Officer Goldberg responds to a reported assault. He gathers the following information:

Location:	700 Ocean Way
Time:	7:00 P.M.
Victim:	Steve Kelly
Injury:	three broken teeth
Weapon:	television remote control
Suspect:	Darren Kelly, victim's brother
Status of Suspect:	arrested

Officer Goldberg is writing his report on the incident. Which of the following expresses the information most clearly and accurately?

A. At 7:00 P.M., Steve Kelly's brother Darren broke three of his teeth by hitting him with a television remote control at 700 Ocean Way. Mr. Kelly was arrested.

B. Steve Kelly reported that at 7:00 P.M. at 700 Ocean Way, his brother Darren struck him with a television remote control, breaking three of his teeth. Darren Kelly was arrested.

C. Darren Kelly, who hit his brother Steve with a television remote control at 7:00 P.M. at 700 Ocean Way, breaking three of his teeth, was arrested shortly thereafter.

D. Three of his teeth were broken after Steve Kelly's brother Darren struck him with a television remote control at 700 Ocean Way at 7:00 P.M. Darren Kelly was arrested.

73. A man lives and hunts in State X, whose laws strictly prohibit the possession of a rifle without a permit. After a brief hunting excursion, the man stops at a fast-food restaurant for lunch, takes his rifle into the restaurant, and lays it on the table beside his food. A worker at the restaurant calls the police. When Officer Henry arrives at the restaurant in response to the call, he asks the man if he has a license for the rifle. The man says he does not have a license, but that he will be happy to take the rifle back out to his car. He says he meant no harm but was nervous about leaving it unattended in a place for fear that it might be stolen. What should Officer Henry do first?

A. check to see if the rifle is loaded

B. tell the man to take the rifle out to his car and interview workers at the restaurant while the man is outside

C. arrest the man for possessing a weapon without a permit

D. call the precinct to see if the man has an arrest record or any outstanding warrants

74. Officer Ray is dispatched to the scene of an automobile accident, where she gathers the following information:

Location:	intersection of Apple and Pear Streets
Time:	5:30 P.M.
Drivers:	Perry Jones and Diane Jordan
Cause of Accident:	Diane Jordan's car rear-ended Perry Jones's car
Damage:	minor; both cars operational
Action Taken:	Diane Jordan received a traffic ticket

    Officer Ray is writing a report on the incident. Which of the following expresses the information most clearly and accurately?

    A. At 5:30 P.M., two cars driven by Diane Jordan and Perry Jones hit one another in the rear of Perry Jones's car. Diane Jordan received a traffic ticket. The damage was minor.

    B. At 5:30 P.M. at the intersection of Apple and Pear Streets, Diane Jordan's car rear-ended Perry Jones's car. The damage was minor, and both cars are operational. Diane Jordan received a traffic ticket.

    C. At the intersection of Apple and Pear Streets, Diane Jordan caused a rear-end accident between her car and Perry Jones's car. Diane Jordan received a traffic ticket, and both cars were operational.

    D. At the intersection of Apple and Pear Streets, Diane Jordan's car rear-ended Perry Jones. His car and her car were operational and received only minor damage. She received a traffic ticket.

75. In State X, a person is guilty of **RIOT IN THE SECOND DEGREE** when, simultaneous with four or more other persons, he engages in tumultuous and violent conduct and thereby intentionally or recklessly causes, or creates a grave risk of causing, public alarm. Based solely upon this definition, which of the following is the best example of Riot in the Second Degree?

    A. After a big victory, Digby and his teammates open champagne bottles, yell, and jump on one another in the locker room.

    B. Protesting the recent firing of a beloved member of his school's faculty, Louis stands during an assembly and shouts "FIRE! Everybody run!" to a crowd of more than 200 students.

    C. Ben and five of his friends simultaneously jump into a crowded swimming pool, splashing water everywhere, which causes several people to slip and fall.

    D. Tanya and four of her friends, upset by the closing of their neighborhood park, empty bags of broken glass on the sidewalk, scream obscenities, and randomly shove people down.

76. Officer Lopez answers a call to a hotel where a room has reportedly been damaged. At the hotel, he gathers the following information:

Location:	The Heart of Town Hotel
Person Reporting Incident:	Helen Peters, manager
Incident:	damaged hotel room
Damage:	$10,000 worth
Suspect:	room was registered to Tommy Johnson, whose location is unknown
Witnesses:	none

Officer Lopez is writing his report. Which of the following expresses the information most clearly and accurately?

A. A man registered as Tommy Johnson damaged $10,000 worth of a hotel room at The Heart of Town Hotel, according to manager Helen Peters. His location is unknown since he damaged the hotel room.

B. Helen Peters, the manager at The Heart of Town Hotel, reported that $10,000 worth of damage was done to a hotel room registered to Tommy Johnson. There were no witnesses, and Mr. Johnson's location is unknown.

C. Tommy Johnson's location is unknown after he reportedly damaged his hotel room at The Heart of Town Hotel, according to manager Helen Peters.

D. A room at The Heart of Town Hotel was damaged by a man registered as Tommy Johnson, whose location is unknown. There were no witnesses. The damage is worth $10,000.

77. In the area he patrols, Officer Ipolito has observed that most public drunkenness occurs near the Flat Street Saloon. He has also observed that most of the robberies occur between Ford and Huron on Lakeside Drive and that most of the carjackings occur around Northam Square. The greatest incidence of public drunkenness is on Saturdays between midnight and 3:00 A.M. Most robberies occur on weekdays between 2:00 A.M. and 7:30 A.M., and most carjackings occur between 5:00 A.M. and 8:00 A.M.

Given this information, which of the following patrol schedules would most effectively enable Officer Ipolito to reduce the number of robberies?

A. Ford and Huron on Lakeside Drive, Mondays and Fridays, 2:00 A.M. to 7:30 A.M.

B. Northam Square, weekdays, midnight to 8:00 A.M.

C. Ford and Huron on Lakeside Drive, weekdays, 1:30 A.M. to 8:00 A.M.

D. Northam Square, Mondays, Tuesdays, and Fridays, 8:00 A.M. to 4:00 P.M.

78. Given the information in Question 77, which of the following patrol schedules would most effectively enable Officer Ipolito to reduce the incidence of public drunkenness?

A. Flat Street Saloon area, Fridays and Saturdays, midnight to 5:00 A.M.

B. Northam Square, Fridays, 10:00 P.M. to 3:00 A.M.

C. Flat Street Saloon area, Saturdays, 1:00 A.M. to 3:00 A.M.

D. Northam Square, weekdays, 2:00 A.M. to 7:30 A.M.

79. Given the information in Question 77, which of the following is the most logical statement?

A. All the people arrested for public drunkenness in Officer Ipolito's patrol area drink at the Flat Street Saloon.

B. Officer Ipolito is less concerned about carjackings than he is about robberies or public drunkenness.

C. There are several different types of crimes regularly occurring in Officer Ipolito's patrol area.

D. People who live near the Flat Street Saloon should be more concerned about their safety than people who live near Northam Square.

80. In State X, a person is guilty of **CREATING A HAZARD** when, having discarded a container with a compartment of more than one and one-half cubic feet capacity and a door that locks automatically when closed and that cannot easily be opened from the inside in any place where it might attract children, he fails to remove the door or locking device. Based solely upon this definition, which of the following is the best example of Creating a Hazard?

A. Mr. Sampson uses an old refrigerator, with a capacity of 10 cubic feet, as a backyard planter by removing the door, filling the refrigerator with dirt, and planting tomatoes in it.

B. Mrs. Gomez buys a new freezer and leaves her antique freezer, with a door that locks automatically when shut and a 15 cubic feet capacity, by the curb for trash pickup. She does not remove the door, but puts a warning sign on the freezer that reads "Do Not Open."

C. Gabriel keeps his tool carrier, which has a 6 cubic foot capacity, on his front stoop. The carrier does not lock automatically when closed and can easily be opened from the inside.

D. Finbar finds a storage container with a capacity of 3 cubic feet and a lid that locks automatically when shut. He removes the automatic locking mechanism and keeps the container, which he uses to hold kindling in his yard.

81. Officer Brown reports to the scene of a slip-and-fall accident at a liquor store, where she gathers the following information:

    Location: Best Liquors
    Time: 10:00 P.M.
    Victim: Lisa Andrews
    Incident: victim slipped on a wet spot on the floor and fell
    Injury: sprained ankle
    Action Taken: woman taken to the hospital by ambulance, Best Liquor store owner Mr. Caldwell offered to pay her hospital bills

    Officer Brown is writing her report. Which of the following expresses the information most clearly and accurately?

    A. At 10:00 P.M., a woman at Best Liquors slipped and fell on a wet spot on the floor named Lisa Andrews. Mr. Caldwell, the owner of the store, offered to pay the hospital bills after Lisa Andrews, who has a sprained ankle, was taken by ambulance to the hospital.

    B. Mr. Caldwell offered to pay for the hospital bills for Lisa Andrews who fell on a wet spot on his floor at Best Liquors and sprained her ankle and was taken to the hospital by ambulance shortly after 10:00 P.M.

    C. Mr. Caldwell, who owns Best Liquors where Lisa Andrews fell after slipping on a wet spot on the floor and sprained her ankle, offered to pay for her hospital bills, where she was taken by ambulance.

    D. At 10:00 P.M., Lisa Andrews slipped on a wet spot on the floor at Best Liquors and fell, spraining her ankle. She was taken by ambulance to the hospital. Mr. Caldwell, the owner of Best Liquors, offered to pay her hospital bills.

82. After work one evening, John Mallius decided to walk home. As he reached an overpass, he was attacked from behind, and his wallet was stolen. Officer Hamby interviewed several witnesses, who gave him the following descriptions of the suspect. Which of the following descriptions should Officer Hamby consider most likely to be accurate?

    A. black male, wearing a black suit with no tie

    B. white male, wearing a black suit with a red tie

    C. black male, wearing a blue suit with a black tie

    D. black male, wearing a black suit with a black tie

83. Officer Cleveland answers a call to a residence where a man reports that his bicycle has been stolen, and he gathers the following information:

Location:	5819 18th Street
Time:	5:30 P.M.
Crime:	larceny
Victim:	Paul Finch
Item Missing:	green 10-speed bicycle
Suspect:	white female, about 14 years old, with a black ponytail
Location of Suspect:	fled on the bike, direction unknown

Officer Cleveland has to write a report on the incident. Which of the following expresses the information most clearly and accurately?

A. At 5:30 P.M., a report of a stolen bicycle was made by Paul Finch. The bicycle is green and 10-speed and was stolen by a teenager that Mr. Finch describes as female, around 14 years old, with a black ponytail.

B. Paul Finch stated that at 5:30 P.M. at his residence at 5819 18th Street, his green 10-speed bicycle was stolen by a suspect Mr. Finch describes as a white female, about 14 years old, with a black ponytail. The suspect fled on the bicycle in an unknown direction.

C. Paul Finch's green 10-speed bicycle was stolen by a teenager from 5819 18th Street at 5:30 P.M. by a teenager who rode off in an unknown direction on the bike.

D. A green 10-speed bicycle was stolen from Paul Finch at 5819 18th Street at 5:30 P.M. by a teenager described as female, 14 years old, with a ponytail. The teenager and the bike took off in an unknown direction.

84. On a routine patrol of a quiet area, Officer Glenby observes a man removing the hubcaps from a car parked on the shoulder of the road. The man explains that he has to trade the hubcaps to a repair company in return for the repair company towing his car away and fixing it. He says the keys to his car are at the repair shop. What should Officer Glenby do first?

A. ask for the name and number of the repair shop so he can verify the man's story

B. ask to see the man's identification

C. arrest the man for attempting to steal the hubcaps

D. call the precinct to find out if the man has an arrest record or any outstanding warrants

85. In State X, a person is guilty of **ARSON IN THE SECOND DEGREE** when he intentionally damages a building by starting a fire, and when another person who is not a participant in the crime is present in such building at the time, and the defendant knows that fact, or the circumstances are such as to render the presence of such a person therein a reasonable possibility. Based solely upon this definition, which of the following is the best example of Arson in the Second Degree?

    A. Leroy starts a fire on the first floor of a condemned and apparently empty building, while two homeless people are sleeping in a hidden corridor on the second floor.

    B. While her father is in his apartment having dinner, Sue sets fire to his apartment.

    C. Leonardo and his friend Patch start a fire in their school at midnight. Patch is trapped inside when a set of fire doors closes.

    D. Perry, who is babysitting his two younger brothers, starts a fire in his family's wood-burning stove, even though he has been told not to do so without supervision. Sparks ignite the carpet and a fire spreads through the house.

86. Officer Leroy is dispatched to the scene of an assault, where he gathers the following information:

Location:	Shakes and Sodas
Address:	45 Clyde Street
Time:	1:30 P.M.
Incident:	a diner assaulted another diner with a knife
Victim:	Stephanie Reynolds
Injury:	superficial cuts on her arms
Suspect:	Ingrid Fahey
Action Taken:	suspect confessed and was arrested

    Officer Leroy must write his report. Which of the following expresses the information most clearly and accurately?

    A. A diner, Stephanie Reynolds, stated that at 1:30 P.M. at Shakes and Sodas, which is located at 45 Clyde Street, Ingrid Fahey, another diner, attacked her. Ms. Reynolds suffered superficial cuts on her arms, and Ms. Fahey confessed and was arrested.

    B. Stephanie Reynolds stated that at 1:30 P.M. at Shakes and Sodas, which is located at 45 Clyde Street, Ingrid Fahey, another diner, attacked her with a knife. Ms. Reynolds suffered superficial cuts on her arms.

    C. A diner, Stephanie Reynolds, stated that at Shakes and Sodas, while she was dining, another diner attacked her with a knife. Ms. Reynolds suffered superficial cuts on her arms, and Ms. Fahey, the other diner, confessed and was arrested.

    D. Stephanie Reynolds stated that at 1:30 P.M., while she was dining at Shakes and Sodas, which is located at 45 Clyde Street, Ingrid Fahey, another diner, attacked her with a knife. Ms. Reynolds suffered superficial cuts on her arms, and Ms. Fahey confessed and was arrested.

87. Officer Alonzo is dispatched to the scene of a reported purse-snatching, and she gathers the following information:

Location:	corner of Porter Street and Third Avenue
Time:	12:30 P.M.
Victim:	Lucy Gonzalez
Item Missing:	purse
Suspect:	black male, 5'10"
Status of Suspect:	fled north on Third Avenue on foot

Officer Alonzo is writing her report. Which of the following expresses the information most clearly and accurately?

A. At 12:30 P.M., a black male who is 5'10" snatched a purse from Lucy Gonzalez, who reported that she was at the corner of Porter Street and Third Avenue. The suspect fled north on foot.

B. At the corner of Porter Street and Third Avenue at 12:30 P.M., reportedly a black male, 5'10", stole Lucy Gonzalez's purse and then fled north on Third Avenue on foot.

C. A black male who is 5'10", according to victim Lucy Gonzalez, stole her purse at the corner of Porter Street and Third Avenue at 12:30 P.M. before fleeing north on Third Avenue with her purse on foot.

D. Lucy Gonzalez reported that at 12:30 P.M. at the corner of Porter Street and Third Avenue, a man she described as a 5'10" black male stole her purse and then fled north on Third Avenue on foot.

88. Officer Sanders arrives at a recreation center shortly after a man has reportedly been injured. Officer Sanders gathers the following information:

Location:	West End Recreation Center
Time:	5:45 P.M.
Injured Party:	Johnny Thompson
Incident:	accident; Mr. Thompson was hit in the eye by a racquetball
Action Taken:	Mr. Thompson was seen by the rec. center nurse, is okay

Officer Sanders must write a report on the incident. Which of the following expresses the information most clearly and accurately?

A. At 5:45 P.M., a racquetball accidentally hit Johnny Thompson in the eye. He is okay.

B. At the West End Recreation Center, a racquetball was accidentally hit into Mr. Thompson's eye. He was seen by the recreation center nurse, and is okay.

C. The nurse at the West End recreation center saw Johnny Thompson after he was accidentally hit in the eye by a racquetball at the center, and is okay. The accident occurred at 5:45 P.M.

D. At 5:45 P.M. at the West End Recreation Center, Johnny Thompson was accidentally hit in the eye with a racquetball. Mr. Thompson was seen by the nurse at the West End Recreation Center, and he is okay.

89. In State X, a person is guilty of **INSURANCE FRAUD IN THE SECOND DEGREE** when he commits a fraudulent insurance act and thereby wrongfully takes or withholds, or attempts to wrongfully take or withhold, property with a value in excess of $50,000. A person is guilty of **INSURANCE FRAUD IN THE FIRST DEGREE** when he commits a fraudulent insurance act and thereby wrongfully takes or withholds, or attempts to wrongfully take or withhold, property with a value in excess of $1 million.

    Based solely upon the above definitions, if Mr. Roth commits a fraudulent insurance act and thereby wrongfully withholds his yacht, which is worth $1,150,000, which of the following is true?

    A. Mr. Roth should be charged with Insurance Fraud in the First Degree.

    B. Mr. Roth should be charged with Insurance Fraud in the Second Degree.

    C. Mr. Roth should be charged with Insurance Fraud in the Third Degree.

    D. Mr. Roth should be charged with Insurance Fraud in the First Degree and Second Degree.

90. Officer Peters is dispatched to a night club, which is filled beyond its legal capacity. At the club, Officer Peters gathers the following information:

Location:	After Hours Club
Time:	1:00 A.M.
Crime:	club is filled beyond legal capacity
Legal Limit:	500 people
Club Owner:	Stanley Mitchell
Action Taken:	Fire Marshall contacted, club evacuated and closed for the night, owner fined

    Officer Peters is writing his report. Which of the following expresses the information most clearly and accurately?

    A. At 1:00 A.M., the After Hours Club was found to be filled beyond its legal capacity of 500 people. The Fire Marshall was contacted, the club was evacuated and closed for the night, and the club's owner, Stanley Mitchell, was fined.

    B. Stanley Mitchell, who owns the club called the After Hours Club that was filled beyond its 500-person capacity, was fined and the club was evacuated and the club was closed for the night after the club was found to have too many people in it at 1:00 A.M. The Fire Marshall was contacted.

    C. At 1:00 A.M., the After Hours Club was fined, closed for the night, and evacuated after it was found to be filled beyond its legal capacity of 500 people. Stanley Mitchell is the owner.

    D. Stanley Mitchell was fined after his club was discovered to be filled beyond its capacity of 500 people at 1:00 A.M. The club was closed for the night, evacuated, and he was fined.

PRACTICE TEST 2 ANSWER KEY

1. A	26. C	51. C	76. B
2. B	27. A	52. C	77. C
3. A	28. C	53. B	78. A
4. C	29. C	54. B	79. C
5. D	30. C	55. B	80. B
6. C	31. D	56. D	81. D
7. C	32. A	57. A	82. D
8. D	33. A	58. A	83. B
9. C	34. C	59. A	84. B
10. B	35. D	60. B	85. B
11. C	36. A	61. C	86. D
12. C	37. B	62. B	87. D
13. D	38. C	63. A	88. D
14. B	39. D	64. C	89. A
15. A	40. C	65. C	90. A
16. C	41. D	66. C	
17. D	42. B	67. D	
18. C	43. B	68. D	
19. A	44. B	69. C	
20. A	45. C	70. B	
21. A	46. A	71. B	
22. B	47. A	72. B	
23. B	48. C	73. C	
24. C	49. B	74. B	
25. C	50. A	75. D	

PRACTICE TEST 2 ANSWERS AND EXPLANATIONS

1. Only **A** is accurate, as there is information missing from the other three statements.

2. **B** is correct. Since noise pollution and excessive noise are "strictly regulated," Officer Juarez has given Mr. Gold more than enough latitude and should arrest him if he has defied Officer Juarez's instructions.

3. B and C are unclear, and there is information missing from D (Mrs. Fields's address), so **A** is correct.

4. **C** is correct, as it is the only situation in which someone "steals property."

5. **D** is correct, as the description of the suspect in the "third robbery only" could apply to the man in custody.

6. **C** contains the most repeaters. Note that the number "1702" is a repeater, appearing in two of the descriptions of the tag number, while "1751" and "1703" each appear only once. This means that each of the four digits in "1702" is more likely to be correct than any differing digit in "1751" or "1703."

7. **C** is the clearest and most accurate statement.

8. **D** contains the most repeaters. Note that the phrases "Chevy Blazer" and "Ford Explorer" each appear twice, canceling each other out, so neither can be used to eliminate any descriptions.

9. There is information missing from A and D, and B is unclear (note the awkward phrase "two bikers, riding bicycles…"), so **C** is correct.

10. **B** is correct, as the descriptions of the suspects in the "first and third rapes only" could apply to the man in custody. Note that "pockmarks on his throat," as were attributed to the suspect in the first rape and the man in custody, could be covered by a "full beard," as was attributed to the suspect in the third rape; so those descriptions could apply to the same man at different times. Therefore, the suspects in the first, third, and fourth rapes could be the same, since their heights, weights, and hairlines match.

11. **C** is the clearest and most accurate statement. Note that in D, the statement "At 809 Heard Street at 8:15 P.M., there were gunshots" implies that the gunshots were at Mrs. Sandra Stephens's home, which is inaccurate; that is simply where she was when she heard them.

12. **C** is correct. Preferential treatment should not be given to anyone who is committing a crime.

13. **D** is correct. Chris attempts to talk his brother into committing a misdemeanor, and Wayne attempts to talk him into committing a felony, so "Chris should be charged with Criminal Solicitation in the Fifth Degree, and Wayne should be charged with Criminal Solicitation in the Fourth Degree."

14. **B** is the best answer. Although an officer might contact a supervisor in any of the given situations, B is the situation in which an officer would be most likely to require assistance from a supervisor.

15. The first step the officer should take to determine whether the boy actually has a right to be there would be to "ask the boy for identification," so **A** is correct. Note the importance of the word "first" in this question.

16. **C** is correct. A and D have unclear wording, and there is information missing (Mr. Austin's address) from B.

17. **D** is correct. Hats are stolen from the shopping district on Thursdays between 10:00 A.M. and 4:00 P.M., and the patrol schedule given in D is the only one of the four that provides coverage of that area on that day of the week at that time.

18. **C** is correct. Bicycles are stolen from the high school quad on Wednesdays and Fridays between 1:00 P.M. and 3:30 P.M., and the patrol schedule in C is the only one of the four that does not provide coverage at that time. Note that this question asks which patrol schedule would be least effective, rather than most effective.

19. **A** is the best answer, as it is the only situation in which someone "alters any object in such a manner that it appears to have an antiquity, rarity, source, or authorship that it does not in fact possess." Neither Stephen, the tile maker (B), nor Sahara, the air-brush artist (D), claims that their wares are anything other than what they are. And Regan, the book store owner (C), is honest about the forged Hemingway signatures.

20. B and C are unclear, and there is information missing from D, so **A** is correct.

21. **A** is correct. June "impersonates another and does an act in such assumed character with intent to…defraud another." Steven Sanborn (B) is imitating the president to receive a benefit, but he is not doing so with the expectation that anyone will really believe he is the president. Loretta (C) and Phil (D) have not done anything unlawful.

22. There is information missing or unclear wording in every statement except **B**, which is correct.

23. **B** is the best answer. If she follows and loses the vehicle but has already notified the precinct that she has spotted it, then there is a greater chance that another officer can locate the vehicle. Contacting the owners (D) would be premature and unwise.

24. **C** is the best answer, as it is the only situation in which someone does not forcibly steal property.

25. **C** is correct. Everything about the situation indicates that the man was committing a crime and that he is now lying. Interviewing the woman at the precinct in her own language will provide more information.

26. **C** is correct. Prostitutes gather at Sugar's Underground on Saturdays and Sundays between 11:00 A.M. and 5:30 P.M., and the patrol schedule given in C is the only one of the four that provides coverage of that location on those days of the week at that time. Note that A is incorrect because it only includes weekdays.

27. **A** is correct. Violent gang members gather at Sugar's East on Fridays between 10:00 P.M. and 1:00 A.M., and the patrol schedule in A is the only one of the four that does not provide coverage at that time. Note that this question asks which patrol schedule would be least effective, rather than most effective.

28. **C** is the best answer. Violet intends to "blow up her sister's car" with a "case of dynamite" that she has bought. Note, in B, Jimmy possesses a knife, not an explosive, so B is incorrect.

29. **C** is correct. Note, in A, the inaccurate phrase "a fire caused by faulty wiring." While faulty wiring is suspected, the cause is under investigation and has not been determined.

30. The only situation in which someone "offers to engage in sexual conduct with another person in return for a fee" is given in **C**, so C is the correct answer. Note that while Sara (B), who "approaches an unmarked police car on a dark street corner," may be a prostitute, she is not committing a crime in the given situation.

31. **D** contains the most repeaters. Note that the phrase "30 years old" (A and D) appears only two times, but since it is the only age description that is repeated, it is most likely to be correct. Remember that a phrase has to appear only twice to be considered a repeater.

32. The fact that the Monte Carlo was impounded is not included in B, and C and D are unclearly stated, so **A** is correct.

33. **A** is the best answer. The public is and should be informed about robberies that have occurred, but Officer Albright should not divulge information about the undercover operation.

34. **C** is the best answer. While a student has no business pulling a weapon in class and is breaking laws in most states by carrying a concealed weapon and by having that weapon on school grounds, he is not doing so with the intent to harm anyone or anyone's property. The other three situations include an immediate threat of danger and would be more likely to compel an officer to remove his weapon from his holster.

35. **D** is correct; A and C are residents of the 15th floor, and B is a police fingerprint specialist.

36. **A** is correct. The arrest took place "three days after the second burglary," on December 9.

37. **B** is correct.

38. **C** is correct.

39. **D** is correct, as it is the only situation in which someone "recklessly" causes "the death of another person." A is an example of murder. B is clearly an accident, and the car accident in C does not injure or kill anyone but the driver, so there is not "another person."

40. **C** is correct, as the descriptions of the suspects in the "first and third fires only" could apply to the woman in custody. Note that "black hair," as was attributed to the suspects in the first and third fires, could be dyed to be "blonde hair with black roots," as was attributed to the woman in custody, so those descriptions could apply to the same woman at different times. Therefore, the suspects in the first, third, and fourth fires could be the same, since their race and height match.

41. **D** is correct. There is not enough evidence for any assumptions to be made.

42. In **B**, the information is presented in the clearest and most logical order. The first thing an officer receiving an alert for a missing child would want to know would be the child's name and description.

43. **B** is correct. Note that while Cass is damaging someone else's property "by means of an explosive," he has permission to do so. In each of the other situations, the individual damaging the property of another does not have permission to do so.

44. **B** is correct. Note that each of the two watches is valued at $1,800, while the three rings are given a total value of $2,700.

45. **C** is correct.

46. **A** is the clearest and most accurate statement.

47. **A** is the best answer. Although all four individuals "cause serious physical injury to another person," A is the only situation in which the individual has not acted with "intent to cause" that injury.

48. **C** is correct, as the descriptions of the suspects in the "second and third larcenies only" could apply to the man in custody. Note that the first suspect is at least a foot taller than the other three suspects, so A and B are incorrect. Also note that D is incorrect because it does not include the suspect in the second larceny.

49. **B** is the best answer. Note that while A and D present situations in which someone is breaking the law, the situation in B, in which "a dozen teenage boys begin setting off fireworks in the middle of the crowd," is the only answer in which there is an immediate threat of danger.

50. **A** is correct. An officer "should not do special favors instead of his [or her] assigned duties." Making decisions based on the desire to avoid blame as in B ("if the man were robbed it would be Officer De Nova's fault"), giving in to an inaccurate stereotype as in C ("rich people tend to look down on police officers"), or "defying a direct order from a supervisor" (D) are not justifiable actions for an officer to take.

51. **C** is the best answer, since Jerry did not obtain "written permission" to bring his weapon to class.

52. **C** is the clearest and most accurate statement.

53. The only assumption that can be made at this point is that the man "does not want the police department to know who he is, for any number of reasons," so the correct answer is **B**. The man's actions, which consist of turning in a wallet and refusing to identify himself, do not suggest any more than what is stated in B, even though any of the other assumptions given could eventually prove to be true.

54. **B** is correct. Since the runaway is described as 5'2" and 110 pounds and has been missing for seven days, B makes the most sense. She is not described as being pregnant or having a child (A), and she would probably not have found a situation that would include "carrying a briefcase and talking on a cellular phone" (C), nor would she have gained 30 pounds (D) in seven days. But she could easily have removed her earrings, shaved her head, and lost five pounds (B).

55. **B** is the best answer. While Joe may later return the disk, he has, according to the definition and the given scenario, committed larceny. The other possible answers include situations in which individuals may have committed a crime or been neglectful, but to which the given definition of larceny does not apply.

56. **D** is the clearest and most accurate statement. Note, in B, Greg Lewis's name is not stated.

57. **A** is the best answer. Until Officer Punch gathers more information, arresting Patricia Story (B), encouraging Mr. Grand to "dismiss Patricia Story" (C), or getting a warrant to "search Patricia Story's belongings, car, and home" (D) would be premature and unjustified—especially given Ms. Story's insistence that "she does not have access to the cash registers."

58. There is information missing from every statement except **A**, which is correct.

59. **A** is correct, since Oscar "intentionally destroys...part of a vehicle without the permission of the owner." Note that while Oscar has committed the act before, he has not been "previously convicted," so B and C are incorrect, and D is illogical.

60. **B** alone presents a situation in which a child has been endangered or obviously mistreated, so it is the best answer. Note that while the caller reported that a man was mistreating his child, Officer Reingold should be most concerned about the situation that warrants the most concern, regardless of what the caller said or believed about the parent's gender. The caller may have been reporting an entirely different parent, who could have left the park before Officer Reingold arrived or who may have been playing some sort of joke.

61. **C** is the clearest and most accurate statement.

62. **B** is correct. Most assaults with broken bottles occur on Sixth Street between Whistler and Boone on Wednesdays between midnight and 4:00 A.M., and the patrol schedule given in B is the only one of the four that provides coverage of that location on that day of the week at that time. Note that D is incorrect because it does not include the hours between 2:00 A.M. and 4:00 A.M.

63. **A** is correct. Most assaults with chains occur on Thursdays, Fridays, Saturdays, and Sundays between 1:00 P.M. and 10:00 P.M., and A is the only day and time that occurs outside of the above window on any of the above days. Note that this is very similar to questions that ask which patrol schedule is least likely to reduce the incidence of the given crime.

64. **C** is the best answer, since Lysette herself stole the card from her roommate. None of the other situations involves an individual attempting to pay for anything with a card he or she knows is stolen.

65. **C** is the clearest and most accurate statement.

66. **C** is the best answer. All four men, even the one walking the dog (A), could be the suspect, but the man who "begins to run when he sees Officer Fugard" is the most likely.

67. **D** is the clearest and most accurate statement. Note, in A, the awkward and confusing phrase "after striking the cheekbone and breaking it of Sheila Carter."

68. **D** is correct. Of the four individuals, only Sela has "the intent to sell" the recordings she has made.

69. **C** is correct. Most robberies occur on Saturday and Sunday mornings between 4:00 A.M. and 6:30 A.M., and most assaults occur on Friday and Sunday mornings between midnight and 3:00 A.M. The patrol schedule given in C is the only one of the four that provides coverage on those days at those times.

70. **B** is the most logical answer. There is no evidence to suggest that any of the other three statements are true.

71. **B** is the best answer. Note that while A includes a situation in which a club is a gathering place for "purposes of engaging in unlawful conduct," the owner "is unaware of the fact," so A is incorrect. The groups gathering in C and D are not doing so in order to engage in unlawful conduct, so neither C nor D is correct.

72. **B** is the clearest and most accurate statement. Note, in A, the confusing sentence "Mr. Kelly was arrested." Since both the victim and the suspect are named Mr. Kelly, it is unclear which one was arrested.

73. **C** is the best answer. The man should be arrested, since the possession of a rifle without a permit is "strictly prohibited." Note the importance of the word "first" in this question.

74. There is information missing from every statement except **B**, which is correct.

75. **D** is the best answe, as it is the only situation in which a "grave risk of public alarm" is caused by someone acting with "four or more persons." Note B is not correct because Louis shouts to the crowd alone.

76. A is unclear, and there is information missing from C and D, so **B** is correct.

77. **C** is correct. Most robberies occur between Ford and Huron on Lakeside Drive on week-days between 2:00 A.M. and 7:30 A.M., and the patrol schedule given in C is the only one of the four that provides coverage on those days at that time. Note A is incorrect because it does not include Tuesdays, Wednesdays, and Thursdays.

78. **A** is correct. The greatest incidence of public drunkenness occurs near the First Street Saloon on Saturdays between midnight and 3:00 A.M., and the patrol schedule given in A is the only one of the four that provides coverage on that day of the week at that time. Note that C is incorrect because it does not include the hour between midnight and 1:00 A.M.

79. **C** is the most logical statement. There is no evidence to suggest that any of the other three statements are true.

80. **B** is correct. Mrs. Gomez is the only individual whose actions meet the criteria given in the definition.

81. **D** is the clearest and most accurate statement. Note, in A, the phrase "fell on a wet spot on the floor named Lisa Andrews," which implies that Lisa Andrews is the name of the wet spot, rather than the name of the victim.

82. **D** contains the most repeaters.

83. There is information missing from A (Mr. Finch's address), and C and D are unclear, so **B** is correct.

84. **B** is the best answer. Note the importance of the word "first" in this question. Establishing the man's identity first will allow Officer Glenby to verify the man's story (A and D) more effectively. At this point, there is no reason to arrest the man, so C is incorrect.

85. The only situation in which the presence of a person inside the building should seem to be a "reasonable possibility" is **B**. Note that C is incorrect because Patch, who is "trapped inside when a set of fire doors closes," is a participant in the crime.

86. **D** is the only statement that contains all the information.

87. **D** is the clearest and most accurate statement.

88. There is information missing from A and B, and C is unclear, so **D** is correct.

89. **A** is correct. Mr. Roth should be charged with Insurance Fraud in the First Degree, because his yacht is worth more than $1,000,000.

90. **A** is correct. The wording in B is confusing, and there is information missing from C and D.

Practice Test 3

ANSWER SHEET FOR PRACTICE TEST 3

For each question, select the best answer choice. Use the answer sheet to mark your choices. Answers and explanations follow the test.

1. Ⓐ Ⓑ Ⓒ Ⓓ
2. Ⓐ Ⓑ Ⓒ Ⓓ
3. Ⓐ Ⓑ Ⓒ Ⓓ
4. Ⓐ Ⓑ Ⓒ Ⓓ
5. Ⓐ Ⓑ Ⓒ Ⓓ
6. Ⓐ Ⓑ Ⓒ Ⓓ
7. Ⓐ Ⓑ Ⓒ Ⓓ
8. Ⓐ Ⓑ Ⓒ Ⓓ
9. Ⓐ Ⓑ Ⓒ Ⓓ
10. Ⓐ Ⓑ Ⓒ Ⓓ
11. Ⓐ Ⓑ Ⓒ Ⓓ
12. Ⓐ Ⓑ Ⓒ Ⓓ
13. Ⓐ Ⓑ Ⓒ Ⓓ
14. Ⓐ Ⓑ Ⓒ Ⓓ
15. Ⓐ Ⓑ Ⓒ Ⓓ
16. Ⓐ Ⓑ Ⓒ Ⓓ
17. Ⓐ Ⓑ Ⓒ Ⓓ
18. Ⓐ Ⓑ Ⓒ Ⓓ
19. Ⓐ Ⓑ Ⓒ Ⓓ
20. Ⓐ Ⓑ Ⓒ Ⓓ
21. Ⓐ Ⓑ Ⓒ Ⓓ
22. Ⓐ Ⓑ Ⓒ Ⓓ
23. Ⓐ Ⓑ Ⓒ Ⓓ
24. Ⓐ Ⓑ Ⓒ Ⓓ
25. Ⓐ Ⓑ Ⓒ Ⓓ

26. Ⓐ Ⓑ Ⓒ Ⓓ
27. Ⓐ Ⓑ Ⓒ Ⓓ
28. Ⓐ Ⓑ Ⓒ Ⓓ
29. Ⓐ Ⓑ Ⓒ Ⓓ
30. Ⓐ Ⓑ Ⓒ Ⓓ
31. Ⓐ Ⓑ Ⓒ Ⓓ
32. Ⓐ Ⓑ Ⓒ Ⓓ
33. Ⓐ Ⓑ Ⓒ Ⓓ
34. Ⓐ Ⓑ Ⓒ Ⓓ
35. Ⓐ Ⓑ Ⓒ Ⓓ
36. Ⓐ Ⓑ Ⓒ Ⓓ
37. Ⓐ Ⓑ Ⓒ Ⓓ
38. Ⓐ Ⓑ Ⓒ Ⓓ
39. Ⓐ Ⓑ Ⓒ Ⓓ
40. Ⓐ Ⓑ Ⓒ Ⓓ
41. Ⓐ Ⓑ Ⓒ Ⓓ
42. Ⓐ Ⓑ Ⓒ Ⓓ
43. Ⓐ Ⓑ Ⓒ Ⓓ
44. Ⓐ Ⓑ Ⓒ Ⓓ
45. Ⓐ Ⓑ Ⓒ Ⓓ
46. Ⓐ Ⓑ Ⓒ Ⓓ
47. Ⓐ Ⓑ Ⓒ Ⓓ
48. Ⓐ Ⓑ Ⓒ Ⓓ
49. Ⓐ Ⓑ Ⓒ Ⓓ
50. Ⓐ Ⓑ Ⓒ Ⓓ

51. Ⓐ Ⓑ Ⓒ Ⓓ
52. Ⓐ Ⓑ Ⓒ Ⓓ
53. Ⓐ Ⓑ Ⓒ Ⓓ
54. Ⓐ Ⓑ Ⓒ Ⓓ
55. Ⓐ Ⓑ Ⓒ Ⓓ
56. Ⓐ Ⓑ Ⓒ Ⓓ
57. Ⓐ Ⓑ Ⓒ Ⓓ
58. Ⓐ Ⓑ Ⓒ Ⓓ
59. Ⓐ Ⓑ Ⓒ Ⓓ
60. Ⓐ Ⓑ Ⓒ Ⓓ
61. Ⓐ Ⓑ Ⓒ Ⓓ
62. Ⓐ Ⓑ Ⓒ Ⓓ
63. Ⓐ Ⓑ Ⓒ Ⓓ
64. Ⓐ Ⓑ Ⓒ Ⓓ
65. Ⓐ Ⓑ Ⓒ Ⓓ
66. Ⓐ Ⓑ Ⓒ Ⓓ
67. Ⓐ Ⓑ Ⓒ Ⓓ
68. Ⓐ Ⓑ Ⓒ Ⓓ
69. Ⓐ Ⓑ Ⓒ Ⓓ
70. Ⓐ Ⓑ Ⓒ Ⓓ
71. Ⓐ Ⓑ Ⓒ Ⓓ
72. Ⓐ Ⓑ Ⓒ Ⓓ
73. Ⓐ Ⓑ Ⓒ Ⓓ
74. Ⓐ Ⓑ Ⓒ Ⓓ
75. Ⓐ Ⓑ Ⓒ Ⓓ

76. Ⓐ Ⓑ Ⓒ Ⓓ
77. Ⓐ Ⓑ Ⓒ Ⓓ
78. Ⓐ Ⓑ Ⓒ Ⓓ
79. Ⓐ Ⓑ Ⓒ Ⓓ
80. Ⓐ Ⓑ Ⓒ Ⓓ
81. Ⓐ Ⓑ Ⓒ Ⓓ
82. Ⓐ Ⓑ Ⓒ Ⓓ
83. Ⓐ Ⓑ Ⓒ Ⓓ
84. Ⓐ Ⓑ Ⓒ Ⓓ
85. Ⓐ Ⓑ Ⓒ Ⓓ
86. Ⓐ Ⓑ Ⓒ Ⓓ
87. Ⓐ Ⓑ Ⓒ Ⓓ
88. Ⓐ Ⓑ Ⓒ Ⓓ
89. Ⓐ Ⓑ Ⓒ Ⓓ
90. Ⓐ Ⓑ Ⓒ Ⓓ

1. Officer Moore pulls over a motorist for exceeding the speed limit by a small margin and determines that the motorist, a man who lives in another state, was honestly unaware of the posted speed limit. Officer Moore should:

   A. issue a warning to the motorist and advise him to be more careful.

   B. issue the man a traffic ticket, since the city can use all the revenue it can get.

   C. give the man a warning, but follow him to his destination to make sure that he drives safely.

   D. issue the man a traffic ticket in order to discourage him from ever visiting the city again.

2. Officer Whitcomb responds to a report of an assault and gathers the following information:

   Location: 490 Pearl Lane
   Time: 8:15 P.M.
   Victim: Sam Valens
   Injury: broken rib
   Weapon: baseball bat
   Suspect: tall male wearing a thick gold chain
   Status of Suspect: fled on foot

   Officer Whitcomb must write his report. Which of the following expresses the information most clearly and accurately?

   A. At 8:15 P.M., Sam Valens, who is tall and wears a thick gold chain, was struck by a baseball bat, breaking his rib. The suspect fled on foot from 490 Pearl Lane, the place where he was struck.

   B. Sam Valens reported that at 8:15 P.M. at 490 Pearl Lane, a tall male wearing a thick gold chain struck him with a baseball bat. Sam Valens suffered a broken rib. The suspect fled on foot.

   C. At 8:15 P.M. at 490 Pearl Lane, a tall male struck him with a baseball bat, breaking his rib. The suspect fled on foot.

   D. Sam Valens reported that at 490 Pearl Lane, a tall male wearing a thick gold chain struck him with a baseball bat. Sam Valens suffered a broken rib. The suspect fled on foot.

3. During a family trip, the Smiths drove through a tunnel. As they emerged from the tunnel, someone threw a large rock through their windshield. Officer Guitterez was sent to investigate. Of the following descriptions of the suspect given to Officer Guitterez by witnesses, which should he consider most likely to be correct?

   A. 5'8" teenage girl, wearing black jeans and an orange sweater

   B. 5'1" teenage girl, wearing blue jeans and a blue sweater

   C. 5'8" teenage boy, wearing blue jeans and an orange sweater

   D. 5'8" teenage girl, wearing blue jeans and an orange sweater

4. In State X, someone who intentionally damages a building or motor vehicle by starting a fire or causing an explosion is guilty of **ARSON IN THE THIRD DEGREE**. Given this definition alone, which of the following is the best example of Arson in the Third Degree?

    A. Hoping to destroy the building and collect the insurance, Jean detonates an explosive in the basement of her building, and the resulting fire engulfs the structure.

    B. Gas fumes from Amelia's car, which is in need of a new exhaust system, are ignited when she throws a lit cigarette on the ground in her garage. The fire destroys her house.

    C. Penelope tests the lighter in her new car and drops it on the passenger seat, resulting in a small fire that burns the upholstery.

    D. Harris sets off fireworks in his backyard, and one of them singes his father's favorite baseball hat.

5. Officer Greely is dispatched to the scene of a collision, where she gathers the following information:

Location:	corner of Elm and First Avenue
Time:	9:00 A.M.
Drivers and Vehicles:	Mr. Cho, driving a black Ford Taurus, and Mrs. Alexander, driving a green Honda Accord
Driver at Fault:	Mrs. Alexander ran a red light, causing the collision
Action Taken:	Mrs. Alexander was given a traffic ticket
Injuries:	none

    Officer Greely must complete her report. Which of the following expresses the information most clearly and accurately?

    A. Mrs. Alexander, who was driving a black Honda Accord, ran a red light at the corner of Elm and First Avenue, causing a collision with a green Ford Taurus, driven by Mr. Cho, at 9:00 A.M. There were no injuries. Mrs. Alexander was given a traffic ticket.

    B. Mrs. Alexander, who was driving a green Honda Accord, ran a red light at the corner of Elm and First Avenue, causing a collision with a black Ford Taurus, driven by Mr. Cho, at 9:00 P.M. There were no injuries. Mrs. Alexander was given a traffic ticket.

    C. Mrs. Alexander, who was driving a green Honda Accord, ran a red light at the corner of Elm and First Avenue, causing a collision with a black Ford Taurus, driven by Mr. Cho, at 9:00 A.M. There were no injuries. Mrs. Alexander was given a traffic ticket.

    D. Mrs. Alexander, who was driving a green Honda Accord, ran a red light at the corner of Elm and First Avenue, causing a collision with a black Ford Taurus, driven by Mr. Cho, at 9:00 A.M. There were no injuries. Mr. Cho was given a traffic ticket.

6. Officer Brody has observed that, within his patrol area, most rapes occur on Fourth Street between Hightower and Branch, most larcenies on Radcliffe Place near Pride Park, and most robberies on the four blocks adjacent to Heritage Square. Most rapes occur on Thursdays, larcenies on Mondays and Fridays, and robberies on Fridays, Saturdays, and Sundays. Most rapes take place between 4:00 P.M. and 6:30 P.M., most larcenies between 10:00 A.M. and 1:00 P.M., and most robberies between 8:00 P.M. and 10:45 P.M.

Given this information, which of the following patrol schedules would enable Officer Brody to most effectively reduce the number of larcenies?

A. Radcliffe Place near Pride Park, Mondays and Fridays, 10:00 A.M. to 3:00 P.M.

B. the four blocks adjacent to Heritage Square, Fridays, 10:00 A.M. to 1:00 P.M.

C. Radcliffe Place near Pride Park, weekdays, 10:00 P.M. to 1:00 A.M.

D. the four blocks adjacent to Heritage Square, Mondays and Fridays, 10:00 P.M. to 1:00 A.M.

7. Given the information in Question 6, which of the following patrol schedules would enable Officer Brody to most effectively reduce the number of rapes?

A. Radcliffe Place near Pride Park, Thursdays, 4:00 P.M. to 6:30 P.M.

B. Fourth Street between Hightower and Branch, Saturdays, 8:00 P.M. to 10:45 P.M.

C. Radcliffe Place near Pride Park, Saturdays, 4:00 P.M. to 10:45 P.M.

D. Fourth Street between Hightower and Branch, Thursdays, 4:00 P.M. to 8:30 P.M.

8. Given the information in Question 6, which of the following would be the most advisable day and time for someone who does not wish to be robbed to walk around the four blocks adjacent to Heritage Square?

A. Sunday between 4:00 P.M. and 9:30 P.M.

B. Saturday between 6:00 P.M. and 7:30 P.M.

C. Friday between 9:00 P.M. and midnight

D. Friday or Saturday between 5:30 P.M. and 8:30 P.M.

9. Officer Land was sent to investigate a reported larceny and gathered the following information:

Location: 80 Prince Street
Time: between 8:00 P.M. and 1:00 A.M.
Police Contacted by: Harriet Leroy, resident
Item Missing: expensive set of antique china

Officer Land is writing his report. Which of the following expresses the information most clearly and accurately?

A. Harriet Leroy reported that an expensive set of antique china was stolen from her residence sometime after 8:00 P.M. She lives at 80 Prince Street.

B. Between 8:00 P.M. and 1:00 A.M., Harriet Leroy reported that some dishes were stolen from her residence.

C. An expensive set of antique china was stolen from 80 Prince Street between 8:00 P.M. and 1:00 A.M.

D. Harriet Leroy reported that, between 8:00 P.M. and 1:00 A.M., an expensive set of antique china was stolen from her residence at 80 Prince Street.

10. In State X, a person is guilty of **MANSLAUGHTER IN THE SECOND DEGREE** when he recklessly causes the death of another person. Based solely upon this definition, which of the following is not an example of Manslaughter in the Second Degree?

A. Practicing his "ninja" moves, Eduardo hurls throwing stars into a tree at a crowded playground, and one of them misses the tree and strikes a man, killing him instantly.

B. Sarah swings on a rope across a creek while holding her baby. The baby falls out of her grasp and drowns in the creek.

C. Charles repeatedly fires his new pistol into the air to celebrate his birthday, and a neighbor is struck by one of the bullets and dies.

D. Peter prepares a peanut butter sandwich for his aunt, who has an unprecedented allergic reaction to the peanut butter and dies.

11. The best way for police officers to treat witnesses to a crime is:

A. to respectfully ask for their cooperation in the investigation.

B. to forcefully establish that the police are in charge and that the witnesses must cooperate.

C. to completely ignore all witnesses whose information is not crucial to the investigation.

D. to threaten to arrest any witness who does not immediately compose a written and signed statement as to what he or she saw.

12. Officer Garcia responded to a report of vandalism and gathered the following information:

Location: Gentleman's Clothing
Police Contacted by: Mr. Mead, the manager
Incident: when he arrived at work at 9:00 A.M., Mr. Mead discovered that the store's windows had been spray-painted
Suspect: unknown

Officer Garcia is writing his report. Which of the following expresses the information most clearly and accurately?

A. Mr. Mead reported that when he arrived at work at 9:00 A.M. at Gentlemen's Clothing, where he is the manager, he discovered that the store's windows had been spray-painted. The suspect is unknown.

B. Mr. Mead discovered it at 9:00 A.M. The windows of the store he manages were spray-painted. He called the police. It was at Gentleman's Clothing. The suspect who did it, possibly, is unknown.

C. At 9:00 A.M., Mr. Mead went to work at Gentleman's Clothing, which he manages, and discovered that an unknown suspect had spray-painted the store's windows at Gentleman's Clothing. He reported the vandalism of Gentleman's Clothing to the police.

D. At 9:00 A.M. was when he, Mr. Mead, discovered that the windows of Gentleman's Clothing had been spray-painted. He is the manager, not the suspect, who is unknown.

13. As she was walking to school, Amber was robbed by a man in an old car who pulled up next to her, shoved her, and stole her satchel. Amber did not get a very good look at the man, but there were witnesses nearby who saw the vehicle speed away after the robbery. Of the following descriptions of the suspect's vehicle given to investigating Officer House, which should she consider most likely to be accurate?

A. black Chevrolet convertible with a white top
B. white Chevrolet convertible with a white top
C. white Chevrolet convertible with a black top
D. white Ford convertible with a white top

14. Officer McKinney was dispatched to the scene of an auto accident, where he gathered the following information:

Location: the rear exit of Percy's Chicken
Time: 6:15 P.M.
Incident: Eloise Winter drove her car into a neon sign
Injury: Ms. Winter suffered a concussion
Damage: neon sign destroyed

Officer McKinney must complete his report. Which of the following expresses the information most clearly and accurately?

A. Eloise Winter destroyed a neon sign with her car at the rear exit of Percy's Chicken, causing herself a concussion.

B. At 6:15 P.M., Eloise Winter drove her car into a neon sign at the rear exit of Percy's Chicken, destroying the neon sign. Ms. Winter suffered a concussion.

C. The neon sign at the rear exit of Percy's Chicken was destroyed when Eloise Winter drove her car into it at 6:15 P.M.

D. Percy's Chicken was the place where, at the rear exit, Eloise Winter got a concussion hitting a neon sign in her car.

15. Officer Henry is instructed to work a series of late night shifts as part of a departmental effort to reduce late-night crime. Officer Henry, who has a new baby at home, is displeased with the assignment. What should Officer Henry do?

A. refuse the assignment

B. quit his job, since the department obviously does not take his needs into consideration

C. speak with a supervisor about his situation

D. complain loudly to his colleagues until someone offers to take the shifts to which he has been assigned

16. In State X, a person is guilty of **PETIT LARCENY** when he steals property. Based solely upon this definition, which of the following is the best example of Petit Larceny?

A. Sandra borrows her mother's hair dryer and forgets to return it.

B. Elizabeth takes a portable CD player from a stranger's bag while the stranger is not looking.

C. Josannah takes her friend's car, with her friend's permission, but forgets to return it until the following morning.

D. Nat borrows a video game from a friend and gets involved in a month-long marathon game.

17. Officer Fine is sent to investigate a report of a missing person. She gathers the following information:

Police Contacted by:	Mr. Branch
Person Missing:	Judd Branch, Mr. Branch's uncle
Description of Person Missing:	elderly man with white hair and a long white beard
Person Last Seen:	at 75 Hill Boulevard at 4:00 P.M.

Officer Fine must write her report. Which of the following expresses the information most clearly and accurately?

A. Mr. Branch reported that his uncle, Judd Branch, who is an elderly man with white hair and a long white beard, is missing. He was last seen at 75 Hill Boulevard, at 4:00 P.M.

B. Judd Branch is an elderly man with white hair and a long white beard whose uncle, Mr. Branch, was reported missing after being last seen at 75 Hill Boulevard at 4:00 P.M.

C. Mr. Branch's uncle, Judd Branch, is missing from 75 Hill Boulevard, where he was last seen at 4:00 P.M. The missing person, Judd Branch, has a long white beard. The missing person, Judd Branch, is also described as elderly with white hair.

D. Judd Branch is the uncle of Mr. Branch who says that Judd Branch was last seen at 4:00 P.M. but is now missing. He is elderly with white hair and a long white beard. That description applies to Judd Branch.

18. In which of the following situations would an officer be least likely to call for backup?

A. during a high-speed car chase
B. upon observing a bank robbery in progress
C. while arresting a suspect who is too drunk to stand up straight
D. upon discovering that an armed suspect has taken a hostage

19. A man is paroled from prison after serving nearly all of a 20-year sentence for a violent crime. Officer Jimenez learns from an informant that citizens in the community where the parolee's family still lives plan to ambush him if he attempts to return and settle there. What should Officer Jimenez do first?

A. report the rumor to his superiors
B. warn the parolee not to return home to his family
C. visit the family and inform them of the possible plan
D. do nothing, as the man probably deserves whatever fate may befall him

20. Officer Jenkins was sent to investigate a report of domestic violence. He gathered the following information:

Location:	100 Peak Street, Apt. A
Time:	12:15 A.M.
Police Contacted by:	a neighbor who refused to identify herself
Incident:	screams and crashing sounds coming from above address; it was discovered that a fight had taken place between Anna Sand and her husband, Richard Sand
Victim:	Anna Sand
Injuries:	broken arm, cuts on her torso
Suspect:	Richard Sand
Status of Suspect:	he was arrested

Officer Jenkins is writing his report. Which of the following expresses the information most clearly and accurately?

A. Richard Sand and his wife Anna Sand had a fight that was reported as screams and crashing sounds by a neighbor who refused to identify herself at 12:15 A.M. Richard Sand was arrested. Anna Sand suffered cuts on her torso.

B. At 12:15 A.M., a neighbor, who refused to identify herself, reported screams and crashing sounds coming from 100 Peak Street, Apt. A. It was discovered that a fight had taken place between Anna Sand and her husband, Richard Sand. Anna Sand suffered a broken arm and cuts on her torso. Richard Sand was arrested.

C. Anna Sand suffered a broken arm and cuts on her torso after a fight with her husband, Richard Sand, who was arrested. This was at 12:15 A.M. at 100 Peak Street, Apt. A.

D. Coming from 100 Peak Street, Apt. A, a neighbor who refused to identify herself heard screams and crashing sounds that were discovered to have been the sounds of a fight between Anna Sand and her husband, Richard, who was arrested. Anna Sand suffered a broken arm.

21. In State X, a person is guilty of **UNLAWFULLY POSTING ADVERTISEMENTS** when, having no right to do so, he affixes to the property of another person any advertisement or other matter designed to benefit a person other than the owner of the property. Based solely upon this definition, which of the following is the best example of Unlawfully Posting Advertisements?

A. Emmanuelle puts a "Happy Birthday" sticker on a friend's notebook on the morning of that friend's birthday.

B. Marcus affixes a poster urging voters to elect Mr. French to a post for which Mr. French is a candidate to Mr. French's front door.

C. Werner affixes a poster advertising his band's upcoming performance on the window of a copy shop owned by Mr. Fassim, whom Werner does not know.

D. Joanie puts a sticker advertising her favorite radio station on the rear windshield of her car.

22. Officer Greer is offered a free two-week vacation at a beachfront condominium belonging to the father of a man who was recently arrested by Officer Greer and who is still in custody. The father insists that there are "no strings attached." What should Officer Greer do?

    A. refuse the offer and report it to his superiors

    B. take the vacation, but be careful not to let the father's generosity affect the outcome of the investigation involving his son

    C. accept the offer, but insist on taking the trip after the investigation involving the man's son has been completed

    D. tell the father he needs to think about it, and plan to accept the offer if and when the man's son is cleared of any charges against him

23. Officer Guerre pulled a motorist over while patrolling a busy street. He noted the following information:

    Location: intersection of Tenth Street and Live Avenue
    Time: 4:30 P.M.
    Driver: Ms. Petrie
    Violation: exceeding the speed limit
    Action Taken: Ms. Petrie was given a traffic ticket

    Officer Guerre must write his report. Which of the following expresses the information most clearly and accurately?

    A. Ms. Petrie was given a traffic ticket. This was because she exceeded the speed limit, occurring at 4:30 P.M. at the intersection of Tenth Street and Live Avenue.

    B. At the intersection of Tenth Street and Live Avenue, Ms. Petrie was exceeding the speed limit.

    C. At 4:30 P.M., Ms. Petrie exceeded the speed limit at the corner of Tenth Street and Live Avenue and was given a traffic ticket.

    D. Ms. Petrie got a ticket for exceeding the speed limit at the intersection of Tenth and Live.

24. On a quiet night, Officer Carroll overhears an argument between a teenager and her mother. The mother is insisting that the teenager go home and do her homework before she goes out with her friends. In response, the teenager calls her mother an obscene name and yells at her in front of a crowd of people. The mother sees Officer Carroll and asks him to take the teenager away because she can no longer deal with her own child. What should Officer Carroll do?

    A. comply with the mother's wishes and take the teenager into custody

    B. arrest the teenager for being cruel to her mother

    C. explain to the mother that he cannot interfere in their family problems, and recommend a place she and her daughter can go for counseling

    D. ignore the mother and the situation, since the police have much more important issues at hand

25. A man who is dressed entirely in black and whose face is covered by a mask walks into a bank, announces that he has "had it with outrageous service charges," and opens fire on all the tellers. The man then flees the bank on foot. During the course of his investigation, Officer Reynolds interviews several witnesses. Of the following descriptions of the suspect's voice given to him by the witnesses, which should Officer Reynolds consider most likely to be correct?

A. deep and nasal with a British accent

B. high and nasal with a British accent

C. deep and booming with a British accent

D. deep and nasal with no accent

26. Officer Isaacson reported to the scene of a robbery, where she gathered the following information:

Location: Number One Bar
Time: 11:30 P.M.
Victim: Mr. Yow, owner
Incident: suspect held a gun to the victim's head and forced him to hand over all the money in the register, which totaled $600
Suspect: short male wearing a blue ski mask

Officer Isaacson must write her report. Which of the following expresses the information most clearly and accurately?

A. Mr. Yow reported that at 11:30 P.M. at the Number One Bar, which he owns, a short male wearing a blue ski mask held a gun to his head and forced him to hand over all the money in the register, which totaled $600.

B. $600 in cash was stolen from Mr. Yow at the Number One Bar, which he owns, by a short male wearing a blue ski mask who held a gun to his head and forced him to hand over all the money in the register.

C. At 11:30 P.M. at the Number One Bar, which Mr. Yow owns, a short male wearing a blue ski mask forced him to hand over all the money in the register, which totaled $600.

D. At the Number One Bar, which he owns, a short male wearing a blue ski mask held a gun to Mr. Yow's head and forced him to hand over all the money in the register, which totaled $600.

To answer Questions 27, 28, 29, and 30, use the information in the following passage.

Officers Scanlon and McCoy were in a patrol car when they were called to the scene of a vehicle/pedestrian accident at the intersection of 14th Avenue and Cavalcade Street. When the officers arrived at the scene, they saw that the injured pedestrian was being tended to by paramedics. Several people were gathered at the corners of the intersection. The driver of the car had parked to the side on Cavalcade Street. Officers in another patrol car began directing traffic, and Officers Scanlon and McCoy interviewed the driver and the witnesses.

The driver, Mr. Pierre Toulouse, said he'd been driving his Ford Taurus northbound on Cavalcade. As he neared the intersection, the light turned yellow; he'd just noticed this when the pedestrian ran in front of the car. Mr. Toulouse said he slammed on the brakes, but was unable to stop. He said he wasn't sure exactly how fast he was traveling, but was certain that it was no more than 30 mph. His insurance and registration were current, but his driver's license had expired on his last birthday. Mr. Toulouse said he'd simply forgotten to renew it; a license check showed no outstanding violations.

Several of the bystanders said they'd witnessed the incident. Ms. Amy Presser said she'd been waiting at the southeast corner to cross Cavalcade. She happened to be looking south and saw the Taurus approaching the intersection. She stated that the car's speed was "about normal" and that she'd seen the light turn yellow just as the car entered the intersection. She had not seen the pedestrian until the car began braking and struck him.

Mr. Augustin Lantos also had been waiting to cross Cavalcade but on the corner opposite Ms. Presser. He said he'd seen the Ford "out of the corner of his eye," but he couldn't tell how fast it had been traveling. He had seen the pedestrian approaching the corner; Mr. Lantos said the young man was running along the sidewalk, carrying a basketball. The young man glanced both ways at the intersection, but ran into the street without pausing. Mr. Lantos turned his head as the pedestrian left the curb and did not see the collision. Mr. Lantos said he'd seen young people jaywalking at this intersection many times, often headed for the basketball courts in the nearby park, and he had been "expecting something like this to happen one of these days."

Mr. Ben Klein had been standing at the bus stop on the west side of Cavalcade, about midway down the block. He had noticed the Taurus as it went through the intersection of Cavalcade and 13th Avenue; he said the car seemed to be traveling at a moderate speed. His view of the collision was blocked by parked cars.

Ms. Nanette Guidry had left the deli at the southeast corner of Cavalcade and 14th Avenue shortly before the Taurus struck the pedestrian. She said the young man had brushed against her as he was running toward the intersection, and she was irritated that he didn't apologize. She was about to cross 14th Avenue and had turned to the left to check traffic when she saw the young man had been struck by the Taurus; she said that just prior to the collision, she'd seen the Taurus out of the corner of her eye, and it had been "flying along very fast."

Before the paramedics took the pedestrian to the hospital, one of them reported to Officer McCoy. The pedestrian's name was Lenny McGraw; he had a broken femur and possible internal injuries. He was conscious but unable to answer any questions.

27. Who was driving the Ford Taurus involved in the incident?
    A. Mr. Ben Klein
    B. Mr. Pierre Toulouse
    C. Mr. Augustin Lantos
    D. Mr. Lenny McGraw

28. In which direction was the driver traveling?

    A. northbound on Cavalcade

    B. northbound on 14th Avenue

    C. eastbound on Cavalcade

    D. southbound on 14th Avenue

29. How many people witnessed the accident?

    A. four people, all of whom witnessed the car strike the pedestrian

    B. four people, three of whom witnessed the car strike the pedestrian

    C. four people, two of whom witnessed the car strike the pedestrian

    D. four people, none of whom witnessed the car strike the pedestrian

30. Based on the information in the passage, should any citations be issued, and if so, to whom?

    A. The driver should receive citations for speeding, driving without a license, and expired insurance.

    B. The pedestrian should receive a citation for jaywalking.

    C. The driver should receive a citation for driving with an expired license.

    D. The driver should receive a citation for speeding and the pedestrian should receive a citation for jaywalking.

31. Of the following experiences, which would be the least significant in preparing someone for a career as a police officer?

    A. being a member of the Boy Scouts, Girl Scouts, or other group that stresses leadership and civic responsibility

    B. taking criminal justice and psychology courses at the undergraduate level

    C. hunting deer or other animals

    D. working as a volunteer at a crisis hotline

32. Officer Brighton is approached by a man who, loudly and in an upset manner, asks him a question in a language Officer Brighton does not understand. What should Officer Brighton do?

    A. turn and walk away from the man, since he clearly can do nothing to help him

    B. attempt to understand the man's question, since it may be urgent.

    C. arrest the man for assaulting him

    D. shake the man until he calms down

33. In State X, a person is guilty of **GRAND LARCENY IN THE THIRD DEGREE** when he steals property and when the value of the property exceeds $3,000. Based solely upon this definition, which of the following is the best example of Grand Larceny in the Third Degree?

    A. Gracie steals a car valued at $3,100.

    B. Julio steals a boat worth $2,900.

    C. Ike steals a computer valued at $1,200.

    D. Marcie buys a stolen stereo system valued at $3,500.

34. Officer Black arrived at the scene of a reported assault, where she gathered the following information:

    Location: First Street Garden
    Time: 3:00 P.M.
    Incident: victim was struck from behind
    Victim: Adelaide Murphy
    Injury: badly bruised neck
    Weapon: shovel
    Suspect: unknown

    Officer Black is writing her report. Which of the following expresses the information most clearly and accurately?

    A. At 3:00 P.M. at the First Street Garden, someone struck someone else from behind with a shovel.

    B. Adelaide Murphy reported that at the First Street Garden, someone struck her from behind with a shovel. The suspect is unknown who gave her a badly bruised neck.

    C. At 3:00 P.M., someone struck Adelaide Murphy from behind with a shovel, giving her a badly bruised neck. The suspect struck her from behind.

    D. Adelaide Murphy reported that at 3:00 P.M. at the First Street Garden, someone struck her from behind with a shovel. Ms. Murphy suffered a badly bruised neck. The suspect is unknown.

35. During a nightly patrol of a section of town in which violent crimes regularly occur, Officer Feldman observes a man and a woman who are yelling, screaming, punching, and pulling at one another in a dimly lit front yard. The most logical assumption for Officer Feldman to make is:

    A. the man and the woman are married.

    B. the man is trying to steal something from the woman.

    C. the man and the woman are practicing some sort of martial art together.

    D. the man and the woman are fighting.

36. Officer Henry answers a call to a residence where a strange odor has been reported. She gathers the following information:

Location:	35 Time Street
Time:	6:30 P.M.
Police Contacted by:	Muriel Stevens, resident
Incident:	strange odor
Action Taken:	a dead squirrel was discovered under the house's front steps

    Officer Henry must write her report. Which of the following expresses the information most clearly and accurately?

    A. At 6:30 P.M., Muriel Stevens reported a strange odor at her residence at 35 Time Street. A dead squirrel was discovered under the house's front steps.

    B. Muriel Stevens reported a strange odor at 6:30 A.M. at her residence at 35 Time Street. A dead squirrel was discovered under the house's front steps.

    C. A dead chipmunk was the cause of the strange smell reported by Muriel Stevens at 6:30 P.M. that she said was coming from her home at 35 Time Street.

    D. At 35 Time Avenue, resident Muriel Stevens reported a strange smell, which turned out to be a dead squirrel under the house's back steps.

37. In State X, a person is guilty of **FALSIFYING BUSINESS RECORDS IN THE SECOND DEGREE** when, with intent to defraud, he makes or causes a false entry in the business records of an enterprise. Based solely upon this definition, which of the following is not an example of Falsifying Business Records in the Second Degree?

    A. To avoid paying taxes, Arnold alters the daily totals for his clothing store in order to make it look like the store has not made a profit.

    B. Lorenzo keeps an authentic copy of his business records in a safe at his house, but keeps a copy with inaccurate figures at the office to show his investors so they will not take away their funding.

    C. Caspar enters an exaggerated amount into his business ledger for one week's total sales so that his weekly bonus will be higher than usual.

    D. Josephine, an art dealer, overcharges a customer for a sculpture.

38. Officer Payne finds a gun on the sidewalk next to a trail of blood. What should Officer Payne do first?

    A. pick up the gun and determine whether it has been discharged
    B. follow the trail of blood
    C. call in to report the gun and the blood
    D. fire a warning shot into the air to clear away any spectators, who may be in danger

39. Officer Alejandro found a small child wandering through an industrial park. He noted the following information:

    Location: Harris Industrial Park
    Time: 4:30 P.M.
    Incident: child found wandering in the area
    Action Taken: a name tag in the child's shirt identified her as Meg Willis; her parents were contacted and picked her up at the precinct

    Officer Alejandro is writing his report. Which of the following expresses the information most clearly and accurately?

    A. The name tag in the shirt of Meg Willis provided her name so her parents could be contacted after she was found wandering in Harris Industrial Park. The parents were contacted. They picked her up at the precinct after the girl, Meg Willis, was found at 4:30 P.M.
    B. At 4:30 P.M., a child was found wandering in Harris Industrial Park. A name tag in the girl's shirt identified her as Meg Willis. Her parents were contacted and picked her up at the precinct.
    C. A child named Meg Willis was found wandering in Harris Industrial Park, and this is known due to a name tag in her shirt. Her parents, who later picked her up at the precinct, were contacted. The child was found, who turned out to be Meg Willis, at 4:30 P.M.
    D. Her parents picked up the child found at 4:30 P.M. wandering in Harris Industrial Park after a name tag in her shirt identified her as Meg Willis. She was picked up at the precinct.

40. Officer Daniels overhears a conversation between two of his supervisors in which they discuss the fact that forensic evidence points to a particular well-to-do suspect in a rape case, but that the individual has a solid alibi for the time of the rape. Believing that his supervisors are dragging their heels because of political pressure, Officer Daniels calls a reporter from the local newspaper and anonymously gives the reporter the information, which the reporter runs on the front page of the newspaper the next morning. Later that day, the suspect dies from a self-inflicted gunshot wound to the head.

    Officer Daniels's actions were

    A. proper, because the man's suicide proved that he was, indeed, guilty.

    B. improper, because leaking any aspect of an investigation to the media without permission from a supervisor is unethical and dangerous.

    C. proper, because the force can now concentrate its efforts on other investigations.

    D. It is impossible to determine whether Officer Daniels's actions were proper without knowing whether the forensic evidence may have pointed to the wrong man.

41. In the parking lot adjacent to the diner where she works, Ada was robbed by a suspect who struck her with a board and stole her purse. Officer Grant spoke to several witnesses who were passing by at the time of the robbery. Of the following descriptions of the suspect given to Officer Grant by witnesses, which should he consider most likely to be correct?

    A. female, about 5'2" and 250 pounds, wearing black cowboy boots

    B. male, about 5'2" and 250 pounds, wearing red cowboy boots

    C. female, about 6'2" and 250 pounds, wearing red cowboy boots

    D. male, about 5'2" and 150 pounds, wearing red cowboy boots

42. Police departments often assign a percentage of their officers to undercover duty. Of the following circumstances, which would be most likely to warrant the assignment of undercover officers?

    A. A group is rioting outside of a courthouse in response to a verdict with which the crowd disagrees.

    B. Several professors at the local college are suspected of selling drugs to their students.

    C. The CEO of a large corporation has stepped out onto the 20-story ledge of his office building and is threatening to jump.

    D. Traffic is constantly backing up at a busy intersection of two four-lane avenues.

43. Officer Haynes responded to a report of a missing item and gathered the following information:

    Location: 610 Fir Street
    Time: 9:15 P.M.
    Police Contacted by: Mr. Herman, resident
    Item Missing: leaf blower

    Officer Haynes must write his report. Which of the following expresses the information most clearly and accurately?

    A. A leaf blower was reported missing by Mr. Herman from his residence. He lives at 610 Fir Street.
    B. Mr. Herman reported that his leaf blower was missing from his residence. He reported this at 9:15 P.M.
    C. 610 Fir Street is the address where Mr. Herman lives and from which he reported at 9:15 that some property was missing.
    D. At 9:15 P.M., Mr. Herman reported that a leaf blower was missing from his residence at 610 Fir Street.

44. In State X, a person is guilty of **ROBBERY IN THE SECOND DEGREE** when he forcibly steals property and when he is aided by another person actually present. Based solely upon the above definition, which of the following is the best example of Robbery in the Second Degree?

    A. Ramona steals her grandmother's hidden supply of cash after receiving a letter from her cousin explaining where the money is hidden.
    B. Fletcher steals a chair from a neighbor with the help of his friend, Christy, who holds a gun to the neighbor's head while Fletcher takes the chair.
    C. Lisette steals an assortment of lipsticks from a drug store, then gives them to her friends.
    D. Hugh strikes a car owner with a club, steals his car, then drives to his girlfriend's house.

45. A truck driver making deliveries for a beer distributor reports that his truck has been stolen while he was on his route; his delivery book was inside the truck, so he isn't sure exactly how much merchandise is missing. When he picked up the truck in the morning, the full load was worth $15,000, and the driver estimates he'd made about one-quarter of his deliveries. About how much was the beer in the stolen truck worth?

    A. $ 7,500
    B. $10,000
    C. $11,250
    D. $12,500

46. Officer Wells is interviewing a suspect whom he believes is guilty of assaulting a nurse as she walked from the hospital to her car. The suspect refuses to answer Officer Wells's questions and behaves belligerently toward him. Officer Wells should:

    A. hit the suspect one time, and make sure the blow is hard enough to get the suspect's attention and respect.

    B. continue with the interview without using physical force.

    C. release the suspect, since he obviously is not going to confess.

    D. injure the suspect in exactly the same way the nurse was injured in order to jar the suspect's memory.

47. Officer Dallas was dispatched to the scene of a collision, where she gathered the following information:

Location:	the intersection of Whitesville and Excelsior Streets
Time:	2:00 P.M.
Drivers and Vehicles:	Miss Moynihan, driving a red Toyota truck, and Mr. Davis, driving a gray Ford sedan
Incident:	Mr. Davis failed to yield the right-of-way, causing the collision
Injury:	Miss Moynihan suffered a broken nose
Action Taken:	Mr. Davis was given a traffic ticket

    Officer Dallas is writing her report. Which of the following expresses the information most clearly and accurately?

    A. Mr. Davis, who was driving a gray Ford sedan, failed to yield the right-of-way, causing a collision with a red Toyota truck, driven by Miss Moynihan, who suffered a broken nose, at 2:00 P.M.

    B. At 2:00 P.M. at the intersection of Whitesville and Excelsior Streets, Mr. Davis, who was driving a gray Ford sedan, failed to yield the right-of-way, causing a collision with a red Toyota truck, driven by Miss Moynihan, who suffered a broken nose. Mr. Davis was given a traffic ticket.

    C. After failing to yield the right-of-way at the intersection of Whitesville and Excelsior Streets at 2:00 P.M., Mr. Davis caused his gray Ford sedan to collide with Miss Moynihan's truck, a red Toyota, causing her to have a broken nose and causing him, Mr. Davis, to get a traffic ticket.

    D. Mr. Davis caused his gray Ford sedan to collide with Miss Moynihan's truck, a red Toyota, causing her to have a broken nose at 2:00 P.M. Mr. Davis was given a traffic ticket.

48. In Officer Duarte's jurisdiction, fishing without a license is strictly prohibited. During a routine patrol, Officer Duarte encounters a man fishing from a bridge without a license. The man offers Officer Duarte $20 to let him continue fishing. Officer Duarte should:

    A. refuse the money, but let the man continue fishing, as it is clearly very important to him.

    B. accept the money and continue with his patrol; such a small sum would hardly be considered a bribe, and the man obviously needs to continue fishing.

    C. refuse the money and arrest the man for fishing without a license and for attempting to bribe him.

    D. tell the man to increase the amount of money he is offering because $20 is an insult.

49. Officer Smith is dispatched to the scene of a reported assault, where he gathers the following information:

Location:	Sherry's Grill
Time:	3:00 P.M.
Victim:	Sherry Hamby, owner
Incident:	a customer threw a bowl of hot soup on Ms. Hamby
Suspect:	short male wearing jeans and cowboy boots

    Officer Smith must write his report. Which of the following expresses the information most clearly and accurately?

    A. At Sherry's Grill, which she owns, Sherry Hamby reported that at 3:00 P.M. a customer described as a short male wearing jeans and cowboy boots threw a hot bowl on her. This was at her grill.

    B. Owner Sherry Hamby reported that at 4:00 P.M. at Sherry's Grill, which she owns, a customer threw a hot bowl of soup on her.

    C. At 3:00 P.M. at Sherry's Grill, which Sherry Hamby owns, a customer described as a short male wearing jeans and cowboy boots threw a hot bowl of soup on Sherry Hamby, the owner of the place and the one who reported it.

    D. Sherry Hamby reported that at 3:00 P.M. at Sherry's Grill, which she owns, a customer described as a short male wearing jeans and cowboy boots threw a hot bowl of soup on her.

50. Of the following structures in Officer Johnston's patrol area, which should he consider the least likely to be a gathering place for high school students who are skipping school?

    A. the school playground

    B. a video game arcade

    C. a shopping mall

    D. an amusement park

51. In State X, a person is guilty of **CRIMINAL POSSESSION OF A CONTROLLED SUBSTANCE IN THE THIRD DEGREE** when he knowingly and unlawfully possesses a narcotic drug with intent to sell it. Based solely upon this definition, which of the following is the best example of Criminal Possession of a Controlled Substance in the Third Degree?

    A. Johnny possesses a small bag of a narcotic drug, which he plans to inject into his bloodstream as soon as he gets home.

    B. Ford obtains a prescribed dose of a narcotic drug, which he has been instructed by his physician to take for postoperative pain.

    C. Jason takes a small container of a narcotic drug from the locked drug cabinet at the hospital where he works, hoping to sell it to a drug addict who lives on his block.

    D. Hilda finds a bag of a white, powdered substance on her doorstep. She takes it to the police, and they identify the substance as a narcotic drug.

52. An officer's primary goal while directing an evacuation of an elementary school that has received a bomb threat should be:

    A. to instill in the children a healthy respect for and fear of explosives.

    B. to find the bomb and remove it from the building.

    C. to find the person who planted the bomb.

    D. to get the children and faculty out quickly and safely, while keeping them calm.

53. Officer Robards observed a reckless motorist, pulled the driver over, and noted the following information:

Location:	Hyperion Street near Twelfth Avenue
Time:	8:30 P.M.
Incident:	Mrs. Terry changed lanes three times quickly and without signaling
Action Taken:	Mrs. Terry was given a traffic ticket

    Officer Robards is writing her report. Which of the following expresses the information most clearly and accurately?

    A. At 8:30 P.M., Mrs. Terry changed lanes three times quickly and without signaling on Hyperion Street near Twelfth Avenue. She was given a traffic ticket.

    B. Mrs. Terry was given a traffic ticket. She changed lanes ten times quickly and without signaling on Hyperion Street near Twelfth Avenue at 8:30 P.M.

    C. On Hippocrates Street near Tenth Avenue, Mrs. Terry changed lanes three times quickly and without signaling at 8:30. She was given a traffic ticket.

    D. At 8:30 P.M., Mrs. Terry changed lanes three times quickly and without signaling on Hyperion Street near Twelfth Avenue. She was arrested.

54. Ingrid was riding her bicycle in the far right section of the right lane of a relatively busy street. As she rounded a curve, she was struck by a yellow truck that sped off after hitting her. There were several witnesses who spoke with Officer Geary as he investigated the incident. Of the following descriptions of the truck's license plate number given to him by witnesses, which should he consider most likely to be correct?

A. TR 17609
B. TZ 77609
C. DR 17809
D. TR 19619

55. If Officer Lahore believes that a dangerous female suspect, whom he has been pursuing by himself, is hiding in the women's restroom of a busy restaurant, which of the following should he do first?

A. fire his gun into the restroom
B. send a female diner into the restroom to see if the suspect is there
C. wait outside the restroom for the suspect to emerge
D. call for backup

56. Officer Weeks was dispatched to the scene of a robbery. There, she gathered the following information:

Location:	High and Dry Laundry
Time:	11:30 P.M.
Victim:	Mrs. Lehigh, owner
Injury:	Mrs. Lehigh suffered a fractured skull
Weapon:	a rock
Items Missing:	a television and DVD player
Suspect:	a short female wearing overalls and a black turtleneck

Officer Weeks is writing her report. Which of the following expresses the information most clearly and accurately?

A. Mrs. Lehigh reported that at 11:30 A.M., a short female wearing black overalls struck her with a rock and stole a television and DVD player from High and Dry Laundry, which she owns. Mrs. Lehigh suffered a fractured skull.

B. Mrs. Lehigh reported that at 11:30 P.M. at High and Dry Laundry, which she owns, a short female wearing overalls and a black turtleneck struck her with a rock and stole a television and DVD player. Mrs. Lehigh suffered a fractured skull.

C. At 11:30 P.M. at High and Dry Laundry, which Mrs. Lehigh owns, a short female wearing overalls and a black turtleneck struck Mrs. Lehigh with a club and stole a television. Mrs. Lehigh suffered a fractured skull.

D. At 11:30 P.M. at High and Dry Laundry, which she owns, a short female wearing overalls and a black turtleneck struck her at High and Dry Laundry with a rock and stole a television and DVD player from High and Dry Laundry. Mrs. Lehigh suffered a fractured arm.

57. Officer Jansen is instructed to watch for a tall, middle-aged male who is suspected of stealing garden tools from area homes. Of the following individuals, on which should Officer Jansen focus his attention most closely during his evening patrol of the area?

    A. a 30-year-old man mowing a lawn

    B. a teenaged girl pulling a wagon full of garden tools down the sidewalk

    C. a 40-year-old man parking his windowless van in a dark corner of an empty lot

    D. a 50-year-old woman buying a toolbox at a hardware store

58. In State X, a person is guilty of **RECKLESS ENDANGERMENT OF PROPERTY** when he recklessly engages in conduct that creates a substantial risk of damage to the property of another person in an amount exceeding $250. Based solely upon this definition, which of the following is the best example of Reckless Endangerment of Property?

    A. George, an inexperienced cyclist, rides his brother's $300 bicycle down a rocky mountainside during a heavy rainstorm.

    B. Phyllis goes swimming in a chlorinated swimming pool while wearing her friend's silk dress, which her friend purchased for $180.

    C. Ralph uses his father's $200 television as a step stool on which he stands in order to climb into his girlfriend's window.

    D. Nathan borrows his brother's $225 guitar for band practice, then uses it as a snowboard after several inches of snow accumulate overnight.

59. Officer Spencer is sent to investigate a report of a missing person and gathers the following information:

Time:	4:45 P.M.
Police Contacted by:	Serena Hernandez
Person Missing:	Keith Hernandez, Serena's younger brother
Description:	Keith Hernandez is four years old and has short black hair
Person Last Seen:	entering a bathroom at Crosstown Mall at 4:15 P.M.

    Officer Spencer must write her report. Which of the following expresses the information most clearly and accurately?

    A. At 4:45 P.M., Serena Hernandez reported that her brother, Keith Hernandez, who is described as four years old with short black hair, was missing. He was last seen entering a bathroom at Crosstown Mall at 4:15 P.M.

    B. Keith Hernandez is four with black hair and went to the bathroom at 4:15 P.M. at Crosstown Mall. At 4:45 P.M. his sister said he was missing. She, Serena Hernandez, reported him missing.

    C. Crosstown Mall's bathroom was where Keith Hernandez, age four and having short black hair, entered and was last seen at 4:15 P.M. before being reported missing by his sister, Serena Hernandez, at 4:45 P.M.

    D. Serena Hernandez reports her brother missing after being last seen entering a bathroom at Crosstown Mall at 4:15 P.M. Her report was made at 4:45 P.M. The brother who is missing is Keith Hernandez, four years old, short black hair.

60. If an off-duty police officer observes a flash flood swelling across a busy thoroughfare, he should first:

   A. assume a position in the middle of the street and direct traffic around the flood.

   B. do nothing, as he is off duty.

   C. call in and report the flood.

   D. instruct the nearest citizen to contact the police department.

61. Assume that one element of grand larceny involves theft of cash, merchandise, or goods worth more than $500. Based only on this information, which of the following incidents would not be considered grand larceny?

   A. Joe Mulligan hotwires a used car with a blue-book value of $750.

   B. Clarice Patterson shoplifts 12 evening bags with a retail value of $65 each.

   C. Freddie Lydon steals a leather attaché case, worth $300, expecting to find expensive jewelry inside. The jewelry is fake, and worth less than $200.

   D. Denise Smigel breaks into an apartment and steals electronic equipment worth nearly $2,000.

62. Officer Chase is sent to investigate a noise complaint. He gathers the following information:

Location:	80 Windsor Place
Time:	12:30 A.M.
Complaint:	loud music coming from 82 Windsor Place
Person Making Complaint:	Sara Richards
Action Taken:	John Shaeffer, the resident at 82 Windsor Place, answered the door while smoking an illegal substance and was arrested

   Officer Chase must write his report. Which of the following expresses the information most clearly and accurately?

   A. Sara Richards, of 80 Windsor Place, reported that loud music was coming from 82 Windsor Place. John Shaeffer, the resident at 82 Windsor Place, answered the door while smoking an illegal substance and was arrested.

   B. At 12:30 A.M., Sara Richards reported that loud music was coming from 82 Windsor Place. John Shaeffer, the resident at 82 Windsor Place, answered the door while smoking an illegal substance and was arrested.

   C. At 12:30 A.M., Sara Richards, of 80 Windsor Place, reported that loud music was coming from 82 Windsor Place. John Shaeffer, the resident at 82 Windsor Place, answered the door while smoking an illegal substance and was arrested.

   D. At 12:30 A.M., Sara Richards, of 80 Windsor Place, reported that loud music was coming from 82 Windsor Place. The resident at 82 Windsor Place answered the door while smoking an illegal substance and was arrested.

63. In State X, a person is guilty of **CRIMINAL TRESPASS IN THE SECOND DEGREE** when he knowingly enters or remains unlawfully in a building. Based solely upon this definition, which of the following is the best example of Criminal Trespass in the Second Degree?

   A. Stacy goes to work at her new job a few minutes early to look over the list of the specials of the day.

   B. After an announcement is made over the mall's loudspeaker that the mall has closed for the night, Carmen hides in the restroom because she does not want to go home.

   C. Adam waits in his father's office for his father to return from a meeting.

   D. Selena, an elderly woman who suffers from memory loss and confusion, enters a stranger's house and watches television.

64. Officer Chavez responds to a report of a larceny. He gathers the following information:

Location:	1800 Park Avenue
Time:	between 2:00 P.M. and 6:30 P.M.
Police Contacted by:	Luke Jones, resident
Items Missing:	a camera and tripod
Suspect:	unknown

   Officer Chavez must write his report. Which of the following expresses the information most clearly and accurately?

   A. Luke Jones reported that a camera and tripod were stolen from his residence at 1800 Park Avenue between 2:00 P.M. and 6:30 P.M. The suspect is unknown.

   B. A camera and tripod were reported stolen by Luke Jones from his residence. The objects were stolen between 2:00 P.M. and 6:30 P.M., and the suspect is unknown.

   C. The camera and tripod that were at his residence at 1800 Park Avenue were stolen from Luke Jones, he reported, and that must have happened between 2:00 P.M. and 6:30 P.M. The suspect is unknown.

   D. Luke Jones reported at a camera and tripod were stolen from his residence at 1800 Park Avenue by a suspect who is unknown.

65. Jamie witnessed an assault and called the police. When Officer Worth arrived at the scene, he found Jamie waiting with the victim and three other witnesses. Of the following descriptions of the suspect given to Officer Worth by the witnesses, which should she consider most likely to be correct?

   A. short female, between 40 and 45 years of age, wearing a black dress

   B. short female, between 40 and 45 years of age, wearing a black suit

   C. tall female, between 40 and 45 years of age, wearing a black suit

   D. short female, between 30 and 35 years of age, wearing a black suit

66. Officer Gerard responds to a report of a hit-and-run. She gathers the following information:

Location: corner of Ponce and Greene Streets
Time: 2:00 P.M.
Crime: hit-and-run
Victim: JoAnn Bunson
Injury: a broken ankle
Description of Vehicle: yellow Honda Prelude

Officer Gerard must write a report. Which of the following expresses the information most clearly and accurately?

A. At 2:00 A.M. on Ponce Street, JoAnn Bunson was struck by a yellow Honda Prelude that did not stop. She suffered a broken ankle.

B. JoAnn Bunson stated that at 2:00 P.M. at the corner of Ponce and Greene Streets, she was struck by a yellow Honda Prelude that did not stop. Ms. Bunson suffered a broken ankle.

C. A yellow Honda Prelude was the reported car that hit JoAnn Bunson at the corner of Ponce and Greene Streets at 2:00 P.M., breaking her leg.

D. Her ankle was broken after a yellow Honda Accord struck her at the corner of Ponce and Greenwich Streets at 2:00 P.M., says JoAnn Bunson.

67. As he patrols a rural area on the outskirts of town, Officer Sellers sees a great deal of smoke rising from a house in the distance. Officer Sellers should first:

A. attempt to maneuver into the driveway of the house to make sure that there is actually a fire.

B. contact the fire department.

C. turn on his sirens to wake up the residents who live nearby.

D. drive back to the precinct and request a pair of binoculars, with which he can get a closer look at the smoke without endangering himself.

68. Between January and April, three robberies have occurred on the north side of town. The suspect in the first robbery is described as a tall female with long blonde hair and a scar on her left cheek. The suspect in the second robbery is described as a short female with short blonde hair and no visible scars. The suspect in the third robbery is described as a tall female with short black hair and a scar on her left cheek.

In May, a fourth robbery occurs, and an arrest is made. The person in custody is a tall female with short blonde hair and a scar on her left cheek. In addition to the robbery for which she was arrested, for which of the following should investigating officers consider the woman in custody a suspect?

A. the first robbery only

B. the second robbery only

C. the third robbery only

D. the first and third robberies only

69. Given the information in Question 68, which of the following is the most logical assumption?

    A. Most of the robberies on the north side of town are committed by women.

    B. Between January and May, the woman in custody might have changed her appearance in order to avoid arrest and continue committing robberies.

    C. It is easy for female criminals to avoid arrest because police officers are less likely to be suspicious of women than men.

    D. All female criminals are less dangerous than male criminals.

70. If an officer finds himself physically struggling with an armed suspect, his primary concern should be:

    A. to disarm the suspect.

    B. to shoot the suspect.

    C. to render the suspect unconscious.

    D. to get away as quickly as possible.

71. Officer Beal was dispatched to a local park to investigate reports that a man was approaching children. There, he gathered the following information:

Location:	Clearwater Park
Time:	5:15 P.M.
Complaint:	a man had offered candy to several children and invited them into his car
Police Contacted by:	Denise Ramirez, a parent
Action Taken:	the man fled the park; a radio alert was sent out

    Officer Beal is writing his report. Which of the following expresses the information most clearly and accurately?

    A. Denise Ramirez, who is a parent, reported that a man at Clearwater Park had offered candy to several children and invited them into his car. The man fled the park, and a radio alert was sent out.

    B. A man who was reported by parent Denise Ramirez as having offered candy to several children at Clearwater Park and invited them into his car fled after she reported him. A radio alert was sent out.

    C. Clearwater Park was the scene of a man inviting several children into his car. Denise Ramirez, a parent, reported this at 5:15 P.M. The man fled the park, and an alert was sent out over the radio.

    D. At 5:15 P.M., Denise Ramirez, a parent, reported that a man at Clearwater Park had offered candy to several children and invited them into his car. The man fled the park, and a radio alert was sent out.

72. In State X, a person is guilty of **CUSTODIAL INTERFERENCE IN THE SECOND DEGREE** when, being a relative of a child less than 16 years old, with intent to hold the child permanently or for a long period, knowing he has no legal right to do so, he takes the child from his lawful custodian. Based solely upon this definition, which of the following is the best example of Custodial Interference in the Second Degree?

    A. Roberta picks up her five-year-old grandson from day care and takes care of him until his mother comes home from work.

    B. Rose receives a call from her 11-year-old sister's school advising her that her sister is ill, so she picks her sister up and brings her home.

    C. Felicia quietly enters her sister's apartment while her sister is sleeping and, without her sister's permission, takes her nephew, who is 17, on a year-long vacation.

    D. Jan takes her 14-year-old son from the home of her ex-husband, who has full custody of the boy, and runs away to Canada with him so they can start over together without her husband's interference.

73. Officer Ritter has been instructed by a supervisor to watch for an armed and dangerous suspect, who is described as a tall female with black hair and blue eyes. Given this information, on which of the following people should Officer Ritter most closely focus her attention?

    A. a 6'1" man with black hair and blue eyes, carrying a briefcase

    B. a 4'11" woman with black hair and sunglasses, carrying a cello case

    C. a 5'9" woman with blonde hair and blue eyes, wearing a heavy coat

    D. a 5'2" man with blonde hair and sunglasses, wearing slacks and a blazer

74. Officer Franklin is dispatched to the scene of an auto accident, where he gathers the following information:

Location:	51st Street and West End Avenue
Time:	1:45 P.M.
Incident:	auto collision
Drivers and Vehicles:	Mrs. Stanley, driving a Chevrolet Malibu, and Mrs. Early, driving a Buick Regal
Witness:	Harold Krups stated that Mrs. Stanley ran a red light, causing the collision
Action Taken:	Mrs. Stanley admitted running the red light; she was given a traffic ticket

Officer Franklin must write his report. Which of the following expresses the information most clearly and accurately?

A. At 1:45 P.M., Harold Krups stated that Mrs. Stanley ran a red light causing a collision between her Chevrolet Malibu and Mrs. Early in her Buick Regal. Mrs. Stanley admitted running the red light and was given a traffic ticket.

B. An auto collision occurred at 51st Street and West End Avenue. Harold Krups stated that he saw Mrs. Stanley run a red light and cause the collision. She got a traffic ticket after admitting that she ran the red light.

C. Harold Krups stated that at 1:45 P.M. at 51st Street and West End Avenue, he saw Mrs. Stanley run a red light in a Chevrolet Malibu, causing a collision with Mrs. Early, who was driving a Buick Regal. Mrs. Stanley admitted running the red light and received a traffic ticket.

D. Mrs. Stanley ran a red light in a Chevrolet Malibu at 1:45 P.M. causing a collision with Mrs. Early, who was driving a Buick Regal, according to Harold Krups who saw the whole thing, he said. Mrs. Stanley admitted running the red light. Due to this she received a traffic ticket.

75. Officer Landon encounters a young man, who appears to be under the legal drinking age and is leaving a liquor store with a bottle of vodka under his arm. Officer Landon asks the young man to show his identification, and the young man complies. His identification proves that he is over the legal drinking age, so Officer Landon thanks him and tells him he is free to go.

Officer Landon's actions were:

A. proper, because he had reason to believe that the young man was breaking the law.

B. improper, because he should have interrogated both the young man and the store clerk.

C. proper, but only because the young man complied with his request.

D. improper, because he had no business bothering the young man, who was not breaking the law.

76. In State X, a person is guilty of **CRIMINAL POSSESSION OF STOLEN PROPERTY IN THE FIRST DEGREE** when he knowingly possesses stolen property, with intent to benefit himself or a person other than an owner thereof or to impede recovery by an owner, and when the value of the property exceeds $1,000,000. Based solely upon this definition, which of the following is the best example of Criminal Possession of Stolen Property in the First Degree?

    A. Juanita agrees to help her brother hide a stolen ancient artifact, which is valued at $750,000, so that the owners will not be able to find it.

    B. Anthony obtains a stolen platinum and diamond necklace worth at least $1,000,000 and arranges for its sale to a foreign buyer of stolen property.

    C. Not realizing that it was stolen from a gallery in Europe, Mr. Vega, a wealthy man who has recently begun collecting art, buys a $1.5 million painting from a dealer.

    D. Gina receives a stolen sports car, valued at $190,000, as a gift from her father-in-law.

77. Officer Rainey responded to a report of an assault and gathered the following information:

    Location: Al's Steak House
    Time: 6:45 P.M.
    Incident: a waiter punched a customer
    Victim: Ruby Samuels
    Injury: black eye
    Suspect: Tom Jennings, a waiter there
    Status of Suspect: confessed and was arrested

    Officer Rainey is writing his report. Which of the following expresses the information most clearly and accurately?

    A. At 6:45 P.M. at Al's Steak House, Tom Jennings, a waiter there, punched Ruby Samuels. She suffered a black eye. Mr. Jennings confessed.

    B. After it happened, Ruby Samuels reported that at Al's Steak House, Tom Jennings, a waiter there, punched her. She suffered a black eye. Mr. Jennings confessed and was arrested.

    C. Ruby Samuels reported that at 6:45 P.M. at Al's Steak House, Tom Jennings, a waiter there, punched her. She suffered a black eye. Mr. Jennings confessed and was arrested.

    D. At Al's Steak House, Tom Jennings, a waiter there, punched Ruby Samuels. She suffered a black eye. Mr. Jennings was arrested.

78. If a factory that employs a large percentage of a town's population announces that it will be closing soon, police officers in the town should be least concerned about which of the following?

    A. the chance that crime will increase due to general frustration and the loss of income

    B. the possibility that violent actions may be taken against the factory owners in response to the closing

    C. the chance that the loss of the factory may damage the town's reputation as an economic center

    D. the possibility that lost income and benefits could give rise to domestic disputes due to increased financial strain on families of factory workers

79. Ernest was waiting in line to buy subway fare when he felt his wallet slide out of his back pocket. As he turned around, he saw a man running up the subway stairs but was unable to catch the man due to heavy foot traffic on the stairwell. Officer Gilroy responded to the reported theft and took statements from several witnesses. Which of the following descriptions of the suspect given to him by witnesses should Officer Gilroy consider most likely to be accurate?

    A. tall male with a mustache, wearing a black denim jacket and red bandanna

    B. tall male with no facial hair, wearing a black denim jacket and red bandanna

    C. short male with a mustache, wearing a black denim jacket and red bandanna

    D. tall male with a mustache, wearing a blue denim jacket and red bandanna

80. Officer Collins was dispatched to the scene of a shooting and gathered the following information:

Location: 700 Broad Street (home of both the victim and witness)
Time: 8:00 P.M.
Incident: victim was shot in the stomach
Victim: Wes Henry
Witness: Meg Henry, Wes Henry's daughter, said the gun went off while he was cleaning it
Action Taken: Mr. Henry was hospitalized; incident is under investigation

Officer Collins is writing his report. Which of the following expresses the information most clearly and accurately?

A. Meg Henry stated that at 8:00 P.M. at their home at 700 Broad Street, her father, Wes Henry, was shot in the stomach when the gun he was cleaning went off. Mr. Henry was hospitalized, and the incident is under investigation.

B. Wes Henry's gun shot him in the stomach when he was cleaning it. This was according to his daughter, Meg Henry, who said it happened at 8:00 P.M. at their home at 700 Broad Street. He was hospitalized, the victim. The incident is under investigation.

C. While it was being cleaned by him, the gun shot Mr. Henry in the stomach. His name is Wes Henry. His daughter, Meg, said this happened at 8:00 P.M. at their home at 700 Broad Street. The incident is under investigation.

D. Meg Henry's father, Wes Henry, was shot in the stomach while cleaning his gun when it went off at 8:00 P.M. at the house where they live at 700 Broad Street. The matter is under investigation after his being hospitalized.

81. In State X, discharging a loaded firearm at an aircraft while such aircraft is in motion or stationary is a **PROHIBITED USE OF A FIREARM**. This is a Class E felony, unless such action endangers the safety of any person, in which case it is a Class D felony.

Angry that he missed her 18th birthday party because he was flying, Brandy points a loaded rifle at her father's plane, which sits empty in an airfield, and discharges the weapon. The bullet misses the plane but punctures the right hand of the owner of another plane parked on the airfield.

Based solely upon the above definition, which of the following is true?

A. Brandy should be charged with the Prohibited Use of a Firearm as a Class E felony.

B. Brandy should be charged with the Prohibited Use of a Firearm as a Class D felony.

C. Brandy should be charged with the Prohibited Use of a Firearm as a Class D and Class E felony.

D. It is impossible to determine how Brandy should be charged without knowing the extent of the plane owner's injuries.

82. Officer Lopez responded to a report of a larceny in a residential area, where she gathered the following information:

Location:	65 Port Place, Mr. Davidson's residence
Time:	between 4:00 P.M. and midnight
Police Contacted by:	Mr. Davidson
Missing Items:	two 10-speed bicycles that were on the front porch
Suspect:	unknown

    Officer Lopez is writing her report. Which of the following expresses the information most clearly and accurately?

    A. Between 4:00 P.M. and noon, according to Mr. Davidson, someone stole two 10-speed bicycles from the front porch of his residence at 65 Port Place. The suspect is unknown.

    B. Mr. Davidson reported that between 4:00 P.M. and midnight, someone stole two 10-speed bicycles from the front porch of his residence at 65 Port Place. The suspect is unknown.

    C. From his residence at 65 Port Place, Mr. Davidson reported that between 4:00 P.M. and midnight, someone stole two 5-speed bicycles from the front porch. The suspect is unknown.

    D. Mr. Davidson reported that between 4:00 P.M. and midnight, someone stole two 10-speed bicycles from the back porch of his residence at 65 Port Place. The suspect is unknown.

83. Officer Clyde has noted certain crimes occur more commonly in certain sections of his patrol area on certain days of the week. Most robberies occur near Loveless Park, most rapes on Battery Street around Jackson Square, and most assaults between First and Fifth Streets on Third Avenue. Robberies take place most often on Mondays and Saturdays, rapes on Thursdays, and assaults on Sundays.

    Given this information, which of the following patrol schedules would enable Officer Clyde to most effectively reduce the number of rapes?

    A. Battery Street around Jackson Square on Mondays

    B. between First and Fifth Streets on Third Avenue on Mondays

    C. Battery Street around Jackson Square on Thursdays

    D. between First and Fifth Streets on Third Avenue on Thursdays

84. Given the information in Question 83, which of the following patrol schedules would enable Officer Clyde to most effectively reduce the number of assaults?

    A. near Loveless Park on Mondays and Thursdays

    B. between First and Fifth Streets on Third Avenue on Sundays

    C. near Loveless Park on Sundays

    D. between First and Fifth Streets on Third Avenue on Mondays and Thursdays

85. Given the information in Question 83, which of the following would be the best day or days of the week for someone who wishes to avoid being robbed to walk near Loveless Park?

    A. Mondays

    B. Fridays and Saturdays

    C. Thursdays and Fridays

    D. Saturdays

86. Officer Guild responded to a report of a kidnapping, where she gathered the following information:

Police Contacted by:	Ella Salzburg
Incident:	Mrs. Salzburg's child was kidnapped from school
Name and Description of Child:	Sue Salzburg, seven years old with short blonde hair
Suspect:	Marcus Salzburg, the child's father (estranged from mother)
Action Taken:	an alert was sent out over the radio

    Officer Guild is writing her report. Which of the following expresses the information most clearly and accurately?

    A. Ella Salzburg kidnapped her child from the child's father, Marcus Salzburg, who is estranged from her, while the child was at school. The child, Sue Salzburg, is seven years old and has short blonde hair. An alert was sent out over the radio.

    B. Sue Salzburg was reportedly kidnapped by her father, Marcus Salzburg, according to her estranged mother. An alert was sent out over the radio for the child, who is seven years old and has short blonde hair.

    C. Ella Salzburg reported that her child, Sue Salzburg, who is seven years old and has short blonde hair, was kidnapped from school. The suspect is Marcus Salzburg, the child's father, who is estranged from Ella Salzburg. An alert was sent out over the radio.

    D. Sue Salzburg was reported to be kidnapped by her father, Marcus Salzburg, from school. She is seven years old and has short blonde hair and an alert was sent out over the radio.

87. In State X, a person is guilty of **CRIMINAL POSSESSION OF A WEAPON IN THE THIRD DEGREE** when he possesses any loaded firearm, except if such possession occurs in the person's home or place of business. Based solely upon this definition, which of the following is the best example of Criminal Possession of a Weapon in the Third Degree?

    A. Lars carries his loaded pistol with him when he visits Disney World during a vacation.

    B. Seneca keeps a loaded rifle under her desk at the insurance company where she works.

    C. When her husband is out of the country on business, Diana loads their shotgun and props it next to their bed for protection.

    D. Amanda keeps a loaded revolver under a potted plant in her office.

88. Of the following pieces of information given to the police during a homicide investigation, which would be least important to that investigation?

    A. an eyewitness account of the homicide

    B. the ages of the victim's children

    C. a description of the suspect

    D. an alias used by the suspect

89. Officer Jackson responds to a report of an assault at an expensive restaurant. Upon arriving at the restaurant, Officer Jackson begins to interview the victim. Which of the following is least likely to be among Officer Jackson's questions?

    A. "Did the assailant say anything to you?"

    B. "What did the assailant look like?"

    C. "Do you know the assailant?"

    D. "Where do you work?"

90. Officer Andrews was patrolling a downtown street when he saw someone cross the street at a point where there was no crosswalk. He noted the following information:

    Location: the middle of the 800 block of Simmons Street
    Time: 3:00 P.M.
    Violation: jaywalking
    Action Taken: Curtis Hamm, the jaywalker, was given a verbal warning

    Officer Andrews is completing his report. Which of the following expresses the information most clearly and accurately?

    A. At 3:00 P.M., Curtis Hamm crossed the street in the middle of the 800 block of Simmons Street. He was given a verbal warning for jaywalking.

    B. Curtis Hamm received a traffic ticket for jaywalking after crossing the street in the middle of the 800 block of Simmons Street at 3:00 P.M.

    C. At 3:00 P.M., Curtis Hamm crossed the street in the middle of the 1800 block of Simmons Street and received a verbal warning for jaywalking. This was at 5:00 P.M.

    D. Curtis Hamm jaywalked. He crossed the street in the middle of the 800 block of Simmons Street, so he was given a verbal warning.

PRACTICE TEST 3 ANSWER KEY

1. A	26. A	51. C	76. B
2. B	27. B	52. D	77. C
3. D	28. A	53. A	78. C
4. A	29. C	54. A	79. A
5. C	30. C	55. D	80. A
6. A	31. C	56. B	81. B
7. D	32. B	57. C	82. B
8. B	33. A	58. A	83. C
9. D	34. D	59. A	84. B
10. D	35. D	60. C	85. C
11. A	36. A	61. C	86. C
12. A	37. D	62. C	87. A
13. B	38. C	63. B	88. B
14. B	39. B	64. A	89. D
15. C	40. B	65. B	90. A
16. B	41. B	66. B	
17. A	42. B	67. B	
18. C	43. D	68. D	
19. A	44. B	69. B	
20. B	45. C	70. A	
21. C	46. B	71. D	
22. A	47. B	72. D	
23. C	48. C	73. C	
24. C	49. D	74. C	
25. A	50. A	75. A	

PRACTICE TEST 3 ANSWERS AND EXPLANATIONS

1. **A** is the best answer. Police officers have a certain amount of latitude when it comes to applying traffic laws; they can use their judgment to determine whether motorists should be given traffic tickets or warnings, or whether they should be arrested. Note following the man (C) "to make sure that he drives safely" would be unnecessary.

2. **B** is the clearest and most accurate statement. Choice A contains inaccurate information; note that the description of the suspect is inaccurately attributed to the victim, Sam Valens. There is information missing from C and D.

3. **D** contains the most repeaters.

4. **A** is correct. It is the only instance in which someone "intentionally damages a building or motor vehicle by starting a fire or causing an explosion."

5. **C** is the only accurate statement. There is inaccurate information in each of the other three statements; the colors of the vehicles are reversed in A, the time is given as "9:00 P.M." rather than "9:00 A.M." in B, and D states "Mr. Cho was given a traffic ticket," which is incorrect.

6. **A** is correct. Most larcenies occur on Radcliffe Place near Pride Park on Mondays and Fridays between 10:00 A.M. and 1:00 P.M., and the patrol schedule in A is the only one of the four that provides coverage of that area on those days at that time.

7. **D** is correct. Most rapes occur on Fourth Street between Hightower and Branch on Thursdays between 4:00 P.M. and 6:30 P.M., and the patrol schedule in D is the only one of the four that provides coverage of that area on that day at that time.

8. **B** is correct. Most robberies occur on Fridays, Saturdays, and Sundays between 8:00 P.M. and 10:45 P.M., and the window of time in B is the only one of the four that occurs outside of the window during which most robberies occur.

9. **D** is the only accurate statement. There is information missing from each of the other three statements.

10. **D** is the best answer. Giving the sandwich to his aunt, who had never had an allergic reaction to peanut butter, could not be seen as a reckless act on Peter's part, while the actions of the individuals in each of the other three instances were clearly reckless.

11. **A** is the best answer.

12. **A** is the clearest and most accurate statement. The wording in each of the other three statements is unclear and confusing. Note, in C, the unnecessary repetition of the name of the business.

13. **B** contains the most repeaters. Note that the word "convertible" appears in all four descriptions, so it can not be used to eliminate any possible answers.

14. **B** is the only statement that contains all the information.

15. **C** is the best answer. An officer should always discuss issues with a supervisor, rather than rashly refusing to carry out instructions (A), quitting the force (B), or attempting to maneuver out of an unpleasant assignment by manipulating colleagues (D).

16. **B** is correct, as it is the only instance in which someone "steals property." In each of the other three circumstances, the individual kept the property simply because he or she forgot to return it.

17. The only statement that conveys all the information accurately and without unnecessary repetition is **A**.

18. **C** is the best answer. While trying to deal with the drunken suspect might be difficult, each of the other three situations presents an immediate danger to the public.

19. **A** is the best answer. Since the rumor indicates that a potentially dangerous situation could arise, informing his superiors before taking any other action is the wisest step for Officer Jimenez to take. Alarming either the parolee (B) or his family (C) before speaking with his supervisors would be unwarranted, and ignoring the situation (D) would be irresponsible.

20. Only **B** contains all the information.

21. **C** is correct. Note that A and B are incorrect because, in each instance, the affixed matter is designed to benefit the owner of the property.

22. **A** is correct. Accepting the offer under any of the circumstances given in B, C, and D would compromise Officer Greer's integrity as an officer.

23. **C** is the clearest and most accurate statement. Choice A is worded in a confusing manner, and there is information missing from B and D.

24. **C** is the best answer. The teenager does not seem to be breaking the law, so A and B are incorrect, but referring the mother to "a place she and her daughter can go for counseling" (C) would be helpful. Ignoring the situation would be unnecessary, especially since it is a "quiet night."

25. **A** contains the most repeaters.

26. **A** is the only accurate statement. There is information missing from each of the other three statements.

27. **B** is correct.

28. **A** is correct.

29. **C** is correct.

30. **C** is correct. Only one witness mentions the driver's speed as possibly excessive, so it's unlikely he was speeding; there are no outstanding warrants on his record, and both insurance and registration are up to date.

31. **C** is the best answer. While "hunting deer or other animals" might improve someone's marksmanship, it would not be as significant in preparing someone for a career as a police officer as the other types of experiences. Choice A would instill an understanding of leadership, teamwork, and responsibility; B would provide an understanding of criminality and psychology; D would provide direct exposure to the sorts of crises that police officers deal with on a daily basis.

32. **B** is correct. The other answers are illogical, and C is absurd, since no assault has occurred.

33. **A** is the best answer. Note that while the "stolen stereo system" in D is worth more than $3,000, Marcie does not steal the stereo. She buys stolen property, but she is not guilty of the crime in question.

34. **D** is the only statement that contains all the information.

35. **D** is the most logical assumption. While any of the other three answers could be possible, there is no reason to assume that any of them are; however, the evidence clearly suggests that "the man and the woman are fighting."

36. **A** is the clearest and most accurate statement. There is inaccurate information in each of the other three statements. Note, in C, that the dead animal is incorrectly identified as a "chipmunk."

37. **D** is correct.

38. **C** is correct. Before proceeding into a potentially dangerous situation, Officer Payne should call in to report the situation and to receive instructions. Also, the blood probably indicates that someone will need medical attention, and an ambulance could be dispatched as a result of the call.

39. **B** is the only statement that is worded in a clear manner. Note, in C, the awkwardness of the last sentence, "The child was found, who turned out to be Meg Willis, at 4:30 P.M."

40. **B** is correct. Officer Daniels's actions were absolutely and obviously improper. The fact that the suspect killed himself is not a factor; an officer should never give information material for an investigation to the media without the permission of a supervisor.

41. **B** contains the most repeaters. Note the descriptions of the suspect's gender each appear twice, canceling each other out, so neither can be used to eliminate any descriptions.

42. **B** is correct. A and C require immediate attention, and assigning undercover officers would not be advantageous to dealing with the situations in either A, C, or D.

43. **D** is the only statement that contains all the information.

44. **B** is correct. It is the only instance in which someone "forcibly steals property" and is "aided by another person actually present." Note that, in addition to the fact that they committed their crimes alone, the individuals in A and C did not "forcibly" steal anything.

45. **C** is correct. Three-quarters, or 75 percent, of the merchandise remained in the truck; 75 percent of $15,000 is $11,250.

46. **B** is the best answer. A police officer should never use undue physical force against any suspect, so A and D are incorrect. C is illogical, since a confession is not necessary to establishing whether the suspect is guilty.

47. **B** is the clearest and most accurate statement. There is information missing from A and D, and C is worded in an unclear and confusing manner.

48. **C** is correct. The other possible answers are illogical, and B and D are unethical.

49. **D** is the clearest and most accurate statement. Note the awkward and confusing wording in C.

50. **A** is correct. Students skipping school would stand a greater chance of being caught if they gathered on "the school playground" than at any of the other three locations.

51. **C** is correct. It is the only instance in which the individual "possesses a narcotic drug with intent to sell it." While Johnny (A) is probably breaking another law by possessing "a small bag of a narcotic drug, which he plans to inject into his bloodstream," he is not guilty of Criminal Possession of a Controlled Substance in the Third Degree according to the given definition.

52. **D** is the best answer. Choice A is simply illogical. B is incorrect because finding the bomb and deciding how to deal with it would be secondary to getting the children and faculty out safely, and those are tasks that would probably be handled by a bomb squad. C is incorrect because, while finding the person responsible for planting the bomb would be a goal of the ensuing investigation, it should not be the primary goal of an officer who is directing an evacuation of the school.

53. **A** is the only accurate statement. The other statements each contain incorrect information.

54. **A** contains the most repeaters.

55. **D** is the most logical choice. If the dangerous suspect is, in fact, hiding in the restroom, the public is at risk, and the officer will need assistance in securing all exits from the restaurant while protecting the public.

56. **B** is the only accurate statement. There is incorrect information in each of the other three statements. Also, note the unnecessary repetition of the name of the business in D.

57. **C** is correct. The individual fits the limited description of the suspect, and his vehicle and the relatively suspicious nature of its location could indicate that he is the suspect.

58. **A** is correct. In each of the other examples, the property in question is not "in an amount exceeding $250."

59. **A** is the clearest and most accurate statement. The wording in each of the other three statements is unclear.

60. **C** is correct. Reporting the situation as soon as possible could prevent property damage and protect the safety of those driving on or living near the road that has been flooded.

61. **C** is correct.

62. **C** is the only statement that contains all the information.

63. **B** is the best answer. Note, while Selena, in D, "enters" and "remains unlawfully in a building," she probably does not do so "knowingly," since she "suffers from memory loss and confusion."

64. **A** is the clearest and most accurate statement. There is information missing from B and D, and C is worded in an unclear and confusing manner.

65. **B** contains the most repeaters.

66. **B** is the clearest and most accurate statement.

67. **B** is correct. The fire department always needs as much time as possible to deal with fires.

68. **D** Is correct. The woman in custody could have changed her hair length and color, thus fitting the descriptions of the suspects in the first and third robberies; however, she could not have changed her height or the existence of her scar, so she does not fit the description of the suspect in the second robbery.

69. **B** is the most logical assumption. There is no evidence to suggest that any of the other three statements might be true.

70. **A** is correct. Disarming the suspect should be an officer's primary concern in such a situation, as it is the best way to protect himself and the public from harm. The other three possible answers are illogical. Note, in B and C, specific types of physical harm to the suspect are given as objectives, which should never be the case.

71. **D** is the only statement that contains all the information.

72. **D** is correct. Neither of the individuals in A and B acts with the "intent to hold the child permanently or for a long period," and the child in C is older than 16 years old.

73. **C** is the best answer. The individuals in A and D are male, so neither could be the suspect, and the individual in B is not tall. Note that the "heavy coat" worn by the individual in C could probably conceal a weapon.

74. **C** is the clearest and most accurate statement. There is information missing from A and B, and D is worded in an unclear and confusing manner.

75. **A** is correct. Officer Landon acted properly in asking the young man for his identification; this would be true whether or not "the young man complied with his request" (C). B and D are illogical. Officer Landon would have had reason to question the store clerk If the young man had been unable to provide identification or if his identification had proven that he was not old enough to purchase an alcoholic beverage.

76. **B** is the best answer, because it is the only instance in which someone "knowingly possesses stolen property," the value of which "exceeds $1,000,000."

77. The only statement that includes all the information is **C**.

78. **C** is the best answer. Police officers should be least concerned with their "town's reputation as an economic center," especially when such a concern is contrasted with worries for public health and safety.

79. **A** contains the most repeaters. Note the phrase "red bandanna" appears in all four descriptions, so it cannot be used to eliminate any possible answers.

80. **A** is the clearest and most accurate statement. Note, in B and C, that the phrases "Wes Henry's gun shot him in the stomach" and "the gun shot Mr. Henry in the stomach" imply that the gun actively chose to shoot Mr. Henry, which is obviously inaccurate.

81. **B** is correct.

82. **B** is the only accurate statement. There is incorrect information in each of the other four statements.

83. **C** is the best answer. Most rapes occur on Battery Street around Jackson Square on Thursdays, and the patrol schedule in C is the only one of the four that provides coverage of that area on that day of the week.

84. **B** is correct. Most assaults occur between First and Fifth Streets on Third Avenue on Sundays, and the patrol schedule in B is the only one of the four that provides coverage of that area on that day of the week.

85. **C** is the best answer. Of all the days given, Thursdays and Fridays would be the safest days to walk near Loveless Park, since most robberies occur there on Mondays and Saturdays.

86. **C** is the clearest and most accurate statement. There is incorrect information in A, and there is information missing from B and D. A, B, and D also are worded in a confusing manner.

87. **A** is correct. In each of the other instances, the loaded weapon is kept at "the person's home or place of business."

88. **B** is the best answer. While "the ages of the victim's children" might be significant, it is unlikely that the information would be as crucial to the investigation as each of the other three possible answers.

89. **D** is the best answer. While knowing where the victim works could be useful to Officer Jackson, the answers to the other questions are much more pertinent to the investigation.

90. **A** is the only accurate statement. There is incorrect or incomplete information in each of the other three statements.

Practice Test 4

ANSWER SHEET FOR PRACTICE TEST 4

For each question, select the best answer choice. Use the answer sheet to mark your choices. Answers and explanations follow the test.

1. Ⓐ Ⓑ Ⓒ Ⓓ	26. Ⓐ Ⓑ Ⓒ Ⓓ	51. Ⓐ Ⓑ Ⓒ Ⓓ	76. Ⓐ Ⓑ Ⓒ Ⓓ
2. Ⓐ Ⓑ Ⓒ Ⓓ	27. Ⓐ Ⓑ Ⓒ Ⓓ	52. Ⓐ Ⓑ Ⓒ Ⓓ	77. Ⓐ Ⓑ Ⓒ Ⓓ
3. Ⓐ Ⓑ Ⓒ Ⓓ	28. Ⓐ Ⓑ Ⓒ Ⓓ	53. Ⓐ Ⓑ Ⓒ Ⓓ	78. Ⓐ Ⓑ Ⓒ Ⓓ
4. Ⓐ Ⓑ Ⓒ Ⓓ	29. Ⓐ Ⓑ Ⓒ Ⓓ	54. Ⓐ Ⓑ Ⓒ Ⓓ	79. Ⓐ Ⓑ Ⓒ Ⓓ
5. Ⓐ Ⓑ Ⓒ Ⓓ	30. Ⓐ Ⓑ Ⓒ Ⓓ	55. Ⓐ Ⓑ Ⓒ Ⓓ	80. Ⓐ Ⓑ Ⓒ Ⓓ
6. Ⓐ Ⓑ Ⓒ Ⓓ	31. Ⓐ Ⓑ Ⓒ Ⓓ	56. Ⓐ Ⓑ Ⓒ Ⓓ	81. Ⓐ Ⓑ Ⓒ Ⓓ
7. Ⓐ Ⓑ Ⓒ Ⓓ	32. Ⓐ Ⓑ Ⓒ Ⓓ	57. Ⓐ Ⓑ Ⓒ Ⓓ	82. Ⓐ Ⓑ Ⓒ Ⓓ
8. Ⓐ Ⓑ Ⓒ Ⓓ	33. Ⓐ Ⓑ Ⓒ Ⓓ	58. Ⓐ Ⓑ Ⓒ Ⓓ	83. Ⓐ Ⓑ Ⓒ Ⓓ
9. Ⓐ Ⓑ Ⓒ Ⓓ	34. Ⓐ Ⓑ Ⓒ Ⓓ	59. Ⓐ Ⓑ Ⓒ Ⓓ	84. Ⓐ Ⓑ Ⓒ Ⓓ
10. Ⓐ Ⓑ Ⓒ Ⓓ	35. Ⓐ Ⓑ Ⓒ Ⓓ	60. Ⓐ Ⓑ Ⓒ Ⓓ	85. Ⓐ Ⓑ Ⓒ Ⓓ
11. Ⓐ Ⓑ Ⓒ Ⓓ	36. Ⓐ Ⓑ Ⓒ Ⓓ	61. Ⓐ Ⓑ Ⓒ Ⓓ	86. Ⓐ Ⓑ Ⓒ Ⓓ
12. Ⓐ Ⓑ Ⓒ Ⓓ	37. Ⓐ Ⓑ Ⓒ Ⓓ	62. Ⓐ Ⓑ Ⓒ Ⓓ	87. Ⓐ Ⓑ Ⓒ Ⓓ
13. Ⓐ Ⓑ Ⓒ Ⓓ	38. Ⓐ Ⓑ Ⓒ Ⓓ	63. Ⓐ Ⓑ Ⓒ Ⓓ	88. Ⓐ Ⓑ Ⓒ Ⓓ
14. Ⓐ Ⓑ Ⓒ Ⓓ	39. Ⓐ Ⓑ Ⓒ Ⓓ	64. Ⓐ Ⓑ Ⓒ Ⓓ	89. Ⓐ Ⓑ Ⓒ Ⓓ
15. Ⓐ Ⓑ Ⓒ Ⓓ	40. Ⓐ Ⓑ Ⓒ Ⓓ	65. Ⓐ Ⓑ Ⓒ Ⓓ	90. Ⓐ Ⓑ Ⓒ Ⓓ
16. Ⓐ Ⓑ Ⓒ Ⓓ	41. Ⓐ Ⓑ Ⓒ Ⓓ	66. Ⓐ Ⓑ Ⓒ Ⓓ	
17. Ⓐ Ⓑ Ⓒ Ⓓ	42. Ⓐ Ⓑ Ⓒ Ⓓ	67. Ⓐ Ⓑ Ⓒ Ⓓ	
18. Ⓐ Ⓑ Ⓒ Ⓓ	43. Ⓐ Ⓑ Ⓒ Ⓓ	68. Ⓐ Ⓑ Ⓒ Ⓓ	
19. Ⓐ Ⓑ Ⓒ Ⓓ	44. Ⓐ Ⓑ Ⓒ Ⓓ	69. Ⓐ Ⓑ Ⓒ Ⓓ	
20. Ⓐ Ⓑ Ⓒ Ⓓ	45. Ⓐ Ⓑ Ⓒ Ⓓ	70. Ⓐ Ⓑ Ⓒ Ⓓ	
21. Ⓐ Ⓑ Ⓒ Ⓓ	46. Ⓐ Ⓑ Ⓒ Ⓓ	71. Ⓐ Ⓑ Ⓒ Ⓓ	
22. Ⓐ Ⓑ Ⓒ Ⓓ	47. Ⓐ Ⓑ Ⓒ Ⓓ	72. Ⓐ Ⓑ Ⓒ Ⓓ	
23. Ⓐ Ⓑ Ⓒ Ⓓ	48. Ⓐ Ⓑ Ⓒ Ⓓ	73. Ⓐ Ⓑ Ⓒ Ⓓ	
24. Ⓐ Ⓑ Ⓒ Ⓓ	49. Ⓐ Ⓑ Ⓒ Ⓓ	74. Ⓐ Ⓑ Ⓒ Ⓓ	
25. Ⓐ Ⓑ Ⓒ Ⓓ	50. Ⓐ Ⓑ Ⓒ Ⓓ	75. Ⓐ Ⓑ Ⓒ Ⓓ	

1. In State X, a person is guilty of **APPEARANCE IN PUBLIC UNDER THE INFLUENCE OF NARCOTICS OR A DRUG OTHER THAN ALCOHOL** when he appears in a public place under the influence of narcotics or a drug other than alcohol to the degree that he may endanger himself or other persons or property, or annoy persons in his vicinity.

   Stavros drinks eight cans of beer and swallows several capsules of a narcotic drug then walks from his house down a sidewalk, all the while screaming and throwing berries at people, until he arrives at his friend's apartment. Based solely upon the above definition, which of the following is true?

   A. Stavros should be charged with the Appearance in Public Under the Influence of Narcotics or a Drug Other Than Alcohol, since he was under the influence of narcotics and was in a public place while he walked to his friend's apartment.

   B. Stavros should not be charged with the Appearance in Public Under the Influence of Narcotics or a Drug Other Than Alcohol because he had been drinking alcohol.

   C. Stavros should not be charged with the Appearance in Public Under the Influence of Narcotics or a Drug Other Than Alcohol because he was not in a public place; he went from home to a friend's apartment.

   D. Stavros should be charged with Appearance in Public Under the Influence of Narcotics or a Drug Other Than Alcohol only if it is determined that he had more narcotics in his bloodstream than alcohol.

2. Officer Sebastian arrived at the scene of an auto accident, where she gathered the following information:

Location:	intersection of High Street and North Avenue
Time:	8:45 A.M.
Drivers and Vehicles:	Penny Coleman, driving a black BMW, and Mark Ryan, driving a yellow Mazda
Driver at Fault:	Mark Ryan drifted into Ms. Coleman's lane, causing a collision between their vehicles
Injuries:	none
Action Taken:	Mr. Ryan was given a traffic ticket

Officer Sebastian is writing her report. Which of the following expresses the information most clearly and accurately?

A. At the intersection of High Street and North Avenue, Mark Ryan, driving a yellow Mazda, drifted into the lane occupied by Penny Coleman, who was driving a black BMW, causing a collision between their vehicles. There were no injuries, and Mr. Ryan was given a traffic ticket.

B. At 8:45 A.M. at the intersection of High Street and North Avenue, Penny Coleman, driving a yellow Mazda, drifted into the lane occupied by Mark Ryan, who was driving a black BMW, causing a collision between their vehicles. There were no injuries. Ms. Coleman was given a traffic ticket.

C. At 8:45 A.M. at the intersection of High Street and North Avenue, Mark Ryan, driving a yellow Mazda, drifted into the lane occupied by Penny Coleman, who was driving a black BMW, causing a collision between their vehicles. There were no injuries. Mr. Ryan was given a traffic ticket.

D. Mark Ryan, driving a yellow Mazda, drifted into the lane on High Street that was occupied by Penny Coleman, who was driving a black BMW, causing a collision between their vehicles. Mr. Ryan was given a traffic ticket.

3. Officer Chin is dispatched to the scene of an apparent suicide. Upon arriving, he notices drops of blood on a tree outside of the apartment where the apparent suicide seems to have taken place. Officer Chin should:

A. touch the blood to see if it is still warm.

B. ignore the blood, since it probably is unrelated to the suicide.

C. immediately alert a supervisor, since the blood could be crucial to the investigation.

D. wipe the blood off the tree so that the case can be wrapped up as quickly as possible; suicides are open-and-shut cases.

4. Officer Heather was dispatched to the scene of a reported assault, where she gathered the following information:

Location:	Smith's Salon
Time:	10:00 A.M.
Incident:	customer struck stylist with her shoe
Victim:	Stacy Sumner, stylist
Injury:	bruised left cheek
Suspect:	Ms. Horne, a customer
Action Taken:	Ms. Horne confessed and was arrested

    Officer Heather is writing her report. Which of the following expresses the information most clearly and accurately?

    A. Stacy Sumner reported that at Smith's Salon, where she works as a stylist, Ms. Horne, a customer, struck her with her shoe. Ms. Sumner suffered a bruised left cheek, and Ms. Horne confessed and was arrested.

    B. Stacy Sumner reported that at 10:00 A.M. at Smith's Salon, where she works as a stylist, Ms. Horne struck her with her shoe. Ms. Horne confessed and was arrested.

    C. Stacy Sumner reported that at 10:00 A.M., Ms. Horne, a customer, struck her with her shoe. Ms. Sumner suffered a bruised left cheek, and Ms. Horne confessed and was arrested.

    D. Stacy Sumner reported that at 10:00 A.M. at Smith's Salon, where she works as a stylist, Ms. Horne, a customer, struck her with her shoe. Ms. Sumner suffered a bruised left cheek, and Ms. Horne confessed and was arrested.

5. Officer Marquez is investigating an assault. Of the following types of information, which would be most useful to his investigation?

    A. a physical description of the suspect

    B. the victim's age and weight

    C. the extent of the victim's injuries

    D. whether the victim is a smoker

6. Frank was walking home from school when a man pushed him down and stole his backpack. Several witnesses described the suspect to Officer Tyler, who was sent to investigate. Of the following descriptions of the suspect given to Officer Tyler by witnesses, which should he consider most likely to be accurate?

    A. 6'1" male with long sideburns and only four fingers on his right hand

    B. 5'1" male with long sideburns and only four fingers on his right hand

    C. 6'1" male with no sideburns and only four fingers on his right hand

    D. 6'1" male with long sideburns and only four fingers on his left hand

7. In State X, a person is guilty of **EXPOSURE OF A PERSON** when he appears in a public place in such a manner that the private or intimate parts of his body are unclothed or exposed. Based solely upon this definition, which of the following is not an example of Exposure of a Person?

   A. Jemma sunbathes nude in her backyard, which is surrounded by a high privacy fence.

   B. Francesca takes off her bathing suit top at a public park where nude sunbathing is not allowed.

   C. Larry wears a shirt but no pants or underwear on a college fraternity excursion to the mall.

   D. Hector skis naked down a mountainside in a national park.

8. Officer Burton responded to a report of a larceny and gathered the following information:

Location:	80 Bertrand Avenue
Time:	between 9:30 P.M. and 10:00 P.M.
Police Contacted by:	Mr. Harlowe, resident
Incident:	larceny
Item Missing:	a floor lamp that was on his back porch
Suspect:	unknown

   Officer Burton is writing his report. Which of the following expresses the information most clearly and accurately?

   A. Mr. Harlowe reported that between 9:30 P.M. and 10:00 P.M., a floor lamp was stolen from the back porch of his residence at 80 Bertrand Avenue. The suspect is unknown.

   B. Between 9:30 P.M. and 10:00 P.M. was the time or times when a floor lamp was stolen from the back porch. Mr. Harlowe lives at 80 Bertrand Avenue, where it was stolen by a suspect who is unknown.

   C. Mr. Harlowe, of 80 Bertrand Avenue, reported a stolen floor lamp from his back porch at that residence. This was, he said, between 9:30 P.M. and 10:00 P.M. by an unknown suspect, who it is believed stole the lamp.

   D. A floor lamp was stolen from the back porch, between 9:30 P.M. and 10:00 P.M., at 80 Bertrand Avenue, where Mr. Harlowe lives and where he said the floor lamp was. More specifically, it was on the back porch. The suspect is unknown.

9. After being promoted, a police officer should:

   A. spend more time with those officers with whom he is equally ranked, and less with those who rank below him.

   B. immediately begin to get to know those who will determine whether he will be promoted again, and use flattery to gain their favor.

   C. assume his new responsibilities and perform his assignments as well as he possibly can.

   D. take advantage of the perks of his new rank, while avoiding any taxing assignments or heavy responsibility.

10. If Officer Edisto wishes to reduce the number of robberies at bank machines in his patrol area, on which of the following locations should he most closely focus his attention?

    A. a bank machine inside a well-lit 24-hour grocery store

    B. a bank machine that is inside a bank and only accessible while the bank is open

    C. a drive-through bank machine across from a police precinct

    D. a drive-through bank machine next to a mall that closes at 9:00 P.M.

11. Officer O'Rourke was dispatched to the scene of an explosion, where he gathered the following information:

Location:	Fountain Park
Time:	3:00 P.M.
Incident:	a fountain exploded
Injuries:	three people were hospitalized
Witness:	Mr. Barber saw a tall man wearing blue jeans place a small box in the water a few minutes before the explosion
Status of Suspect:	left the park on foot; current location unknown

    Officer O'Rourke must write his report. Which of the following expresses the information most clearly and accurately?

    A. At 3:00 P.M., a fountain exploded. Three people were injured and hospitalized. Mr. Barber stated that he saw a tall man place a small box in the water a few minutes before the explosion. The suspect then left the park on foot; his current location is unknown.

    B. At 3:00 P.M., a fountain at Fountain Park exploded. Three people were injured and hospitalized. Mr. Barber stated that he saw a tall man wearing blue jeans place a small box in the water a few minutes before the explosion. The suspect left the park on foot; his current location is unknown.

    C. Three people were injured and hospitalized as a result of an explosion at Fountain Park, just before which Mr. Barber stated that he saw a tall man wearing blue jeans place a small box in the water. The suspect's current location is unknown.

    D. At 3:00 P.M., three people were injured and hospitalized after a fountain at Fountain Park exploded, which happened just a few minutes after a tall man wearing blue jeans placed a small box in the water, according to a witness. The suspect then left the park on foot.

12. During a thunderstorm, Mrs. Evans was driving home on a one-way street when she collided with a vehicle that was traveling in the wrong direction. The suspect sped off after colliding with Mrs. Evans's vehicle, but several other motorists were able to offer descriptions of the suspect's vehicle's license plate number to Officer Morehouse. Of the following descriptions of the license plate number given to Officer Morehouse by these witnesses, which should she consider most likely to be correct?

    A. T 9901

    B. F 9901

    C. F 9802

    D. F 8911

13. Several rapes have occurred in Officer Jackson's patrol area during the past few weeks. On a late-night patrol of this area, Officer Jackson should be most concerned about which of the following?

    A. a couple walking down the street, holding hands

    B. a man dressed in black who is following a female pedestrian down the sidewalk

    C. a man and woman arguing loudly on their stoop

    D. two teenage boys camped in a tent in their backyard

14. Officer Hamm responded to a report of gunshots in a residential area, where he gathered the following information:

Location:	35 Green Place
Time:	11:45 P.M.
Police Contacted by:	Mildred Anson
Complaint:	gunshots heard near her house
Action Taken:	sounds were traced to a backfiring utility truck

    Officer Hamm must write his report. Which of the following expresses the information most clearly and accurately?

    A. At 11:45 A.M., Mildred Anson reported hearing gunshots near her house at 35 Green Place. The sounds were traced to a backfiring utility truck.

    B. Mildred Green reported hearing gunshots near her house at 35 Anson Place at 11:45 P.M. The sounds were traced to a backfiring utility truck.

    C. At 11:45 P.M., Mildred Anson reported hearing gunshots near her house at 35 Green Place. The sounds were traced to a backfiring utility truck.

    D. Myrtle Anson reported hearing gunshots coming from her house at 35 Anson Place at 11:45 P.M. The sounds were traced to a backfiring police car.

15. In State X, a person is guilty of **EAVESDROPPING** when he unlawfully engages in wiretapping, mechanical overhearing of a conversation, or intercepting or accessing of an electronic communication. Based solely upon this definition, which of the following is the best example of Eavesdropping?

    A. Marlena installs microphones behind the mirrors in her tenants apartments so she can listen to their private conversations.

    B. Steve overhears a loud argument between his neighbor and his neighbor's wife.

    C. A credit card company records all its customer service calls and makes this practice known to all its customers.

    D. Josiah testifies in court that he heard the defendant threaten to injure someone.

16. Officer Seymour responded to a report that a child was driving a car through a neighborhood. He gathered the following information:

Location:	Castle Island subdivision
Time:	4:15 P.M.
Police Contacted by:	Dr. Ronald, a resident
Incident:	a child was seen driving a yellow convertible through the neighborhood
Action Taken:	the child and vehicle in question were not found

    Officer Seymour is writing his report. Which of the following expresses the information most clearly and accurately?

    A. At 4:15 P.M., Dr. Ronald, a resident of Castle Island subdivision, reported seeing a child driving a yellow convertible through the neighborhood. The child and vehicle in question were not found.

    B. Dr. Ronald, a resident of Castle Island subdivision, reported seeing a child driving a yellow convertible through the neighborhood. The time that Dr. Ronald reported this was at 4:15 P.M. The child and vehicle in question, as described by Dr. Ronald, were not found.

    C. In Castle Island subdivision, Dr. Ronald, a resident, reported seeing a child driving a convertible through the neighborhood. The child and vehicle in question were not found.

    D. A child driving a yellow convertible through Castle Island subdivision were reported by Dr. Ronald, a resident there, at 4:15 P.M. The child was not found who was reported to have been doing the driving.

17. Officer Gianini sees a man using a credit card to open a dead-bolt lock on a house's front door. What should Officer Gianini do first?

    A. ask the man for his identification

    B. remove his weapon from its holster

    C. call in and request backup

    D. shoot the man

18. After purchasing a new drill at a home improvement store, Mr. Bellows was robbed as he carried his new drill into his house. The suspect struck Mr. Bellows and stole the drill, then ran off. Officer Jefferson interviewed several people at the scene and found that many of them had witnessed the incident. Of the following descriptions of the suspect given to Officer Jefferson by the witnesses, which should he consider most likely to be accurate?

A. tall male, wearing a black suit with a blue bow tie

B. short male, wearing a gray suit with a blue bow tie

C. tall male, wearing a gray suit with a blue bow tie

D. tall male, wearing a gray suit with a blue necktie

19. A storage warehouse manager discovers one of the storage spaces has been broken into and robbed. When he files the report, he gives the officer a document written by the storage space tenant, listing the items stolen and their value.

Three men's suits	$ 300 (each)
One men's tuxedo	$ 500
One women's fur coat	$1,500
One leather love seat	$ 750
One box collectible coins	$1,000
Four Victorian lamps	$ 750 (total)
One box antique china & silver	$ 500

What is the total value of the missing merchandise?

A. $9,050

B. $5,300

C. $5,900

D. $8,150

20. Officer Schofield responds to a report of a robbery and gathers the following information:

Location:	Anderson Arms Apartments, manager's office
Time:	5:00 P.M.
Incident:	victim was robbed at knifepoint
Victim:	Henry Anderson, assistant manager
Amount Stolen:	$3,000 from the office's petty cash drawer
Suspect:	short female wearing black coveralls

    Officer Schofield must write her report. Which of the following expresses the information most clearly and accurately?

    A. Henry Anderson stated that at 5:00 at the manager's office at Anderson Arms Apartments, where he is the assistant manager, he was robbed at knifepoint by a short female wearing black coveralls, who stole $3,000 from the office's petty cash drawer.

    B. Henry Anderson stated that at 5:00 P.M. at the manager's office at Anderson Arms Apartments, where he is the assistant manager, he was robbed at knifepoint by a short female wearing black coveralls, who stole $3,000 from the office's petty cash drawer.

    C. Henry Anderson stated that at 5:00 P.M. at the manager's office at Anderson Arms Apartments, he was robbed at knifepoint by a short female wearing black coveralls, who stole $3,000 from the office's petty cash drawer.

    D. Henry Anderson stated that at 5:00 P.M. at the manager's office at Anderson Arms Apartments, where he is the assistant manager, he was robbed by a short female wearing black coveralls, who stole $3,000 from the office's petty cash drawer.

21. Officer Lamont is watching for an armed robbery suspect who is described as a short, bald male with large biceps. On which of the following individuals should Officer Lamont most closely focus his attention?

    A. a short man with long hair and skinny arms
    B. a tall man with long hair and large biceps
    C. a short man with long hair and large biceps
    D. a short woman with short hair and skinny arms

22. After a weekend fishing trip, Mr. Haskell was driving home with his son when he was sideswiped by a vehicle that did not stop after hitting him. Officer Zed began his investigation by speaking with Mr. Haskell and his son, then proceeded to interview several witnesses. Of the following descriptions of the suspect and the suspect's vehicle given to Officer Zed by witnesses, which should he consider most likely to be correct?

    A. a teenage girl driving a blue Mazda Miata
    B. a teenage boy driving a blue Mazda Miata
    C. a teenage boy driving a blue Mazda 626
    D. a teenage boy driving a green Mazda Miata

23. Officer Julia was dispatched to the scene of an apparent suicide attempt. There, he gathered the following information:

Location:	179 Hopper Lane, Ford residence
Time:	11:15 P.M.
Police Contacted by:	Sally Ford
Victim:	Megan Ford, Sally Ford's daughter
Incident:	mother found victim unconscious; victim had ingested a bottle of sleeping pills; is currently hospitalized
Action Taken:	incident is under investigation

    Officer Julia is writing his report. Which of the following expresses the information most clearly and accurately?

    A. At 11:15 P.M., Sally Ford reported that she had found her daughter, Megan Ford, unconscious. The victim had ingested a bottle of pills and is currently hospitalized. The incident is under investigation.
    B. Sally Ford reported finding her daughter unconscious at their residence at 179 Hopper Lane. This was reported at 11:15 P.M. The victim is hospitalized and the incident is under investigation.
    C. At 11:15 P.M., Sally Ford reported that she found her daughter, Megan Ford, unconscious at their residence at 179 Hopper Lane. The victim had ingested a bottle of sleeping pills and is currently hospitalized. The incident is under investigation.
    D. Sally Ford reported at 11:15 P.M. that she had found her daughter unconscious at their residence at 179 Hopper Lane. Her daughter, the victim, is Megan Ford, who had ingested a bottle of pills that were sleeping pills and who was unconscious then, and currently, hospitalized. The incident is under investigation.

24. Officer Nesbaum sees a man shove an apparently homeless woman into the gutter. Officer Nesbaum should:

    A. congratulate the man, since homeless people get on everyone's nerves.

    B. ignore the situation, since the woman probably deserved to be shoved.

    C. detain the man for questioning about the incident.

    D. arrest the woman for harassing the man.

25. In State X, a person is guilty of **PROSTITUTION** when such person engages or agrees or offers to engage in sexual conduct with another person in return for a fee. Based solely upon this definition, which of the following is the best example of Prostitution?

    A. Yolanda accepts overtime for attending a late-night dinner meeting with several male clients at a club that features strippers.

    B. Helen offers to give her husband a massage every night for a month if he will buy her a new pair of pearl earrings.

    C. Ricardo and Earline agree to meet at Ricardo's apartment at midnight for a sexual encounter.

    D. Annie offers to have sexual intercourse with a stranger in exchange for $500.

26. Officer Vitti pulled a motorist over for exceeding the speed limit and noted the following information:

Location:	the 900 block of Broadway
Time:	4:15 P.M.
Driver:	Sam Sanborne
Vehicle:	tan Chevrolet Impala
Violation:	exceeding the speed limit by 20 miles per hour
Action Taken:	Mr. Sanborne was given a traffic ticket

    Officer Vitti is writing her report. Which of the following expresses the information most clearly and accurately?

    A. Sam Sanborne was exceeding the speed limit by 20 miles per hour and was, as a result, given a traffic ticket. This was at 4:15 P.M. and was at the 900 block of Broadway, where he was driving and speeding in a tan Chevrolet Impala.

    B. At 4:15 P.M. at the 900 block of Broadway, Sam Sanborne, who was driving a tan Chevrolet Impala, was given a traffic ticket for exceeding the speed limit by 20 miles per hour.

    C. At the 900 block of Broadway, Sam Sanborne speeded by 20 miles per hour and was given a traffic ticket at 4:15 P.M. He was driving a tan Chevrolet Impala, in which he did the speeding.

    D. In a tan Chevrolet Impala, Sam Sanborne exceeded the speed limit by 20 miles per hour and was given a traffic ticket at 4:15 P.M. This was at the 900 block of Broadway where he both sped and was given the ticket.

27. Officer Messina responded to a report of vandalism and gathered the following information:

Location:	Holy Union School
Time:	7:30 A.M.
Incident:	a former student was found spray-painting the mirrors in a boys' restroom
Police Contacted by:	Headmaster Stokes, who caught the suspect
Suspect:	Fred Wimbley
Status of Suspect:	he was arrested

    Officer Messina is writing her report. Which of the following expresses the information most clearly and accurately?

    A. Headmaster Stokes stated that at 7:30 A.M., he caught Fred Wimbley, a former student, spray-painting the mirrors in a boys' restroom at Holy Union School. Mr. Wimbley was arrested.

    B. At 7:30 A.M., the headmaster caught Fred Wimbley, a former student, spray-painting the mirrors in a boys' restroom at Holy Union School. Mr. Wimbley was arrested.

    C. Headmaster Stokes stated that he caught Fred Wimbley, a former student, spray-painting the mirrors in a boys' restroom at Holy Union School. Mr. Wimbley was arrested.

    D. At 7:30 A.M., Headmaster Stokes caught Fred Wimbley, a former student, spray-painting the mirrors at Holy Union School. Mr. Wimbley was arrested.

28. A few days after a red Camaro is reported stolen, Officer Buford sees a similar Camaro in the parking lot of a convenience store. Officer Buford calls in the car's license plate and determines that the Camaro is, indeed, the stolen car. Officer Buford should next:

    A. enter the store and announce that he is there to arrest the driver of the Camaro.

    B. fire shots into the Camaro's tires so that the suspect will be unable to flee in the car.

    C. call for backup and wait in an inconspicuous location for the suspect to return to the car so that the suspect can be caught.

    D. drive around the block, looking for suspicious individuals.

29. Mrs. Osborne was the victim of a hit-and-run while pushing her grocery cart to her car. Officer Murray interviewed many witnesses who saw incident and were able to describe the suspect's vehicle. Of the following descriptions of the suspect's vehicle given to Officer Murray by witnesses, which should she consider most likely to be correct?

    A. burgundy Dodge minivan

    B. red Dodge minivan

    C. burgundy Ford minivan

    D. burgundy Dodge truck

30. Officer Dailey is dispatched to the scene of a fire, where she gathers the following information:

Location: Fifth Street Gallery
Address: 665 Fifth Street
Incident: the third floor was destroyed by fire
Cause of Fire: believed to have been faulty wiring inside a vintage lamp, but is still under investigation

Officer Dailey must write her report. Which of the following expresses the information most clearly and accurately?

A. The third floor of the Fifth Street Gallery, at 665 Fifth Street, was destroyed by a fire that is believed to have been caused by faulty wiring inside a vintage lamp.

B. The third floor of the Fifth Street Gallery, at 665 Fifth Street, was destroyed by a fire that is believed to have been caused by faulty wiring inside a vintage lamp, but which is still under investigation.

C. A fire that is believed to have been caused by faulty wiring, but which is still under investigation, destroyed the third floor of the Fifth Street Gallery, located at 665 Fifth Street.

D. A fire that destroyed the third floor of the Fifth Street Gallery is under investigation. The gallery is located at 665 Fifth Street and the third floor was destroyed, it is believed, by a fire caused by faulty wiring inside a vintage lamp.

31. If, while she is patrolling on foot, Officer Wilson sees a citizen strike his partner in the face, Officer Wilson should:

A. fire warning shots over the citizen's head to protect his partner.

B. subdue and arrest the citizen.

C. attack the citizen from behind and deliver multiple crushing blows to the citizen's body.

D. shoot the citizen in the ankle.

32. In State X, a person is guilty of **TRESPASS** when he knowingly enters or remains unlawfully in or upon premises. Based solely upon this definition, which of the following is not an example of Trespass?

A. Envious of his property, Jane walks through a rich citizen's yard and takes a nap in his rose garden.

B. Uncertain of the location of the property line between her father's estate and that of a neighbor's, Sharon crosses into the neighbor's property and walks on the neighbor's land for several hours.

C. Yvette sneaks into a movie theater at night through an open door to enjoy the smell of popcorn.

D. Walt, who needs a place to sleep, hides behind a tapestry so he will be locked inside a carpet store when it closes for the evening.

33. Officer O'Brien was sent to investigate a report of an aggressive stray dog in a parking lot and gathered the following information:

    Location: Big Movies' parking lot
    Time: 1:30 P.M.
    Incident: an aggressive stray dog was seen there
    Police Contacted by: Ralph Miller, an employee
    Action Taken: animal was found and animal control was notified

    Officer O'Brien is writing his report. Which of the following expresses the information most clearly and accurately?

    A. Ralph Miller reported seeing an aggressive stray dog in the parking lot of Big Movies, where he works. The animal was found and animal control was notified.

    B. At 1:30 P.M., Ralph Miller reported seeing a stray dog in the parking lot of Big Movies, where he works. The animal was found and animal control was notified.

    C. Ralph Miller reported at 1:30 P.M. that he had seen an aggressive stray dog in the parking lot of Big Movies. The animal was found.

    D. At 1:30 P.M., Ralph Miller reported seeing an aggressive stray dog in the parking lot of Big Movies, where he works. The animal was found and animal control was notified.

34. After a child is bitten by a dog, several neighbors who saw the dog bite the child offer descriptions of the animal to Officer Withers. Of the following descriptions of the dog, which should he consider most likely to be correct?

    A. medium-sized, black dog with droopy ears and a black tongue
    B. medium-sized, brown dog with droopy ears and a spotted tongue
    C. large, brown dog with droopy ears and a black tongue
    D. medium-sized, brown dog with droopy ears and a black tongue

35. Of the following witnesses to an auto collision, who would be the most credible?

    A. a passenger in one of the two cars involved
    B. the driver of one of the two cars involved
    C. the wife of one of the drivers of the two cars involved, who was several car lengths behind her husband, but was not involved in the collision
    D. a pedestrian who was standing on the side of the road where the collision occurred

36. Officer Albright is diagnosed with a painful and chronic disease. He should:

    A. tell his supervisors about the diagnosis and work with them to arrange a comfortable and appropriate schedule if he is able to continue working.

    B. keep the information to himself until the disease progresses to the point where he cannot work.

    C. resign from the police department immediately.

    D. say nothing and hope that his supervisors will figure it out on their own to save him from having to confront them with it.

37. Officer Monroe arrived at the scene of an auto accident, where he gathered the following information:

Location:	corner of Hickory Street and First Avenue
Time:	5:00 P.M.
Driver and Vehicle:	Mr. Rasmussen, driving a white Ford minivan
Incident:	a falling rock crashed through Mr. Rasmussen's windshield, causing him to drive off the road into a ditch
Injuries:	Mr. Rasmussen suffered cuts and bruises

    Officer Monroe is writing his report. Which of the following expresses the information most clearly and accurately?

    A. Mr. Rasmussen stated that at 5:00 P.M. at the corner of Hickory Street and First Avenue, a falling rock crashed through the windshield of his white Ford minivan, causing him to drive off the road into a ditch. He suffered cuts and bruises.

    B. At 5:00 P.M., a falling rock crashed through the window of Mr. Rasmussen's white Ford minivan, causing him to drive off the road into a ditch, and causing him to suffer cuts and bruises.

    C. At the corner of Hickory Street and First Avenue, a falling rock crashed through the windshield of the white minivan, Ford brand, that was driven by Mr. Rasmussen, who suffered cuts and bruises. As a result of the rock and the incident, Mr. Rasmussen drove off the road into a ditch.

    D. A falling rock crashed through his windshield, according to Mr. Rasmussen, at 5:00 P.M., causing him to drive off the road into a ditch in his white Ford minivan and giving him, as a result, cuts and bruises. This was at the corner of Hickory Street where it meets up with First Avenue.

38. Officer Yin hears a woman's screams coming from a duplex apartment. The most logical assumption for him to make is:

    A. someone is attempting to kill the woman.

    B. the woman is involved in a violent argument with her husband.

    C. the woman may need assistance.

    D. someone has broken into the woman's apartment, and she is terrified.

39. Harriet was mowing her lawn on a hot afternoon when a beer bottle thrown from a passing truck struck her in the head and knocked her off of her riding mower. Officer Daintry interviewed several neighbors who saw the incident. Of the following descriptions of the suspect's vehicle given to Officer Daintry by the witnesses, which should he consider most likely to be correct?

    A. a white Chevrolet truck with a New Jersey license plate

    B. a white Chevrolet truck with a New Hampshire license plate

    C. a white Ford truck with a New Hampshire license plate

    D. a yellow Chevrolet truck with a New Hampshire license plate

40. Officer Lewis responded to a report of a man exposing himself to groups of diners at a mall food court. He gathered the following information:

    Location: the food court at Municipal Mall
    Time: 8:00 P.M.
    Police Contacted by: Mr. Raj, a mall merchant
    Incident: a man was exposing his naked body to diners
    Action Taken: the suspect, who had no identification, was arrested

    Officer Lewis is writing his report. Which of the following expresses the information most clearly and accurately?

    A. Mr. Raj, a customer at Municipal Mall, reported that a man was exposing his naked body to diners at the food court at Municipal Mall. The suspect, who had no identification, was arrested.

    B. Mr. Raj reported that a man was exposing his naked body to workers at Municipal Mall at the food court at 8:00 P.M. The suspect, who had no identification, was arrested

    C. At 8:00 P.M., Mr. Raj reported that a man was exposing himself to diners at the food court at Municipal Mall, where Mr. Raj is a merchant. The suspect, who had no identification, was arrested.

    D. At 8:00 A.M., Mr. Raj reported that a man was exposing himself to diners at the food court at Municipal Mall, where Mr. Raj is a merchant. The suspect, who had no identification, was not arrested.

41. After seeing a woman who fits the description of a suspect in a murder investigation, Officer Leary should first:

    A. contact the District Attorney and let her know that the suspect has been found.

    B. call the victim's family and tell them that the suspect has been found.

    C. call the precinct and report the situation, taking care not to lose sight of the woman.

    D. fire three warning shots in the woman's direction to let her know that she has been caught.

42. In State X, a person is guilty of **HINDERING PROSECUTION IN THE THIRD DEGREE** when he intentionally harbors or conceals a person who has committed a felony.

    Xavier is guilty of a felony and is running from the police. Based solely upon the above definition, which of the following is the best example of Hindering Prosecution in the Third Degree?

    A. Xavier's mother goes to her condo at the beach for the weekend, and Xavier hides in her basement, without her knowledge, while she is gone.

    B. Xavier's former business partner pays for Xavier's wife to have her teeth fixed out of consideration to her and her family.

    C. Xavier's brother picks Xavier up at their mother's house and takes him to his house, where he hides Xavier in a secret underground apartment.

    D. Xavier's former parole officer provides the police with records, phone numbers, and addresses of all of Xavier's known associates.

43. Officer Roth observed a vehicle with an outdated tag on a city street, pulled the driver of the vehicle over, and noted the following information:

Location:	Everett Street between Finley and Hurt Boulevards
Time:	7:00 P.M.
Driver and Vehicle:	Mr. Solano in a brown Lincoln
Incident:	driving with an outdated tag
Action Taken:	Mr. Solano was given a traffic ticket

    Officer Roth is writing his report. Which of the following expresses the information most clearly and accurately?

    A. At 7:00 P.M. on Everett Street between Finley and Hurt Boulevards, Mr. Solano was given a traffic ticket for driving his brown Lincoln with an outdated tag.

    B. At 7:00 P.M. on Everett Street between Finley and Hurt Boulevards, Mr. Solano was given a traffic ticket for driving his Lincoln with an outdated tag.

    C. On Everett Street and Hurt Boulevard at 7:00 P.M., Mr. Solano was given a traffic ticket for driving his brown Lincoln with an outdated tag.

    D. On Everett Street between Finley and Hurt Boulevards, Mr. Solano was driving his brown Lincoln with an outdated tag.

44. A man who was involved in and won many fistfights when he was a teenager would be:

    A. a welcome candidate for the police department regardless of his other abilities, since his fighting prowess has been tested and proven.

    B. an unwelcome candidate for the police department, since he has proven that he has a short temper.

    C. a welcome candidate for the police department if he has matured and learned from his past experiences and if he is qualified in other areas.

    D. an unwelcome candidate for the police department regardless of his other abilities, since the police department only hires people who have never been involved in any sorts of disputes.

45. Rodney was shopping at an outdoor market when someone grabbed his shopping bag, which was filled with soaps and candles that he had just purchased, and ran off. Officer Withrow arrived moments later and interviewed several witnesses. Of the following descriptions of the suspect given to Officer Withrow by witnesses, which should he consider most likely to be correct?

    A. heavyset female, wearing a blue T-shirt and gray corduroy pants

    B. thin female, wearing a black T-shirt and gray corduroy pants

    C. heavyset male, wearing a black T-shirt and gray corduroy pants

    D. heavyset female, wearing a black T-shirt and gray corduroy pants

46. Officer Cassel responded to a report of a dispute. He gathered the following information:

Location:	Dizzy's Vintage Records
Time:	3:15 P.M.
Police Contacted by:	Dizzy Smith, owner
Incident:	two customers were fighting over a record
Action Taken:	customers were removed from the store

    Officer Cassel is writing his report. Which of the following expresses the information most clearly and accurately?

    A. Dizzy Smith's Dizzy's Vintage Records was the scene of two customers fighting over a record who were, after it was reported at 3:15 P.M., removed from the store, Dizzy's Vintage Records.

    B. At 3:15 P.M., two customers' fighting, over a record, was reported by Dizzy Smith, the owner of Dizzy's Vintage Records, where the fight was. The customers who were doing the said fighting were removed from the store.

    C. Dizzy Smith reported at 3:15 that his store, Dizzy's Vintage Records, was where two customers were fighting over a record who were later removed from the store after he reported the fight.

    D. At 3:15 P.M., Dizzy Smith reported that two customers were fighting over a record at Dizzy's Vintage Records, which he owns. The customers were removed from the store.

To answer Questions 47, 48, and 49, use the information in the following passage.

At 1:30 P.M. on September 14, Officers Maxwell and Nathan were called to the scene of a vehicle/bicycle accident on Pelletier Avenue, a one-way northbound street. William Lyman and his wife, Claire Lyman, were double-parked in the far left lane of Nelson Avenue; Mr. Lyman was in the driver's seat of their car, a Lexus sedan. Ms. Ellie Ochoa was riding her bicycle north on Pelletier Avenue, also in the far left lane. As Ms. Ochoa passed the Lexus on the right, Mrs. Lyman opened her car door. Ms. Ochoa, who was not wearing a helmet, struck the door and was thrown into the adjoining lane on the right; she landed on her head and was knocked unconscious. Two pedestrians, Mike Cargill and Fletcher Ingram, saw the accident and carried Ms. Ochoa to the sidewalk, where she regained consciousness. Mr. Cargill called the police on his cellular phone, and Mr. Ingram called an ambulance on his.

Officers Maxwell and Nathan took statements from Mr. and Mrs. Lyman, Mr. Cargill, Mr. Ingram, and another witness, Gladys Pinkerton. Mr. Lyman showed the officers his driver's license, registration, and insurance; all were up to date. A license check showed no outstanding warrants. He said he and his wife were returning from lunch, and he had double-parked in front of the building where she worked to drop her off. He said he'd turned on the car's flashing lights to indicate that he was temporarily parked. Mrs. Lyman said she couldn't remember if she'd looked behind the car before she opened her door, but she hadn't seen Ms. Ochoa until she hit the car door. Mr. Cargill and Mr. Ingram, who did not know one another, had been walking south on the west side of Pelletier Avenue. Neither man had noticed the Lexus before the accident; both heard the sound of Ms. Ochoa striking the car door and turned in time to see her land in oncoming traffic. Mr. Ingram said, "It was a loud thunk, and then this really hollow sound—like when Letterman would drop watermelons off of buildings—and car brakes screeching and everything." They then rushed out and carried the woman to safety. Mr. Cargill said he tried to retrieve Ms. Ochoa's bicycle, but "a garbage truck had run over it, and it was just totally flattened."

Ms. Pinkerton had just crossed Pelletier Avenue midblock; she said she'd noticed the Lexus because "it was just parked there, without flashers on or anything. I was wondering if they were going to get a ticket." Ms. Pinkerton confirmed the men's account, and she also said that a yellow cab had nearly struck Ms. Ochoa and hadn't stopped; she gave Officer Maxwell the cab's number. Officer Nathan later went to the emergency room to take a statement from Ms. Ochoa. She remembered seeing the car door open in front of her and trying to brake the bicycle; she had a vague recollection of sitting on the sidewalk, but couldn't clearly remember anything that happened before she arrived in the emergency room. According to the doctor treating her, Ms. Ochoa had a mild concussion and a broken nose; she would be treated and, unless more serious injuries were revealed on a CAT scan, released later that afternoon.

47. In what direction was the bicyclist traveling?

    A. north

    B. south

    C. east

    D. west

48. How did Ms. Ochoa sustain her injuries?

    A. falling against the curb after losing control of her bike

    B. landing on the pavement after striking the car door

    C. being struck by a yellow cab

    D. being struck by a garbage truck

49. Who notified the police of the accident?

    A. William Lyman

    B. Gladys Pinkerton

    C. Mike Cargill

    D. Fletcher Ingram

50. Officer Arias observed a collision at a busy intersection and noted the following information:

Location:	Washington Avenue near Bell Park
Time:	2:45 P.M.
Drivers and Vehicles:	Mary Suffolk, driving a white Acura, and Peter Stone, driving a gray Toyota
Incident:	Peter Stone was driving the wrong way down Washington Avenue, a one-way street, causing a head-on collision
Injuries:	both drivers hospitalized for observation
Action Taken:	Mr. Stone was given a traffic ticket

    Officer Arias is writing his report. Which of the following expresses the information most clearly and accurately?

    A. At 2:45 P.M., Peter Stone, driving a gray Toyota, and Mary Suffolk, driving a white Acura, were involved in a head-on collision caused by Mr. Stone, who was driving the wrong way down a one-way street. The collision occurred on Washington Avenue near Bell Park. Both drivers were hospitalized for observation, and Mr. Stone was given a traffic ticket.

    B. Peter Stone, driving a gray Toyota, and Mary Suffolk, driving a white Acura, were involved in a head-on collision caused by Mr. Stone, who was driving the wrong way down Washington Avenue, a one-way street. The collision occurred on Washington Avenue near Bell Park. Both drivers were hospitalized for observation, and Mr. Stone was given a traffic ticket.

    C. At 2:45 P.M., Peter Stone and Mary Suffolk were involved in a head-on collision caused by Mr. Stone, who was driving the wrong way down Washington Avenue, a one-way street. The collision occurred on Washington Avenue near Bell Park. Both drivers were hospitalized for observation, and Mr. Stone was given a traffic ticket.

    D. At 2:45 P.M., Peter Stone, driving a gray Toyota, and Mary Suffolk, driving a white Acura, were involved in a head-on collision caused by Mr. Stone. The collision occurred on Washington Avenue near Bell Park. Both drivers were hospitalized for observation, and Mr. Stone was given a traffic ticket.

51. After eating more than $250 worth of food and drinks, three people left an expensive restaurant without paying. The restaurant manager reported the incident to the police. Officer Javier was dispatched to investigate and interviewed several witnesses at the restaurant. Of the following descriptions of the suspects given to Officer Javier by the witnesses, which should he consider most likely to be correct?

    A. three brunette males, each wearing a blue suit

    B. two brunette males and one brunette female, each wearing a blue suit

    C. three brunette males, each wearing a black suit

    D. three red-haired males, each wearing a red suit

52. In State X, a person is guilty of **CRIMINAL SALE OF A FIREARM IN THE FIRST DEGREE** when he unlawfully sells to another 20 or more firearms.

    Darius, who is not a licensed firearms dealer, unlawfully sells ten shotguns and ten handguns to an anonymous buyer. Based solely upon the above definition, which of the following is true?

    A. Darius should be charged with Criminal Sale of a Firearm in the First Degree because he unlawfully sold 20 or more firearms.

    B. Darius should not be charged with Criminal Sale of a Firearm in the First Degree because he did not unlawfully sell 20 or more of the same type of firearm.

    C. Darius should be charged with Criminal Sale of a Firearm in the First Degree only if the buyer was an undercover officer, since the testimony of an "anonymous buyer" would probably not be credible.

    D. It is impossible to decide whether Darius should be charged with Criminal Sale of a Firearm in the First Degree without knowing more about the exchange between Darius and the buyer.

53. Officer Welch was dispatched to the scene of a reported assault, where she gathered the following information:

Location:	Puente Real Estate Agency
Time:	6:00 P.M.
Police Contacted by:	Ellie Puente, owner
Incident:	a prospective renter struck Realtor John Sears in the face
Injury:	black eye
Suspect:	Cary Kearns
Location of Suspect:	unknown

    Officer Welch is writing her report. Which of the following expresses the information most clearly and accurately?

    A. At Puente Real Estate Agency, which Ellie Puente owns, and where she reported the incident, a prospective renter named Cary Kearns struck Realtor John Sears. He, Mr. Sears, was struck in the face, causing him to end up with a black eye. The suspect's location is unknown.

    B. At 6:00 P.M. at Puente Real Estate Agency, a prospective renter named Cary Kearns, whose location is unknown now, struck Realtor John Sears in the face. This was reported by Ellie Puente, who happens to own Puente Real Estate, where it happened and which employs Mr. Sears as the Realtor who suffered a black eye. The suspect's location is unknown.

    C. Ellie Puente reported that at 6:00 P.M. at Puente Real Estate Agency, which she owns, a prospective renter named Cary Kearns struck Realtor John Sears in the face. Mr. Sears suffered a black eye. The suspect's location is unknown.

    D. Ellie Puente reported that at 4:00 P.M. at Puente Real Estate Agency, which she owns, a prospective renter named Cary Kearns, whose location is unknown, struck tenant John Sears in the face. Mr. Sears suffered a black eye.

54. If, during the course of an investigation, an officer reviews a suspect's criminal record and discovers that the suspect has been convicted of a crime similar to the one being investigated, which of the following would be the most logical assumption for the officer to make?

A. The suspect is definitely guilty of the crime being investigated.

B. The suspect might be guilty of the crime being investigated.

C. The suspect is not guilty of the crime being investigated.

D. The suspect will commit another such crime, whether or not he is guilty of the crime being investigated.

55. Officer Cox has noticed that certain crimes regularly occur in certain sections of his patrol area. Larcenies occur on Reese Road between Griffin and Cooper Streets, rapes occur on Frederick Boulevard near Common Harbor, and robberies occur near the northwest corner of the Sunny Skies subdivision. Larcenies occur on Sundays and Fridays between 2:00 P.M. and 8:30 P.M., rapes on Wednesdays between 1:00 A.M. and 7:00 A.M., and robberies on Tuesdays and Thursdays between 8:30 A.M. and 2:00 P.M.

Given this information, which of the following patrol schedules would enable Officer Cox to most effectively reduce the number of larcenies?

A. Reese Road between Griffin and Cooper Streets, Wednesdays, 1:00 A.M. to 7:00 A.M.

B. Frederick Boulevard near Common Harbor, Wednesdays, 1:00 A.M. to 7:00 A.M.

C. Reese Road between Griffin and Cooper Streets, Sundays and Fridays, noon to 8:30 P.M.

D. Frederick Boulevard near Common Harbor, Sundays and Fridays, noon to 8:30 P.M.

56. Given the information in Question 55, which of the following patrol schedules would enable Officer Cox to most effectively reduce the number of rapes?

A. Frederick Boulevard near Common Harbor, Wednesdays and Sundays, midnight to 7:00 A.M.

B. the northwest corner of the Sunny Skies subdivision, Wednesdays, midnight to 7:00 A.M.

C. Frederick Boulevard near Common Harbor, Sundays, 1:00 A.M. to 7:00 A.M.

D. the northwest corner of the Sunny Skies subdivision, Wednesdays and Sundays, 7:00 A.M. to noon

57. Given the information in Question 55, which of the following patrol schedules would enable Officer Cox to most effectively reduce the number of robberies?

    A. Reese Road between Griffin and Cooper Streets, Sundays and Fridays, 8:30 A.M. to 2:00 P.M.

    B. near the northwest corner of the Sunny Skies subdivision, Sundays and Fridays, 8:30 A.M. to 2:00 P.M.

    C. Reese Road between Griffin and Cooper Streets, Tuesdays and Thursdays, 2:00 P.M. to 8:30 P.M.

    D. near the northwest corner of the Sunny Skies subdivision, Tuesdays and Thursdays, 8:30 A.M. to 2:00 P.M.

58. Given the information in Question 55, which of the following is the most logical assumption?

    A. Officer Cox is responsible for patrolling a potentially dangerous area.

    B. Robberies, larcenies, and rapes are the only crimes that occur in Officer Cox's patrol area.

    C. The victims of most robberies are young women.

    D. Frederick Boulevard near Common Harbor would be a safe place for someone who wished to avoid being robbed to reside.

59. Officer Middleton arrived at the scene of a reported larceny, where she gathered the following information:

Location:	#4 Tanner Court
Time:	between 6:00 A.M. and noon
Police Contacted by:	Steve Lowery, resident
Missing Items:	skis and ski poles
Suspect:	Mr. Lowery suspects his ex-wife, Hanna Lowery, who still has a key to the apartment
Action Taken:	Ms. Lowery is being sought for questioning

Officer Middleton is writing her report. Which of the following expresses the information most clearly and accurately?

A. Between 6:00 A.M. and noon, skis and ski poles were reported by Steve Lowery as stolen from his residence at #4 Tanner Court. He suspects that the skis and ski poles, which were stolen, were stolen by his ex-wife, who still has keys to the apartment. Her name, the ex-wife, who is being sought for questioning, is Hanna Lowery.

B. Steve Lowery reported that between 6:00 A.M. and noon, skis and ski poles were stolen from his residence at #4 Tanner Court, where he lives. His ex-wife, Hanna Lowery, is who he suspects because she still has a key to #4 Tanner Court, where Mr. Lowery lives, and is, therefore, being sought for questioning.

C. Between 6:00 A.M. and noon, Hanna Lowery is the suspect who may have stolen skis and ski poles from Steve Lowery, her ex-husband, that were at his residence at #4 Tanner Court, to which she still has keys. Hanna Lowery is being sought for questioning.

D. Steve Lowery reported that between 6:00 A.M. and noon, skis and ski poles were stolen from his residence at #4 Tanner Court. He indicated that he suspects his ex-wife, Hanna Lowery, who still has keys to the apartment. Ms. Lowery is being sought for questioning.

60. A man driving a yellow truck and pulling a boat on a trailer side swiped a family in an RV that was driving in the adjacent lane, and then sped off. Officer Kane interviewed many witnesses to the incident and found that several of their accounts differed when it came to describing the suspect's boat. Of the following descriptions of the suspect's boat given to Officer Kane by witnesses, which should he consider most likely to be accurate?

A. a blue-bottomed speedboat with green seats

B. a blue-bottomed bass boat with blue seats

C. a blue-bottomed speedboat with blue seats

D. a white-bottomed speedboat with blue seats

61. Officer Chamberlain was sent to investigate a report of a missing child. He gathered the following information:

Time:	9:00 P.M.
Police Contacted by:	Fiona Starr
Person Missing:	Helen Starr, Ms. Starr's daughter
Description:	seven years old, with blonde hair and a red dress
Last Seen:	playing at The Arbor playground at 8:15 P.M.

Officer Chamberlain is writing his report. Which of the following expresses the information most clearly and accurately?

A. Fiona Starr reported her daughter, Helen Starr, missing. The child, described as seven years old with blonde hair and a red dress, was last seen playing at The Arbor playground at 8:15 P.M.

B. At 9:00 P.M., Fiona Starr reported Helen Starr missing. The child, described as seven years old with blonde hair and a red dress, was last seen playing at The Arbor playground at 8:15 P.M.

C. Fiona Starr reported her daughter, Helen Starr, missing at 9:00 P.M. The child, described as seven years old with blonde hair, was last seen playing at The Arbor playground at 8:15 P.M.

D. At 9:00 P.M., Fiona Starr reported her daughter, Helen Starr, missing. The child, described as seven years old with blonde hair and a red dress, was last seen playing at The Arbor playground at 8:15 P.M.

62. In State X, a person is guilty of **CRIMINAL POSSESSION OF A WEAPON IN THE FOURTH DEGREE** when he possesses a rifle or shotgun and has been convicted of a felony. Based solely upon this definition, which of the following is the best example of Criminal Possession of a Weapon in the Fourth Degree?

A. Monty, a convicted felon, is found in possession of a pistol.

B. Ira, a convicted felon, is found in possession of a shotgun.

C. Opal, a convicted felon, is found in possession of a knife.

D. Pierce, a convicted felon, is found in possession of a shotgun and rifle catalog.

63. Officer Coburn is dispatched to the scene of a hit-and-run, where he gathers the following information:

Location:	the corner of Janice and Herald Streets
Time:	2:15 P.M.
Incident:	hit-and-run
Victim:	Maureen Cash
Injury:	broken right arm
Suspect's Vehicle:	gold Camaro

Officer Coburn must write his report. Which of the following expresses the information most clearly and accurately?

A. Maureen Cash reported that at 2:15 P.M. at the corner of Janice and Herald Streets, she was the victim of a hit-and-run. Ms. Cash, who suffered a broken right arm, describes the suspect's vehicle as a gold Camaro.

B. Victim Maureen Cash reported that at the corner of Janice and Herald Streets, she was the victim of a hit-and-run. Ms. Cash suffered a broken right arm.

C. Maureen Cash reported that at 2:15 A.M. at the corner of Janice and Herald Streets, she was the victim of a hit-and-run. Ms. Cash, who suffered a broken right arm, describes the suspect's vehicle as a silver Camaro.

D. Maureen Cash reported that at 2:15 P.M., she was the victim of a hit-and-run. Ms. Cash, who suffered a broken right arm, describes the suspect's vehicle as a gold Camaro.

64. If an armed off-duty officer encounters a man who fits the description of a dangerous escaped felon for whom the department has been searching, the officer should first:

A. ask the man for identification.

B. pull his gun and fire warning shots in the man's direction.

C. call in and report the situation.

D. resolve to let someone know when he is back on duty.

65. Officer Rush was off duty, unarmed, and eating lunch on the third-floor terrace of a restaurant when he witnessed a robbery on the first floor of a business across the street. Officer Rush immediately reported the robbery by using his cellular phone to call the precinct and was instructed to follow the suspect and stay in touch with the precinct. Officer Rush did as he was instructed, maintaining a safe distance since he was unarmed, but the suspect eluded him when he ran into a crowd of people.

Officer Rush's actions were:

A. improper, because the suspect got away.

B. proper, because he reported the crime and followed the instructions of his supervisor.

C. improper, because he should have had a gun with him.

D. proper, but only because he was not hurt.

66. Officer Lon responded to a report of a robbery and gathered the following information:

Location:	Center City Library
Time:	11:30 A.M.
Incident:	victim was robbed at gunpoint
Victim:	John Stinson
Item Missing:	wristwatch
Suspect:	short male wearing black pants and a purple jacket

Officer Lon is writing his report. Which of the following expresses the information most clearly and accurately?

A. At the Center City Library at 11:30 A.M., there was a gunpoint robbery of a wristwatch by a short male wearing black pants and a purple jacket from John Stinson, according to John Stinson, the victim.

B. John Stinson stated that at 11:30 A.M. at the Center City Library, he was robbed at gunpoint by a short male wearing black pants and a purple jacket, who stole his wristwatch.

C. At 11:30 A.M. at the Center City Library was when and where a wristwatch was stolen at gunpoint by a short male wearing black pants and a purple jacket from John Stinson, as stated after the incident by Mr. Stinson.

D. A wristwatch was stolen after a gunpoint robbery by a short male wearing black pants and a purple jacket robbed it from John Stinson at 11:30 A.M. at the Center City Library, where they were, the victim and the suspect.

67. During his investigation of a hit-and-run accident, Officer Moon spoke with several witnesses. Of the following descriptions of the suspect and vehicle given to her by the witnesses, which should Officer Moon consider most likely to be correct?

A. a blonde woman driving a Cadillac

B. a blonde man driving a Lincoln

C. a brunette man driving a Cadillac

D. a blonde man driving a Cadillac

68. Officer Sheridan is instructed to remove any dangerous accessories or items from a suspect who is in an interrogation room awaiting questioning. Officer Sheridan should be least concerned about which of the following?

A. a silver letter opener

B. a book of matches

C. an eight-inch nail file

D. a six-inch silk ribbon

69. Officer Stuart observes a struggle between two men in a parking garage, and he notes the following information:

Location: Downtown Parking Garage
Time: 7:45 A.M.
Incident: physical struggle between two men
Action Taken: both men were arrested when they refused to stop fighting

Officer Stuart must write his report. Which of the following expresses the information most clearly and accurately?

A. At 7:45 A.M., two men were observed in a physical struggle with one another at the Downtown Parking Garage. The men refused to stop fighting and were subsequently arrested.

B. There was a struggle between three men at the Downtown Parking Garage at 7:45, causing them all to be arrested after they refused to stop fighting.

C. Two men were observed in a physical struggle with one another at the Uptown Parking Garage at 7:45 A.M. The men refused to stop fighting and were subsequently arrested.

D. After refusing to stop fighting, two men who were observed in a physical struggle with one another at the Downtown Parking Garage at 8:45 A.M. were arrested.

70. Officer Stacy is investigating a report of a missing child and asks the child's parents many questions pertaining to the situation. Of the following questions, which would Officer Stacy be least likely to ask the child's parents?

A. "What does your child look like?"

B. "May we have a picture of your child?"

C. "Are any of your neighbors shifty looking?"

D. "Where did you last see your child?"

71. In State X, a person is guilty of **MANSLAUGHTER IN THE SECOND DEGREE** when he intentionally aids or causes another person to commit suicide. Based solely upon this definition, which of the following is the best example of Manslaughter in the Second Degree?

A. Rose breaks up with her devoted boyfriend, Tonio, and Tonio is so distraught that he kills himself.

B. Winston helps his friend, Kim, hold a gun to her head while she pulls the trigger, and she dies.

C. Clay buys his sister a new car, and she crashes it into a tree and dies.

D. Andy shoots his sleeping father in the head, killing him instantly.

72. During a church service, someone threw rocks through a large stained-glass window, scattering glass across dozens of pews and injuring many parishioners. Officer Lamar interviewed several witnesses who were passing by the church at the time that the incident occurred. They said that they heard the sound of breaking glass and then saw a vehicle speed out of the parking lot. Of the following descriptions of the suspect's vehicle given to Officer Lamar by these witnesses, which should she consider most likely to be correct?

    A. a blue Land Cruiser with a luggage rack
    B. a black Land Cruiser with a luggage rack
    C. a blue Range Rover with a luggage rack
    D. a blue Land Cruiser with no luggage rack

73. Officer Bonham responded to a report of a man firing a pistol in the air at a public park and gathered the following information:

Location:	Fourth Street Park
Time:	7:30 P.M.
Police Contacted by:	Mr. Orestes, a park attendant
Incident:	a man was repeatedly firing a pistol into the air
Injuries:	none
Action Taken:	the man, Joseph Church, was arrested

    Officer Bonham is writing his report. Which of the following expresses the information most clearly and accurately?

    A. Mr. Orestes reported that a man was repeatedly firing a pistol into the air at the Fourth Street Park, where Mr. Orestes is a park attendant. The man, Joseph Church, was arrested.
    B. At 7:30 P.M., Mr. Orestes reported that a man was repeatedly firing a pistol into the air. There were no injuries. The man, Joseph Church, was arrested.
    C. Mr. Orestes reported at 7:30 P.M. that a man was repeatedly firing a pistol into the air at the Fourth Street Park, where Mr. Orestes is a park attendant. The man, Joseph Church, was arrested.
    D. At 7:30 P.M., Mr. Orestes reported that a man was repeatedly firing a pistol into the air at the Fourth Street Park, where Mr. Orestes is a park attendant. There were no injuries. The man, Joseph Church, was arrested.

74. A newly instituted departmental program to encourage children to stay in school includes a series of visits to area schools by police officers. Officer Jefferson is particularly interested in participating in this part of the program, since he has a background in childhood education and is a father himself. What should Officer Jefferson do?

    A. ask to be included in that part of the program
    B. insist on being included in that part of the program
    C. appear at the schools that are being visited whether he is officially involved in that part of the program or not
    D. wait to be asked to be included in that part of the program, without mentioning his interest to anyone

75. If a supervisor gives an officer instructions that the officer does not fully understand, the officer should:

    A. ask for assistance from other officers, but not the supervisor.

    B. ask the supervisor to explain the instructions.

    C. carry out the instructions to the point at which they cease to make sense, then ask for clarification.

    D. figure out what to do without asking anyone.

76. Officer Hennessy was dispatched to the scene of a reported assault, where she gathered the following information:

Location:	Leggy's Crab Shack
Address:	10 Oceanside Boulevard
Incident:	victim was using the pay phone and was struck in the face by the suspect, who was waiting to use the phone
Victim:	Lester Herman
Suspect:	Paul Bertels
Action Taken:	suspect confessed and was arrested

    Officer Hennessy is writing her report. Which of the following expresses the information most clearly and accurately?

    A. Lester Herman stated that, while Paul Bertels was waiting for him to finish using the pay phone at Leggy's Crab Shack, which is located at 10 Oceanside Boulevard, which Mr. Herman was using and which he wanted to use, Paul Bertels struck him in the face. Mr. Bertels confessed and was arrested.

    B. While using the pay phone at Leggy's Crab Shack, which is located at 10 Oceanside Boulevard, he, the victim, whose name is Lester Herman and who reported the incident, was struck in the face by Paul Bertels, who was waiting to use the phone. Mr. Bertels confessed and was arrested.

    C. Lester Herman stated that, while using the pay phone at Leggy's Crab Shack, which is located at 10 Oceanside Boulevard, he was struck in the face by Paul Bertels, who was waiting to use the phone. Mr. Bertels confessed and was arrested.

    D. While using the pay phone at Leggy's Crab Shack, which is located at 10 Oceanside Boulevard, Lester Herman reported that he was struck in the face by Paul Bertels, who was waiting to use the phone. Mr. Bertels confessed to having been waiting and then striking Mr. Herman in the face, as Mr. Herman reported it, and he, Mr. Bertels, was arrested.

77. During recent weeks, three assaults have occurred in Officer Moore's patrol area. The suspect in the first assault is described as a tall male with curly black hair and no mustache. The suspect in the second assault is described as a short male with curly blonde hair and a blonde mustache. The suspect in the third assault is described as a tall female with curly black hair.

    After a fourth assault, an arrest is made. The suspect in custody is a tall male with curly black hair and a black mustache. In addition to the crime for which the suspect was arrested, for which, if any, of the previous assaults should he be considered a suspect?

    A. the first assault only
    B. the second assault only
    C. the first and second assaults only
    D. none of the previous assaults

78. Given the information in Question 77, if a fifth assault occurs and a tall male with curly black hair and a black mustache is arrested, which of the following is the most logical assumption?

    A. The suspect arrested for the fourth assault is obviously innocent and should be released.
    B. There are more assaults in Officer Moore's patrol area than in any other area in the city.
    C. Officer Moore is not good at apprehending criminals.
    D. Either suspect currently in custody might be guilty of committing at least one assault.

79. After a long and trying court battle with his ex-wife, Officer McDonald is given joint custody of his two children. Almost immediately, however, he is asked to work extra shifts at night and on the weekends as part of a departmental effort to reduce crime. Officer McDonald should:

    A. find another job, since the department is obviously concerned only with its own objectives.
    B. speak with a supervisor about the situation, since there are clearly special circumstances in his life that could be taken into consideration.
    C. blatantly refuse to work any extra shifts.
    D. liquidate his assets and try to use the money to pay other police officers to take his extra shifts.

80. Officer Gossett responded to a report of a missing person and gathered the following information:

Time: 8:45 A.M.
Location: St. Francis Hospital
Police Contacted by: Dr. Elmore
Person Missing: Juan Thompson, a patient recovering from heart surgery
Description: 76 years old, with a large, freshly sutured incision on his chest, wearing a hospital gown and bracelet
Person Last Seen: in the Intensive Care Unit at the hospital at 8:30 A.M.

Officer Gossett is writing his report. Which of the following expresses the information most clearly and accurately?

A. At 8:45 A.M., Dr. Elmore reported Juan Thompson, a patient recovering from heart surgery who is 76 years old, with a large, freshly sutured incision on his chest and wearing a hospital gown and bracelet, as missing from the St. Francis Hospital. Dr. Elmore reported this after the patient, again named Juan Thompson, was last seen in the Intensive Care Unit at St. Francis Hospital at 8:30 A.M.

B. At 8:45 A.M., Dr. Elmore reported Juan Thompson, a patient recovering from heart surgery, missing. The patient is described as 76 years old, with a large, freshly sutured incision on his chest and wearing a hospital gown and bracelet. He was last seen in the Intensive Care Unit at St. Francis Hospital at 8:30 A.M.

C. At 8:45 A.M., Dr. Elmore reported a patient recovering from heart surgery missing. The patient is described as 76 years old, with a large, freshly sutured incision on his chest and wearing a hospital gown and bracelet. He was last seen in the Intensive Care Unit at St. Francis at 8:30 A.M.

D. At 8:45 A.M., Juan Thompson, a patient recovering from heart surgery, was reported missing. The patient is described as 76 years old, with a large, freshly sutured incision on his chest and wearing a hospital gown and bracelet. He was last seen in the Intensive Care Unit at St. Francis Hospital at 8:30 A.M.

81. Dr. Farrow left the hospital at the end of a long day and found that his car was not in his parking space. Suspecting that it might have been stolen, Dr. Farrow contacted the police, and Officer Turner was dispatched to investigate. She interviewed several witnesses who said they saw two people break into the doctor's car and drive away with it. Of the following descriptions of the suspects given to Officer Turner by the witnesses, which should she consider most likely to be accurate?

A. a male and a female, each wearing white shorts and tennis shoes
B. two females, each wearing yellow shorts and tennis shoes
C. a male and a female, each wearing yellow shorts and tennis shoes
D. two males, each wearing yellow shorts and running shoes

82. Assume a study shows 1.5 percent of the drivers on the road on New Year's Eve are driving while impaired by alcohol or drugs. According to this study, if a police department stops 4,200 drivers on New Year's Eve, how many of these drivers would be impaired?

    A. 4.2
    B. 21
    C. 42
    D. 63

83. Officer Richardson is offered a second job working as a security guard for a small business. Officer Richardson's department does not have a policy against "moonlighting," so he accepts the second job to earn extra money. During a shift at this new job, he observes his new boss engaging in illegal activities. What should Officer Richardson do?

    A. Decide which job he cares about the most and quit the other, since the two jobs are obviously incompatible.
    B. Ignore the illegal activities, since his boss was kind enough to hire him, and continue working.
    C. Report the illegal activities and quit the second job.
    D. Confront his boss with what he knows and demand compensation for his silence.

84. In State X, a person is guilty of **FRAUDULENTLY OBTAINING A SIGNATURE** when, with intent to defraud or to acquire a substantial benefit, he obtains a signature of a person to a written instrument by means of any misrepresentation of fact that he knows to be false.

    Cassandra tells her boss that the paper she has placed in front of him is another copy of his consent form for his son's class trip, when she knows that the paper is actually a revised copy of her employment contract. This revised contract, which she has not discussed with her boss, grants her a substantial cash bonus immediately upon being signed, in addition to an immediate one-month vacation. Based solely upon the above definition, which of the following is true?

    A. Cassandra should be charged with Fraudulently Obtaining a Signature.
    B. Cassandra should not be charged with any crime.
    C. Cassandra should be charged with Fraudulently Obtaining a Signature only if she attempts to claim any of the benefits granted to her in the revised contract.
    D. Cassandra should be charged with Fraudulently Obtaining a Signature only if, upon looking over the contract, her boss determines that she does not deserve the perks outlined in the new contract.

85. Officer Blackmon was dispatched to the scene of a bicycle accident, where she gathered the following information:

Location: the corner of Redwood Lane and Court Street
Time: 9:00 P.M.
Police Contacted by: Elaine Womack, witness
Incident: two cyclists collided as each rounded the corner and slid on the road, which was wet due to a recent storm
Injuries: both suffered several broken bones and are currently hospitalized

Officer Blackmon is writing her report. Which of the following expresses the information most clearly and accurately?

A. At 9:00 P.M., Elaine Womack reported seeing two cyclists collide as each rounded a corner and slipped on the road, which was wet due to a recent storm. Both cyclists suffered several broken bones and are currently hospitalized.

B. Elaine Womack reported seeing two cyclists collide as each rounded the corner of Redwood Lane and Court Street and slipped on the road, which was wet due to a recent storm. Both cyclists suffered several broken bones and are currently hospitalized.

C. At 9:00 P.M., Elaine Womack reported seeing two cyclists slip on the road and collide as each rounded the corner of Redwood Lane and Court Street, which was wet due to a recent storm. Both cyclists suffered several broken bones and are currently hospitalized.

D. Elaine Womack reported at 9:00 P.M. that she had seen two cyclists collide as each rounded the corner of Redwood Lane and Court Street. Both cyclists suffered several broken bones and are currently hospitalized.

86. Of the following, which is the least important skill or attribute for a police officer to possess?

A. generations of family history in the community
B. good marksmanship
C. courage
D. compassion

87. Officer Austin is hiking on a nature trail on his day off when he nearly stumbles over a partially decomposed corpse. Officer Austin does not have a cellular phone with him. What should Officer Austin do first?

A. complete his hike and use the nearest phone at the end of the trail to report the situation
B. run to the nearest phone and report the situation
C. do nothing, since he is off duty, and the person cannot be helped anyway
D. drag the corpse to the nearest outpost

88. While checking out of his hotel, Mr. Conroy turned from the desk clerk to find that his briefcase was missing. Convinced that his briefcase had been stolen, Mr. Conroy called the police, and Officer Patel soon arrived to investigate. Many witnesses volunteered to speak with Officer Patel. Of the following descriptions of the suspect given to Officer Patel by the witnesses, which should he consider most likely to be correct?

    A. tall, middle-aged man, wearing a solid blue suit

    B. tall, young man, wearing a tan pinstriped suit

    C. short, young man, wearing a blue pinstriped suit

    D. tall, young man, wearing a blue pinstriped suit

89. Officer Bartholomew was sent to investigate a report that two men had attempted to sneak into a movie, and he gathered the following information:

Location:	Big Twelve Cineplex
Time:	7:15 P.M.
Police Contacted by:	Lamar Rankin, manager
Incident:	two men attempted to sneak into a movie without paying
Suspects:	Joe and Jonathan Levy
Action Taken:	both men confessed and were arrested

    Officer Bartholomew is writing his report. Which of the following expresses the information most clearly and accurately?

    A. At 7:15 P.M., Lamar Rankin reported that two men had attempted to sneak into a movie without paying at Big Twelve Cineplex, which Mr. Rankin manages. The two men, Joe and Jonathan Levy, confessed and were arrested.

    B. Joe and Jonathan Levy were caught by Big Twelve Cineplex manager Lamar Rifkin trying to sneak into a movie without paying. The men confessed and were arrested.

    C. At 7:15 A.M., Lamar Rankin, the manager, reported that Joe and Jonathan Levy attempted to sneak into a movie at Big Twelve Cineplex without paying. Both men confessed and were arrested.

    D. Joe and Jonathan Levy were caught by Big Twelve Cineplex manager Lamar Rankin trying to sneak into a movie without paying. Mr. Rankin reported the incident at 7:15 P.M.

90. Officer Long is concerned about the increasing amount of unlawful consumption of alcohol by minors in her patrol area. In an effort to combat this trend, on which of the following locations should Officer Long most closely focus her attention?

    A. a church outreach program that hosts all-night parties for teens

    B. a large, popular bar whose policy about admitting minors and allowing them to drink is reputed to be extremely relaxed

    C. a skating rink in which alcoholic beverages are prohibited

    D. the home of a minor whose parents allow him and his underage friends to drink

PRACTICE TEST 4 ANSWER KEY

1. A	26. B	51. A	76. C
2. C	27. A	52. A	77. A
3. C	28. C	53. C	78. D
4. D	29. A	54. B	79. B
5. A	30. B	55. C	80. B
6. A	31. B	56. A	81. C
7. A	32. B	57. D	82. D
8. A	33. D	58. A	83. C
9. C	34. D	59. D	84. A
10. D	35. D	60. C	85. C
11. B	36. A	61. D	86. A
12. B	37. A	62. B	87. B
13. B	38. C	63. A	88. D
14. C	39. B	64. C	89. A
15. A	40. C	65. B	90. B
16. A	41. C	66. B	
17. A	42. C	67. D	
18. C	43. A	68. D	
19. C	44. C	69. A	
20. B	45. D	70. C	
21. C	46. D	71. B	
22. B	47. A	72. A	
23. C	48. B	73. D	
24. C	49. C	74. A	
25. D	50. A	75. B	

PRACTICE TEST 4 ANSWERS AND EXPLANATIONS

1. **A** is correct.

2. **C** is the clearest and most accurate statement. There is information missing from A and D, and B contains inaccurate information (the drivers' names are reversed).

3. **C** is correct.

4. **D** is the only accurate statement; there is information missing from each of the other three statements.

5. **A** is the best answer. While the other pieces of information might be useful, they would not be as immediately important to Officer Marquez's investigation as a "physical description of the suspect."

6. **A** contains the most repeaters.

7. **A** is correct. The backyard with the "high privacy fence" is not a "public place," so Jemma is not breaking the law in question.

8. Only **A** is stated clearly and in a logical order.

9. **C** is obviously correct.

10. **D** is correct. The bank machine "next to a mall that closes at 9:00 P.M." presents the greatest opportunity for criminals to rob bank machine customers without being observed.

11. **B** is the only statement that contains all of the information.

12. **B** contains the most repeaters.

13. **B** is correct. The man's behavior makes the situation very suspicious.

14. **C** is the only accurate statement. Each of the other statements contains incorrect information; for example, in A, the time is given as "11:45 A.M." rather than "11:45 P.M."

15. **A** is the best answer. It is the only instance in which someone "unlawfully engages" in "overhearing of a conversation."

16. **A** is the only statement that contains all the information without unnecessary repetition.

17. **A** is correct. The man may simply have misplaced his keys and could be entering his own house. Asking the man for identification will enable Officer Gianini to determine whether further action is warranted.

18. **C** contains the most repeaters. Note that the color of the tie is the same in each of the four descriptions, so it cannot be used to eliminate possible answers.

19. **C** is correct. Notice *three* men's suits were stolen, each with a value of $300 (or $900 total). The total amount for the four Victorian lamps is provided ($750).

20. **B** is the only statement that contains all the information. Note that the only information missing from A is the designation "P.M." This is easy to overlook.

21. **C** is correct. The suspect, who is a "short, bald man with large biceps" could easily don a wig to become a "short man with long hair and large biceps" (C), but he could not easily alter his appearance to look like the other three individuals.

22. **B** contains the most repeaters.

23. **C** is the clearest and most accurate statement. There is information missing from A and B, and the wording in D is unclear and confusing.

24. **C** is correct.

25. **D** is correct. The conduct in A and B is not sexual, and C is an example of two adults consenting to engage in a sexual act without the exchange of a fee.

26. Only **B** is worded in a clear and logical manner.

27. **A** is the only statement that contains all the information.

28. **C** is the best answer. Now that the car has been located, finding the person who stole the car is Officer Buford's primary goal, but he should proceed carefully so he does not alert the suspect to his presence too soon.

29. **A** contains the most repeaters.

30. **B** is the clearest and most accurate statement. There is information missing from A and C, and D is worded in an unclear and confusing manner. Note, in D, the unnecessary repetition of the fact that the "third floor was destroyed."

31. **B** is correct. Each of the other three actions would be violations of the citizen's civil rights.

32. **B** is correct, since Sharon did not know where the property line was and, therefore, did not "knowingly" enter or remain "unlawfully" upon the premises.

33. **D** is the only statement that contains all the information.

34. **D** contains the most repeaters. Note the phrase "droopy ears" appears in all four descriptions, so it cannot be used to eliminate possible answers.

35. **D** is the best answer. A "pedestrian who was standing on the side of the road" would have had a good vantage point and would be more likely to be impartial than anyone involved in the collision (A and B) or related to anyone involved (C).

36. **A** is the best answer. Supervisors of an officer in such a situation would want to assist and accommodate the officer in any way possible.

37. **A** is the clearest and most accurate statement. There is information missing from B, and C and D are worded in a confusing and unclear manner.

38. **C** is the most logical assumption. Given the officer's limited observation of the situation, there is no evidence to suggest that any of the others would be true.

39. **B** contains the most repeaters.

40. **C** is the only accurate statement. There is inaccurate information in each of the other three statements; for example, in A, Mr. Raj is identified as "a customer" rather than as "a merchant."

41. **C** is correct. A and B would be terribly premature, and D would be dangerous and irresponsible.

42. **C** is correct. In A, his mother does not know that he is hiding at her house. In B, the "business partner" is simply doing Xavier's wife a favor, and that favor does not serve to "harbor or conceal" Xavier. In D, the "former parole officer" is assisting the police rather than assisting Xavier.

43. **A** is the only statement that contains all the information. Note, in B, that the only missing information is the color of Mr. Solano's vehicle. This is easy to overlook.

44. **C** is correct. Note, in D, the use of the word "never"; this is usually an indication that a statement is exaggerated or incorrect, as is the case here.

45. **D** contains the most repeaters. Note that the phrase "gray corduroy pants" appears in all four descriptions, so it cannot be used to eliminate any possible answers.

46. **D** is the clearest statement. The wording in each of the other three statements is unclear and confusing. Note, in B, the awkward wording of the phrase "who were doing the said fighting."

47. **A** is correct.

48. **B.** is correct

49. **C** is correct.

50. **A** is the only statement that contains all the information.

51. **A** contains the most repeaters. Note, while it appears only twice, the phrase "blue suit" is a repeater.

52. **A** is correct.

53. **C** is the clearest and most accurate statement. The wording in A and B is unclear and confusing, and there is inaccurate information in D.

54. **B** is correct. There is no reason to assume that any of the other statements might be true.

55. **C** is correct. Larcenies occur on Reese Road between Griffin and Cooper Streets on Sundays and Fridays between 2:00 P.M. and 8:30 P.M., and the patrol schedule in C is the only one of the four that provides coverage of that area on those days at that time.

56. **A** is correct. Rapes occur on Frederick Boulevard near Common Harbor on Wednesdays between 1:00 A.M. and 7:00 A.M., and the patrol schedule in A is the only one of the four that provides coverage of that area on that day of the week at that time.

57. **D** is correct. Robberies occur near the northwest corner of the Sunny Skies subdivision on Tuesdays and Thursdays between 8:30 A.M. and 2:00 P.M., and the patrol schedule in D is the only one of the four that provides coverage of that area on those days at that time.

58. **A** is the only logical assumption. There is no reason to think that any of the other statements are true.

59. **D** is the only statement that is worded clearly and in a logical order. Note, in B, the unnecessary repetition of the fact that #4 Tanner Court is Mr. Lowery's residence.

60. **C** contains the most repeaters.

61. **D** is the only statement that contains all the information.

62. **B** is correct. Noticing the last word of the sentence in D, which is "catalog," is crucial to determining whether or not D is correct.

63. **A** is the clearest and most accurate statement.

64. **C** is the best answer. The department should be notified in such a situation before any further action is taken by any individual officer, on or off duty. In addition, B would unnecessarily endanger the lives of civilians and the man in question, whose identity has not been established. D would simply be irresponsible.

65. **B** is correct.

66. **B** is the only clearly worded statement.

67. **D** contains the most repeaters.

68. **D** is correct. A "six-inch silk ribbon" is unlikely to be used by the suspect as a harmful device.

69. **A** is the only accurate statement. There is incorrect information in each of the other statements.

70. **C** is correct. Encouraging the family to point fingers at neighbors who might be "shifty looking" would not be part of Officer Stacy's agenda during an interview with them.

71. **B** is clearly the only instance in which someone "intentionally aids or causes another person to commit suicide." Note that D is not such an instance; since the victim did not participate, it does not seem likely that his death was a suicide.

72. **A** contains the most repeaters.

73. **D** is the only statement that contains all the information.

74. **A** is the best answer. An officer should feel comfortable indicating a particular interest in any departmental program, since anyone who is excited about participating in a program is likely to bring a good measure of enthusiasm to that program.

75. **B** is the best answer. Completely understanding instructions is key to an officer's ability to carry them out.

76. **C** is the clearest statement. The wording in each of the other statements is unclear and confusing.

77. **A** is correct. The suspect in custody matches the description of the suspect in the first assault, except for the mustache, which he could have grown after the first assault. His description does not match the descriptions of the other two suspects.

78. **D** is the only logical assumption. Note that the fact that a fifth assault has been committed does not necessarily mean that the suspect arrested for the fourth assault is "obviously innocent and should be released" (A).

79. **B** is correct. It is always advisable for an officer to discuss with a supervisor any scheduling problems or personal issues pertaining to that officer's performance.

80. **B** is the clearest and most accurate statement. It is the only statement that accurately conveys all the information without unnecessary repetition.

81. **C** contains the most repeaters. Note, while it only appears twice, the phrase "a male and a female" is a repeater.

82. **D** is correct. To calculate 1.5% of 4,200, multiple 0.015 by 4,200. This equals 63.

83. **C** is correct.

84. **A** is correct. Cassandra definitely had intent "to acquire substantial benefit" and obtained a signature by means of a "misrepresentation of fact," which she knew to be false.

85. **C** is the only statement that contains all the information.

86. **A** would be the least important attribute, as each of the others would materially contribute to an officer's ability, while a "family history" would not.

87. **B** is correct. Note that D is incorrect because removing the corpse could compromise any evidence that may be present on or near the victim.

88. **D** contains the most repeaters.

89. **A** is the clearest and most accurate statement. Note, in B, the name of the theater manager is misspelled.

90. **B** is the best answer. While "the home of a minor whose parents allow him and his underage friends to drink" (D) would be a location at which underage consumption of alcohol occurs, it would affect a much smaller number of minors than the "large, popular bar" in B.

Practice Test 5

ANSWER SHEET FOR PRACTICE TEST 5

For each question, select the best answer choice. Use the answer sheet to mark your choices. Answers and explanations follow the test.

1. Ⓐ Ⓑ Ⓒ Ⓓ	26. Ⓐ Ⓑ Ⓒ Ⓓ	51. Ⓐ Ⓑ Ⓒ Ⓓ	76. Ⓐ Ⓑ Ⓒ Ⓓ
2. Ⓐ Ⓑ Ⓒ Ⓓ	27. Ⓐ Ⓑ Ⓒ Ⓓ	52. Ⓐ Ⓑ Ⓒ Ⓓ	77. Ⓐ Ⓑ Ⓒ Ⓓ
3. Ⓐ Ⓑ Ⓒ Ⓓ	28. Ⓐ Ⓑ Ⓒ Ⓓ	53. Ⓐ Ⓑ Ⓒ Ⓓ	78. Ⓐ Ⓑ Ⓒ Ⓓ
4. Ⓐ Ⓑ Ⓒ Ⓓ	29. Ⓐ Ⓑ Ⓒ Ⓓ	54. Ⓐ Ⓑ Ⓒ Ⓓ	79. Ⓐ Ⓑ Ⓒ Ⓓ
5. Ⓐ Ⓑ Ⓒ Ⓓ	30. Ⓐ Ⓑ Ⓒ Ⓓ	55. Ⓐ Ⓑ Ⓒ Ⓓ	80. Ⓐ Ⓑ Ⓒ Ⓓ
6. Ⓐ Ⓑ Ⓒ Ⓓ	31. Ⓐ Ⓑ Ⓒ Ⓓ	56. Ⓐ Ⓑ Ⓒ Ⓓ	81. Ⓐ Ⓑ Ⓒ Ⓓ
7. Ⓐ Ⓑ Ⓒ Ⓓ	32. Ⓐ Ⓑ Ⓒ Ⓓ	57. Ⓐ Ⓑ Ⓒ Ⓓ	82. Ⓐ Ⓑ Ⓒ Ⓓ
8. Ⓐ Ⓑ Ⓒ Ⓓ	33. Ⓐ Ⓑ Ⓒ Ⓓ	58. Ⓐ Ⓑ Ⓒ Ⓓ	83. Ⓐ Ⓑ Ⓒ Ⓓ
9. Ⓐ Ⓑ Ⓒ Ⓓ	34. Ⓐ Ⓑ Ⓒ Ⓓ	59. Ⓐ Ⓑ Ⓒ Ⓓ	84. Ⓐ Ⓑ Ⓒ Ⓓ
10. Ⓐ Ⓑ Ⓒ Ⓓ	35. Ⓐ Ⓑ Ⓒ Ⓓ	60. Ⓐ Ⓑ Ⓒ Ⓓ	85. Ⓐ Ⓑ Ⓒ Ⓓ
11. Ⓐ Ⓑ Ⓒ Ⓓ	36. Ⓐ Ⓑ Ⓒ Ⓓ	61. Ⓐ Ⓑ Ⓒ Ⓓ	86. Ⓐ Ⓑ Ⓒ Ⓓ
12. Ⓐ Ⓑ Ⓒ Ⓓ	37. Ⓐ Ⓑ Ⓒ Ⓓ	62. Ⓐ Ⓑ Ⓒ Ⓓ	87. Ⓐ Ⓑ Ⓒ Ⓓ
13. Ⓐ Ⓑ Ⓒ Ⓓ	38. Ⓐ Ⓑ Ⓒ Ⓓ	63. Ⓐ Ⓑ Ⓒ Ⓓ	88. Ⓐ Ⓑ Ⓒ Ⓓ
14. Ⓐ Ⓑ Ⓒ Ⓓ	39. Ⓐ Ⓑ Ⓒ Ⓓ	64. Ⓐ Ⓑ Ⓒ Ⓓ	89 Ⓐ Ⓑ Ⓒ Ⓓ
15. Ⓐ Ⓑ Ⓒ Ⓓ	40. Ⓐ Ⓑ Ⓒ Ⓓ	65. Ⓐ Ⓑ Ⓒ Ⓓ	90. Ⓐ Ⓑ Ⓒ Ⓓ
16. Ⓐ Ⓑ Ⓒ Ⓓ	41. Ⓐ Ⓑ Ⓒ Ⓓ	66. Ⓐ Ⓑ Ⓒ Ⓓ	
17. Ⓐ Ⓑ Ⓒ Ⓓ	42. Ⓐ Ⓑ Ⓒ Ⓓ	67. Ⓐ Ⓑ Ⓒ Ⓓ	
18. Ⓐ Ⓑ Ⓒ Ⓓ	43. Ⓐ Ⓑ Ⓒ Ⓓ	68. Ⓐ Ⓑ Ⓒ Ⓓ	
19. Ⓐ Ⓑ Ⓒ Ⓓ	44. Ⓐ Ⓑ Ⓒ Ⓓ	69. Ⓐ Ⓑ Ⓒ Ⓓ	
20. Ⓐ Ⓑ Ⓒ Ⓓ	45. Ⓐ Ⓑ Ⓒ Ⓓ	70. Ⓐ Ⓑ Ⓒ Ⓓ	
21. Ⓐ Ⓑ Ⓒ Ⓓ	46. Ⓐ Ⓑ Ⓒ Ⓓ	71. Ⓐ Ⓑ Ⓒ Ⓓ	
22. Ⓐ Ⓑ Ⓒ Ⓓ	47. Ⓐ Ⓑ Ⓒ Ⓓ	72. Ⓐ Ⓑ Ⓒ Ⓓ	
23. Ⓐ Ⓑ Ⓒ Ⓓ	48. Ⓐ Ⓑ Ⓒ Ⓓ	73. Ⓐ Ⓑ Ⓒ Ⓓ	
24. Ⓐ Ⓑ Ⓒ Ⓓ	49. Ⓐ Ⓑ Ⓒ Ⓓ	74. Ⓐ Ⓑ Ⓒ Ⓓ	
25. Ⓐ Ⓑ Ⓒ Ⓓ	50. Ⓐ Ⓑ Ⓒ Ⓓ	75. Ⓐ Ⓑ Ⓒ Ⓓ	

1. A residential section of Officer Chokkar's patrol area has been hit by a string of recent robberies. Most of the items stolen have been HDTVs and video game machines. Of the following scenarios observed by Officer Chokkar during a routine patrol of the area, about which should he be most concerned?

   A. a teenage couple renting video games at a video rental store
   B. two large men riding bicycles through the area near sundown
   C. three large men in a windowless panel truck slowly circling a block in the area
   D. a man helping a worker unload a boxed HDTV from a department store van

2. In State X, a person is guilty of **ROBBERY IN THE SECOND DEGREE** when he forcibly steals property and when the property consists of a motor vehicle. Based solely upon this definition, which of the following is the best example of Robbery in the Second Degree?

   A. Leo notices that someone has left a new car in a parking deck with the windows down and the keys in the ignition. Leo steals the car.
   B. Sela punches a young man and pulls him from behind the wheel of his car, then steals the car.
   C. Jimmy holds a knife to a man's throat and steals his wallet.
   D. Carlos threatens to beat a small boy unconscious if he does not give him all of his money.

3. Officer Frasier was dispatched to the scene of a robbery, where she gathered the following information:

Location:	Tex's Barbeque
Time:	8:00 P.M.
Incident:	an unsatisfied customer sprayed barbeque sauce in the eyes of Joe Baltran, a cook
Suspect:	tall male wearing a flannel shirt and jeans
Location of Suspect:	unknown

   Officer Frasier is writing her report. Which of the following expresses the information most clearly and accurately?

   A. Joe Baltran, a cook at Tex's Barbeque, threw barbeque sauce at 8:00 P.M. into the eyes of an unsatisfied customer described as a tall male wearing a flannel shirt and jeans whose location is unknown.
   B. At 8:00 P.M., Joe Baltran reported that an unsatisfied customer at Tex's Barbeque, where Mr. Baltran is a cook, threw barbeque sauce in his eyes. The suspect is described as a tall male wearing a flannel shirt and jeans, and his location is unknown.
   C. At Tex's Barbeque, an unsatisfied customer threw barbeque sauce in the eyes of Joe Baltran, a cook there. He is a tall male wearing a flannel shirt and jeans. His location is unknown.
   D. Barbeque sauce was thrown into the eyes of Joe Baltran, a cook, at 8:00 A.M. This was at Tex's Barbeque and the person doing the throwing was a tall, unsatisfied male customer wearing a flannel shirt and jeans whose location is unknown.

4. The description of a vehicle that has reportedly been involved in a hit-and-run matches Officer Dale's wife's car. What should Officer Dale do first?

   A. ask a supervisor or an officer investigating the hit-and-run for more information about the incident and the suspect's vehicle
   B. proceed to his wife's workplace and arrest her
   C. call his wife and tell her to get out of town immediately
   D. file for divorce

5. Estelle was picking out fabric for a dress she planned to make for her sister's wedding. She heard footsteps behind her, but did not turn around in time to see the face of the person who struck her on the back of her head and stole her purse. During the course of his investigation, Officer Winchester interviewed many witnesses, all of whom saw the incident and reported that the suspect fled from the store. Of the following descriptions of the suspect given to Officer Winchester by witnesses, which should he consider most likely to be correct?

   A. tall male with a red birthmark on his right cheek
   B. tall female with a red birthmark on her left cheek
   C. short male with a red birthmark on his left cheek
   D. short male with a brown mole on his left cheek

6. Officer Singh responds to a report of a drowning and gathers the following information:

Location:	City Pools
Time:	3:00 P.M.
Police Contacted by:	Steve Greer, a lifeguard
Incident:	James Wheeler, an elderly man, drowned
Action Taken:	victim's family was contacted

   Officer Singh must write his report. Which of the following expresses the information most clearly and accurately?

   A. At City Pools, where Steve Greer is a lifeguard, Mr. Greer stated that an elderly man named James Wheeler drowned.
   B. Steve Greer reported that at 3:00 P.M., an elderly man named James Wheeler drowned at City Pools. Mr. Wheeler's family was contacted.
   C. Steve Greer reported that at 3:00 P.M. at City Pools, where he is a lifeguard, an elderly man named James Wheeler drowned. Mr. Wheeler's family was contacted.
   D. James Wheeler drowned at 3:00 P.M. at City Pools, and his family was notified, according to lifeguard Steve Greer.

7. Officer Mundy is patrolling an area near an elementary school. Which of the following individuals should Officer Mundy consider to be suspicious?

   A. a middle-aged woman driving into the school parking lot in a minivan

   B. an elderly man walking his dog on the sidewalk that runs in front of the school

   C. a young woman who brings several trays of cupcakes to the school for a bake sale

   D. a middle-aged man who takes pictures of children playing on the playground and then beckons for them to come and see the pictures

8. In State X, a person is guilty of **MURDER IN THE SECOND DEGREE** when, with intent to cause the death of another person, he causes the death of such person or of a third person. Based solely upon this definition, which of the following is the best example of Murder in the Second Degree?

   A. Emilio aims his gun, which he believes is not loaded, at his wife, then pulls the trigger. A bullet is fired from the gun, and his wife is shot and dies.

   B. Deandra stabs her mother in the palm of her hand, hoping to get her attention. Due to the shock of the puncture, Deandra's mother has a heart attack and dies.

   C. Roger aims his loaded shotgun at his wife's ex-boyfriend and, intending to kill him, shoots him in the head, fatally wounding him.

   D. Georgette shoots herself in the head and dies from the wound.

9. Officer Smith was dispatched to the scene of an auto accident, where he gathered the following information:

Location:	South Terrace Street near Beaver Lake
Time:	11:15 P.M.
Driver and Vehicle:	Velma Johnson, driving a Ford Probe
Incident:	hit a deer
Injury:	severely bruised ribs
Action Taken:	Ms. Johnson was hospitalized; the car was towed away

   Officer Smith is writing his report. Which of the following expresses the information most clearly and accurately?

   A. At 11:15 P.M. at South Terrace Street near Beaver Lake, Velma Johnson hit a deer. She suffered severely bruised ribs and was hospitalized, and her car was towed away.

   B. Velma Johnson stated that at 11:15 P.M., she hit a deer while driving her Ford Probe. She suffered severely bruised ribs and was hospitalized. Her car was towed away.

   C. At 11:15 P.M., Velma Johnson hit a deer in her Ford Probe at South Terrace Street near Beaver Lake. She was hospitalized, and her car was towed away.

   D. Velma Johnson stated that at 11:15 P.M. at South Terrace Street near Beaver Lake, she hit a deer while driving her Ford Probe. She suffered severely bruised ribs and was hospitalized, and her car was towed away.

10. Officer Desoto has observed that certain crimes regularly occur in some sections of the area he patrols. Robberies occur on the south side of Tucker Field, assaults on Briggs Street between Sands and Pace Avenues, and arsons on Tripoli Street between Forest and Lawn Streets. Robberies occur on Mondays and Saturdays, assaults on Fridays and Sundays, and arsons on Mondays and Wednesdays. Robberies take place between noon and 6:00 P.M., assaults between 2:00 P.M. and 5:00 P.M., and arsons between 9:00 P.M. and midnight.

    Given this information, which of the following patrol schedules would enable Officer Desoto to most effectively reduce the number of assaults?

    A. Tripoli Street between Forest and Lawn Streets, Fridays, 2:00 P.M. to 5:00 P.M.

    B. Briggs Street between Sands and Pace Avenues, Fridays, 2:00 P.M. to 5:00 P.M.

    C. Tripoli Street between Forest and Lawn Streets, Fridays and Saturdays, 2:00 P.M. to midnight

    D. Briggs Street between Sands and Pace Avenues, Fridays and Sundays, 2:00 P.M. to midnight

11. Given the information in Question 10, which of the following patrol schedules would enable Officer Desoto to most effectively reduce the number of arsons?

    A. the south side of Tucker Field, Mondays and Wednesdays, 9:00 P.M. to midnight

    B. Tripoli Street between Forest and Lawn Streets, Mondays and Wednesdays, 9:00 P.M. to midnight

    C. the south side of Tucker Field, Wednesdays, noon to 6:00 P.M.

    D. Tripoli Street between Forest and Lawn Streets, Wednesdays, noon to 6:00 P.M.

12. Given the information in Question 10, which of the following would be the most advisable day and time for someone who wishes to avoid being robbed to walk along the south side of Tucker Field?

    A. Wednesday at 3:00 P.M.

    B. Saturday at 3:00 P.M.

    C. Monday at 5:00 P.M.

    D. Saturday at 5:30 P.M.

13. Given the information in Question 10, which of the following is the most logical statement?

    A. Officer Desoto's patrol area is one of the most dangerous areas of town.

    B. The south side of Tucker Field is a very affluent area.

    C. In Officer Desoto's patrol area, arsons occur at night.

    D. It is easier for Officer Desoto to catch robbers than arsonists.

14. If an off-duty officer observes a fistfight between two men on a street corner, he should:

    A. do nothing, since he is not being paid for his time while he is off duty.

    B. jump into the fight and break it up.

    C. announce that he is a police officer and demand that the men stop fighting.

    D. wait until the fight is over and call an ambulance if either of the men is seriously injured.

15. If witnesses to an assault offered the following descriptions of the suspect's weapon to Officer Hendricks, which should he consider most likely to be accurate?

    A. a long, black club with a white logo on the handle

    B. a short, black club with a red logo on the handle

    C. a long, black club with a red logo on the handle

    D. a long, brown club with a red logo on the handle

16. Officer Lai encountered a stranded motorist and gathered the following information:

Location:	700 block of Main Street
Driver and Vehicle:	Sally Ramos, driving a Mercury Cougar
Incident:	Ms. Ramos was in her car on the shoulder of the road
Action Taken:	Ms. Ramos explained that her car had stalled; she was driven home, and a wrecker was called to tow her car to a garage

    Officer Lai must write his report. Which of the following expresses the information most clearly and accurately?

    A. Sally Ramos was found in her Mercury Cougar on the shoulder of the road at the 700 block of Main Street. She explained that her car had stalled. She was driven home, and a wrecker was called to tow her car to a garage.

    B. A Mercury Cougar containing Sally Ramos was found stalled on the shoulder of the road. Ms. Ramos was given a ride home, and a wrecker was called to tow her car to a shop.

    C. A wrecker was called to tow the Mercury Cougar in which Sally Ramos was found because it had stalled on the shoulder of the road at the 700 block of Main Street.

    D. At Main Street, Sally Ramos was found in her stalled Mercury Cougar. She explained that the car had stalled, and she was given a ride home, and a wrecker was called to tow her car to a garage.

17. Officer Joyce responded to a report of a larceny and gathered the following information:

Location: 6600 Hill Street
Police Contacted by: Prudence Tyrrell, resident
Complaint: a new wheelbarrow had been stolen from her yard
Time: between 9:00 A.M. and 5:45 P.M., while she was at work

Officer Joyce is writing her report. Which of the following expresses the information most clearly and accurately?

A. Between 9:00 A.M. and 5:45 P.M., someone stole a new wheelbarrow from the yard at 6600 Hill Street that belongs to Prudence Tyrrell, the resident, and the person who contacted the police. She was at work at the time.

B. A new wheelbarrow that belonged to Prudence Tyrrell, the complainer, was stolen between 9:00 A.M. and 5:45 P.M., while Ms. Tyrrell was at work, from her residence at 6600 Hill Street.

C. Prudence Tyrrell stated that between 9:00 A.M. and 5:45 P.M., while she was at work, a new wheelbarrow was stolen from her yard at 6600 Hill Street.

D. 6600 Hill Street, her residence, is where the reportedly stolen new wheelbarrow, belonging to Prudence Tyrrell, was stolen from, reportedly, while she was at work between 9:00 A.M. and 5:45 P.M.

18. In State X, a person is guilty of **KIDNAPPING IN THE SECOND DEGREE** when he abducts another person. A person is guilty of **KIDNAPPING IN THE FIRST DEGREE** when he abducts another person and when the person abducted dies during the abduction or before he is able to return or be returned to safety.

Gerald abducts his boss's wife. After Gerald's boss agrees to give Gerald a promotion upon the safe return of his wife, Gerald drives her to a predetermined meeting place. Upon arrival at the site, but before Gerald's boss arrives, Gerald's boss's wife has a mysterious seizure and dies. Based solely upon the above definitions, which of the following is true?

A. Gerald should be charged with Kidnapping in the First Degree only.

B. Gerald should be charged with Kidnapping in the Second Degree only.

C. Gerald should be charged with Murder.

D. Gerald should not be charged with any crime until the cause of the woman's seizure can be determined.

19. Officer Hill is dispatched to deal with an unruly crowd outside of a department store. There, she gathers the following information:

Location:	Deals Department Store parking lot
Time:	2:00 P.M.
Incident:	unhappy shoppers were yelling because they were not able to get inside the crowded store to take advantage of a one-hour sale
Police Contacted by:	Mandy Simmons, a clerk at the store
Action Taken:	the crowd was dispersed, and the store closed early to avoid further problems

Officer Hill must write her report. Which of the following expresses the information most clearly and accurately?

A. At 2:00 P.M., Mandy Simmons reported that a crowd of unhappy shoppers were yelling in the parking lot of Deals Department Store because they were not able to get inside the crowded store to take advantage of a one-hour sale. The crowd was dispersed, and the store closed early to avoid further problems.

B. At 2:00 P.M., a clerk reported that a crowd of unhappy shoppers were yelling in the parking lot of Deals Department Store because they were not able to get inside the crowded store to take advantage of a one-hour sale. The crowd was dispersed, and the store closed early to avoid further problems.

C. At 2:00 P.M., Mandy Simmons reported that a crowd of unhappy shoppers were yelling in the parking lot of Deals Department Store, where she is a clerk, because they were not able to get inside the crowded store to take advantage of a one-hour sale. The crowd was dispersed, and the store closed early to avoid further problems.

D. At 2:00 P.M., Mandy Simmons reported that a crowd of unhappy shoppers were yelling in the parking lot of Deals Department Store, where she is a clerk, because they were not able to get inside the crowded store to take advantage of a sale. The crowd was dispersed, and the store closed early to avoid further problems.

20. During a thunderstorm, a vehicle slid across three lanes of traffic, crashed through a guardrail, and then sped off through a cornfield. Officer Mulgrew interviewed many motorists who saw the incident. Of the following descriptions of the suspect's vehicle given to her by witnesses, which should Officer Mulgrew consider most likely to be correct?

A. blue Nissan Pathfinder with red fog lights
B. blue Nissan Pathfinder with pink fog lights
C. blue Ford Explorer with red fog lights
D. black Nissan Pathfinder with red fog lights

21. Officer Keaton observed a pair of cars racing on an empty city street. He gathered the following information:

Time: 3:30 A.M.
Incident: road racing
Location: Cane Street between Julian and Worth
Drivers and Vehicles: Tom Stanton and Hank Flame, both driving Volvo wagons
Action Taken: both men were arrested

Officer Keaton must write his report. Which of the following expresses the information most clearly and accurately?

A. At 3:30 A.M., Tom Stanton and Hank Flame, both driving Volvo wagons, were observed road racing on Cane Street between Julian and Worth. Both men were arrested.

B. Tom Stanton and Hank Flame were road racing in their Volvo wagons when they were observed. This was at 3:30 A.M. Where it was was Cane Street between Julian and Worth. Both men were arrested.

C. Both men, Tom Stanton and Hank Flame, were arrested after being observed road racing at 3:30 A.M. in each of their Volvo wagons on Cane Street between Julian and Worth.

D. Between Julian and Worth on Cane Street, two men, Tom Stanton and Hank Flame, were arrested after 3:30 A.M. which was when they were observed road racing in their Volvo wagons, which each of them was driving.

22. Officer Hinton sees a shabbily dressed man sitting on a street curb about 50 yards away. Which is the most logical assumption for Officer Hinton to make about the man?

A. He will hurt someone if he is allowed to remain on the curb.
B. He is a criminal.
C. He is a drug addict and currently possesses illegal drugs.
D. He is probably not a wealthy person.

23. As he was pulling out of his driveway, Albert accidentally struck a skateboarder who fell, then jumped back on his board and sped off. Concerned about the safety of the skateboarder, who had left a blood stain on the asphalt where he had fallen, Albert called the police. Officer Edgar interviewed several witnesses in the area. Of the following descriptions of the victim given to Officer Edgar by witnesses, which should he consider most likely to be correct?

A. male, wearing a large olive-green T-shirt and baggy black shorts
B. female, wearing a large olive-green T-shirt and tight-fitting black shorts
C. female, wearing a tight-fitting olive-green T-shirt and baggy black shorts
D. female, wearing a large olive-green T-shirt and baggy black shorts

24. Officer Burke was dispatched to the scene of an assault, where he gathered the following information:

    Location: T-Ball Paradise
    Time: 6:45 P.M.
    Incident: victim was struck with a bat
    Victim: Mr. Lucas
    Injury: bruised thigh
    Suspect: Mr. Todd
    Action Taken: suspect confessed and was arrested

    Officer Burke is writing his report. Which of the following expresses the information most clearly and accurately?

    A. Mr. Todd stated that at 6:45 P.M. at T-Ball Paradise, Mr. Lucas struck him with a bat, bruising his thigh. Mr. Lucas confessed and was arrested.

    B. Mr. Lucas stated that at 6:45 P.M., Mr. Todd struck him at T-Ball Paradise with a bat, bruising his shoulder. Mr. Todd confessed and was arrested.

    C. Mr. Lucas stated that at 6:45 P.M. at T-Ball Paradise, Mr. Todd struck him with a bat, bruising his thigh. Mr. Todd confessed and was arrested.

    D. Mr. Lucas stated that at 4:45 P.M. at T-Ball Paradise, Mr. Todd struck him with a bat, bruising his thigh. Mr. Todd confessed and was arrested.

25. Officer Gross is searching for clues at a dormitory from which a woman has been kidnapped. Of the following messages that were recently left on the abductee's answering machine, on which should Officer Gross most closely focus his attention?

    A. a message from a movie store asking for the prompt return of an overdue tape

    B. a message from the abductee's mother asking her to call home

    C. a message from the front desk attendant announcing that she has a guest

    D. a message from a credit card company offering an increase in her credit limit

26. In State X, a person is guilty of **GRAND LARCENY IN THE SECOND DEGREE** when he steals property and when the value of the property exceeds $50,000. Based solely upon this definition, which of the following is the best example of Grand Larceny in the Second Degree?

    A. Antoinette steals a speedboat valued at $46,000.

    B. Upon being released from jail after serving his sentence for stealing a car valued at $35,000, Vinnie steals a necklace valued at $16,000.

    C. Michelle kidnaps a child and demands $75,000 as ransom.

    D. Walter steals a painting valued at $60,000.

27. Officer Beatty observes and pulls over a motorist who is driving erratically. He notes the following information:

Location: Broad Street between Carson and First Avenues
Time: 9:00 P.M.
Driver: Sandy Falwell
Violation: changed lanes without signaling, drove over a curb
Action Taken: driver arrested on suspicion of driving while intoxicated

Officer Beatty must write his report. Which of the following expresses the information most clearly and accurately?

A. At 9:00 P.M., Sandy Falwell was observed changing lanes without signaling and driving over a curb at Broad Street between Carson and First Avenues and was subsequently arrested on suspicion of driving while intoxicated.

B. Sandy Falwell was observed changing lanes without signaling and driving over a curb at Broad Street between Carson and First Avenues and was subsequently arrested on suspicion of driving while intoxicated.

C. At 9:00 P.M., Sandy Falwell was observed changing lanes without signaling at Broad Street between Carson and First Avenues and was subsequently arrested on suspicion of driving while intoxicated.

D. At 9:00 P.M., Sandy Falwell was observed changing lanes without signaling and driving over a curb at Broad Street between Carson and First Avenues and was subsequently arrested.

28. If an officer pulls over a motorist who is a friend of the officer's family, the officer should:

A. warn the motorist to be careful, no matter what the violation, since the motorist is a family friend.

B. act according to the severity of the violation and the motorist's explanation as the officer would if the motorist were a stranger.

C. give the motorist a traffic ticket, no matter what the violation, to prove his impartiality.

D. call another officer in to deal with the motorist, since he would probably be unable to act with complete impartiality.

29. Officer McClure is dispatched to a crime scene, where he is instructed to interview three potential witnesses. Officer McClure should:

    A. see to it that the potential witnesses are kept apart until each can be interviewed individually.

    B. bring the potential witnesses into a room to discuss what happened with them as a group.

    C. give each individual a short-answer questionnaire pertaining to the crime and instruct each of them to take the questionnaire home, complete it, and mail it to the precinct.

    D. ask each potential witness to summarize what he or she saw in fewer than 500 words.

30. The owner of an appliance store reported a break-in and gave the following list of items stolen and their value:

Five microwaves	$100 (each)
Two 27" televisions	$350 (each)
Seven 13" televisions	$250 (each)
Twelve hand-held blenders	$240 (total)

    What is the total value of the missing merchandise?

    A. $ 940

    B. $3,190

    C. $4,140

    D. $6,910

31. Mrs. Blue drove to the hobby shop to have her favorite antique doll repaired, but was involved in a hit-and-run accident on the way to the shop and had to be hospitalized. Mrs. Blue never saw the car that hit her, but Officer Kitchen, who was dispatched to the scene to investigate, interviewed many witnesses who did. Of the following descriptions of the suspect's car given to Officer Kitchen by witnesses, which should she consider most likely to be correct?

    A. yellow sedan with a tree-shaped air freshener

    B. green sedan with a tree-shaped air freshener

    C. yellow station wagon with a tree-shaped air freshener

    D. yellow sedan with a basketball-shaped air freshener

32. Officer Russo is dispatched to the scene of a fire, where he gathers the following information:

Location: Fletcher Herb Nursery
Time: 5:15 P.M.
Incident: a fire in the nursery's seed room
Action Taken: fire department was contacted; nursery was evacuated

Officer Russo must write his report. Which of the following expresses the information most clearly and accurately?

A. At 5:15 P.M., a fire was reported at the Fletcher Herb Nursery. The fire department was contacted, and the nursery was evacuated.

B. A fire at the Fletcher Herb Nursery, which was in the seed room, was reported. The fire department was contacted, and the nursery was evacuated.

C. At 5:15 P.M., a fire was reported in the seed room of the Fletcher Herb Nursery. The fire department was contacted, and the nursery was evacuated.

D. A fire in the pesticide room of the Fletcher Herb Nursery was reported at 5:15 A.M. The fire department was contacted, and the nursery was evacuated.

33. Officer Wainwright was interrogating a suspect who told her that he would confess to committing the crime about which he was being questioned if she promised not to tell his family what he did. Officer Wainwright told the suspect that if he confessed or was found guilty of the crime, the situation would become a matter of public record, so his family could not be prevented from finding out about it.

Officer Wainwright's actions were:

A. improper, because she should restrict their conversation to questions and answers directly pertaining to the commission of the crime in question.

B. proper if the suspect really committed the crime, but improper if he did not.

C. improper, because he asked her for such a small favor in return for the quick and simple solution to her investigation.

D. proper, because she truthfully informed the suspect of the facts with regard to her inability to keep such information from his family.

34. Officer Curtis is dispatched to an apartment building where a man is reportedly threatening to jump from a high ledge. There, Officer Curtis gathers the following information:

Location:	Uptown Towers
Time:	10:00 P.M.
Police Contacted by:	Mrs. Ernestine, a resident
Incident:	Claude Franklin was on the ledge of his 19th-floor apartment, threatening to jump
Action Taken:	negotiators were able to talk Mr. Franklin into coming back inside, and he was taken to a local hospital for psychiatric evaluation

    Officer Curtis must write his report. Which of the following expresses the information most clearly and accurately?

    A. Mrs. Ernestine reported that at the Uptown Towers, where she lives, Claude Franklin was on the ledge of his 19th-floor apartment, threatening to jump. Negotiators were able to talk him into coming back inside, and he was taken to a local hospital for psychiatric evaluation.

    B. At 10:00 P.M., Mrs. Ernestine reported that at the Uptown Towers, where she lives, Claude Franklin was on the ledge of his 19th-floor apartment, threatening to jump. Negotiators were able to talk him into coming back inside, and he was taken to a local hospital for psychiatric evaluation.

    C. Mrs. Ernestine reported at 10:00 P.M. that at the Uptown Towers, where she lives, Claude Franklin was on the ledge of his apartment, threatening to jump. Negotiators were able to talk him into coming back inside, and he was taken to a local hospital for psychiatric evaluation.

    D. At 10:00 P.M., Mrs. Ernestine reported that at the Uptown Towers, where she lives, Claude Franklin was on the ledge of his 19th-floor apartment, threatening to jump. Negotiators were able to talk him into coming back inside.

35. Officer Ignatius encounters an obviously sick dog in a public park. The dog lays down in a bed of fallen leaves, and Officer Ignatius notices two tiny puppies laying next to the dog. Officer Ignatius should:

    A. shoot the dog to put her out of her misery, and take the puppies to the animal shelter.

    B. take all three animals to the animal shelter.

    C. shoot all three animals to put them out of their misery, since they are all probably stricken with the same illness.

    D. contact animal control, since the dogs should be handled by animal experts.

36. In State X, a person is guilty of **CRIMINAL POSSESSION OF A CONTROLLED SUBSTANCE IN THE SECOND DEGREE** when he knowingly and unlawfully possesses a stimulant and said stimulant weighs 10 grams or more. Based solely upon this definition, which of the following is the best example of Criminal Possession of a Controlled Substance in the Second Degree?

   A. Fran is caught with 15 grams of an illegal stimulant in her pants pocket, which, it is later determined, was slipped into her pocket by her ex-husband without her knowledge.

   B. Spencer is caught with 5 grams of an illegal stimulant that he had just purchased from a dealer.

   C. Tatum is found in possession of 9 grams of an illegal stimulant, which she was preparing to ingest.

   D. Hank is caught with 20 grams of an illegal stimulant that he had just purchased from a dealer.

To answer Questions 37, 38, 39, and 40, use the information in the following passage.

While on foot patrol early one weekday morning, Officers Fulton and Watkins are walking through Hilltop Park when they hear shouting, followed by a woman's screams. They run to the site of the incident, at the western edge of the park along Addison Avenue at Pine Street. (The park is bordered by Addison Avenue on the west, Oak Street on the north, Beverly Avenue on the east, and Ash Street on the south. Pine Street dead-ends at the western edge of the park.) Two women are standing on the sidewalk just outside the park gate. One of the women is holding the side of her neck, which is bleeding profusely. Both women are screaming. A bystander has taken off his shirt and is pressing it against the bleeding woman's neck. Another bystander tells the officers that she's called an ambulance on her cell phone.

Officer Fulton reports the incident, while Officer Watkins tends to the woman's injury. She's been cut on the right side of the neck; the cut is approximately six inches long, but fortunately has missed the major blood vessels. The ambulance arrives and as the paramedics tend to the victim, the officers interview the two bystanders and the victim's friend.

The friend is Maureen McGowan; she tells the officers that the victim is her roommate, Kelley Masters. They live at 475 Oak Street, two blocks east of the park; they usually leave for work together and walk through the park to the bus stop at the corner of Addison Avenue and Ash Street. This morning, they'd followed their usual routine. As they reached the gate at Pine Street, they saw a man who often loitered on their block. Ms. McGowan said they know him only as Chill. She isn't sure where he lives; a neighbor told her Chill had recently been released from prison and moved in with his grandmother somewhere nearby. Chill had a large male dog that he walked without a leash; Ms. Masters also has a dog, a medium-sized female. Over the past several months, Ms. Masters has had many arguments with Chill; his dog regularly snarled and lunged at her dog and once had torn her dog's ear. He refused to leash the dog or keep it off hers. Ms. McGowan said the most recent argument had occurred early this morning. Ms. Masters had taken her dog out for a walk and had returned very angry; she had seen Chill, who immediately started yelling at her. He said his dog had been taken away by Animal Control and he blamed Ms. Masters for calling the city. Ms. Masters denied it, but he continued shouting at her, following her to the door of her building. Ms. Masters and Ms. McGowan discussed what to do; Ms. Masters said she would call the precinct house when she arrived at work.

Ms. McGowan said Chill had been waiting for them behind the bushes near the Pine Street gate. "He just jumped out and grabbed Kelley's arm and started yelling at her," she said. Both Ms. McGowan and Ms. Masters shouted at him to leave them alone. Ms. McGowan said she saw Chill step back and thought he was leaving, until he lunged forward with the knife. After slashing Ms. Masters's neck, he ran away; Ms. McGowan did not see which direction he took.

The male witness, Clancy Washington, said he'd just returned from buying a newspaper and some juice at the deli across Addison Avenue when he saw the man and two women shouting. "I thought it was some kind of boyfriend/girlfriend thing at first," he said. "Then when he stepped back and pulled out the knife, I thought, 'Oh, man, this is serious.'" He said he began running toward the man, but before he could reach him, the man slashed Ms. Masters and ran away. Mr. Washington said he'd run north, toward Oak Street; he wasn't sure if the man had turned at Oak or continued north. By then, he was trying to help Ms. Masters stanch the blood from her cut.

The female witness, Marisol Alvarez, did not see the slashing incident. She was walking south along the park on the eastern edge of Addison Avenue, heading for the bus stop at Addison and Ash. She heard shouting, then screaming, and a man came running toward her. "He almost knocked me down," she said. "He smelled bad, too, like he hadn't bathed in days. And his eyes were all red and crazy. He was scary." Ms. Alvarez said she turned and watched him run north then cut through the northwest corner of the park, heading east on Oak Street. The screaming continued and when she got past the bushes near the Pine Street gate, she saw that a woman had been injured, so she called for an ambulance on her cell phone.

Ms. Alvarez, Mr. Washington, and Ms. McGowan gave the officers a description of Chill: white male, late 20s, approximately 5'8" and 160 pounds, shaved head, multiple ear piercings and several large tattoos on his forearms, including an eagle clutching a swastika on his left forearm.

37. Who notified the precinct house of the slashing incident?

    A. Marisol Alvarez

    B. Clancy Washington

    C. Maureen McGowan

    D. Officer Fulton

38. Who witnessed the attack on Kelley Masters?

    A. Clancy Washington and Marisol Alvarez

    B. Clancy Washington and Maureen McGowan

    C. Marisol Alvarez and Maureen McGowan

    D. Clancy Washington, Marisol Alvarez, and Maureen McGowan

39. Why didn't the two women avoid Chill that morning?

    A. Ms. McGowan had once dated him, and they didn't think he'd really hurt them.

    B. They felt that avoiding him would encourage him to escalate his behavior.

    C. They didn't see him until he'd already grabbed Ms. Masters.

    D. They were so frightened at the sight of him that they couldn't move.

40. What triggered the attack?

    A. Ms. Masters's dog bit Chill's dog, puncturing its ear.

    B. Ms. Masters reported Chill for walking his dog without a leash.

    C. Chill's dog was taken away, and he blamed Ms. Masters.

    D. Chill's building had no hot water that morning, and he couldn't shower.

41. Harvey and Hector were standing in line to buy movie tickets when a woman behind them was attacked by an apparently stray dog. The dog ran off. Of the following descriptions of the animal given to investigating Officer Murphy by witnesses, which should he consider most likely to be correct?

    A. small, with wiry, brown hair and floppy ears

    B. medium-sized, with wiry, brown hair and pointed ears

    C. medium-sized, with wiry, black hair and floppy ears

    D. medium-sized, with thick, brown hair and pointed ears

42. Officer Whaley was patrolling a residential area when he saw smoke coming from a house. He noted the following information:

Location: 80 Herald Street
Time: 7:15 P.M.
Incident: smoke coming from the top floor of the house
Action Taken: fire department notified; residents alerted to the smoke
Injuries: none; the fire was easily contained by the fire department

Officer Whaley is writing his report. Which of the following expresses the information most clearly and accurately?

A. Smoke was seen coming from the top floor so the fire department was notified and residents alerted who lived there, which was at 80 Herald Street. The fire was easily contained by the fire department, and there were no injuries due to it.

B. At 80 Herald Street, there was a fire indicated by smoke coming from the top floor of the house at that address, and so the fire department came and easily contained the fire, preventing injuries, after being notified and after the residents of that house were alerted to the smoke.

C. At 7:15 P.M., smoke was seen coming from the top floor of the house at 80 Herald Street. The fire department was notified, and residents of the house were alerted to the smoke. The fire was easily contained by the fire department, and there were no injuries.

D. A fire at 80 Herald Street was easily contained by the fire department, so there were no injuries, after the department was notified after the residents of the house there, where smoke was seen coming from the top floor, were alerted to the smoke.

43. Officer Hale has been saving money for months for a family vacation. The day before he is to leave for this vacation, Officer Hale is offered $50 to overlook a man's minor traffic violation. What should Officer Hale do?

    A. refuse the money and arrest the man for attempting to bribe him

    B. take the money, since it is a small amount, and the man's violation is minor

    C. take the money and give the man a traffic ticket just to teach him a lesson about who is in control

    D. explain to the man that he would not take the money under normal circumstances, but that he will accept it for the sake of his family, and take the money

44. Of the following, which would be the most appropriate way to deal with an uncooperative suspect?

    A. threaten to fabricate additional charges against him if he does not cooperate

    B. threaten the suspect with physical force unless he agrees to cooperate

    C. beat the suspect, causing painful but minor injuries, until he agrees to cooperate

    D. use departmentally approved interrogation tactics that do not violate the suspect's civil rights

45. Officer Levy responded to a report of a robbery and gathered the following information:

Location:	Soldier's Pier
Time:	8:00 P.M.
Police Contacted by:	Ronald Place, victim
Incident:	victim was robbed at gunpoint
Item Missing:	his wallet, containing $200 in cash
Suspect:	a short man with a gray mustache

    Officer Levy is writing her report. Which of the following expresses the information most clearly and accurately?

    A. Ronald Place reported that at 8:00 P.M. at Soldier's Pier, a short man with a gray mustache robbed him at gunpoint. Mr. Place stated that his wallet, containing $200 in cash, was stolen.

    B. Ronald Place reported that at Soldier's Pier, a short man with a gray mustache robbed him at gunpoint. Mr. Place stated that his wallet, containing $200 in cash, was stolen.

    C. A short man with a gray mustache reported that at 8:00 P.M. at Soldier's Pier, Ronald Place robbed him at gunpoint. The victim stated that his wallet, containing $200 in cash, was stolen.

    D. Ronald Place reported that at 8:00 P.M. at Soldier's Pier, a short man with a gray mustache robbed him at gunpoint, stealing, at gunpoint, his wallet, containing $200 in cash, which was stolen with the wallet, according to Mr. Place.

46. Just as Officer O'Neal pulled a motorist over for exceeding the speed limit by seven miles per hour, a car sped by him from which a passenger was firing bullets in random directions. Officer O'Neal got back into his patrol car and called in to report the situation as he turned on his lights and sirens and began pursuing the speeding vehicle.

Officer O'Neal's actions were:

A. improper, as his first order of business was to complete his exchange with the motorist he had pulled over.

B. proper, as he reported the dangerous situation and took immediate action to protect the public from it.

C. improper, as he should have immediately begun firing shots at the passenger who was firing the bullets from the second car.

D. It is impossible to determine whether his actions were proper or improper without knowing more about the outcome of the situation.

47. During a child's pizza party, an enraged teenager overturned the child's table, dumping pizza and presents all over the child, his parents, and their guests. The teenager then fled. The manager of the pizza parlor called the police, and Officer Diego soon arrived and began interviewing witnesses. Of the following descriptions of the teenager given to Officer Diego by witnesses, which should he consider most likely to be correct?

A. 6'2" and 175 pounds, with straight, black hair and green eyes

B. 6'2" and 145 pounds, with straight, black hair and brown eyes

C. 5'2" and 145 pounds, with straight, blonde hair and brown eyes

D. 6'2" and 145 pounds, with curly, black hair and green eyes

48. Officer Mueller responded to a report of an assault and gathered the following information:

Location:	Bowl-lots
Time:	10:45 P.M.
Police Contacted by:	Rosetta Stamey, a witness
Incident:	victim was struck in the stomach with a bowling ball
Victim:	Jack Cook
Suspect:	Les Cook, who is being sought for questioning

Officer Mueller is writing his report. Which of the following expresses the information most clearly and accurately?

A. Les Cook, who is being sought for questioning, struck Jack Cook in the stomach with a bowling ball according to Rosetta Stamey who reported this, as she saw it, to the police at 10:45 P.M., including in her report the fact that this allegedly occurred at Bowl-lots.

B. Jack Cook was struck in the stomach by Les Cook. Mr. Cook used a bowling ball. Rosetta Stamey saw it all and reported it at 10:45 P.M. from Bowl-lots, where it happened, she said. Being sought for questioning is Les Cook.

C. A bowling ball was the weapon used to strike Jack Cook in the stomach by Les Cook, who was reported for this by Rosetta Stamey who was at Bowl-lots, where she said it happened, and he, Les Cook, is now being sought for questioning as a result.

D. Rosetta Stamey reported that at 10:45 P.M. at Bowl-lots, she saw Les Cook strike Jack Cook in the stomach with a bowling ball. Les Cook is being sought for questioning.

49. In State X, a person is guilty of **PERJURY IN THE FIRST DEGREE** when he swears falsely and when his statement consists of testimony and is material to the action, proceeding, or matter in which it is made. Based solely upon this definition, which of the following is not an example of Perjury in the First Degree?

A. Fifi, who is being tried on robbery charges, swears under oath that she was in another state on the evening that the crime in question was committed, when she actually was not.

B. Sally is being questioned under oath as to the nature of her relationship with the defendant in a murder trial. She falsely states that she does not know him, when, in fact, they are lovers.

C. Ramon, who is testifying at his brother's divorce hearing, is asked as a matter of course whether or not he has a job. He swears that he does, when, in fact, he quit his job that morning.

D. Stefan testifies that he witnessed the crime for which the defendant is being tried, when he really did not.

50. According to historical data, car thefts in a particular jurisdiction are reported at an annual rate of 2.5 thefts per 1,000 cars. If this year's car registration records show 150,000 cars, how many car thefts would be expected?

    A. 375
    B. 3,750
    C. 37.5
    D. 300

51. Officer Ferrara is sent to investigate a report of a missing person. He gathers the following information:

Location:	4523 Guadalupe Street
Time:	8:45 P.M.
Police Contacted by:	Serena Palmer, resident
Person Missing:	J. J. Palmer, her 12-year-old son
Action Taken:	J. J. Palmer came home as Ms. Palmer was filling out the report; he had been fishing with a friend and had lost track of time

    Officer Ferrara must write his report. Which of the following expresses the information most clearly and accurately?

    A. Serena Palmer, of 4523 Guadalupe Street, reported that her 12-year-old son, J. J. Palmer, was missing. As she was filling out the report, J. J., who was thought to be missing, came home. He had been fishing with a friend and had lost track of time.

    B. At 8:45 P.M., Serena Palmer, of 4523 Guadalupe Street, reported that her 12-year-old son, J. J. Palmer, was missing. As she was filling out the report, J. J. Palmer came home. He had been fishing with a friend and had lost track of time.

    C. Serena Palmer, of 4523 Guadalupe Street, reported that her 12-year-old son was missing. As she was filling out the report, he came home. He had been fishing with a friend and had lost track of time.

    D. At 8:45 P.M., Serena Palmer reported that her 12-year-old son, J. J. Palmer, was missing. As she was filling out the report, J. J. Palmer came home to where they live at 4523 Guadalupe Street.

52. As part of a departmental effort to reduce the number of robberies in the town's business center, Officer Conlon is instructed to watch for suspicious situations. Of the following, about which should Officer Conlon be most concerned?

    A. a man applying for a license to own a handgun
    B. two men in suits looking over a blueprint of an office building's layout
    C. a boy who is selling candy bars to people on the street to raise money for summer camp
    D. a man and woman who have slowly been circling an office park and photographing entrances and exits

53. If an officer is asked to work on a holiday weekend, he should:

    A. refuse to work unless a supervisor guarantees that he will have the next holiday off.

    B. comply with the request.

    C. ignore the request and hope that the supervisor asks someone else.

    D. agree to come in, then call in sick.

54. At the end of a busy day, the manager of an upscale boutique discovered that one of the shop's very expensive silk scarves was missing. Officer Pierce interviewed as many of the customers who had been in the shop that day as possible in the course of her investigation. Of the following descriptions of the suspect given to Officer Pierce by witnesses, which should she consider most likely to be accurate?

    A. gray-haired female, wearing an ivory sweaterdress and burgundy stiletto heels

    B. black-haired female, wearing an ivory sweaterdress and burgundy stiletto heels

    C. gray-haired female, wearing an ivory pantsuit and burgundy stiletto heels

    D. gray-haired female, wearing an ivory sweaterdress and burgundy sandals

55. Officer Abraham arrives at the scene of a collision, where she gathers the following information:

Location:	corner of Lock Street and Brandywine Avenue
Time:	2:15 P.M.
Incident:	auto collision
Drivers and Vehicles:	Miss Tennyson, driving a black Ford truck, and Mr. Luis, driving a green Chevrolet convertible
Driver at Fault:	Miss Tennyson ran a stop sign, causing the collision
Action Taken:	Miss Tennyson was given a traffic ticket

    Officer Abraham must write her report. Which of the following expresses the information most clearly and accurately?

    A. Miss Tennyson ran a stop sign in a black Ford truck, colliding with a green Chevrolet convertible driven by Mr. Luis. Miss Tennyson received a traffic ticket. This was at the corner of Lock Street and Brandywine Avenue.

    B. A collision with a green Chevrolet convertible driven by Mr. Luis was caused by Miss Tennyson, who ran a stop sign in her black Ford truck. She was given a traffic ticket.

    C. At 2:15 P.M. at the corner of Lock Street and Brandywine Avenue, Miss Tennyson ran a stop sign in a black Ford truck, causing a collision with a green Chevrolet convertible driven by Mr. Luis. Miss Tennyson was given a traffic ticket.

    D. Miss Tennyson ran a stop sign in a black Ford truck, causing a collision with a green Chevrolet convertible driven by Mr. Luis. Miss Tennyson was given a traffic ticket. This happened at 2:15 P.M.

56. Officer Greenleaf observed two men fighting in a restaurant parking lot and, upon closer inspection of the situation, determined that both men were armed. Officer Greenleaf called for backup and then announced to the men he was a police officer and demanded they stop fighting. The men refused to stop fighting. Officer Greenleaf and the backup officers, who arrived at the scene in minutes, broke up the fight by physically restraining the men, neither of whom reached for his weapon at any point during the fight.

    Officer Greenleaf's actions were:

    A. bad, because he should have attempted to break up the fight by himself before the other officers arrived.

    B. good, because the two armed men presented a danger to themselves, each other, the public, and Officer Greenleaf, and were better dealt with by more than one officer.

    C. bad, because he should have let them settle their dispute on their own.

    D. good, but only because no one got shot.

57. Officer Glaser responds to a report of a larceny and gathers the following information:

Location:	Burger Central
Time:	between 1:00 A.M. and 7:15 A.M., when the restaurant was closed and empty
Police Contacted by:	Joe Bridge, owner
Item Missing:	40 pounds of hamburger meat that was in the freezer
Suspect:	unknown

    Officer Glaser must write her report. Which of the following expresses the information most clearly and accurately?

    A. Joe Bridge, the owner of Burger Central, reported that between 1:00 A.M. and 7:15 A.M., when the restaurant was closed and empty, 40 pounds of hamburger meat was stolen from the restaurant's freezer. The suspect is unknown.

    B. At Berger Central, according to owner Joe Bridge, 40 pounds of hamburger meat was stolen by an unknown suspect from the restaurant's freezer between 1:00 A.M. and 7:15 A.M., when the restaurant was closed and empty.

    C. Burger Central's 40 pounds of frozen hamburger meat was stolen from the freezer between 1:00 A.M. and 7:15 A.M., when the restaurant was closed and empty, by an unknown suspect.

    D. Between 1:00 A.M. and 7:15 A.M., when Burger Central was closed and empty, Joe Bridge stole 40 pounds of hamburger meat from the freezer.

58. In State X, a person is guilty of **ASSAULT IN THE FIRST DEGREE** when, with intent to cause serious physical injury to another person, he causes such injury to such person or to a third person by means of a deadly weapon. Based solely upon this definition, which of the following is the best example of Assault in the First Degree?

    A. While Martina is shooting at a target on her property, her neighbor steps into her line of fire and is shot in the head.

    B. Julio is chopping greens at his restaurant with a long, sharp knife when one of his employees stumbles into the knife, causing a deep gash in his chest, from which he bleeds to death.

    C. Knowing that his ex-girlfriend is deathly allergic to wheat, Marcus sprinkles copious amounts of wheat germ into the punch at her wedding. The groom, who is also allergic, drinks 12 cups of the punch and goes into respiratory arrest as a result.

    D. Franklin fires his automatic weapon at his mother, but his bullets hit a passerby who steps between them instead, and the passerby is permanently disabled as a result.

59. During a Sunday afternoon at the park, Martin pulled out his wallet to buy something cold to drink. Just as he reached into his wallet for his money, someone grabbed his wallet and then raced off on a bicycle. Officer Lee interviewed Martin and several witnesses, all of whom described the suspect as a short man wearing black shorts and a black tank top. Of the following descriptions of the suspect's bicycle given to Officer Lee by witnesses, which should she consider most likely to be correct?

    A. gold mountain bike with a white water bottle

    B. silver road bike with a white water bottle

    C. gold road bike with a red water bottle

    D. gold road bike with a white water bottle

60. Officer Johnson is dispatched to the scene of a collapsed bridge, where he gathers the following information:

Location:	Veterans' Bridge
Time:	1:15 P.M.
Incident:	the section of the bridge between its two central supports collapsed
Injuries:	dozens of motorists taken to the hospital
Cause of Collapse:	under investigation

Officer Johnson must write his report. Which of the following expresses the information most clearly and accurately?

A. The section of Veterans' Bridge between the bridge's two central supports collapsed. Dozens of motorists were taken to the hospital, and the cause of the collapse is under investigation.

B. At 1:15 P.M., the section of Veterans' Bridge between the bridge's two central supports collapsed. Dozens of motorists were taken to the hospital. The cause of the collapse is under investigation.

C. A section of Veterans' Bridge collapsed at 1:15 P.M. As a result, dozens of motorists were taken to the hospital, and the precise cause of the bridge's collapse is currently under investigation.

D. At 1:15 P.M., the section between the bridge's two central supports collapsed, causing dozens of motorists to be taken to the hospital. The cause of the collapse is under investigation at this time.

61. Officer Levy is patrolling a section of town where there are a large number of night clubs and bars when he receives an alert that an armed and dangerous female suspect may be in the area. The suspect is described as a tall female with curly, blonde hair and dark brown eyes. Of the following individuals, on which should Officer Levy most closely focus his attention?

A. a tall man with curly, blonde hair and dark brown eyes who is carrying a briefcase

B. a tall woman with a curly, blonde ponytail and dark brown eyes who is carrying a small purse

C. a short woman with curly, blonde hair and dark brown eyes who is carrying a backpack

D. a tall woman with straight, blonde hair and blue eyes who is dressed in a bodysuit and is not carrying any sort of bag

62. If an officer accidentally shoots a suspect whom he knows was guilty of a violent crime after a lengthy pursuit of the suspect, that officer should:

    A. accurately relate what happened to his supervisors.

    B. tell his supervisors that the suspect was about to shoot him and that he shot the suspect in self-defense.

    C. put his gun in the suspect's hand and pull the trigger, so it will appear that the suspect stole the officer's gun and shot himself.

    D. do nothing and hope that investigators do not discover the truth.

63. Officer Lenox drives a pregnant woman to the hospital and gathers the following notes:

Incident:	pregnant woman went into labor on a bench in Harbor Park
Time:	10:30 A.M.
Name of Woman:	Ida Reed
Action Taken:	woman driven to the emergency room at Crews' Hospital
Status:	baby was delivered at the hospital; mother and child are healthy

    Officer Lenox must write his report. Which of the following expresses the information most clearly and accurately?

    A. A pregnant woman named Ida Reed went into labor on a bench in Harbor Park at 10:30 A.M. She was driven to the emergency room at Crews' Hospital, where the baby was delivered. Both mother and child are healthy.

    B. Both mother and child are healthy after a pregnant woman named Ida Reed went into labor on a bench in Harbor Park, and she was driven to the emergency room at Crews' Hospital, where the baby was delivered.

    C. A pregnant woman went into labor on a bench in Harbor Park at 10:30 A.M. She was driven to the emergency room at Crews' Hospital, where the baby was delivered. Both mother and child are healthy.

    D. Both mother and child are healthy after a pregnant woman named Ida Reed went into labor on a bench in Harbor Park at 10:30 P.M. She was driven to the emergency room at Chambers' Hospital, where the baby was delivered.

64. Officer Reynaldo is investigating a hit-and-run that occurred at a busy intersection. Of the following pieces of physical evidence, which would be most important to his investigation?

    A. a drop of the victim's blood found on the road at the intersection

    B. the victim's driver's license

    C. paint from the suspect's car found on the victim

    D. a rotten apple found in a ditch near the intersection

65. Oscar took the trash out on a cold morning before he showered for school. As he chased the lid to one of his family's trash cans into the street, he was hit by a vehicle traveling at a high rate of speed. The car did not stop. During his investigation, Officer Moody interviewed several neighbors who saw the incident through their windows. Of the following descriptions of the suspect's vehicle's license plate number given to him by witnesses, which should Officer Moody consider most likely to be accurate?

A. HAN 991
B. HEK 900
C. HAN 901
D. KAH 801

66. After a series of robberies is reported, a woman approaches an officer on patrol and asks him to recommend a security company in the city. The officer should:

A. tell her not to waste her money on a security company's services, since the police department is well trained and well staffed.
B. recommend the company where his brother-in-law works.
C. offer to sell her a shotgun from his private collection.
D. recommend that she check with the Better Business Bureau and talk to her neighbors about whom they use.

67. Officer Anderson responds to a report of a robbery and gathers the following information:

Location:	Fourth Street Florists
Time:	7:30 P.M.
Incident:	victim was jumped from behind and robbed
Victim:	Mrs. Flander, the manager
Missing Item:	the night's deposit, totaling $1,500
Suspect:	unknown; the victim did not see the suspect

Officer Anderson must write his report. Which of the following expresses the information most clearly and accurately?

A. Mrs. Flander stated that at 7:30 P.M., she was jumped from behind and robbed. The night's deposit for Fourth Street Florists, totaling $1,500, was stolen. The suspect is unknown.
B. Mrs. Flander stated that at 7:30 P.M. at Fourth Street Florists, where she is the manager, she was jumped from behind and robbed. The night's deposit, totaling $1,500, was stolen. The suspect is unknown, as the victim did not see the suspect.
C. At 7:30 P.M. at Fourth Street Florists, where Mrs. Flander is the manager, she was jumped from behind and robbed, according to her statement. The night's deposit was stolen. The suspect is unknown, as the victim did not see the suspect.
D. Mrs. Flander stated that at 7:30 P.M. at Fourth Street Florists, where she is the manager, she was jumped from behind and robbed. The night's deposit, totaling $2,500, was stolen. The suspect is unknown, as the victim did not see the suspect.

68. As he was walking home from his shift, Officer Esposito, who was not in uniform, encountered a child who appeared to be walking home from school. Officer Esposito had a bag of homemade cookies in his backpack and considered offering one to the child. However, Officer Esposito decided to continue walking without offering a cookie to the child. Officer Esposito's actions were:

    A. improper, because the child might have been hungry.

    B. proper, because children should not be encouraged to accept food from strangers.

    C. improper, because he missed an opportunity to teach a child to trust the police.

    D. It is impossible to determine whether Officer Esposito acted properly without knowing how old the child was.

69. In State X, a person is guilty of **CONSPIRACY IN THE SIXTH DEGREE** when, with intent that conduct constituting a crime be performed, he agrees with one or more persons to engage in or cause the performance of such conduct. Based solely upon this definition, which of the following is the best example of Conspiracy in the Sixth Degree?

    A. Joe writes a letter to his mother telling her that he is going to rob a liquor store.

    B. Horace and Julia agree to steal $1,000 from her mother's purse.

    C. Sylvia brags to a crowd of drunken strangers that she will "do some evil tomorrow" and proceeds to kill a man the next morning.

    D. Lorenzo steals his uncle's car after his uncle warned him not to touch it.

70. Officer Cohen is dispatched to the scene of a dispute, where he gathers the following information:

Location:	Green Golf Course
Time:	9:45 A.M.
Police Contacted by:	Herb Spotto, course manager
Incident:	Mr. Jasper and Dr. Fine were arguing over their tee times; play on the course was held up
Action Taken:	both men were removed from the course and barred from returning

    Officer Cohen must write his report. Which of the following expresses the information most clearly and accurately?

    A. At 9:45 A.M., Herb Spotto reported that at Green Golf Course, where he is the course manager, Mr. Jasper and Dr. Fine were arguing over their tee times, holding up play on the course. Both men were removed from the course and barred from returning.

    B. Herb Spotto, the course manager at Green Golf Course, where this happened, reported at 9:45 A.M. that Mr. Jasper and Dr. Fine were holding up play on the course, which resulted in them being removed from the course and barred from returning, because they were arguing over their tee times.

    C. Mr. Jasper and Dr. Fine were arguing over their tee times at Green Golf Course at 9:45 A.M., according to course manager Herb Spotto, who reported this to the police, who removed both men from the course as a result (Mr. Jasper and Dr. Fine being the two men), and then the men were barred from returning.

    D. The two men, Mr. Jasper and Dr. Fine, who held up play on the course at Green Golf Course, according to course manager Herb Spotto, were removed from the course and barred from returning after this was reported to the police at 9:45 A.M.

71. Officer Parsons pulls over a motorist who is exceeding the speed limit by a dangerous margin. The motorist identifies herself as the governor's sister. What should Officer Parsons do?

    A. apologize and send her on her way without giving her a traffic ticket

    B. give her a traffic ticket just to make an example out of her, since she is a prominent citizen

    C. offer to let her go if she promises to get an autographed picture of her brother for him

    D. give her a traffic ticket if her violation warrants such an action

72. If a male veteran officer feels more confident working with male rather than female officers, he should:

    A. expect to be allowed to work with whichever officer or officers he chooses, since he is a veteran.

    B. feel free to announce his preference to a supervisor and other officers, but expect to follow the supervisor's instructions.

    C. overcome his lack of confidence in female officers, since they are vital members of his department.

    D. refuse to work with any female officers, since his "hunch" about avoiding them could save his life.

73. A clerk at a 24-hour copy store was robbed at gunpoint. The suspect stole the cash from the store's register, as well as the clerk's watch and wallet. Officer Henry interviewed the passersby who said they saw someone carrying a bag and a gun, leaving the store in a hurry about the time that the robbery occurred. Of the following descriptions of the suspect given to Officer Henry by witnesses, which should he consider most likely to be accurate?

    A. thin female, wearing blue shorts and a white shirt

    B. thin male, wearing blue shorts and a white shirt

    C. heavyset female, wearing a blue skirt and a white shirt

    D. thin female, wearing blue shorts and a tan shirt

74. A juror in a criminal case was chased by someone in a speeding car who repeatedly bashed the juror's car, forcing it off the road. Several motorists in the oncoming lane of traffic saw the suspect's vehicle and were interviewed by Officer Webster, who was dispatched to the scene to investigate. Of the following descriptions of the suspect's vehicle given to Officer Webster by witnesses, which should he consider most likely to be correct?

    A. red Nissan Maxima with tinted windows and an Ohio license plate

    B. red Toyota Cressida with tinted windows and an Ohio license plate

    C. maroon Nissan Maxima with untinted windows and an Ohio license plate

    D. red Nissan Maxima with tinted windows and an Indiana license plate

75. Officer Esposito observed a weaving motorist and pulled her over. He noted the following information:

Location:	Feather Street between First and Second Avenues
Time:	11:15 A.M.
Driver:	Helen Kincaid
Incident:	driver was weaving from lane to lane
Action Taken:	driver was in medical distress; an ambulance was called, which took her to the hospital, where she is in stable condition

Officer Esposito is writing his report. Which of the following expresses the information most clearly and accurately?

A. At 11:15, a driver was observed weaving from lane to lane on Feather Street between First and Second Avenues. The driver, Helen Kincaid, was determined to be in medical distress. An ambulance was called, which took her to the hospital, where she is in stable condition.

B. At 11:15 A.M., a driver was observed weaving from lane to lane on Feather Street between First and Second Avenues. The driver, Helen Kincaid, was determined to be in medical distress. An ambulance was called, which took her to the hospital, where she is in stable condition.

C. A driver was observed weaving from lane to lane on Feather Street between First and Second Avenues. The driver, Helen Kincaid, was determined to be in medical distress. An ambulance was called, which took her to the hospital, where she is in stable condition.

D. A driver was observed weaving from lane to lane on Feather Street between First and Second Avenues at 11:15 A.M. The driver, Helen Kincaid, was determined to be in medical distress. She is in the hospital in stable condition.

76. Officer Rodriguez is told to watch for an armed and dangerous male suspect who has just robbed a liquor store while holding a rifle to the head of the store clerk. Of the following individuals, on which should Officer Rodriguez most closely focus his attention?

A. a woman in a business suit, carrying a steamer trunk

B. a man in camouflage clothes, carrying a rifle and a dead rabbit

C. a man in shorts and a T-shirt, with a noticeable bulge in the right pocket of his shorts

D. a man in jeans and a work shirt, wearing a tool belt and carrying a hammer

77. Officer Dahl was sent to investigate a report of a larceny. She gathered the following information:

Location: 992 Pickford Lane
Time: between 10:00 P.M. and 11:00 P.M.
Police Contacted by: Loretta Washington, resident
Item Missing: red motorized scooter that was in the carport
Suspect: Tommy Jasper, her nephew
Location of Suspect: unknown

Officer Dahl is writing his report. Which of the following expresses the information most clearly and accurately?

A. Tommy Jasper reported that between 10:00 P.M. and 11:00 P.M., a red motorized scooter was stolen from the carport at his residence at 992 Pickford Lane. Mr. Jasper stated that he suspects that his aunt, Loretta Washington, whose location is unknown, stole the scooter.

B. Loretta Washington reported that between 10:00 a.m. and 11:00 a.m., a green motorized scooter was stolen from the carport at her residence at 992 Pickford Lane. Ms. Washington stated that she suspects that her nephew, Tommy Jasper, whose location is unknown, stole the scooter.

C. Loretta Washington reported that between 10:00 P.M. and 11:00 P.M., a red motorized scooter was stolen from the carport at her residence at 992 Pickford Lane. Ms. Washington stated that she suspects that her nephew, Tommy Jasper, whose location is unknown, stole the scooter.

D. Loretta Washington reported that a red motorized scooter was stolen from the carport at her residence at 902 Pickford Avenue between 10:00 P.M. and 11:00 P.M. Ms. Washington stated that she suspects that her nephew, Tommy Jasper, whose location is unknown, stole the scooter.

78. In State X, a person is guilty of **FALSE IMPERSONATION** or **FALSE PERSONATION** when, after being informed of the consequences of such act, he knowingly misrepresents his actual name, date of birth, or address to a police officer or peace officer with intent to prevent the officer from ascertaining such information.

After being stopped on the street for questioning by a police officer in search of a dangerous suspect, Richie Harris tells the officer that his name is Rickie Hardaway. The officer informs him of the circumstances of misinforming a police officer, and Mr. Harris again identifies himself as Rickie Hardaway. Based solely upon the above definition, which of the following statements is true?

A. Richie Harris should be charged with False Personation.

B. Richie Harris should not be charged with any crime.

C. Richie Harris should be charged with False Personation only if it is established that he is the dangerous suspect for whom the officer has been searching.

D. It is impossible to determine whether Richie Harris should be charged with any crime in the absence of further information about the dangerous suspect for whom the officer has been searching.

79. Officer Fargas responds to a report of a deliberately poisoned animal and gathers the following information:

Location: 8 Farns Way
Time: 9:00 A.M.
Police Contacted by: Mrs. Lopez, resident
Incident: Mrs. Lopez claims that her neighbor, Mr. Samuels, deliberately poisoned her cat
Action Taken: a feline autopsy revealed that the cat had been poisoned, and Mr. Samuels is being sought for questioning

Officer Fargas must write his report. Which of the following expresses the information most clearly and accurately?

A. Mrs. Lopez, of 8 Farns Way, stated at 9:00 A.M. that she believed that her neighbor, Mr. Samuels, had deliberately poisoned her cat. A feline autopsy revealed that the cat had been poisoned, and Mr. Samuels is being sought for questioning.

B. Mr. Samuels poisoned the cat of Mrs. Lopez, of 8 Farns Way, according to a feline autopsy. Mr. Samuels, a neighbor, is being sought for questioning after Mrs. Lopez accused him at 9:00 A.M.

C. At 9:00 A.M., Mrs. Lopez stated that she believed that her neighbor, Mr. Samuels, had deliberately poisoned her cat. A feline autopsy revealed that the cat had been poisoned, and Mr. Samuels is being sought for questioning.

D. At 8 Farns Way, Mrs. Lopez stated that she believed that her neighbor, Mr. Samuels, had deliberately poisoned her cat. A feline autopsy revealed that the cat had been poisoned, and Mr. Samuels is being sought for questioning.

80. When patrolling a quiet residential area, a uniformed officer should keep his weapon:

A. safely in its holster.
B. in his hand, but with the safety mechanism on.
C. in his hand, ready to fire.
D. hidden in his sock, under the leg of his uniform pants.

81. Officer Blair was dispatched to the scene of a hit-and-run, where she gathered the following information:

Location:	intersection of Peters and Anselm Streets
Time:	4:00 P.M.
Crime:	hit-and-run
Victim:	Charity Falcon
Witness:	Susan Gonzalvez
Suspect's Vehicle:	gold Dodge Colt

    Officer Blair is writing her report. Which of the following expresses the information most clearly and accurately?

    A. Susan Gonzalvez stated that at 4:00 P.M. at the intersection of Peters and Anselm Streets, she witnessed a hit-and-run. The victim was struck by a vehicle described as a gold Dodge Colt.

    B. Susan Gonzalvez stated that at the intersection of Peters and Anselm Streets, she witnessed a hit-and-run. The victim was Charity Falcon, and the suspect's vehicle is described as a gold Dodge Colt.

    C. Susan Gonzalvez stated that at 4:00 P.M. at the intersection of Peters and Anselm Streets, she witnessed a hit-and-run. The victim was Charity Falcon, and the suspect's vehicle is described as a gold Dodge Colt.

    D. Susan Gonzalvez stated that at 4:00 P.M. at the intersection of Peters and Anselm Streets, she witnessed a hit-and-run. The victim was Charity Falcon, and the suspect's vehicle is described as a Dodge Colt.

82. Officer Jeffries has noticed that, over the past few months, certain crimes have occurred with a certain regularity in a few sections of the area that he patrols. Rapes happen in Harris Park, assaults on Dougherty Street between Tenth and Twelfth Avenues, and larcenies happen on the west end of Walker Avenue. Rapes occur on Tuesdays and Saturdays, assaults on Wednesdays and Fridays, and larcenies on Sundays. Rapes occur between 1:00 P.M. and 8:00 P.M., assaults between 5:00 P.M. and 10:30 P.M., and larcenies between 10:00 A.M. and noon.

    Given this information, which of the following patrol schedules would enable Officer Jeffries to most effectively reduce the number of larcenies?

    A. the west end of Walker Avenue, Sundays and Mondays, 10:00 A.M. to 1:00 P.M.

    B. Harris Park, Sundays, 10:00 A.M. to 1:00 P.M.

    C. the west end of Walker Avenue, Tuesdays and Saturdays, 5:00 P.M. to 10:30 P.M.

    D. Harris Park, Tuesdays, 5:00 P.M. to 10:30 P.M.

83. Given the information in Question 82, which of the following patrol schedules would enable Officer Jeffries to most effectively reduce the number of rapes?

    A. the west end of Walker Avenue, Tuesdays and Saturdays, 1:00 P.M. to 8:00 P.M.
    B. Harris Park, Tuesdays and Saturdays, 1:00 P.M. to 8:00 P.M.
    C. the west end of Walker Avenue, Saturdays and Sundays, 5:00 P.M. to 10:30 P.M.
    D. Harris Park, Saturdays and Sundays, 5:00 P.M. to 10:30 P.M.

84. Given the information in Question 82, which would be the most advisable day and time for someone who wishes to avoid being assaulted to visit Dougherty Street between Tenth and Twelfth Avenues?

    A. Wednesday between 3:00 P.M. and 7:00 P.M.
    B. Friday between 5:00 P.M. and 7:00 P.M.
    C. Wednesday between 1:00 P.M. and 4:00 P.M.
    D. Friday between 9:00 P.M. and midnight

85. A well-known artist was buying painting supplies when she was approached by a man who pretended to be a security guard and asked her to step outside. The artist did not return to the store, and days later a ransom note appeared at the gallery where the artist's work was commonly displayed. Officer Grady retraced the artist's steps on the day of her disappearance, learned about the incident at the store, and interviewed people who were there and who saw the incident take place. Of the following descriptions of the suspect given to Officer Grady by witnesses, which should she consider most likely to be correct?

    A. about 50 years old, with long, gray hair and blue eyes
    B. about 25 years old, with long, black hair and green eyes
    C. about 25 years old, with short, gray hair and blue eyes
    D. about 25 years old, with long, gray hair and green eyes

86. Officer Paul noted the following information after pulling a motorist over for speeding:

Location:	the 900 block of Hart Street
Time:	6:15 A.M.
Driver and Vehicle:	Jack Voorhies, driving a red Volvo
Violation:	exceeding the posted speed limit
Action Taken:	Mr. Voorhies was given a traffic ticket

    Officer Paul is writing his report. Which of the following expresses the information most clearly and accurately?

    A. At 6:15 A.M., Jack Voorhies was observed exceeding the speed limit at the 900 block of Hart Street. Mr. Voorhies was given a traffic ticket.
    B. Jack Voorhies was observed exceeding the speed limit at 6:15 A.M. in a red Volvo at the 900 block of Hart Street. Mr. Voorhies was given a traffic ticket.
    C. At 6:15 A.M., Jack Voorhies was observed running a red light at the 900 block of Hart Street. Mr. Voorhies was given a traffic ticket.
    D. Jack Voorhies was observed exceeding the speed limit at 6:15 A.M. in a red Volvo on Hart Street. Mr. Voorhies was given a traffic ticket.

87. In State X, a person is guilty of **SPORTS BRIBING** when he confers, or agrees to confer, any benefit upon a sports participant with the intent to influence him not to give his best efforts in a sports contest. Based solely upon this definition, which of the following is not an example of Sports Bribing?

    A. Mary Elizabeth offers to give her father her $100 savings bond if he hits a home run during the game he's playing on her birthday.

    B. Frank offers $500 to Catherine, a professional skater, if she intentionally falls during a competition.

    C. Serita gives Joe, a boxer, $1,000 in cash to pretend to be knocked out after the first punch in an important bout.

    D. Scott promises to buy Ricky, a hockey goalie, a new car if he allows three goals to be scored against him during a championship game.

88. Officer Lockhart responds to a report of a robbery and gathers the following information:

    Location: Elmo's Tavern
    Time: 2:15 A.M.
    Victim: Elmo Timmons, owner
    Incident: victim was robbed at gunpoint
    Item Missing: victim's antique pocket watch
    Suspect: short female wearing a pink dress

    Officer Lockhart must write her report. Which of the following expresses the information most clearly and accurately?

    A. Elmo Timmons reported a robbery to him at 2:15 A.M. at Elmo's Tavern, which he is the owner of, from a gun-pointing suspect described as a short female wearing a pink dress. Mr. Timmons's antique pocket watch was stolen.

    B. The owner of Elmo's Tavern was robbed reportedly, according to him, at 2:15 A.M. at the tavern that he owns by a short female wearing a pink dress, who took his antique pocket watch at gunpoint.

    C. Elmo Timmons stated that at 2:15 A.M. at Elmo's Tavern, which he owns, he was robbed at gunpoint by a short female wearing a pink dress who took his antique pocket watch.

    D. At gunpoint, Elmo Timmons was robbed of his antique pocket watch at his owned place, Elmo's Tavern, at 2:15 A.M. by a short female in a pink dress, he said.

89. Many police officers are multilingual. Of the following, which is not an advantage of such an ability?

    A. Multilingual officers can more easily converse with citizens who speak languages other than English.

    B. Citizens who speak languages other than English might feel more comfortable with a multilingual officer than with one who only speaks English.

    C. Officers who can understand languages other than English can absorb information exchanged between citizens who are speaking a language other than English, which might be important to an investigation.

    D. Multilingual officers can converse with each other in a language other than English when they do not want a supervisor who speaks only English to understand what they are saying.

90. If Officer Serrano has been assigned to direct traffic at a busy intersection after the power lines in the area have fallen in a terrible storm, he should be least concerned about which of the following?

    A. an impatient businessman who does not want his passage through the intersection to be delayed

    B. a speeding motorist who narrowly avoids causing a collision with another vehicle and speeds away from the intersection

    C. a woman who approaches the officer and informs him that her mother, who is in a car at the intersection, appears to be having a heart attack

    D. the beginnings of a flash flood at the intersection

PRACTICE TEST 5 ANSWERS AND EXPLANATIONS
ANSWER KEY

1. C	26. D	51. B	76. B
2. B	27. A	52. D	77. C
3. B	28. B	53. B	78. A
4. A	29. A	54. A	79. A
5. C	30. B	55. C	80. A
6. C	31. A	56. B	81. C
7. D	32. C	57. A	82. A
8. C	33. D	58. D	83. B
9. D	34. B	59. D	84. C
10. D	35. D	60. B	85. D
11. B	36. D	61. B	86. B
12. A	37. D	62. A	87. A
13. C	38. B	63. A	88. C
14. C	39. C	64. C	89. D
15. C	40. C	65. C	90. A
16. A	41. B	66. D	
17. C	42. C	67. B	
18. A	43. A	68. B	
19. C	44. D	69. B	
20. A	45. A	70. A	
21. A	46. B	71. D	
22. D	47. B	72. C	
23. D	48. D	73. A	
24. C	49. C	74. A	
25. C	50. A	75. B	

ANSWERS AND EXPLANATIONS

1. **C** is the best answer. The "three large men" in the "windowless panel truck" seem much more likely to be planning and executing robberies in the area than anyone in the other three scenarios.

2. **B** is the best answer. Note, in A, Leo does not "forcibly" steal the car.

3. **B** is the only complete and accurate statement. There is inaccurate information in each of the other three statements. Note, in C, the description of the suspect is not specifically attributed to the suspect, so the description "a tall male wearing a flannel shirt and jeans" could apply to either the victim or the suspect.

4. **A** is the best answer. So many of each make and model of a vehicle are manufactured every year that a basic description of a vehicle is not enough evidence to determine whether or not someone owning a vehicle matching the description of one used in a crime is guilty of committing that crime.

5. **C** contains the most repeaters. Note the descriptions of the suspect's height ("tall" and "short") each appear twice, canceling each other out, so neither can be used to eliminate possible answers.

6. **C** is the clearest and most accurate statement. There is information missing from all the other statements.

7. **D** is obviously correct. A "middle-aged man who takes pictures of children playing on the playground and then beckons for them to come and see the pictures" could very easily be a predator, and he should be questioned about his activities.

8. **C** is correct. A and B are clearly instances in which someone acted without the "intent to cause the death of another person," and D is an example of a suicide, not a murder.

9. **D** is the clearest and most accurate statement.

10. **D** is correct. Assaults occur on Briggs Street between Sands and Pace Avenues on Fridays and Sundays between 2:00 P.M. and 5:00 P.M., and the patrol schedule in D is the only one of the four that provides coverage of this area on those days at that time.

11. **B** is correct. Arsons occur on Tripoli Street between Forest and Lawn Streets on Mondays and Wednesdays between 9:00 P.M. and midnight, and the patrol schedule in B is the only one of the four that provides coverage of that area on those days at that time.

12. The window of time in **A** is the only one of the four that occurs outside of the window during which robberies take place (Mondays and Saturdays, noon to 6:00 P.M.).

13. **C** is correct. There is no reason to assume that any of the other statements are true.

14. **C** is correct. Each of the other three actions is illogical and irresponsible.

15. **C** contains the most repeaters.

16. **A** is the only statement that contains all the information

17. **C** is the only clearly worded statement.

18. **A** is the best answer. The circumstances of the abduction and death of "Gerald's boss's wife" meet the criteria for this crime. Note that C is not correct because neither of the given definitions pertains to Murder, and the answer should be based "solely upon the above definitions."

19. **C** is the only statement that contains all the information.

20. **A** contains the most repeaters.

21. **A** is the only statement that is worded in a clear and logical manner. Note the awkward sentence fragment, "Where it was was Cane Street between Julian and Worth," in B.

22. **D** is the most logical assumption for Officer Hinton to make about the man, given his limited observations of the man's situation.

23. **D** contains the most repeaters. Note the phrases "olive-green T-shirt" and "black shorts" appear in each of the four descriptions, so they cannot be used to eliminate any possible answers.

24. **C** is the only accurate statement. Each of the other three statements contains incorrect information; for instance, in A, the names of the suspect and the victim have been reversed.

25. **C** is correct. A "message from the front desk attendant announcing that she has a guest" indicates that someone was there to see her who could have been the abductor or who might have information about what happened. Also, the voice of the "front desk attendant" can be matched to the personnel at the dormitory to determine if it actually belongs to the attendant who was on duty at the time; if not, it could be the voice of the abductor or an accomplice.

26. **D** is correct. It is the only instance in which the value of the property stolen "exceeds $50,000." Note, in B, the value of the necklace is the only relevant figure since Vinnie has already served his sentence for stealing the $35,000 car. Also note, in C, the crime committed is not larceny since a child is not property.

27. Only **A** contains all the information.

28. **B** is correct. An officer's judgment should not be affected by his personal feelings, so each of the other possible answers is incorrect.

29. **A** is correct. Keeping witnesses apart can be crucial to preserving the authenticity of their recollections.

30. **B** is correct. Except for the 12 hand-held blenders where their total value is provided ($240), the values of the other items are listed per individual item and must be calculated accordingly.

31. **A** contains the most repeaters.

32. **C** is the clearest and most accurate statement. There is information missing from A and B, and D contains inaccurate information.

33. **D** is correct.

34. **B** is the only statement that contains all the information.

35. **D** is the best answer. Since the officer is not a veterinarian, he should not presume that any of the animals should be put out of their "misery" (A and C). For a similar reason, he should not attempt to transport the animals (B), as they might be dangerous to him, and he could accidentally injure them.

36. **D** is correct.

37. **D** is correct.

38. **B** is correct.

39. **C** is correct.

40. **C** is correct.

41. **B** contains the most repeaters. Note the descriptions of the dog's ears ("floppy ears" and "pointed ears") each appear twice, canceling each other out, so neither can be used to eliminate possible answers.

42. **C** is the most clearly and logically worded statement. Note the wording in D presents the events in nearly reverse order, so the statement is unnecessarily confusing.

43. **A** is correct. An officer should not accept a bribe under any circumstances.

44. **D** is correct.

45. **A** is the clearest and most accurate statement. Note, in C, the name of the victim and the description of the suspect have been reversed.

46. **B** is correct.

47. **B** contains the most repeaters. Note the descriptions of the suspect's eye color ("green eyes" and "brown eyes") each appears twice, canceling each other out, so neither can be used to eliminate possible answers.

48. Only **D** is worded in a clear and logical manner. Note, in B, that the use of the name "Mr. Cook" is confusing, since both the victim and the suspect could be referred to in that manner.

49. **C** is correct. Ramon's employment status is not "material to the…matter" of his brother's divorce.

50. **A** is correct. 2.5 is .25% of 1,000. To calculate .25% of 150,000, multiply .0025 by 150,000, which equals 375.

51. **B** is the clearest and most accurate statement.

52. **D** is correct. Note that while a handgun could be used to commit a robbery, the fact that a man is "applying for a license to own a handgun" (A) should not immediately concern Officer Conlon. Neither should the "men in suits looking over a blueprint of an office building's layout" (B), since they may well be contractors or architects. However, the "man and woman who have slowly been circling an office park and photographing entrances and exits" should concern Officer Conlon.

53. **B** is correct. It is necessary for officers to work on holidays to assist with the year-round, 24-hour coverage that police departments offer.

54. **A** contains the most repeaters.

55. **C** is the only statement that contains all the information.

56. **B** is the best answer.

57. **A** is the only statement that accurately conveys all the information. Note, in B, that the restaurant's name is misspelled. Also note, in D, that the owner is given as the suspect.

58. **D** is correct. A and B are clearly accidents, and C is incorrect because "wheat germ" could not be considered a "deadly weapon."

59. **D** contains the most repeaters.

60. **B** is the only statement that contains all the information.

61. **B** is the best answer. The only other individual who may fit the suspect's description is the "tall woman with straight, blonde hair" in D, but her appearance differs in many ways from that of the suspect, while the individual in B fits the description perfectly.

62. **A** is correct. Lying (B), falsifying evidence (C), or omitting information crucial to an investigation (D) would all be unethical and unlawful.

63. **A** is the clearest and most accurate statement. There is information missing from B and C, and D contains inaccurate information.

64. **C** would be the most important piece of physical evidence. Some "paint from the suspect's car found on the victim" could help positively identify the make and model of the suspect's car.

65. **C** contains the most repeaters. Note that while the letter "N" as the third letter in the license plate number only occurs twice, it is still a repeater.

66. **D** is correct. The officer should decline to recommend a particular company, as any such recommendation could be seen as a departmental endorsement. He should definitely not offer to "sell her a shotgun from his private collection" (C), and the idea of him discouraging any citizen from additionally protecting himself or herself with a private security company (A) is absurd.

67. **B** is the clearest and most accurate statement. Note, in D, that the "night's deposit" is given as "$2,500" rather than "$1,500."

68. **B** is correct.

69. **B** is the only instance in which someone "agrees with one or more persons" to commit a crime. Note that the situation in A, in which "Joe writes a letter to his mother" informing her of his criminal plans constitutes someone telling someone else about his criminal intentions rather than someone agreeing with others to commit a crime. Likewise, C presents a situation in which a vague announcement of criminal intentions is made, but this is not the same thing as an agreement to commit a crime.

70. Only **A** is worded in a clear and logical manner.

71. **D** is correct. Every citizen should be treated equally, and every situation should be judged on its own merits and circumstances.

72. **C** is correct. No prejudice should affect an officer's willingness to work with other officers.

73. **A** contains the most repeaters.

74. **A** contains the most repeaters.

75. **B** is the only statement that contains all the information. Note that, in A, the only missing information is the designation "A.M." This is easy to overlook.

76. **B** is the best answer. Even though the man appears to be a hunter, his weapon matches that of the suspect's, so he could be the suspect. The clothing and the dead rabbit could be decoys meant to divert suspicion from the suspect.

77. **C** is the only statement that accurately conveys all the information. Note, in A, that the names of the victim and the suspect have been reversed.

78. **A** is correct. Richie Harris's actions clearly meet the criteria given in the definition of False Personation.

79. **A** is the clearest and most accurate statement. Note, in B, that Mr. Samuels's guilt is stated as an established fact, which is not true. He is simply being sought for questioning. There is information missing from C and D.

80. **A** is the best answer. A uniformed officer should keep his weapon in its holster, where it can be reached if it is needed, but should not remove it from its holster until an appropriate situation arises.

81. **C** is the only statement that contains all the information. Note, in D, the only missing information is the color of the suspect's vehicle. This is easy to overlook.

82. **A** is correct. Larcenies occur on the west end of Walker Avenue on Sundays between 10:00 A.M. and noon, and the patrol schedule in A is the only one of the four that provides coverage of that area on that day of the week at those times.

83. **B** is correct. Rapes occur in Harris Park on Tuesdays and Saturdays between 1:00 P.M. and 8:00 P.M., and the patrol schedule in B is the only one of the four that provides coverage of that area on those days at that time.

84. **C** is correct. It is the only window of time that does not overlap with the window in which assaults occur on Dougherty Street between Tenth and Twelfth Avenues (Wednesdays and Fridays between 5:00 P.M. and 10:30 P.M.).

85. **D** contains the most repeaters. Note that the descriptions of the suspect's eye color ("blue" and "green") each appear twice, canceling each other out, so neither can be used to eliminate any possible answers.

86. **B** is the clearest and most accurate statement. There is information missing from A and D, and C contains inaccurate information.

87. **A** is correct. Mary Elizabeth seems to be encouraging her father to perform well, while, in each of the other three instances, the individual in question acts "with the intent to influence" the participant "not to give his best efforts in a sports contest."

88. Only **C** is worded in a clear and logical manner.

89. **D** is correct.

90. **A** is the least important of the given situations and should concern Officer Serrano the least.

About the Author

During 25 years with the FBI, John Douglas became a leading expert on criminal personality profiling. Early in his career, he served as a recruiter for the Bureau; later, he conducted the first organized study into the methods and motivations of serial criminals, and became known as the pioneer of modern criminal investigative analysis. As a consultant, he continues assisting in criminal investigations and prosecutions throughout the world. An Air Force veteran, Douglas holds a doctorate in adult education, and is the author of numerous articles and presentations on criminology. He coauthored two landmark criminology texts: *Sexual Homicide: Patterns and Motives* and the *Crime Classification Manual*, for which he earned the prestigious Jefferson Award for Academic Excellence. With Mark Olshaker, he's coauthored several best-selling nonfiction books: *Mindhunter: Inside the FBI's Elite Serial Crime Unit; Unabomber: On the Trail of America's Most-Wanted Serial Killer; Journey into Darkness: The FBI's Premier Investigator Penetrates the Minds and Motives of the Most Terrifying Serial Killers; Obsession: The FBI's Legendary Profiler Probes the Psyches of Killers, Rapists, and Stalkers, and Their Victims, and Tells How to Fight Back.* He has also coauthored *Anyone You Want Me to Be: A True Story of Sex and Death on the Internet* and *Inside the Mind of BTK: The True Story Behind the Thirty-Year Hunt for the Notorious Wichita Serial Killer.* Douglas lives in the Washington, D.C., area.